Applied Health Ec

MW00986318

The first edition of *Applied Health Economics* did an expert job of showing how the availability of large-scale datasets and the rapid advancement of advanced econometric techniques can help health economists and health professionals make sense of information better than ever before.

This second edition has been revised and updated throughout, and includes new chapters on the description and modelling of individual health care costs, thus broadening the book's readership to those working on risk adjustment and health technology appraisal. The text also fully reflects the very latest advances in the health economics field and the key journal literature.

Practical applications of the methods are illustrated using data on health from the British Health and Lifestyle Survey (HALS), the British Household Panel Survey (BHPS), the European Community Household Panel (ECHP), the US Medical Expenditure Panel Survey (MEPS) and the Survey of Health, Ageing and Retirement in Europe (SHARE). There is a strong emphasis on applied work, illustrating the use of relevant computer software with code provided for Stata. Familiarity with the basic syntax and structure of Stata is assumed. The Stata code and extracts from the statistical output are embedded directly in the main text and explained at regular intervals.

The book is built around empirical case studies rather than general theory, and the emphasis is on learning by example. It presents a detailed dissection of the methods and results of recent research papers written by the authors and their colleagues. Relevant methods are presented alongside the Stata code that can be used to implement them, and the empirical results are discussed at each stage.

This text brings together the theory and application of health economics and econometrics, and will be a valuable reference for applied economists and students of health economics and applied econometrics.

Andrew M. Jones is Professor of Economics at the University of York, UK, where he is also Head of the Department of Economics and Related Studies.

Nigel Rice is Professor of Health Economics and Director of the Health, Econometrics and Data Group (HEDG) at the Centre for Health Economics, University of York, UK.

Teresa Bago d'Uva is an Associate Professor in the Department of Applied Economics at the Erasmus School of Economics, The Netherlands.

Silvia Balia is an Assistant Professor at the Department of Economics and Business and a researcher at the Centre for North-South Economic Research (CRENoS) at the University of Cagliari, Italy.

Routledge advanced texts in economics and finance

1 **Financial Econometrics**
Peijie Wang

2 **Macroeconomics for Developing Countries**
Second edition
Raghbendra Jha

3 **Advanced Mathematical Economics**
Rakesh Vohra

4 **Advanced Econometric Theory**
John S. Chipman

5 **Understanding Macroeconomic Theory**
John M. Barron, Bradley T. Ewing and Gerald J. Lynch

6 **Regional Economics**
Roberta Capello

7 **Mathematical Finance**
Core theory, problems and statistical algorithms
Nikolai Dokuchaev

8 **Applied Health Economics**
Andrew M. Jones, Nigel Rice, Teresa Bago d'Uva and Silvia Balia

9 **Information Economics**
Urs Birchler and Monika Bütler

10 **Financial Econometrics**
Second edition
Peijie Wang

11 **Development Finance**
Debates, dogmas and new directions
Stephen Spratt

12 **Culture and Economics**
On values, economics and international business
Eelke de Jong

13 **Modern Public Economics**
Second edition
Raghbendra Jha

14 **Introduction to Estimating Economic Models**
Atsushi Maki

15 **Advanced Econometric Theory**
John Chipman

16 **Behavioral Economics**
Edward Cartwright

17 **Essentials of Advanced Macroeconomic Theory**
Ola Olsson

18 **Behavioural Economics and Finance**
Michelle Baddeley

19 **Applied Health Economics**
Second edition
Andrew M. Jones, Nigel Rice, Teresa Bago d'Uva and Silvia Balia

Applied Health Economics

Second edition

Andrew M. Jones, Nigel Rice, Teresa Bago d'Uva and Silvia Balia

LONDON AND NEW YORK

First published 2013
by Routledge
2 Park Square, Milton Park, Abingdon, Oxon OX14 4RN

Simultaneously published in the USA and Canada
by Routledge
711 Third Avenue, New York, NY 10017

Routledge is an imprint of the Taylor & Francis Group, an informa business

© 2013 Andrew M. Jones, Nigel Rice, Teresa Bago d'Uva and
Silvia Balia

The right of Andrew M. Jones, Nigel Rice, Teresa Bago d'Uva and
Silvia Balia to be identified as authors of this work has been asserted
by them in accordance with the Copyright, Designs and Patent Act
1988.

All rights reserved. No part of this book may be reprinted or
reproduced or utilised in any form or by any electronic, mechanical,
or other means, now known or hereafter invented, including
photocopying and recording, or in any information storage or retrieval
system, without permission in writing from the publishers.

Trademark notice: Product or corporate names may be trademarks or
registered trademarks, and are used only for identification and
explanation without intent to infringe.

British Library Cataloguing in Publication Data
A catalogue record for this book is available from the British Library

Library of Congress Cataloging in Publication Data
Applied health economics/by Andrew M. Jones ... [et al.]. – 2nd ed.
    p. cm.
    Includes bibliographical references and index.
    I. Jones, Andrew M., 1960–
    [DNLM: 1. Economics, Medical. 2. Health Care Costs. 3. Statistics
    as Topic. W 74.1]
    338.4'73621–dc23
    2012006760

ISBN: 978-0-415-67681-6 (hbk)
ISBN: 978-0-415-67682-3 (pbk)
ISBN: 978-0-203-10241-1 (ebk)

Typeset in Times New Roman
by Florence Production Ltd, Stoodleigh, Devon

Contents

List of illustrations   viii
Preface   xiii
Acknowledgements   xv
Introduction   xvii

PART I
Describing and summarising data   **1**

1   Data and survey design   3

  1.1   The Health and Lifestyle Survey 3
  1.2   The British Household Panel Survey 5
  1.3   The European Community Household Panel 7
  1.4   The US Medical Expenditure Panel Survey 8
  1.5   Survey of Health, Ageing and Retirement in Europe 10
  1.6   Overview 11

2   Describing the dynamics of health   12

  2.1   Introduction 12
  2.2   Graphical analysis 14
  2.3   Tabulating the data 21
  2.4   Overview 29

3   Describing health care costs   30

  3.1   Introduction 30
  3.2   Data description 31
  3.3   Modelling health care cost data 40
  3.4   Linear regression models 44
  3.5   Overview 65

PART II
Categorical data   **67**

4   Reporting heterogeneity in health   **69**

  4.1   Introduction 69
  4.2   Data 71

4.3 Standard analysis 72

4.4 Using vignettes 75

4.5 Overview 98

Appendix 101

5 Health and lifestyles　　　　　　　　　　　　　　　　　　　**106**

5.1 Introduction 106

5.2 HALS data and sample 107

5.3 Descriptive analysis 113

5.4 Estimation strategy and results 121

5.5 Overview 138

PART III
Duration data　　　　　　　　　　　　　　　　　　　　　　　　　**139**

6 Smoking and mortality　　　　　　　　　　　　　　　　　　141

6.1 Introduction 141

6.2 Basic concepts of duration analysis 141

6.3 The HALS data 143

6.4 Duration data in HALS 145

6.5 Descriptive statistics 149

6.6 Duration models 150

6.7 Overview 181

7 Health and retirement　　　　　　　　　　　　　　　　　　182

7.1 Introduction 182

7.2 Preparing and summarising the data 182

7.3 Dealing with self-reported health 193

7.4 Empirical approach to duration modelling 196

7.5 Stock sampling and discrete-time hazard analysis 201

7.6 Overview 217

PART IV
Panel data　　　　　　　　　　　　　　　　　　　　　　　　　　**219**

8 Health and wages　　　　　　　　　　　　　　　　　　　　221

8.1 Introduction 221

8.2 BHPS sample and variables 222

8.3 Empirical model and estimation 225

8.4 Overview 241

Appendix 243

9 Modelling the dynamics of health　　　　　　　　　　　　　**244**

9.1 Introduction 244

9.2 Static models 251

9.3   Dynamic models 268
9.4   Overview 276

10   Non-response and attrition bias   277

10.1 Introduction 277
10.2 Testing for non-response bias 280
10.3 Estimation 283
10.4 Overview 290
Appendix 290

PART V
Health care data   293

11   Models for count data   295

11.1 Introduction 295
11.2 The Poisson model 296
11.3 The negative binomial model 299
11.4 Zero-inflated models 302
11.5 Hurdle models 308
11.6 Finite mixture/latent class models 311
11.7 Latent class models for panel data 318
11.8 Overview 337
Appendix 337

12   Modelling health care costs   342

12.1 Introduction 342
12.2 Exponential conditional mean models 343
12.3 Generalised linear models 359
12.4 Finite mixture models 370
12.5 Comparing model performance 377
12.6 Overview 380

Bibliography   381
Index   388

Illustrations

FIGURES

2.1	Bar chart for SAH, men	15
2.2	Bar chart for SAH by wave, men	16
2.3	Bar chart for SAH by age group, wave 1, men	17
2.4	Bar chart for SAH by quintile of meaninc, men	18
2.5	Empirical CDFs of meaninc, men	19
2.6	Bar chart for SAH by education, men	20
2.7	Bar chart for SAH by previous SAH, wave 2, men	21
3.1	Distribution of positive costs	35
3.2	Distribution of transformed costs	36
3.3	Box plots of health care costs	37
3.4	Normal probability plots of health care costs	37
3.5	Mean of cost against variance – level of cost (LHS): log of costs (RHS)	40
3.6	Empirical CDFs by insurance status: all expenditures and expenditures < $15,000	43
3.7	Normal probability plot for Box–Cox residuals	64
6.1	Non-parametric functions for smoking initiation	153
6.2	Cox–Snell residuals test – smoking initiation	156
6.3	Log-logistic functions for smoking initiation	160
6.4	Cox–Snell residuals test – smoking initiation for starters	161
6.5	Log-logistic functions for smoking initiation	164
6.6	Non-parametric functions for smoking cessation	167
6.7	Cox–Snell residuals test – smoking cessation	170
6.8	Weibull estimated functions for smoking cessation	171
6.9	Normal probability plot for lifespan	174
6.10	Non-parametric functions for lifespan	176
6.11	Cox–Snell residuals test – lifespan	177
6.12	Gompertz estimated functions for lifespan	181
7.1	Life table estimates of the proportion not retired by health limitations	203
12.1	Normal probability plot for the exponential conditional mean model	345

12.2	Hosmer–Lemeshow plot: nonlinear least squares	348
12.3	Hosmer–Lemeshow plot: Poisson regression	350
12.4	Weibull density functions	351
12.5	Normal pp plot for generalised linear model	364

TABLES

3.1	Description of dataset	32
3.2	Summary statistics of variables	41
3.3	OLS on total expenditures	45
3.4	Maximum likelihood estimation of log-normal model	51
3.5	Heteroskedasticity on log-scale	56
3.6	Square root transformed linear regression	58
3.7	Comparison of approaches for a binary regressor	60
3.8	Comparison of predictions following retransformation	61
3.9	Box–Cox transformed regression	63
3.10	Summary of residuals from Box–Cox transformed regression	64
4.1	Ordered probit for self-reported health in the domain of breathing	73
4.2	Partial effects on the probability of reporting no problems with breathing for reference individual, with homogeneous reporting	74
4.3	Ordered probit for vignette ratings in the domain of *breathing*	80
4.4	Generalised ordered probit for vignette ratings in the domain of *breathing*	82
4.5	Interval regression for self-reported health in the domain of breathing with parallel cut-point shift	88
4.6	Partial effects on the probability of having no problems with breathing for reference individual, with parallel cut-point shift	89
4.7	Interval regression for self-reported health in the domain of breathing with non-parallel cut-point shift	91
4.8	Partial effects on the probability of having no problems with breathing for reference individual, with non-parallel cut-point shift – two-step estimation	91
4.9	HOPIT for self-reported health in the domain of breathing with cut-point shift – one-step estimation	93
4.10	Partial effects on the probability of having no problems with breathing for reference individual in model with non-parallel cut-point shift – one-step HOPIT estimation	98
4.11	Estimated coefficients in latent health index in all models	99
4.12	Partial effects on the probability of reporting no problems with breathing for reference individual in all models	100
5.1	Probit model for mortality – without exclusion restrictions	124
5.2	Probit model for mortality – with exclusion restrictions	125
5.3	Multivariate probit model – without exclusion restrictions	128

5.4	Multivariate probit model – with exclusion restrictions	131
5.5	Average partial effects from alternative models for mortality	137
6.1	Information criteria – smoking initiation	156
6.2	Smoking initiation – coefficients from log-logistic model (AFT)	159
6.3	Information criteria – smoking initiation for starters	161
6.4	Smoking initiation for starters – coefficients from log-logistic model (AFT)	163
6.5	Information criteria – smoking cessation	169
6.6	Smoking cessation – coefficients from Weibull model (AFT)	172
6.7	Information criteria – lifespan	177
6.8	Lifespan – coefficients from Gompertz model	179
6.9	Lifespan – hazard ratio from Gompertz model	180
7.1	Variable names and definitions	187
7.2	Labour market status by wave	191
7.3	Descriptive statistics	192
7.4	Ordered probits for self-assessed health	195
7.5	Life-table for retirement by health limitations	202
7.6	Discrete-time hazard model – no heterogeneity	207
7.7	Complementary log-log model with frailty	210
7.8	Discrete-time duration model with gamma distributed frailty	212
7.9	Discrete-time duration model with Heckman–Singer frailty	214
7.10	Discrete-time duration model with Heckman–Singer frailty	215
7.11	Discrete-time duration models with latent self-assessed health	216
8.1	Variable labels and definitions	226
8.2	Summary statistics for full sample of observations	227
8.3	OLS on full sample of observations	229
8.4	RE on full sample of observations	231
8.5	FE on full sample of observations	233
8.6	Hausman and Taylor IV estimator on full sample of observations	237
8.7	Men – Amemiya and MaCurdy IV estimator on full sample of observations	240
8.8	Men – comparison across estimators	242
9.1	Pooled probit model, unbalanced panel	253
9.2	Pooled probit model, average partial effects	254
9.3	Pooled probit model, balanced panel	255
9.4	Mundlak specification of pooled probit model, unbalanced panel	257
9.5	Random effects probit model, unbalanced panel	259
9.6	Random effects probit model, partial effects	260
9.7	Random effects probit model, balanced panel	264
9.8	Mundlak specification of random effects probit model, unbalanced panel	266
9.9	Conditional logit model, unbalanced panel	268
9.10	Dynamic pooled probit model, unbalanced panel	271
9.11	Dynamic pooled probit model with initial conditions, unbalanced panel	272

9.12	Dynamic random effects probit model with initial conditions, unbalanced panel	273
9.13	Dynamic random effects probit model with initial conditions, partial effects	274
10.1	Dynamic pooled probit with IPW, unbalanced panel	288
10.2	Dynamic pooled probit with IPW, balanced panel	289
11.1	Poisson regression	297
11.2	Average marginal effects from Poisson regression	298
11.3	Poisson regression with robust standard errors	299
11.4	Negative binomial model	301
11.5	Average marginal effects from negative binomial model	301
11.6	Generalised negative binomial model	302
11.7	Zero-inflated Poisson model with constant zero-inflation probability	304
11.8	Average marginal effects from zero-inflated Poisson model with constant zero-inflation probability	304
11.9	Zero-inflated Poisson model with variable zero-inflation probability	305
11.10	Zero-inflated NB model for number of specialist visits with variable zero-inflation probability	306
11.11	Average marginal effects from zero-inflated NB model with variable zero-inflation probability	307
11.12	Logit-NB2 hurdle model	309
11.13	Average marginal effects on probability of receiving some health care from first part of hurdle model (Logit)	310
11.14	Average marginal effects on conditionally positive number of visits from second part of hurdle model (truncated NB2)	311
11.15	LCNB model with two latent classes	313
11.16	Summary statistics of fitted values by latent class (LCNB)	314
11.17	Average marginal effects of continuous regressors from LCNB model – latent class 1	315
11.18	Average marginal effects of continuous regressors from LCNB model – latent class 2	316
11.19	Average marginal effects of continuous regressors from LCNB model	316
11.20	Average incremental effects of male from LCNB model	317
11.21	AIC and BIC of alternative models	317
11.22	LCNB-Pan with two latent classes	323
11.23	Summary statistics of fitted values by latent class (LCNB-Pan)	323
11.24	AIC and BIC of NB, LCNB and LCNB-Pan (with two latent classes)	325
11.25	LCH-Pan (with two latent classes), with constant class membership	329
11.26	AIC and BIC of LCNB-Pan, hurdle and LCH-Pan	330
11.27	LCH-Pan (with two latent classes), with variable class membership	332

11.28	Summary statistics for individual p in LCH-Pan, with variable class membership	333
11.29	Summary statistics of fitted values by latent class in LCH-Pan, with variable class membership	335
11.30	AIC and BIC of LCNB-Pan and LCH-Pan (with two latent classes) with constant and variable class memberships	336
12.1	Nonlinear regression: exponential conditional mean model	344
12.2	Average marginal effects for exponential conditional mean model	346
12.3	Average marginal effects from Poisson regression	349
12.4	Exponential hazard function	353
12.5	Marginal effects from exponential hazard function	354
12.6	Weibull hazard function	356
12.7	Marginal effects from Wcibull hazard function	356
12.8	Link test Weibull hazard function	357
12.9	Generalised gamma	358
12.10	Generalised gamma	360
12.11	Generalised gamma with heteroskedasticity	361
12.12	Generalised linear model; square root link, gamma distribution	363
12.13	Link test for generalised linear model	366
12.14	Summary results for alternative GLMs	367
12.15	Extended estimating equations	369
12.16	Finite mixture model (mixture of gammas)	372
12.17	Finite mixture model information criteria	375
12.18	Finite mixture model (three-component mixture of gammas)	376
12.19	Comparison of model specification and predictive performance	379

Preface

Large-scale survey datasets, in particular complex survey designs such as panel data and surveys linked to administrative data, provide a rich source of information for health economists. Panel data offer the scope to control for individual heterogeneity and to model the dynamics of individual behaviour. The detailed information on individual morbidity characteristics and use of health care services contained in administrative data allows the analyst to model observed heterogeneity. However, the measures of outcome used in health economics do not always lend themselves to straightforward analysis and are often qualitative or categorical or display non-symmetrical and heteroskedastic distributions. These features of outcomes create challenges for estimating econometric models. The dramatic growth in computing power over recent years has been accompanied by the development of methods that help to overcome these challenges. The purpose of this book is to provide a practical guide to the skills necessary to put the required methods into practice.

This book highlights practical applications of econometric methods, illustrated using data on health from the British Health and Lifestyle Survey (HALS), the British Household Panel Survey (BHPS), the European Community Household Panel (ECHP), the US Medical Expenditure Panel Survey (MEPS) and the Survey of Health, Ageing and Retirement in Europe (SHARE). Throughout the book, there is a strong emphasis on applied work, illustrating the use of relevant computer software with code provided for Stata version 12 (www.stata.com). Familiarity with the basic syntax and structure of Stata is assumed. The Stata code and extracts from the statistical output are embedded directly in the main text (using the font Courier New) and explained as we go along, for example:

```
use "c:\stata\data\bhps.dta" , clear
```

The corresponding Stata output appears alongside in a smaller font. The code presented in this book can be downloaded from the web pages of the Health, Econometrics and Data Group (HEDG): www.york.ac.uk/res/herc/research/hedg/.

We do not attempt to provide a review of the extensive health economics literature that makes use of econometric methods (for surveys of the literature see Jones, 2000, 2009). Instead, the book is built around empirical case studies, rather than general theory, and the emphasis is on learning by example. We present a detailed dissection of methods and results of some recent research papers written by the authors and our colleagues. Relevant methods are presented alongside the Stata code that can be used to implement them and the empirical results are discussed as we go along. To our knowledge, no comparable text exists. There are health economics texts and there are econometrics texts but these tend to focus on theory rather than application and tend not to bring the two disciplines together for the benefit of applied economists. The emphasis is on hands-on empirical analysis: the area that econometric texts tend to neglect. The closest in spirit is Angus Deaton's (1997) excellent book on the analysis of household surveys, but that emphasises issues in the economics of development, poverty and welfare rather than health. A general knowledge of microeconometric methods is assumed. For more details, readers can refer to texts such as Baltagi (2005), Cameron and Trivedi (2005), Greene (2003) and Wooldridge (2002b). Cameron and Trivedi (2009) provide a comprehensive source for the use of microeconometrics based on Stata and we have adopted one of their datasets in the analysis presented in Chapters 3 and 12.

As the book is built around case studies, and these reflect the particular interests of the authors, we do not claim to cover the full diversity of topics within applied health economics. However, we hope that these examples provide guidance and inspiration for those working on other topics within the field who want to make use of econometric methods. The book is primarily aimed at advanced undergraduates and postgraduates in health economics, along with health economics researchers in academic, government and private sector organisations who want to learn more about empirical research methods. In addition, the book may be used by other applied economists, in areas such as labour and environmental economics, and by health and social statisticians.

The second edition has been revised and updated throughout and two new chapters, on the description and modelling of individual health care costs, have been added.

Acknowledgements

Data from the British Household Panel Survey (BHPS) were supplied by the UK Data Archive. Neither the original collectors of the data nor the Archive bear any responsibility for the analysis or interpretations presented here. The European Community Household Panel Users' Database (ECHP), version of December 2003, was supplied by Eurostat. Data from the Health and Lifestyle Survey (HALS) were supplied by the UK Data Archive. SHARE data are from release 2.5.0 of wave 1 (2004). The SHARE data collection has been primarily funded by the European Commission through the 5th framework programme (project QLK6-CT-2001-00360 in the thematic programme Quality of Life), through the 6th framework programme (projects SHARE-I3, RII-CT- 2006-062193, COMPARE, CIT5-CT-2005-028857, and SHARELIFE, CIT4-CT-2006-028812) and through the 7th framework programme (SHARE-PREP, 211909 and SHARE-LEAP, 227822). Additional funding from the US National Institute on Aging (U01 AG09740-13S2, P01 AG005842, P01 AG08291, P30 AG12815, Y1-AG-4553-01 and OGHA 04-064, IAG BSR06-11, R21 AG025169) as well as from various national sources is gratefully acknowledged (see www.share-project.org for a full list of funding institutions). The subsample of MEPS data corresponds to that used in Cameron and Trivedi (2009). Instructions on how to download these data are available at the Stata Press website (www.stata-press.com/books/musr.html).

We are very grateful to all of the co-authors of the joint work that we use as case studies: Paul Contoyannis, Martin Forster, Xander Koolman, Owen O'Donnell, Jennifer Roberts and Eddy van Doorslaer. The specific papers that are adapted for the case studies are the following:

Bago d'Uva, T. (2006) 'Latent class models for health care utilisation', *Health Economics*, 15: 329–343.

Bago d'Uva, T. and Jones, A. (2009) 'Health care utilisation in Europe: new evidence from the ECHP', *Journal of Health Economics*, 28: 265–279.

Bago d'Uva, T., O'Donnell, O. and van Doorslaer, E. (2008) 'Differential health reporting by education level and its impact on the measurement of health inequalities among older Europeans', *International Journal of Epidemiology*, 37: 1375–1383.

Balia, S. and Jones, A.M. (2008) 'Mortality, lifestyle and socio-economic status', *Journal of Health Economics*, 27: 1–26.

Balia, S. and Jones, A.M. (2011) 'Catching the habit: a study of inequality of opportunity in smoking-related mortality', *Journal of the Royal Statistical Society Series A*, 174: 175–194.

Contoyannis, P. and Rice, N. (2001) 'The impact of health on wages: evidence from the British Household Panel Survey', *Empirical Economics*, 26: 599–622.

Contoyannis, P., Jones, A.M. and Rice, N. (2004b) 'The dynamics of health in the British Household Panel Survey', *Journal of Applied Econometrics*, 19: 473–503.

Forster, M. and Jones, A.M. (2001) 'The role of tobacco taxes in starting and quitting smoking: duration analysis of British data', *Journal of the Royal Statistical Society Series A*, 164: 517–547.

Jones, A.M. (2011) 'Models for health care', in Hendry, D. and Clements, M. (eds), *Oxford Handbook of Economic Forecasting*, Oxford: Oxford University Press, pp. 625–654.

Jones, A.M., Koolman, X. and Rice, N. (2006) 'Health-related non-response in the BHPS and ECHP: using inverse probability weighted estimators in nonlinear models', *Journal of the Royal Statistical Society Series A*, 169: 543–569.

Jones, A.M., Rice, N. and Roberts, J. (2010) 'Sick of work or too sick to work? Evidence on self-reported health shocks and early retirement from the BHPS', *Economic Modelling*, 27: 866–880.

A draft of the first edition of the book was used as teaching material for a short course named 'Applied Health Economics', which was hosted by the Health, Econometrics and Data Group (HEDG) at the University of York, 19–30 June 2006. This course was part of the Marie Curie Training Programme in Applied Health Economics. We are grateful for the input from other members of HEDG who were involved with the course: Cristina Hernández Quevedo, Eugenio Zucchelli, Silvana Robone, Pedro Rosa Dias and Rodrigo Moreno Serra. Also we would like to thank the course participants for their valuable feedback on the material.

We are particularly grateful to Ranjeeta Thomas for her assistance in preparing the second edition, which included commenting on all of the chapters and the Stata code.

Introduction

This book provides a practical guide to doing applied health economics. It is built around a series of case studies that are based on recent research. The first, which runs through the book, explores the dynamics of self-reported health in the British Household Panel Survey (BHPS). The aim is to investigate socioeconomic gradients in health, persistence of health problems and the difficulties created by sample attrition in panel data (Contoyannnis *et al.*, 2004b; Jones *et al.*, 2006). The data for this and all the other case studies are introduced in Chapter 1, which also introduces some general principles of survey design.

Chapter 2 uses the BHPS sample to show how descriptive techniques, including graphs and tables, can be used to summarise and explore the raw data and provide an intuitive understanding of how variables are distributed and associated with each other. Chapter 3 uses data on the medical expenditures of elderly individuals in the United States from the Medical Expenditure Panel Survey (MEPS) dataset. The chapter describes the challenges that modelling health care costs can present. Individual level data on medical expenditures typically feature a spike at zero, are heavily right skewed, have heavy tails and exhibit heteroskedasticity.

Subjective and self-reported measures of health raise questions of reliability. Chapter 4 explores the issue of reporting bias using French data from the Survey of Health, Ageing and Retirement in Europe (SHARE). The standard ordered probit model is extended to include applications of the generalised ordered model and the 'HOPIT'. These exploit hypothetical 'vignettes' to deal with reporting bias (Bago d'Uva *et al.*, 2008a).

Lifestyle factors, such as smoking and drinking, are thought to have an influence on health. But these health-related behaviours are individual choices that are themselves influenced by, often unobservable, individual characteristics such as time preference rates. Chapter 5 uses data from the Health and Lifestyle Survey (HALS) to show how the multivariate probit model can be used to model mortality, morbidity and lifestyles jointly, taking account of the problem of unobservables (Balia and Jones, 2008). This illustrates the kind of models that can be applied to categorical data in cross-section surveys.

Part III moves from cross-sectional data to longitudinal data, in particular to duration analysis. There are two types of duration data: continuous and discrete time. Chapter 6 takes the analysis of HALS a step further by estimating continuous time duration models for initiation and cessation of smoking and for the risk of death (this draws on work by Forster and Jones, 2001, and Balia and Jones, 2011). Chapter 7 illustrates convenient methods for discrete-time duration analysis. The BHPS is used to investigate the extent to which 'health shocks' are a factor that leads to early retirement, following Roberts and co-workers (2010).

Longitudinal data is the focus of Part IV, which presents linear and nonlinear panel data regression methods. Linear models are covered in Chapter 8, where BHPS data are used to estimate classical Mincerian wage equations that are augmented by measures of self-reported health (Contoyannis and Rice, 2001). Chapter 9 stays with the BHPS but moves to nonlinear dynamic specifications (Contoyannis *et al.*, 2004b). The outcome of interest is a binary measure of health problems and the focus is on socioeconomic gradients in health. Chapter 10 continues this analysis but shifts the emphasis to the potential problems created by sample attrition in panel data (Jones *et al.*, 2006). The chapter shows how to test for attrition bias and illustrates how inverse probability weights provide one way of dealing with the problem.

Part V turns to methods that are suitable for modelling individual data on health care utilisation when that is measured by numbers of visits or by levels of expenditure. Health care utilisation is most frequently modelled using count data regressions. Chapter 11 analyses data on specialist visits taken from the European Community Household Panel (ECHP). The chapter reviews and applies standard methods and also introduces recent developments of the literature that use a latent class specification (Bago d'Uva, 2006). Chapter 12 builds on the earlier analysis of individual health care costs in Chapter 3. It uses the MEPS data to show how nonlinear regression models can augment the standard linear model when the outcome of interest is highly non-normal and it compares the performance of different specifications.

The key methods and Stata commands that are covered in each chapter are summarised below.

Chapter	Key methods	Key Stata commands
2	Descriptive statistics:	
	Summary statistics	`summarize`
	Bar charts	`graph bar`
	Empirical distribution functions	`distplot`
	Frequency tables	`tabulate`
		`xttrans`
3	Descriptive statistics:	
	Histograms	`tw histogram`
	Box-whisker plots	`graph box`
	Normal plots	`pnorm`
	Linear regression:	`regress`
	Predictions	`predict`
		`preserve & restore`

Chapter	Key methods	Key Stata commands
	Diagnostics	`estat hetest`
		`estat ovtest`
		`linktest`
	Box–Cox regression	`boxcox`
4	Ordered probit	`oprobit`
	Generalised ordered probit	`ml`
	Interval regression	`intreg`
	HOPIT	
5	Binary choice:	
	Probit	`probit`
	Multivariate choice:	
	Multivariate probit	`mvprobit`
	Average partial effects	`preserve & restore`
	Information criteria	`estimates store`
		`estimates stats`
6	Continuous time survival models:	`stset`
	Kaplan–Meier and Nelson–Aalen	`sts graph`
	Parametric models (exponential,	`streg`
	Weibull, log-logistic, log-normal,	`stcurve`
	Gompertz)	
	Cox–Snell residuals	`line, gr combine`
7	Discrete time survival models:	
	Life tables	`ltable`
		`sts graph`
	Complementary log-log models	`cloglog`
	Unobserved frailty	`pgmhaz8`
		`xtcloglog`
	Heckman–Singer model	`hshaz`
8	Linear panel data models:	`xtset`
	Random effects	`xtreg, re`
	Fixed effects	`xtreg, fe`
	Hausman tests	`hausman`
	Hausman–Taylor estimator	`xthtaylor`
9	Panel probit models:	`xtsum`
	Pooled	`probit, dprobit`
	Random effects	`xtprobit`
	Average partial effects	`margins`
	Conditional logit	`clogit`
	Dynamic panel probit	`redpace`

Chapter	Key methods	Key Stata commands
10	Attrition bias:	
	Inverse probability weights	`probit`
11	Count data regression:	
	Poisson model	`poisson`
	Negbin model	`nbreg, gnbreg`
	Zero-inflated models	`zip, zinb`
	Hurdle models	`hnblogit, ztnb`
	Finite mixture models	`fmm, ml`
12	Cost regressions:	
	ECM models (nls and ml)	`nl,`
		`poisson`
	Generalised gamma models	`streg`
	GLMs	`glm`
	Extended estimating equations	`pglm`
	Finite mixture models	`fmm`

Part I

Describing and summarising data

1 Data and survey design

SYNOPSIS

This chapter introduces each of the datasets that are used in the practical case studies throughout the book. It discusses some important features of survey design and focuses on the variables that are of particular interest for health economists.

1.1 THE HEALTH AND LIFESTYLE SURVEY

The sample

The Health and Lifestyle Survey (HALS) is an example of a health interview survey. Aspects of the survey are used in Chapters 5 and 6. The HALS was designed as a representative survey of adults in Great Britain (see Cox *et al.*, 1987, 1993). The population surveyed was individuals aged 18 and over living in private households. In principle, each individual should have an equal probability of being selected for the survey. This allows the data to be used to make inferences about the underlying population. HALS was designed originally as a cross-section survey with one measurement for each individual. It was carried out between the autumn of 1984 and the summer of 1985, and information was collected in three stages:

- a one-hour face-to-face interview, which collected information on experience and attitudes towards to health and lifestyle along with general socioeconomic information;
- a nurse visit to collect physiological measures and indicators of cognitive function, such as memory and reasoning;
- a self-completion postal questionnaire to measure psychiatric health and personality.

The HALS is an example of a clustered random sample. The intention was to build a representative random sample of this population but without the excessive costs of collecting a true random sample. Addresses were randomly selected from electoral registers using a three-stage design. First 198 electoral constituencies were selected with the probability of selection proportional to the population of each constituency. Then two electoral wards were selected for each constituency and, finally, 30 addresses per ward. Then individuals were randomly selected from households. This selection procedure gave a target of 12,672 interviews.

Some of the addresses from the electoral register proved to be inappropriate as they were in use as holiday homes, business premises or were derelict. This number was relatively small and only 418 addresses were excluded, leaving a total of 12,254 individuals to be interviewed. The response rate fell more dramatically when it came to success in completing these interviews: 9,003 interviews were completed. This is a response rate of 73.5 per cent. In other words, there was a 1 in 4 chance that an interview was not completed.

The overall response rate is fairly typical of general population surveys. Understandably, the response rate declines for the subsequent nurse visit and postal questionnaire. The overall response rate for those individuals who completed all three stages of the survey is only 53.7 per cent. To get a sense of how well the sample represents the population, it can be compared to external data sources. The most comprehensive of these is the population census which is collected every ten years. Comparison with the 1981 census suggests that the final sample under-represents those with lower incomes and lower levels of education. In general, it is important to bear this kind of unit non-response in mind when doing analysis with any survey data.

The longitudinal follow-up

The HALS was originally intended to be a one-off cross-section survey. However, HALS also provides an example of a longitudinal, or panel, dataset. In 1991/92, seven years on from the original survey, the HALS was repeated. This provides an example of repeated measurements, where the same individuals are re-interviewed. Panel data provide a powerful enhancement of cross-section surveys that allows a deeper analysis of heterogeneity across individuals and of changes in individual behaviour over time. However, because of the need to revisit and interview individuals repeatedly, the problems of unit non-response tend to be amplified. Of the original 9,003 individuals who were interviewed at the time of the first HALS survey, 808 (9 per cent) had died by the time of the second survey, 1,347 (14.9 per cent) could not be traced and 222 were traced but could not be interviewed, either because they had moved overseas or they had moved to geographic areas that were out of the scope of the survey. These cases are examples of attrition – individuals who drop out of a longitudinal survey.

The deaths data

HALS provides an example of a cross-section survey (HALS1) and panel data (HALS1&2). Also it provides a longitudinal follow-up of subsequent mortality and cancer cases among the original respondents. These deaths data can be used for survival analysis. Most of the 9,003 individuals interviewed in HALS1 have been *flagged* on the NHS Central Register. In June 2005, the fifth deaths revision and the second cancer revision were completed. The flagging process was quite lengthy because it required several checks in order to be sure that the flagging registrations were related to the person previously interviewed. About 98 per cent of the sample had been flagged. Deaths account for some 27 per cent of the original sample. This information is used in Chapter 6 for a duration analysis of mortality rates.

1.2 THE BRITISH HOUSEHOLD PANEL SURVEY

The sample

The British Household Panel Survey (BHPS) is a longitudinal survey of private households in Great Britain that provides rich information on socio-demographic and health variables. While HALS has only two waves of panel data, the BHPS has repeated annual measurements from 1991 to the present and is an ongoing survey, which has become part of the larger understanding society study. This provides more scope for longitudinal analysis. The BHPS is used in Chapters 2, and 7 to 10.

The BHPS was designed as an annual survey of each adult (16+) member of a nationally representative sample of more that 5,000 households, with a total of approximately 10,000 individual interviews. The first wave of the survey was conducted between 1 September 1990 and 30 April 1991. The initial selection of households for inclusion in the survey was performed using a two-stage clustered systematic sampling procedure designed to give each address an approximately equal probability of selection (Taylor *et al.*, 1998). The same individuals are re-interviewed in successive waves and, if they split off from their original households are also re-interviewed along with all adult members of their new households.

Measures of health

One measure of health outcomes that is available in the BHPS, and many other general surveys, is self-assessed health (SAH), defined by a response to: 'Please think back over the last 12 months about how your health has been. Compared to people of your own age, would you say that your health has on the whole been excellent/good/fair/poor/very poor?' SAH should therefore be interpreted as indicating a perceived health status relative to the individual's concept of the 'norm' for their age group. SAH has been used widely in previous studies of the relationship between health and socioeconomic status and of the relationship between health and lifestyles. SAH is a simple subjective measure of health that provides an ordinal ranking of perceived health status.

Unfortunately there was a change in the wording of the SAH question at wave 9 of the BHPS. For waves 1–8 and 10 onwards, the SAH variable represents 'health status over the last 12 months'. However, the SF-36 questionnaire was included in wave 9. In this questionnaire, the SAH variable for wave 9 represents 'general state of health', using the question: 'In general, would you say your health is: excellent, very good, good, fair, poor?'. Note that the question is not framed in terms of a comparison with people of one's own age and the response categories differ from the other waves. Item non-response is greater for SAH at wave 9 than for the other waves and these factors would complicate the analysis of non-response rates. Hernandez *et al.* (2004) have explored the sensitivity of models of SAH to this change in the wording.

Other indicators of morbidity are available in the BHPS. The variable health limitations (HLLT) measures self-reported functional limitations and is based on the question 'does your health in any way limit your daily activities compared to most people of your age?' Respondents are left to define their own concepts of health and their daily activities. In contrast, for the variable measuring specified health problems (HLPRB), respondents are presented with a prompt card and asked, 'do you have any of the health problems or disabilities listed on this card?' The list is made up of problems with arms, legs, hands, etc; sight; hearing; skin conditions/allergies; chest/breathing; heart/blood pressure; stomach/ digestion; diabetes; anxiety/depression; alcohol/drug-related; epilepsy; migraine and other (cancer and stroke were added as separate categories in wave 11). Also respondents are asked to report whether they are registered as a disabled person (HLDSBL).

Socioeconomic status

The analysis of the BHPS data discussed in subsequent chapters often focuses on socioeconomic gradients in health. Two main dimensions of socioeconomic status are included in our analyses: income and education. Income is measured as equivalised and RPI-deflated annual household income (INCOME). In our analysis, this variable is often transformed to natural logarithms to allow for concavity of the relationship between health and income. Education is measured by the highest educational qualification attained by the end of the sample period in descending order of attainment (DEGREE, HND/A, O/CSE). NO-QUAL (no academic qualifications) is the reference category for the educational variable. In addition to income and education, variables are included to reflect individuals' demographic characteristics and stage of life: age, ethnic group, marital status and family composition. Marital status distinguishes between WIDOW, SINGLE (never married) and DIVORCED/SEPARATED, with married or living as a couple as the reference category. Similarly, we include an indicator of ethnic origin

(NON-WHITE), the number of individuals living in the household including the respondent (HHSIZE), and the numbers of children living in the household at different ages (NCH04, NCH511, NCH1218). Age is included as a fourth-order polynomial (AGE, AGE2 = $AGE^2/100$, AGE3 = $AGE^3/10000$, AGE4 = $AGE^4/1000000$), where the higher order terms are rescaled to avoid computational problems in the estimation routines.

1.3 THE EUROPEAN COMMUNITY HOUSEHOLD PANEL

The sample

The European Community Household Panel User Database (ECHP-UDB) adds an international dimension and allows a comparison across countries as well as across time. It is used in Chapter 11.

The ECHP was designed and coordinated by Eurostat, the European Statistical Office, and is a standardised multi-purpose annual longitudinal survey carried out at the level of the pre-enlargement European Union (EC-15), between 1994 (wave 1) and 2001 (wave 8). More information about the survey can be found in Peracchi (2002). The survey is based on a standardised questionnaire that involves annual interviewing of a representative panel of households and individuals of 16 years and older in each of the participating EU member states. It covers a wide range of topics including demographics, income, social transfers, health, housing, education and employment. Data are available for the following member states of the EU (waves): Austria (waves 2–8), Belgium (1–8), Denmark (1–8), Finland (3–8), France (1–8), Germany (1–3), Greece (1–8), Ireland (1–8), Italy (1–8), Luxembourg (1–3), Netherlands (1–8), Portugal (1–8), Spain (1–8) and the United Kingdom (1–3). The case study in Chapter 11 is based on Bago d'Uva and Jones (2009), which used data for all countries except France (relevant information on health care use not available), Germany, Luxembourg and the United Kingdom. Sweden did not take part in the ECHP although the living conditions panel is included with the UDB. The ECHP-UDB also includes comparable versions of the older, and still ongoing, British and German panels – BHPS and German Socioeconomic Panel (GSOEP) – between 1994 and 2001. The illustration in Chapter 11 uses Portuguese data from waves 2 to 5.

Health care utilisation

The ECHP contains information on health care use during the past 12 months. Individuals are asked whether they have been admitted to a hospital as an inpatient and the number of nights spent in a hospital. Additionally, they are also asked about the number of consultations with a general practitioner, specialist and dentist (separately, except for wave 1). In Chapter 11, we illustrate the application of count data models to the number of specialist consultations.

Measures of health

In the ECHP self-assessed general health status (SAH) is measured as either very good, good, fair, poor or very poor. Unlike the BHPS, respondents are not asked to compare themselves with others of the same age. In France, a six-category scale was used but this is recoded to the five-category scale in the ECHP-UDB. Responses are also available for the question 'Do you have any chronic physical or mental health problem, illness or disability? (yes/no)' and if so 'Are you hampered in your daily activities by this physical or mental health problem, illness or disability? (no; yes, to some extent; yes, severely).' In this case study, we consider only a dummy variable indicating whether individuals' health in the previous wave as poor or very poor (as opposed to fair, good or very good).

Socioeconomic status and demographic characteristics

The ECHP includes a comprehensive set of information on household and personal income, broken down by source. In our analysis, the principal income measure is total disposable household income per equivalent adult, using the modified Organisation for Economic Cooperation and Development (OECD) equivalence scale (giving a weight of 1.0 to the first adult, 0.5 to the second and each subsequent person aged 14 and over, and 0.3 to each child aged under 14 in the household). Total household income includes all net monetary income received by the household members during the reference year. Bago d'Uva and Jones (2009) also use information not used here, which is the highest level of general or higher education completed (third level education, ISCED 5–7, second stage of secondary level education, ISCED 3–4, or less than second stage of secondary education, ISCED 0–2); marital status (married/living in consensual union, separated/divorced, widowed or unmarried); and activity status (employed, self-employed, student, unemployed, retired, doing housework or 'other economically inactive').

1.4 THE US MEDICAL EXPENDITURE PANEL SURVEY

The sample

The Medical Expenditure Panel Survey (MEPS) is a panel survey conducted in the United States since 1996 covering families and individuals, employers and, importantly for our purposes, information on the use of medical services (doctors, hospitals, pharmacies, etc.). This includes data on health services accessed, frequency of contact, the cost of services used and information on health insurance status. A subset of MEPS data is used in Chapters 3 and 12 to illustrate regression-based approaches to modelling health care costs. MEPS consists of two basic survey components: a Household Component providing data on households and their members with additional data obtained from medical providers; and an Insurance Component providing information on health insurance.

The Household Component collects data on families and individuals in selected areas across the United States drawn from a nationally representative subsample of households that participated in the prior year's National Health Interview Survey (conducted by the US National Centre for Health Statistics). Data is collected through what is termed an overlapping panel design. An initial interview with each respondent is followed by five rounds of interviews over a two-and-a-half-year period. Each year the survey is supplemented by a new sample of households to provide overlapping panels of data. Data are collected on demographic characteristics, health conditions, health status, use of medical services, charges and source of payments, access to care, satisfaction with care, health insurance coverage, income and employment. The Insurance Component includes information from employers on the health insurance plans offered to their employees, such as the number and type of private insurance plans offered, premiums, contributions by employers and employees, eligibility criteria, and the benefits associated with the plans. This is augmented with information on the characteristics of employers.

Health care costs

Health care expenditures in MEPS are defined as the sum of direct payments for care provided during the year, including out-of-pocket payments and payments by private insurance, Medicaid, Medicare and other sources. Annual data are collected on the use of and associated expenditures for office and hospital-based care, home health care, dental services, prescribed medicines, vision aids and other medical supplies and equipment. Payments for over-the-counter drugs, alternative care services and phone contacts with medical providers are not included. Missing data on expenditures are imputed using a weighted sequential hot-deck procedure for medical visits and services. This aims to impute data from events with complete information to events with missing information but with similar characteristics.

Socioeconomic status

The use and intensity of health care consumed is often modelled as a function of socioeconomic characteristics and health status indicators. Among other information, MEPS collects data on respondent age, race (American Indian, Alaska Native, Asian or Pacific Islander, black, white, or other), household income, household poverty status (income relative to poverty thresholds measured as poor, near poor, low income, middle income, high income), region and place of residence (e.g. region: Northeast, Midwest, South, West) and employment status (employed if aged 16 or over, and had a job for pay, owned a business, or worked without pay in a family business). Health status is recorded by asking respondents to rate the health of each person in the family using the following categories: excellent, very good, good, fair, and poor. Health insurance details for individuals under age 65 is categorised as: private health insurance (individuals who had insurance that provides cover for hospital and physician care, other than Medicare, Medicaid, or other public cover); public cover only (individuals not covered by private insurance and were covered by Medicare, Medicaid, or other public cover); and uninsured. Individuals age 65 and over were classified as being insured under Medicare only; Medicare and private insurance; Medicare and other public insurance.

The particular subset of data used in Chapters 3 and 12 is taken from the MEPS sample used in Chapter 3 of Cameron and Trivedi (2009) (Stata dataset mus03data.dta which we have renamed AHE_2ed_Ch_3.dta). Instructions to download these data can be obtained from the Stata Press website: www.stata-press.com/books/musr.html. The data covers the medical expenditures of US citizens aged 65 years and older who qualify for health care under Medicare. Medicare is a federally financed health insurance plan for the elderly, persons receiving Social Security disability payments and individuals with end-stage renal disease. Total annual health care expenditures are measured in US dollars, and this is the outcome of interest in Chapters 3 and 12. Other key variables are age, gender, household income, supplementary insurance status (insurance beyond Medicare), physical and activity limitations and the total number of chronic conditions.

1.5 THE SURVEY OF HEALTH, AGEING AND RETIREMENT IN EUROPE

The sample

The data used in Chapter 4 are taken from the first wave of the Survey of Health, Ageing and Retirement in Europe (SHARE), collected in 2004–2005 (release version 2.5.0). This survey randomly sampled from the population aged 50 years and older (plus younger spouses) in 12 countries (Börsch-Supan and Jürges, 2005). Supplementary samples containing the vignettes data are available for eight countries (Belgium, France, Germany, Greece, Italy, The Netherlands, Spain and Sweden). The case study in Chapter 4 is based on Bago d'Uva *et al.* (2008b), who analyse all eight countries separately. For illustrative purposes, we use here only French data (which had the highest response rate, 77 per cent, resulting in 885 respondents). Questionnaires were administered face-to-face by a computer-assisted personal interview to collect core information like age, gender and education, plus a self-completion drop-off part that covered self-assessments of health and vignette ratings (Börsch-Supan and Jürges, 2005).

Measures of health

Respondents were asked to classify their own health in six domains (mobility, cognition, pain, sleep, breathing, emotional health). The response categories were: 'None', 'Mild', 'Moderate', 'Severe' and 'Extreme'. In addition, for each domain, respondents were asked to evaluate three vignettes, each describing a fixed level of difficulty in that domain, on the same response scale. In the case study in

Chapter 4, we focus on the domain of breathing, while Bago d'Uva *et al.* (2008b) analysed all six health domains. Additionally, SHARE contains a general self-assessed health variable and a battery of more objective health information (including limitations with activities of daily living, mobility problems, existence and age of onset of each of a number of chronic conditions), which are not used in Bago d'Uva *et al.* (2008b) nor here.

Socioeconomic status

The indicator of socioeconomic status in our analysis is educational attainment, based on the International Standard Classification of Education (ISCED 97): (i) finished at most primary education or first stage of basic education (ISCED 0–1); (ii) lower secondary or second stage of basic education (ISCED 2), (iii) upper secondary education (ISCED 3–4) and (iv) recognised third level education, which includes higher vocational education and university degree (ISCED 5–6) (UNESCO, 1997).

1.6 OVERVIEW

All of the datasets used in this book are examples of surveys that are designed to be representative of a specified population. Normally these are collected using multi-stage clustered random samples, for convenience and economy. The simplest design is a cross-section survey in which each individual is measured just once. This may involve face-to-face interviews, medical examinations, telephone interviews or postal questionnaires. Repeated measurements of the same individuals give longitudinal, or panel, data. This provides more scope for analysis of individual heterogeneity and dynamic models.

2 Describing the dynamics of health

SYNOPSIS

This chapter uses a sub-sample of the British Household Panel Survey (BHPS) to show how descriptive techniques, including graphs and tables, can be used to summarise and explore the raw data and provide an intuitive understanding of how variables are distributed and associated with each other.

2.1 INTRODUCTION

Contoyannis *et al.* (2004b) use eight waves of the British Household Panel Survey (BHPS) to model the dynamics of self-assessed health (SAH): their paper forms the basis for the case study reported in this chapter and in Chapters 9 and 10. The main focus of the paper is on the observed persistence in reported health and an assessment of whether this is due to *state dependence* or to *unobservable individual heterogeneity*. The paper also provides evidence on the socioeconomic gradient in health and explores whether health-related attrition is a source of bias in this kind of analysis. The econometric methods are discussed in more detail in Chapters 9 and 10; this chapter concentrates on some preliminary descriptive analysis of the BHPS data and explains the Stata code that can be used to do graphical analysis and to prepare tables of summary statistics.

In this analysis, we use both *balanced samples* of respondents, for whom information on all the required variables is reported at each of the eight waves used here, and *unbalanced samples*, which exploit all available observations for wave 1 respondents. Neither sample includes new entrants to the BHPS; the samples only track all of those who were observed at wave 1. In this sense, the analysis treats the sample as a cohort consisting of all those present at wave 1. To be included in the analysis, individuals must be 'original sample members' (OSMs) who were aged 16 or older and who provided a valid response for the health measures at wave 1. Our broad definition of non-response encompasses all individuals who are missing at subsequent waves.

The first step is to load the Stata data file, called AHE_2ed_Ch_2.dta, which contains the relevant BHPS variables:

```
use "AHE_2ed_Ch_2.dta", clear
```

Then open a log file, AHE_2ed_Ch_2.log, to store a permanent record of the results:

```
capture log close
log using "AHE_2ed_Ch_2.log", replace
```

A sense of the content of the raw dataset can be obtained by running the following commands:

```
describe
codebook, compact
summarize
```

The output of these commands is not displayed here and this is left as an exercise that can be completed using the data on the web page (www.york.ac.uk/res/herc/research/hedg/).

As this is a panel dataset, with repeated time series observations for each individual, it is essential to specify the variables that contain the individual (i) and time (t) indexes indicated by the variables pid and wavenum. These can be used to sort the data prior to analysis:

```
xtset pid wavenum
sort pid wavenum
```

The BHPS includes missing data due to both *unit* and *item non-response* so not all individuals in our dataset are observed at every wave. As described above, this gives two options for the analysis: using the unbalanced panel, which includes all available observations, or the balanced panel, which restricts the sample to those individuals who have a complete set of data for all of the waves.

The following commands provide a simple way of creating indicator variables for whether or not individuals are in the balanced panel and in the unbalanced panel. These indicators can be used to select the sample in the subsequent estimation commands and also play a role in the analysis of attrition, as discussed in Chapter 10. The commands work by first running a model that includes all the variables that are relevant for subsequent estimation in the list of dependent and independent variables. Here we use a pooled ordered probit (oprobit) but the particular form of the model is not important: the dependent variable is y and the list of regressors is included in the global xvarsm, which is defined later in Chapter 9; the details are not important here. The model is run quietly as we are not interested in the regression output per se:

```
quietly oprobit y $xvarsm
```

Having run the model, we can exploit the internally saved result e(sample), which holds a binary indicator of whether an observation has been used in the preceding estimation command. Use this to create an indicator of whether an observation is in the estimation sample for the model or not:

```
generate insampm = 0
recode insampm 0 = 1 if e(sample)
```

Then the dataset is sorted by individual and wave identifiers and a new variable (Ti) is generated that counts the number of waves that each individual is observed in the panel with non-missing observations for the full set of variables that are used in the regression model:

```
sort pid wavenum
generate constant = 1
by pid: egen Ti = sum(constant) if insampm == 1
```

Using this new variable, it is possible to create indicators of whether an individual appears in the next wave (nextwavem) and for whether they appear in the balanced panel (allwavesm). This uses the Stata syntax "." To denote a missing value:

```
sort pid wavenum
by pid: gen nextwavem = insampm[_n+1]
generate allwavesm = .
recode allwavesm . = 0 if Ti ~= 8
recode allwavesm . = 1 if Ti == 8
generate numwavesm = .
replace numwavesm = Ti
```

These new variables are used in the tests for attrition bias that are described in Chapter 10.

2.2 GRAPHICAL ANALYSIS

Now we move on to show the Stata code that produces the graphical analysis of self-assessed health (SAH) from Contoyannis *et al.* (2004b). First, it is useful to attach some meaningful labels to describe the categorical responses to the question:

```
label variable sahex "hlstat=excellent"
label variable sahgood "hlstat=good"
label variable sahfair "hlstat=fair"
```

```
label variable sahpoor "hlstat=poor"
label variable sahvpoor "hlstat=very poor"
```

Contoyannis *et al.* (2004b) use bar charts to illustrate the distribution of SAH split by gender and by the eight waves of the BHPS used in the paper. In the code below, this is preceded by a graph that pools the data for men across all of the waves. An alternative to the use of bar charts would be to graph histograms but their appearance would be less satisfactory for the kind of categorical data used here. The second graph command uses `over(wavenum)` to produce the eight separate plots by wave. The figures are saved as encapsulated postscript (eps) files for subsequent use:

```
graph bar sahex sahgood sahfair sahpoor sahvpoor       ///
      if male==1, title(bar chart for SAH, men)        ///
      ylabel(0 0.1 0.2 0.3 0.4 0.5)
graph export "c:\stata\data\fig1.eps", as(eps)         ///
      preview(on) replace
sort wavenum
graph bar sahex sahgood sahfair sahpoor sahvpoor       ///
      if male==1, over(wavenum)                        ///
      title(Bar chart for SAH by wave, men)            ///
      ylabel(0 0.1 0.2 0.3 0.4 0.5)
graph export "fig2.eps", as(eps) preview(on) replace
```

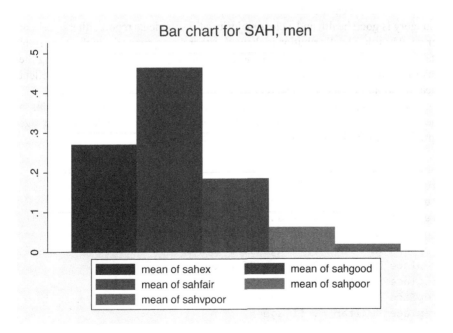

Figure 2.1 Bar chart for SAH, men.

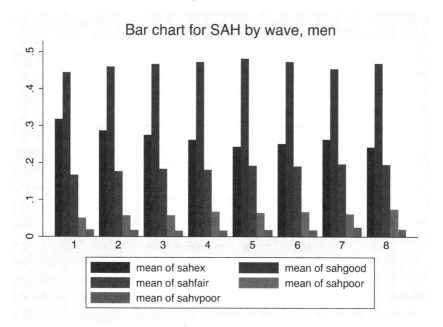

Figure 2.2 Bar chart for SAH by wave, men.

The figures reveal the characteristic shape of the distribution of SAH. The modal category is good health and a clear majority of respondents report either excellent or good health. The distribution is skewed, rather than symmetric, with a long right hand tail of individuals who report fair, poor or very poor health. Comparing the distribution over time, there is a decrease in the proportion reporting excellent health and an increase in those reporting fair or worse health.

The next step is to present the distribution of SAH by age-group. To do this, a new variable (healtab) is created that divides individuals into ten-year age groups. The bar charts are then plotted over these groups:

```
generate healtab=1
replace healtab =2 if age<36 & age>27
replace healtab =3 if age<44 & age>35
replace healtab =4 if age<52 & age>43
replace healtab =5 if age<60 & age>51
replace healtab =6 if age<68 & age>59
replace healtab =7 if age<76 & age>67
replace healtab =8 if age<84 & age>75
replace healtab =9 if age>83
replace healtab =. if age==.
tabulate healtab
```

The table for the new variable `healtab` shows the frequency distribution across age groups:

```
healtab |      Freq.     Percent      Cum.
--------+-----------------------------------
      1 |      9,612       14.85      14.85
      2 |     10,846       16.75      31.60
      3 |     10,121       15.63      47.23
      4 |     10,064       15.55      62.78
      5 |      7,270       11.23      74.01
      6 |      6,200        9.58      83.58
      7 |      5,842        9.02      92.61
      8 |      3,440        5.31      97.92
      9 |      1,346        2.08     100.00
--------+-----------------------------------
  Total |     64,741      100.00
```

These groups are then used in the construction of the bar chart:

```
sort healtab
graph bar sahex sahgood sahfair sahpoor sahvpoor          ///
        if male==1 & wavenum==1, over(healtab)            ///
        title(Bar chart for SAH by age group, wave1, men) ///
        ylabel(0 0.1 0.2 0.3 0.4 0.5 0.6)
```

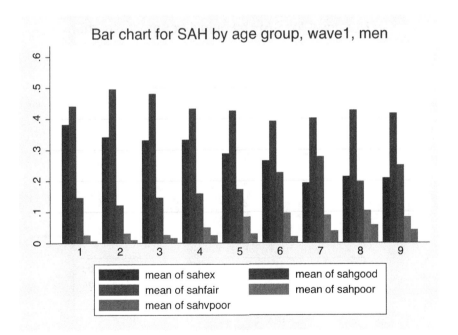

Figure 2.3 Bar chart for SAH by age group, wave 1, men.

The results help to explain the pattern observed in Figure 2.2. Despite the fact that respondents are asked to rate their health relative to someone of their own age, there is a clear pattern of worsening health for the older age groups, with the proportions in the top two categories declining and the bottom three categories increasing as age increases.

To illustrate the socioeconomic gradient in SAH, the distribution can be plotted for different income levels. Respondents are divided into quintiles of the distribution of income, using their average equivalised income over the waves of the panel (meaninc). This can be done using the xtile command to create an indicator of the quintile that individual belongs to:

```
sort pid wavenum
xtile incquim=meaninc if male==1,nquantiles(5)
graph bar sahex sahgood sahfair sahpoor sahvpoor          ///
    if male==1, over(incquim)                             ///
    title(Bar chart for SAH by quintile of meaninc, men)  ///
    ylabel(0 0.1 0.2 0.3 0.4 0.5)
```

The figure shows that there is a clear income-related gradient in SAH. Moving from the poorest quintile (1) to the richest (5) sees an increase in the proportion reporting excellent health and a decline in the proportion reporting very poor health.

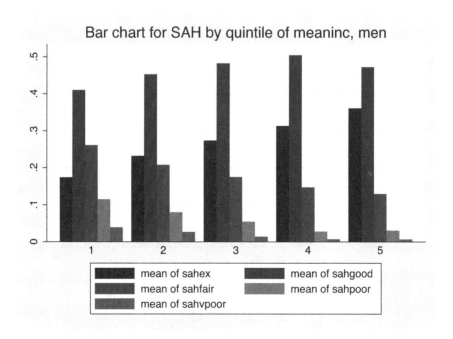

Figure 2.4 Bar chart for SAH by quintile of meaninc, men.

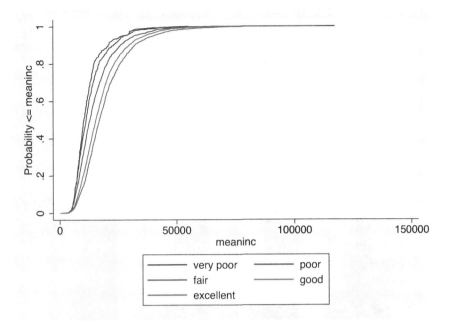

Figure 2.5 Empirical CDFs (cumulative distribution function) of meaninc, men.

Another way of visualising the income-health gradient is to plot the *empirical distribution function* for income, split by levels of SAH. This can be done using the command distplot:

```
distplot meaninc if male==1, over(hlstat)
```

Moving from left to right across the graph allows a comparison of the distribution of income across increasing levels of SAH. This shows evidence of what is known as *first order stochastic dominance*: the empirical distribution functions for income always lie to the right as levels of health improve. Further testing would be required to establish whether the differences between the distributions are statistically significant.

Our second indicator of socioeconomic status is educational attainment, measured by the highest formal qualification achieved. The new variable edatt groups individuals into categories according to increasing levels of qualification:

```
sort pid wavenum
generate edatt=1
replace edatt = 2 if ocse==1
replace edatt = 3 if hndalev==1
replace edatt = 4 if deghdeg==1
sort edatt
```

```
graph bar sahex sahgood sahfair sahpoor sahvpoor          ///
     if male==1, over(edatt)                              ///
     title(Bar chart for SAH by education, men)           ///
     ylabel(0 0.1 0.2 0.3 0.4 0.5)
```

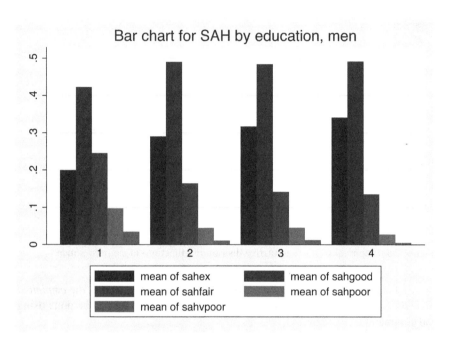

Figure 2.6 Bar chart for SAH by education, men.

One of the aims of Contoyannis *et al.* (2004b) was to investigate the dynamics of health. Descriptive evidence of state dependence is provided by plotting the distribution for current SAH split by levels of SAH in the previous wave (hstatlag):

```
sort pid wavenum
quietly by pid: gen hstatlag=hlstat[_n-1]
sort hstatlag
graph bar sahex sahgood sahfair sahpoor sahvpoor          ///
   if male==1 & wavenum==2, over(hstatlag)                ///
   title(Bar chart for SAH by previous SAH, wave 2, men)  ///
   ylabel(0 0.1 0.2 0.3 0.4 0.5 0.6)
```

Figure 2.7 reveals clear evidence of persistence in self-reported health. The probabilities of making a transition from one end of the distribution (excellent

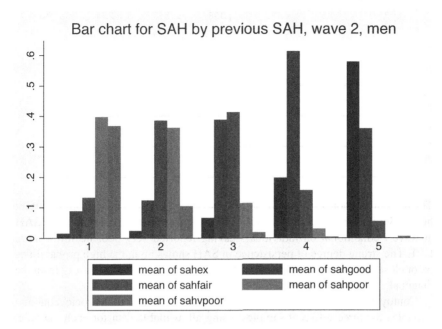

Figure 2.7 Bar chart for SAH by previous SAH, wave 2, men.

health) to the other (poor or very poor) are very small and individuals are most likely to remain close to their previous level of health.

2.3 TABULATING THE DATA

Along with the graphical analysis, it is useful to tabulate some descriptive statistics for the data. Given the emphasis on dynamics and state dependence, we begin with transition matrices. Here these are split by gender and presented for males only:

```
xttrans hlstat if male==1,i(pid) t(wavenum) freq
```

```
           |                       hlstat
  hlstat   |      1         2        3         4        5 |    Total
-----------+---------------------------------------------+---------
        1  |     148       150       59        24        9 |      390
           |   37.95     38.46    15.13      6.15     2.31 |   100.00
-----------+---------------------------------------------+---------
        2  |     152       598      473       169       37 |    1,429
           |   10.64     41.85    33.10     11.83     2.59 |   100.00
-----------+---------------------------------------------+---------
```

3		85	485	2,068	1,597	234	4,469
		1.90	10.85	46.27	35.74	5.24	100.00
4		55	251	1,696	7,402	2,069	11,473
		0.48	2.19	14.78	64.52	18.03	100.00
5		18	65	331	2,324	4,080	6,818
		0.26	0.95	4.85	34.09	59.84	100.00
Total		458	1,549	4,627	11,516	6,429	24,579
		1.86	6.30	18.83	46.85	26.16	100.00

The rows of the table indicate previous health state while the columns show current health. So, for example, the elements of the first row show the distribution of SAH at wave t conditional on individuals having reported very poor health at wave t – 1. The strong degree of persistence in SAH shows up in the high probabilities on or close to the diagonal in these tables and the low probabilities away from the diagonal.

Contoyannis *et al.* (2004b, Table III) show sample means of the socioeconomic variables for three different samples: using all available data for each variable, using the unbalanced sample and using the balanced sample. This gives an indication of whether the more restricted samples are comparable to the full dataset or whether there are systematic differences in terms of observable characteristics. Here the summarize command provides a range of summary statistics, not just the sample means for a set of variables contained in the global list xvars:

```
*  ALL AVAILABLE DATA
* DEFINE GLOBAL FOR VARIABLE LISTS
#delimit ;
global xvars "widowed nvrmar divsep deghdeg hndalev ocse
    hhsize nch04 nch511 nch1218 age age2 age3 age4 yr9293
    yr9394 yr9495 yr9596 yr9697 yr9798 lninc mlninc mwid
    mnvrmar mdivsep mhhsize mnch04 mnch511 mnch1218";
#delimit cr;
summarize $xvars
```

Variable	Obs	Mean	Std. Dev.	Min	Max
widowed	66323	.0881745	.2835507	0	1
nvrmar	66323	.1633672	.3697031	0	1
divsep	66323	.0682116	.2521106	0	1
deghdeg	82112	.0964536	.2952141	0	1
hndalev	82112	.2024552	.4018321	0	1
ocse	82112	.2724084	.4452016	0	1

```
      hhsize |   64741    2.788357   1.329707           1          11
       nch04 |   64741    .1443753   .4196944           0           4
      nch511 |   64741    .2597736   .6145583           0           6
     nch1218 |   64741    .1833151   .4861762           0           4
-------------+----------------------------------------------------------
         age |   64741    46.95723   17.77155          15         100
        age2 |   64741    25.20804   18.17837        2.25         100
        age3 |   64741    15.01471   15.53261       .3375         100
        age4 |   64741    9.658935   12.80088     .050625         100
      yr9293 |   82112        .125   .3307209           0           1
-------------+----------------------------------------------------------
      yr9394 |   82112        .125   .3307209           0           1
      yr9495 |   82112        .125   .3307209           0           1
      yr9596 |   82112        .125   .3307209           0           1
      yr9697 |   82112        .125   .3307209           0           1
      yr9798 |   82112        .125   .3307209           0           1
-------------+----------------------------------------------------------
       lninc |   64101    9.497943   .6664307   -.1312631    13.12998
```

```
* UNBALANCED ESTIMATION SAMPLE
summarize $xvars if insampm==1
```

```
    Variable |     Obs        Mean   Std. Dev.        Min         Max
-------------+----------------------------------------------------------
     widowed |   64053    .0894103   .2853373           0           1
      nvrmar |   64053    .1609605   .3674973           0           1
      divsep |   64053    .0689585   .2533856           0           1
     deghdeg |   64053    .1082385   .3106838           0           1
     hndalev |   64053    .2152436   .4109945           0           1
-------------+----------------------------------------------------------
        ocse |   64053    .2797683   .4488888           0           1
      hhsize |   64053    2.791204   1.329624           1          11
       nch04 |   64053    .1450518   .4206046           0           4
      nch511 |   64053    .2602376   .6154699           0           6
     nch1218 |   64053    .1832701   .4859802           0           4
-------------+----------------------------------------------------------
         age |   64053    46.95126   17.78103          15         100
        age2 |   64053    25.20581   18.18994        2.25         100
        age3 |   64053    15.01587   15.54473       .3375         100
        age4 |   64053    9.662014    12.8131     .050625         100
      yr9293 |   64053     .127535   .3335739           0           1
-------------+----------------------------------------------------------
      yr9394 |   64053    .1228982   .3283229           0           1
      yr9495 |   64053    .1163412   .3206361           0           1
      yr9596 |   64053    .1151702   .3192298           0           1
```

```
     yr9697 |    64053   .1112672   .3144652          0          1
     yr9798 |    64053   .1070207    .309142          0          1
------------|------------------------------------------------------
      lninc |    64053   9.498008    .666476  -.1312631  13.12998
------------|------------------------------------------------------


*  BALANCED ESTIMATION SAMPLE
summarize $xvars if allwavesm==1

   Variable |    Obs      Mean  Std. Dev.    Min    Max
------------|------------------------------------------------------
    widowed |   48992   .079462   .2704612          0          1
     nvrmar |   48992  .1444113   .3515099          0          1
     divsep |   48992  .0676233   .2511009          0          1
    deghdeg |   48992   .114631   .3185793          0          1
    hndalev |   48992  .2261594   .4183478          0          1
------------|------------------------------------------------------
       ocse |   48992  .2867407    .452244          0          1
     hhsize |   48992  2.815051   1.303281          1         10
      nch04 |   48992  .1494121   .4218498          0          4
     nch511 |   48992    .27133   .6221702          0          4
    nch1218 |   48992   .186459   .4884763          0          4
------------|------------------------------------------------------
        age |   48992   46.7817   16.98556         15        100
       age2 |   48992  24.77031   17.23182       2.25        100
       age3 |   48992  14.46847   14.53681      .3375        100
       age4 |   48992  9.104977    11.8005    .050625        100
     yr9293 |   48992      .125   .3307223          0          1
------------|------------------------------------------------------
     yr9394 |   48992      .125   .3307223          0          1
     yr9495 |   48992      .125   .3307223          0          1
     yr9596 |   48992      .125   .3307223          0          1
     yr9697 |   48992      .125   .3307223          0          1
     yr9798 |   48992      .125   .3307223          0          1
------------|------------------------------------------------------
      lninc |   48992  9.530462   .6420103   3.324561    12.9514
------------|------------------------------------------------------
```

The descriptive analysis is taken a stage further in Contoyannis *et al.* (2004b, Table IV). This compares the full sample with sub-groups who are defined according to particular sequences of reported health: those who are always in excellent or good health, those who are always in poor or very poor health, those who make a single transition away from excellent or good health (becoming unhealthy), and those who make a single transition away from poor or very poor health (becoming healthy). The following Stata code defines these groups, for the males in the sample, and runs separate summary statistics for each group:

```
tabulate hlstat if male==1
```

hlstat	Freq.	Percent	Cum.
very poor	560	1.88	1.88
poor	1,838	6.16	8.03
fair	5,501	18.43	26.46
good	13,868	46.45	72.91
excellent	8,087	27.09	100.00
Total	29,854	100.00	

```
generate count1=1
replace count1 =10 if wavenum==2
replace count1 =100 if wavenum==3
replace count1 =1000 if wavenum==4
replace count1 =10000 if wavenum==5
replace count1 =100000 if wavenum==6
replace count1 =1000000 if wavenum==7
replace count1 =10000000 if wavenum==8

 ALWAYS EXCELLENT/GOOD
generate hexgood=sahex==1|sahgood==1
generate use=hexgood* count1
sort pid
egen tot=sum(use), by(pid)
summarize $xvars if (tot==11111111 & male==1)
drop use tot
```

Variable	Obs	Mean	Std. Dev.	Min	Max
widowed	9544	.0209556	.1432431	0	1
nvrmar	9544	.1679589	.3738494	0	1
divsep	9544	.045264	.2078936	0	1
deghdeg	9544	.1684828	.3743141	0	1
hndalev	9544	.3051132	.4604795	0	1
ocse	9544	.2816429	.4498237	0	1
hhsize	9544	2.970138	1.273814	1	10
nch04	9544	.1658634	.4420094	0	3
nch511	9544	.2825859	.637708	0	4
nch1218	9544	.2044216	.5071193	0	3

```
       age |   9544   44.22161   15.50413         15         91
      age2 |   9544   21.95903   15.12651       2.25      82.81
      age3 |   9544   12.01464   12.32994      .3375    75.3571
      age4 |   9544   7.109863    9.71877    .050625   68.57496
     yr9293 |  9544       .125    .3307362        0          1
-----------|-------------------------------------------------------
     yr9394 |  9544       .125    .3307362        0          1
     yr9495 |  9544       .125    .3307362        0          1
     yr9596 |  9544       .125    .3307362        0          1
     yr9697 |  9544       .125    .3307362        0          1
     yr9798 |  9544       .125    .3307362        0          1
-----------|-------------------------------------------------------
     lninc |   9508    9.70625    .6180908   4.493146   12.52561
-----------|-------------------------------------------------------
```

```
ALWAYS POOR/VERY POOR
generate hpovpo=sahpoor==1|sahvpoor==1
generate use=hpovpo*count1
sort pid
egen tot=sum(use), by(pid)
summarize $xvars if (tot==11111111 & male==1)
drop use tot
```

```
   Variable |    Obs      Mean    Std. Dev.       Min        Max
-----------|-------------------------------------------------------
    widowed |    200       .06    .2380828         0          1
     nvrmar |    200       .03    .1710153         0          1
     divsep |    200       .07    .2557873         0          1
    deghdeg |    200       .04    .1964509         0          1
    hndalev |    200        .2    .4010038         0          1
-----------|-------------------------------------------------------
       ocse |    200       .12     .325777         0          1
     hhsize |    200      2.72    1.182621         1          6
      nch04 |    200       .04    .2422673         0          2
     nch511 |    200      .185    .5852243         0          3
    nch1218 |    200       .18    .4886655         0          3
-----------|-------------------------------------------------------
        age |    200      53.3    11.26251        28         84
       age2 |    200    29.671    12.67862       7.84      70.56
       age3 |    200   17.21977   11.38129     2.1952    59.2704
       age4 |    200   10.40312    9.55444    .614656   49.78714
     yr9293 |    200      .125    .3315488         0          1
-----------|-------------------------------------------------------
```

```
    yr9394 |      200        .125    .3315488            0            1
    yr9495 |      200        .125    .3315488            0            1
    yr9596 |      200        .125    .3315488            0            1
    yr9697 |      200        .125    .3315488            0            1
    yr9798 |      200        .125    .3315488            0            1
-----------|-------------------------------------------------------------
     lninc |      200    9.222452   .5673511     7.948007    10.81978
-----------|-------------------------------------------------------------
```

SINGLE TRANSITION FROM EXCELLENT/GOOD
generate use=hexgood*count1
sort pid
egen tot=sum(use), by(pid)
summarize $xvars if   ///
      (tot==1|tot==11|tot==111|tot==1111|tot==11111| ///
      tot==111111|tot==1111111) & male==1
tabulate tot if   ///
      (tot==1|tot==11|tot==111|tot==1111|tot==11111| ///
      tot==111111|tot==1111111) & male==1
drop use tot

```
  Variable |      Obs        Mean   Std. Dev.         Min          Max
-----------|-------------------------------------------------------------
   widowed |     4839   .0440174    .2051549            0            1
    nvrmar |     4839   .2143005    .4103786            0            1
    divsep |     4839   .0560033    .2299519            0            1
   deghdeg |     4839   .1113867    .3146429            0            1
   hndalev |     4839   .2512916    .4338007            0            1
-----------|-------------------------------------------------------------
      ocse |     4839   .2335193    .4231135            0            1
    hhsize |     4839   2.809465    1.328786            1           11
     nch04 |     4839   .1155197    .3815788            0            3
    nch511 |     4839   .2140938    .5747546            0            4
   nch1218 |     4839   .1799959    .4751414            0            3
-----------|-------------------------------------------------------------
       age |     4839   46.62244    18.60908           16           93
      age2 |     4839   25.19878    19.00365         2.56        86.49
      age3 |     4839   15.22316    16.31359        .4096      80.4357
      age4 |     4839   9.960428     13.5342      .065536      74.8052
    yr9293 |     4839   .1425914    .3496919            0            1
-----------|-------------------------------------------------------------
    yr9394 |     4839   .1151064    .3191833            0            1
    yr9495 |     4839   .0913412    .2881235            0            1
    yr9596 |     4839   .0787353     .269353            0            1
```

```
       yr9697 |    4839    .0673693    .2506864         0         1
       yr9798 |    4839    .0557967    .2295523         0         1
--------------|-----------------------------------------------------------
        lninc |    4780    9.521568    .6978869    .0895683  11.75901
--------------|-----------------------------------------------------------
```

The pattern of transitions can be illustrated by tabulating the new variable tot:

```
tabulate tot if                                                  ///
      (tot==1|tot==11|tot==111|tot==1111|tot==11111|             ///
      tot==111111|tot==1111111) & male==1

        tot |     Freq.    Percent      Cum.
------------|--------------------------------------
          1 |       856      17.69     17.69
         11 |       696      14.38     32.07
        111 |       560      11.57     43.65
       1111 |       618      12.77     56.42
      11111 |       479       9.90     66.32
     111111 |       567      11.72     78.03
   11111111 |     1,063      21.97    100.00
------------|--------------------------------------
      Total |     4,839     100.00
```

```
SINGLE TRANSITION FROM POOR/VPOOR
generate use=hpovpo* count1
sort pid
egen tot=sum(use), by(pid)
summarize $xvars if                                              ///
      (tot==1|tot==11|tot==111|tot==1111|tot==11111|             ///
      tot==111111|tot==1111111) & male==1

   Variable |     Obs      Mean   Std. Dev.      Min      Max
------------|-----------------------------------------------------
    widowed |     796  .0753769    .2641645        0        1
     nvrmar |     796  .1984925    .3991157        0        1
     divsep |     796  .1067839    .3090325        0        1
    deghdeg |     796   .071608    .2579999        0        1
    hndalev |     796  .2386935     .426553        0        1
------------|-----------------------------------------------------
       ocse |     796  .2060302    .4047067        0        1
     hhsize |     796  2.497487    1.329394        1       10
      nch04 |     796  .0854271     .317599        0        2
     nch511 |     796   .129397    .3847275        0        2
    nch1218 |     796  .1319095    .4153494        0        3
```

age	796	52.13065	18.19179	16	94
age2	796	30.48131	18.69782	2.56	88.36
age3	796	19.24572	15.81715	.4096	83.0584
age4	796	12.78279	12.79799	.065536	78.0749
yr9293	796	.1344221	.3413197	0	1
yr9394	796	.1155779	.3199191	0	1
yr9495	796	.0954774	.294058	0	1
yr9596	796	.0866834	.2815475	0	1
yr9697	796	.0816583	.2740156	0	1
yr9798	796	.0778894	.268166	0	1
lninc	791	9.421001	.6465908	5.752284	11.65996

tot	Freq.	Percent	Cum.
1	462	58.04	58.04
11	144	18.09	76.13
111	49	6.16	82.29
1111	36	4.52	86.81
11111	25	3.14	89.95
111111	56	7.04	96.98
1111111	24	3.02	100.00
Total	796	100.00	

These tables once again reveal the associations between SAH and socioeconomic characteristics. For example, those who are always in excellent or good health have higher incomes, are more educated and are younger than those in the other groups.

2.4 OVERVIEW

The simple statistical associations between health and socioeconomic status revealed by graphing and tabulating the data are explored in more detail in Chapters 9 and 10. These illustrate the estimation of dynamic panel data models (Chapter 9) and methods to deal with non-response (Chapter 10).

3 Describing health care costs

SYNOPSIS

This chapter uses a sub-sample of the Medical Expenditure Panel Survey (MEPS) to show how descriptive techniques can be used to capture the distinctive characteristics of the distribution of individual health care costs. Linear regression models are introduced to explore the relationship between health care costs and socioeconomic variables.

3.1 INTRODUCTION

Individual data on health care expenditure data are typically non-normally distributed with a skewed and heavy right-hand tail and often with a mass point at zero. Relatively rare or severe events, clinical complications and multiple comorbidities may all contribute to these features of the distribution. It is often the case that a minority of patients account for a large proportion of high costs, rendering the mean larger than the median. These features of expenditure data pose challenges for their econometric modelling. In addition, the relationship between costs and covariates may be nonlinear in models of expenditure data and errors may exhibit substantial heteroskedasticity.

Jones (2011) reviews econometric approaches used by health economists to model health care cost data. The methods are used for a variety of reasons, most notably for prediction, projection and forecasting in the context of risk adjustment, resource allocation, health technology assessment and policy evaluation. The main focus of this chapter is to introduce health care cost data, and describe elements of the data distribution commonly encountered and highlight problems in modelling such data. We then introduce linear regression modelling of untransformed and transformed costs. The chapter is complemented by more advanced techniques, including methods commonly encountered in the health economics literature together with more recent developments described in Chapter 12.

3.2 DATA DESCRIPTION

Throughout we illustrate the distinguishing features of cost data, the methods proposed for its modelling and the evaluation of performance by drawing on an easily accessible but representative sample of health care cost data. The data used are an extract from the Medical Expenditure Panel Survey (MEPS), which has been used by Cameron and Trivedi (2009) in their excellent text on micro-econometrics using Stata and is readily available through their web page. A brief description of the data is provided in Chapter 1.

First load the Stata data file:

```
use "AHE_2ed_Ch_3.dta"
```

Then open a log file to store a permanent record of the outputs:

```
capture log close
log using "AHE_2ed_Ch_3.log", replace
```

Produce a summary of the dataset that will provide information on the coding of the various variables:

```
describe
```

This gives the output in Table 3.1.

The main variable of interest is totexp, which contains information on the total medical expenditures of the sample in MEPS. This cost variable is the focus of the analysis. The sample covers the medical expenses of a sample of elderly individuals who qualify for health care under the US Medicare programme. Before proceeding, create a copy of the variable using the clonevar command as follows:

```
clonevar y=totexp
```

A summary of the expenditure data shows that the sample consists of 3,064 individuals some of whom have no health care expenditures in the period studied:

```
summarize y
```

Variable	Obs	Mean	Std. Dev.	Min	Max
y	3064	7030.889	11852.75	0	125610

We can investigate the proportion of 'users' (with positive expenditures) and 'non-users' (with zero expenditures) by tabulating the variable posexp as follows:

Table 3.1 Description of dataset

```
obs:              3,064
vars:                33                          26 Nov 2008 17:11
size:           723,104 (93.1% of memory free)

storage   display   value
variable name   type    format   label    variable label

dupersid    double  %12.0g              Subject ID
year03      double  %12.0g              =1 if data is from MEPS 2003
age         double  %12.0g              Age
famsze      double  %12.0g              Size of the family
educyr      double  %12.0g              Years of education
totexp      double  %12.0g              Total medical expenditure
private     double  %12.0g              =1 if private supplementary insurance
retire      double  %12.0g              =1 if retired
female      double  %12.0g              =1 if female
white       double  %12.0g              =1 if white
hisp        double  %12.0g              =1 if Hispanic
marry       double  %12.0g              =1 if married
northe      double  %12.0g              =1 if northeast area
```

mwest	double %12.0g	=1 if Midwest area
south	double %12.0g	=1 if south area (West is excluded)
phylim	double %12.0g	=1 if has functional limitation
actlim	double %12.0g	=1 if has activity limitation
msa	double %12.0g	=1 if metropolitan statistical area
income	double %12.0g	annual household income/1000
injury	double %12.0g	=1 if condition is caused by an accident/injury
priolist	double %12.0g	=1 if has medical conditions that are on the priority list
totchr	double %12.0g	# of chronic problems
omc	double %12.0g	=1 if other managed care (Privately insured sample)
hmo	double %12.0g	=1 if private insurance is HMO (Privately insured sample)
mnc	double %12.0g	
ratio	float %9.0g	
posexp	float %9.0g	=1 if total expenditure > 0
suppins	float %9.0g	=1 if has supp priv insurance
hvgg	float %9.0g	=1 if health status is excellent, good or very good
hfp	float %9.0g	=1 if health status is fair or poor
ltotexp	float %9.0g	ln(totexp) if totexp > 0
hins	float %9.0g	Excellent health indicator
hdem	float %9.0g	Demographic group indicator

```
table posexp

=1 if total |
expenditure |
        > 0 |        Freq.     Percent        Cum.
------------|--------------------------------------
         0  |         109         3.56        3.56
         1  |       2,955        96.44      100.00
------------|--------------------------------------
     Total  |       3,064       100.00
```

This shows that 96 per cent of the sample (2,955 individuals) were users of health care and had positive expenditures. Note that when cost data represent the population as a whole, rather than a specific sample of elderly people used here, the distribution of expenditures will typically display a much larger mass point at zero. In the modelling that follows, we will only be concerned with users of health care, with positive expenditures, and as such do not consider models designed to account for observations with zero cost. Accordingly drop observations with zero expenditure from the analysis:

```
drop if y==0
```

Now summarise the expenditure data again, but this time using the option detail we produce a further set of statistics in addition to the mean, standard deviation and minimum and maximum values produced by the standard command. These additional statistics summarise the skewness, kurtosis, the four smallest and largest values, and various percentiles of the cost distribution:

```
summarize y, detail
```

The following output is produced:

```
            Total medical expenditure
-------------------------------------------------------------
        Percentiles       Smallest
  1%            81              3
  5%           300              6
 10%           581              9     Obs                2955
 25%          1433             14     Sum of Wgt.        2955

 50%          3334                    Mean           7290.235
                              Largest  Std. Dev.      11990.84
 75%          7497         104823
 90%         17549         108256     Variance       1.44e+08
 95%         27941         123611     Skewness       4.113807
 99%         62989         125610     Kurtosis       25.64123
```

The mean cost is $7,290, with a minimum of $3 and a maximum of $125,610. The inter-quartile range of $6,064 ($7,497 – $1,433) is quite tight compared to the overall range and the distribution of costs is distinguished by a very heavy right-hand tail. The skewness statistic is 4.1 (compared to 0 for symmetric data) and kurtosis is 25.6 (compared to 3 for normal data). As expected for heavily skewed data, the median cost, $3,334, is less than half the mean cost.

We can observe the distribution of costs in more detail using a two-way histogram and superimposing a kernel density plot. The figures are saved as encapsulated postscript (eps) files for subsequent use:

```
twoway histogram y, color(*.5) || kdensity y ,          ///
    title(MEPS cost data)
graph export "fig1.eps", as(eps) preview(on) replace
```

Figure 3.1 clearly shows the high degree of skewness and the long right-hand tail in the data. A common way of dealing with skewed data is to transform it using, for example, a log or other power transformation. Figure 3.2 plots the distribution after taking the natural logarithm and also a square root of costs. The logarithm of costs exists in the dataset as `ltotexp` and we create a copy (`clonevar lny=ltotexp`), but we need to generate the square root of costs before plotting its distribution: `generate sqrty=y^0.5`.

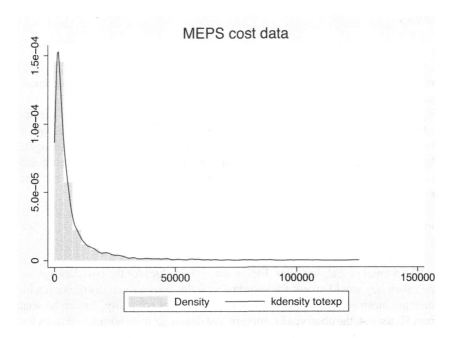

Figure 3.1 Distribution of positive costs.

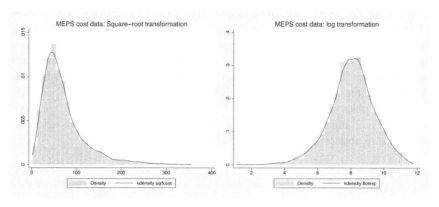

Figure 3.2 Distribution of transformed costs.

It is clear from Figure 3.2 that while a square root transformation pulls in the long right-hand tails in the distribution of costs, it still exhibits significant skewness. The log transformation does a great deal better in producing a more symmetric distribution of expenditures, in fact there is an indication that the distribution is now slightly skewed to the left.

Another way to investigate the distribution of costs graphically is to use box and whisker plots. These can be graphed easily using the Stata command as follows:

```
graph box y, title(Level) saving(boxplot, replace)
```

which saves the plot to 'boxplot'. We can graph similar plots for the log and square root transformed data. This produces the plots in Figure 3.3.

The box plots illustrate once again that the log transformation, and to a lesser extent the square root transformation, has the effect of pulling in the upper tail of the distribution and producing a more symmetric distribution. We can investigate the extent to which transforming the data helps to produce more symmetric and normally distributed data using normal probability plots, for example to plot the observed expenditures:

```
pnorm y, title(normal plot of costs) ytitle(costs)          ///
    xtitle(inverse normal) saving(pnormy, replace)
```

The normal probability plots display the actual values for the cost data against the value they would take if the distribution followed a normal distribution with the same mean and variance. A straight line indicates normality. As can be seen from Figure 3.4, the observed health care cost data is far from normally distributed and the log transformation is superior to the square root transformation for inducing normality.

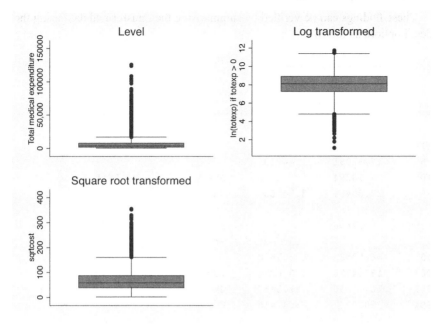

Figure 3.3 Box plots of health care costs.

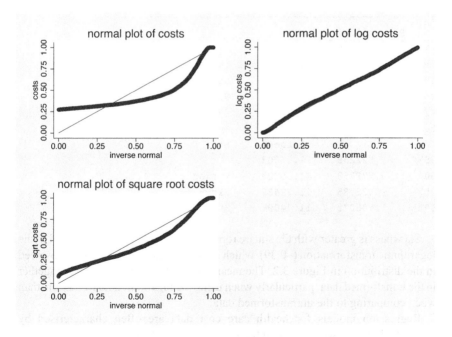

Figure 3.4 Normal probability plots of health care costs.

These findings can be verified by summarising the transformed data using the detail option, as follows:

```
summarize sqrty, detail
```

                                sqrty

	Percentiles	Smallest		
1%	9	1.732051		
5%	17.32051	2.44949		
10%	24.10394	3	Obs	2955
25%	37.85499	3.741657	Sum of Wgt.	2955
50%	57.7408		Mean	70.01143
		Largest	Std. Dev.	48.88193
75%	86.58522	323.7638		
90%	132.4726	329.0228	Variance	2389.443
95%	167.1556	351.5836	Skewness	1.832267
99%	250.9761	354.415	Kurtosis	7.484348

```
summarize lny, detail
```

                ln(totexp) if totexp > 0

	Percentiles	Smallest		
1%	4.394449	1.098612		
5%	5.703783	1.791759		
10%	6.364751	2.197225	Obs	2955
25%	7.267525	2.639057	Sum of Wgt.	2955
50%	8.111928		Mean	8.059866
		Largest	Std. Dev.	1.367592
75%	8.922258	11.56003		
90%	9.772752	11.59225	Variance	1.870308
95%	10.23785	11.72489	Skewness	-.3857887
99%	11.05072	11.74094	Kurtosis	3.842263

Skewness is greater with the square root transformation (1.83) compared to the logarithmic transformation (–0.39), which exhibits negative skewness, as observed in the distribution in Figure 3.2. The mean and median are much closer together in the transformed data, particularly when using the logarithm transformation, than when comparing to the untransformed data.

Regression models for health care cost data are often characterised by heteroskedasticity, where the conditional variance of the error term is a function of the regressors. This is often handled, for example, in the GLM framework that is introduced in Chapter 12, by modelling the variance as a function of the conditional mean. We can investigate the relationship between the mean and the variance in the raw data graphically by considering the relationship between the mean of costs and its variance at different percentiles of the distribution of the conditional mean of costs. These percentiles are based on the fitted values from a simple regression model for costs. This can be achieved using the following set of commands:

```
global qy=20
quietly regress totexp age female income suppins phylim ///
   actlim totchr
predict yf_q, xb
xtile yq=yf_q, nq($qy)

generate yqmean=0
generate yqvar=0

forvalues i=1/$qy {
  quietly summarize totexp if yq==`i', detail
  replace yqmean=r(mean) if yq==`i'
  replace yqvar=r(Var) if yq==`i'
  }

twoway scatter yqvar yqmean , title(Mean and Variance)    ///
      ytitle(variance) xtitle(mean)  saving(mean&var,     ///
      replace)

graph export mean&var.tif, replace
```

This produces the scatter plot on the left of Figure 3.5. While the scale of the *y*-axis is not particularly helpful here, it is clear that the variance of costs increases with the mean across the percentiles of the distribution of fitted values. The figure repeats the exercise for log-transformed costs. Here we see that, in general, the variance decreases with the mean. These figures indicate that our approaches to modelling health care cost data will need to account for the heteroskedastic nature of the data.

The analysis so far has demonstrated the nature of the distribution of costs that is typical of health care expenditure data. The distribution of costs in the MEPS sample is non-symmetric, has heavy tails and is heteroskedastic. Transformations, particularly the logarithmic transformation, help to produce a more symmetric distribution but heteroskedasticity is likely to remain an issue. In the next section, we will consider modelling health care cost data on its observed scale ($) and on a transformed scale and consider the difficulties this creates, particularly for the latter, in forecasting costs and deriving marginal effects.

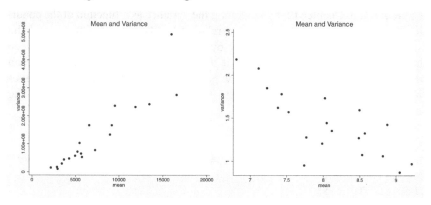

Figure 3.5 Mean of cost against variance – level of cost (LHS): log of costs (RHS).

3.3 MODELLING HEALTH CARE COST DATA

This section introduces regression models to analyse health care cost data. We focus on linear regression techniques including linear regression of transformations of the cost variable. Throughout we follow the basic model specification used by Cameron and Trivedi (2009), which consists of a simple additive specification of the linear index that includes indicators of supplementary private insurance (suppins), physical limitations (phylim), activity limitations (actlim), the number of chronic conditions (totchr), age (age), gender (female), and household income (income: annual income/$1,000) as regressors.

It is important to note that the simple comparison of models presented here uses the same linear index in each specification. In empirical applications, a richer specification will typically be used, with many more covariates and with polynomials and interaction terms, perhaps using a fully saturated model as a starting point if sufficient data are available (Manning *et al.*, 1987). A fuller and fairer comparison of models may entail using different specifications of the regressors for each model so that the best specification of one model is compared with the best specification of another. For example, Veazie *et al.* (2003) discuss the case where a linear specification is appropriate on the square root scale so that a quadratic function would be appropriate on the levels scale. Chapter 12 builds on the methods presented here by extending the modelling of health care costs data by considering nonlinear regression models, generalised linear models and more advanced nonlinear models including finite mixture models. These are illustrated using the same sample of MEPS data presented in this chapter. Table 3.2 summarises the key variables used in the analysis that follows.

The average age of the sample is 74 years, with individuals' age ranging from 65 to 90 years; 58 per cent are women; 59 per cent have supplementary insurance; 44 per cent have some physical limitations; 29 per cent have activity limitations and the average number of chronic conditions in the sample is 1.8, ranging from

Table 3.2 Summary statistics of variables

Variable	Obs	Mean	Std. Dev.	Min	Max
y	2955	7290.235	11990.84	3	125610
lny	2955	8.059866	1.367592	1.098612	11.74094
sqrty	2955	70.01143	48.88193	1.732051	354.415
age	2955	74.24535	6.375975	65	90
female	2955	.5840948	.4929608	0	1
income	2955	22.68353	22.60988	-1	312.46
suppins	2955	.5915398	.4916322	0	1
phylim	2955	.4362098	.4959981	0	1
actlim	2955	.2879865	.4529014	0	1
totchr	2955	1.808799	1.294613	0	7

0 to 7. The average level of income is $22,684. It is notable, however, that the income variable contains negative values. In principle, negative values are possible for income from self-employment or investments. To investigate the extent of these values, we tabulate the income variable restricting the range over which this is displayed. This reveals a single individual with a negative income (–$1,000). In the analysis that follows, we include this observation. However, as Cameron and Trivedi (2009, p. 73) point out, it would be preferable to check the original data source before proceeding to analysis to ensure this is a valid data point.

```
tabulate income if income <= 0.5
```

annual household income/1000	Freq.	Percent	Cum.
-1	1	1.02	1.02
0	81	82.65	83.67
.023	1	1.02	84.69
.069	1	1.02	85.71
.07	1	1.02	86.73
.1	2	2.04	88.78
.12	1	1.02	89.80
.2	1	1.02	90.82
.25	1	1.02	91.84
.309	1	1.02	92.86
.336	1	1.02	93.88
.38	1	1.02	94.90

```
    .425 |          2          2.04        96.94
    .445 |          1          1.02        97.96
    .455 |          2          2.04       100.00
------------|---------------------------------
   Total |         98        100.00
```

One of the key variables in the analysis is the impact of supplementary insurance on the use of health care. We can describe this by summarising the expenditure data by insurance status. This reveals the mean costs for health care is greater for the sub-sample with supplementary insurance ($7,612) compared to those without insurance ($6,824). Indeed, it would appear that the use of health care is greater across the majority of the distribution of expenditures for those with supplementary insurance.

```
sort suppins
by suppins: summarize y , detail

--------------------------------------------------------

-> suppins = 0
                    Total medical expenditure
--------------------------------------------------------

        Percentiles    Smallest
  1%          51            9
  5%         226           14
 10%         427           18     Obs              1207
 25%        1128           20     Sum of Wgt.      1207

 50%        2779                  Mean         6824.303
                    Largest       Std. Dev.    11425.94
 75%        6590        89270
 90%       17937        97447     Variance     1.31e+08
 95%       28569       100419     Skewness     3.868345
 99%       53037       104823     Kurtosis     23.21172

--------------------------------------------------------

-> suppins = 1
                    Total medical expenditure
--------------------------------------------------------

        Percentiles    Smallest
  1%         112            3
  5%         383            6
 10%         715           25     Obs              1748
 25%       1677.5          30     Sum of Wgt.      1748

 50%       3648.5                 Mean         7611.963
                    Largest       Std. Dev.    12358.83
 75%        8065       102303
```

90%	17534	108256	Variance	1.53e+08
95%	27021	123611	Skewness	4.232459
99%	66413	125610	Kurtosis	26.59292

An alternative way of viewing this is to plot the empirical cumulative distribution functions (CDFs) of expenditures by supplementary insurance status. This can be done using the following commands:

```
preserve
sort suppins
cumul y if suppins == 0, generate(insurance_0)
cumul y if suppins == 1, generate(insurance_1)
stack insurance_0 y insurance_1 y, into(c expenditure)    ///
    wide clear
line insurance_0 insurance_1 expenditure,                ///
    sort lpattern (dash)                                 ///
    title(Empirical CDFs of costs by insurance status)   ///
    saving(fig361, replace)
line insurance_0 insurance_1 expenditure if expenditure  ///
    < 15000, sort lpattern(dash)                         ///
    title(Empirical CDFs of costs by insurance status)   ///
    saving(fig362, replace)
restore
graph combine "fig361" "fig362" , ysize(1) xsize(2.3)    ///
    iscale(1)
```

Figure 3.6 displays the resulting empirical CDFs. As the distribution of costs is skewed to the right, it is difficult to observe whether having supplementary

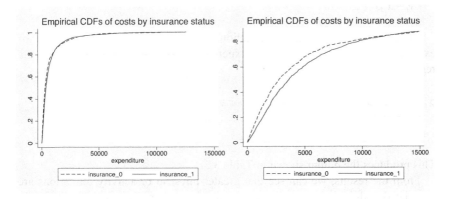

Figure 3.6 Empirical CDFs by insurance status: all expenditures and expenditures
< $15,000.

insurance leads to greater costs in the left-hand figure. The right-hand figure restricts the plots of the CDFs to expenditures less than $15,000 where it becomes more apparent that individuals with supplementary insurance, in general, incur greater health care costs.

3.4 LINEAR REGRESSION MODELS

Regression on observed cost scale

Perhaps the most commonly used regression estimator is ordinary least squares (OLS) on an untransformed dependent variable. The method is attractive due to its ease of implementation and computational simplicity. Estimation operates directly on the 'natural' cost scale (level of cost), measured in dollars or pounds etc., and no prior transformation is required. Since the natural cost scale is used, the marginal effects of covariates are on the same scale and are easy to compute and interpret. Potential disadvantages of OLS are that the distribution of cost data on its natural scale tends to be non-symmetric and heteroskedatic (non-constant variance). This renders OLS regression inefficient. In addition, OLS imposes linearity between the set of regressors and cost, which can lead to out-of-range (negative) predictions. The model can be specified as follows:

$$y_i = x_i \beta + \epsilon_i, \quad i = 1, \ldots, N$$

where, y_i is the measure of health care costs, x_i is a vector of regressors, including a constant term, β is a conformably dimensioned vector of parameters, and ϵ_i is an idiosyncratic error term assumed to be identically and independently distributed and orthogonal to the regressors. The model can be estimated by OLS, and estimates, $\hat{y}$ of the conditional mean of costs, $E[y \mid x]$, are given by

$$\hat{y}_i = x_i \hat{\beta}$$

To estimate the regression function using OLS first specify the set of explanatory regressors predictive of expenditures as a global variable the run the regression:

```
global xvars "age female income suppins phylim actlim
    totchr"
regress y $xvars, robust
```

This produces the output shown in Table 3.3.

From the results, we can see that greater physical or activity limitations are associated with higher expenditures, as are the number of chronic conditions. In general, women appear to incur less expenditure than men in this sample, and older individuals have lower costs than their younger counterparts conditional on the

Table 3.3 OLS on total expenditures

Linear regression

					Number of obs	=	2955
					F(7, 2947)	=	40.58
					Prob > F	=	0.0000
					R-squared	=	0.1163
					Root MSE	=	11285

y	Coef.	Robust Std. Err.	t	P>|t|	[95% Conf. Interval]
age	-85.36264	37.81868	-2.26	0.024	-159.5163	-11.20892
female	-1383.29	432.4759	-3.20	0.001	-2231.275	-535.3044
income	6.46894	8.570658	0.75	0.450	-10.33614	23.27402
suppins	724.8632	427.3045	1.70	0.090	-112.9824	1562.709
phylim	2389.019	544.3493	4.39	0.000	1321.675	3456.362
actlim	3900.491	705.2244	5.53	0.000	2517.708	5283.273
totchr	1844.377	186.8938	9.87	0.000	1477.921	2210.832
_cons	8358.954	2847.802	2.94	0.003	2775.07	13942.84

other regressors. Note that the sample consists of individuals greater than 65 years and there may be a survivor effect here, also the model controls for chronic conditions and measures of morbidity. However, we may have failed to reflect nonlinearities in the relationship between age and health care expenditures with such a simple specification.

Predictions from the model can be computed using Stata's `predict` command. Summarising the predictions illustrates one of the drawbacks of using OLS to model cost data, particularly where interest lies in estimating the conditional mean for purposes of forecasting. In the results below, we see that the four smallest predictions produce negative expenditures.

```
predict yhat, xb
summarize yhat, detail

              Linear prediction
-----------------------------------------------------------
      Percentiles      Smallest
 1%     674.9428      -236.3781
 5%     1716.237      -199.2982
10%     2434.016      -77.67862      Obs              2955
25%     4092.742      -23.68736      Sum of Wgt.      2955

50%     6464.692                     Mean          7290.235
                       Largest       Std. Dev.     4089.624
75%    10199.28       20024.03
90%    13181.78       20131.43       Variance      1.67e+07
95%    14799.29       20790.16       Skewness       .574583
99%    17418.97          22559       Kurtosis      2.656862
```

Clearly, these do not make sense where observed data are restricted to be positive. While the conditional mean estimated using OLS is the same as the actual mean observed in the data ($7,290), this is misleading as an indication of how well OLS performs in predicting costs (this will always be the case when using OLS with an intercept). More revealing is a comparison of the median values (actual: $3,334; predicted: $6,465). This discrepancy, which is large, is due to the skewness in the observed cost data, which OLS fails to model. OLS also performs poorly at predicting high expenditures. The 90th, 95th and 99th percentiles of predicted expenditures are $13,182, $14,799 and $17,419, respectively, and the four largest predictions range from $20,024 to $22,559. The corresponding figures observed in the distribution of actual expenditures are $17,549, $27,941 and $62,989 for the percentiles and $104,823–$125,610 for the range of the four largest observations. The correlation between predicted and actual costs is 0.34 (rank correlation 0.47).

```
correlate y yhat

(obs=2955)
             |         y        yhat
-------------|----------------------------------
         y  |    1.0000
      yhat  |    0.3411     1.0000


spearman y yhat

 Number of obs =   2955
Spearman's rho =      0.4666


Test of Ho: y and yhat are independent
    Prob > |t| =    0.0000
```

Our predictions of costs from our simple specification estimated using OLS do not adequately model high-expenditure patients. In part, the inadequacies in the specification of the regressors and the assumption that these are additive in effects may contribute to the poor performance; however, to simplify the exposition of the various models that follow we persist with this parsimonious model.

Model diagnostics

The specification of the regression model can be checked using a variety of diagnostic tests. These are presented here in the context of the linear cost regression model, but can be extended to models for transformed costs and to the nonlinear regression models introduced in Chapter 12. With individual-level data on health care costs, there will typically be a high degree of heteroskedasticity in the distribution of the error term. This can be detected using relevant diagnostic tests. For the OLS estimator used above, we can use the post-estimation command estat hettest to detect heteroskedasticity. Where there is concern about hetero-scedasticity, the norm is to estimate the model using robust standard errors (as in the above regression) and use these for inference (White, 1980).

A commonly used test of the reliability of the specification of a model is provided by the RESET test (Ramsey, 1969), which is based on re-running the regression with squares and possibly other powers of the fitted (predicted) values included as auxiliary variables. This can be undertaken by, either, manually computing the relevant powers of the fitted values and re-running the model estimation or, for models for which it is supported, by using the postestimation command estat ovtest. In the health economics literature, Pregibon's (1980) link test is widely used as an alternative to the RESET test. The test adds the level of the fitted values (and its square) rather than including the individual regressors and consists of testing the null hypothesis that the coefficient of the square of the fitted values is not significantly different to zero. The test is implemented in Stata using `linktest`. For the OLS regression above we apply these diagnostics as follows:

```
quietly regress y $xvars

estat hettest, fstat     /* Option fstat relaxes assumption
of normality */

Breusch-Pagan / Cook-Weisberg test for heteroskedasticity
        Ho: Constant variance
        Variables: fitted values of y

        F(1 , 2953) =   74.10
        Prob > F    =  0.0000


estat ovtest

Ramsey RESET test using powers of the fitted values of y
        Ho: model has no omitted variables
              F(3, 2944) =    3.18
                Prob > F =   0.0230


linktest

    Source |       SS     df         MS     Number of obs =    2955
---------|------------------------------     F( 2, 2952)  = 196.00
    Model | 4.9789e+10      2  2.4895e+10    Prob > F      = 0.0000
 Residual | 3.7494e+11   2952   127011328    R-squared     = 0.1172
---------|------------------------------     Adj R-squared = 0.1166
    Total | 4.2473e+11   2954   143780269    Root MSE      =  11270


--------------------------------------------------------------------
       y |    Coef.  Std. Err.     t   P>|t|  [95% Conf. Interval]
--------------------------------------------------------------------
    _hat | .6831985  .1891798   3.61  0.000   .3122608   1.054136
  _hatsq | .0000187  .0000108   1.74  0.082  -2.40e-06   .0000398
    _cons |  1002.17  715.5632   1.40  0.161  -400.8831   2405.223
--------------------------------------------------------------------
```

The results indicate substantial heteroskedasticity and evidence of model misspecification. The latter can be seen via the RESET test, although the link test is less clear on this matter – there is insufficient evidence to reject the hypothesis that the square of the fitted values is not zero.

Regression on transformed costs

As outlined earlier, an alternative to modelling cost on its natural scale is to transform the outcome in an attempt to 'pull-in' the upper tail of the distribution and reduce skewness. The log transformation, and to a lesser extent, the square-root transformation are commonly used to this effect. Data with zero expenditures, however, will render the use of the log transformation problematic. A potential solution involves either using two-part specifications or adding an arbitrary constant to the data prior to transformation. The latter is, however, unsatisfactory due to the influence of the specific choice of constant on the subsequent regression and its failure to deal with the mass point at the lower end of the distribution. In general, the results from a log-transformed regression can be sensitive to changes in the left-hand tail of the distribution of cost (see Buntin and Zaslavsky, 2004). In contrast, the square-root transformation does not suffer from a problem with zero costs. These concerns are not relevant for the MEPS sample we are interested in modelling here.

Estimation proceeds via OLS on the transformed outcome. A problem arises when deriving predictions from a model based on a transformed scale. As Manning (1998) points out 'Congress does not appropriate log dollars'. Accordingly, where models are estimated on a transformed outcome, predictions must be retransformed back to the original scale to draw meaningful conclusions relevant for policy purposes.

Logarithmic transformation

An approach to reducing skewness to produce a more symmetric and normally distributed function of costs is to use a logarithmic transformation. Once on the log-scale, OLS regression can be undertaken as follows:

$$\ln(y_i) = x_i\beta + \epsilon_i, \quad i = 1, \ldots, N$$

Estimating models on the log scale is, however, not without problems. Predictions from the above model will provide cost on the log scale, where typically this is not desirable and costs on the observed raw scale are much more useful for policy interpretation. It is a mistake to simply take the exponential of the predictions following estimation on the log scale – this will produce the geometric, rather than the arithmetic mean. We require the expected conditional value of expenditures, $E[y \mid x]$. For a log transformation, this is not equivalent to taking the exponent of the predictions: $E[y \mid x] \neq \exp\{E[\ln(y) \mid x]\}$. Instead it is necessary to apply what is termed a smearing factor to retransform the predicted costs on the log-scale to predictions on the observed raw scale. As we will see this is not always straightforward to implement. More concretely we require an estimate of $E[y \mid x]$ which for the log model: $\ln(y) = x\beta + \epsilon$ is given by:

$$E[y_i \mid x_i] = E\left[\exp(x_i\beta + \epsilon_i) \mid x_i\right] = \exp(x_i\beta) E\left[\exp(\epsilon_i) \mid x_i\right]$$

The latter term in the above expression is the smearing factor. The difficulties in estimating the smearing factor often limits the use of modelling health care cost data of transformed expenditures in practical settings.

The following outlines various approaches to estimating $E[\exp(\epsilon)\,|\,x]$ and recovering predictions on the original cost scale when working with log-trans-formed data. We then extend the approach to the square root transformation of y and finally consider greater flexibility offered through Box–Cox transformations.

For log transformations, assuming homoskedastic and normally distributed errors on the log-scale so that the cost data has a log-normal distribution, it can be shown that $E[\exp(\epsilon)\,|\,x] = \exp(0.5\,\sigma_\epsilon^2)$, where σ_ϵ^2 is the variance of the distribution of the error. Hence, expected cost on the original scale can be recovered using the following retransformation:

$$E\big[y_i\,|\,x_i\big] = \exp\big(x_i\beta + 0.5\sigma_\epsilon^2\big)$$

It follows that the marginal effect for a continuous regressor, x_k, is given by

$$\frac{\partial E\big[y_i\,|\,x_i\big]}{\partial x_{ki}} = \beta_k E\big[y_i\,|\,x_i\big] = \beta_k\,\exp\big(x_i\beta + 0.5\sigma_\epsilon^2\big)$$

Similarly, the incremental effect for a discrete regressor is defined as

$$\frac{\Delta E\big[y_i\,|\,x_i\big]}{\Delta x_{ki}} = \exp\big(x_i\beta^{|x_k=1} + 0.5\sigma_\epsilon^2\big) - \exp\big(x_i\beta^{|x_k=0} + 0.5\sigma_\epsilon^2\big)$$

$$= \big((\exp x_i\beta^{|x_k=1}) - (\exp x_i\beta^{|x_k=0})\big)\exp\big(0.5\sigma_\epsilon^2\big)$$

We can implement this estimator in Stata by writing a program to estimate the log-normal distribution via maximum likelihood estimation.

```
/***************************************************************/
/* Assuming normally distributed and homoskedastic errors*/

program define myreg
   args lnf theta1 theta2
   quietly replace `lnf'=ln(normalden(($ML_y1-`theta1')    ///
      /`theta2')) - ln(`theta2')
end
/***************************************************************/
ml model lf myreg (lny = $xvars) /sigma
ml maximize
```

Estimating the model for the log-normal distribution by maximum likelihood produces the output in Table 3.4.

Table 3.4 Maximum likelihood estimation of log-normal model

```
---------------------------------------------------------------------
                                  Number of obs  =     2955
                                  Wald chi2(7)   =   877.25
Log likelihood = -4733.4476       Prob > chi2    =   0.0000
----------|----------------------------------------------------------
     lny  |     Coef. Std. Err.     z  P>|z| [95% Conf. Interval]
----------|----------------------------------------------------------
eq1       |
     age  |  .0038016   .0036512   1.04  0.298  -.0033545   .0109578
  female  | -.0843275   .0454825  -1.85  0.064  -.1734716   .0048166
  income  |  .0025498    .001018   2.50  0.012   .0005545   .0045451
 suppins  |  .2556428   .0461638   5.54  0.000   .1651634   .3461221
  phylim  |  .3020598   .0568937   5.31  0.000   .1905501   .4135695
  actlim  |  .3560054   .0620276   5.74  0.000   .2344335   .4775774
  totchr  |  .3758201   .0183978  20.43  0.000   .3397612   .4118791
    _cons |  6.703737   .2763851  24.26  0.000   6.162033   7.245442
----------|----------------------------------------------------------
sigma     |
    _cons |    1.2007   .0156186  76.88  0.000   1.170089   1.231312
----------|----------------------------------------------------------
```

If we compare the retransformed predictions from this model to the actual costs on the original scale, we see that the mean predicted cost is greater once we have retransformed the log model predictions. The model also overestimates low cost patients and underestimates high cost patients substantially.

```
predict lyhat, xb
scalar sigma = _b[sigma:_cons]
generate yhatnorm = exp(lyhat)*exp(0.5*sigma^2)
summarize yhatnorm y
```

Variable	Obs	Mean	Std. Dev.	Min	Max
yhatnorm	2955	8233.8	6792.64	1973.09	77571.19
y	2955	7290.235	11990.84	3	125610

Compute the marginal effect of income as follows:

```
generate meincome = _b[income] * yhatnorm
summarize meincome
```

Variable	Obs	Mean	Std. Dev.	Min	Max
meincome	2955	20.99469	17.31999	5.03102	197.7924

The average marginal effect for income is $21, which is substantially greater than that estimated via linear regression in Table 3.3. The average incremental effect for supplementary insurance is given by

```
preserve
quietly replace suppins = 0
quietly predict lyhat0
generate yhatnorm0 = exp(lyhat0)*exp(0.5*sigma^2)
quietly replace suppins = 1
quietly predict lyhat1
generate yhatnorm1 = exp(lyhat1)*exp(0.5*sigma^2)
generate iesuppins = yhatnorm1 - yhatnorm0
summarize iesuppins
```

Variable	Obs	Mean	Std. Dev.	Min	Max
iesuppins	2955	2043.616	1646.669	574.7444	17498.63

```
restore
```

Notice that this code uses the commands preserve and restore. These allow the dataset to be temporarily altered so that the predict command can be re-used with counterfactual values set for the regressor suppins before the original values of the data are restored to be used in subsequent analysis.

The incremental effect on health care costs of having supplementary insurance is estimated as $2,043.6. This is nearly three times the size of the effect estimated via linear regression on untransformed costs in Table 3.3. Note that throughout we do not make claim to estimating causal effects of insurance status as our models are rudimentary, assuming exogeneity, and designed solely to illustrate approaches to modelling expenditure data, rather than informing policy around the provision of supplementary insurance.

Where the distribution of the error is not normally distributed (it is extremely likely that the distribution of expenditures conditional on the regressors is non-normal), but is homoskedastic (has a constant variance) then Duan's smearing estimator (Duan, 1983) can be applied as an alternative as follows:

$$E[y_i|x_i] = \phi \times \exp(x_i\beta)$$

Here an estimate of $E[\exp(\epsilon)\,|\,x_i]$ is given by averaging over the exponentiated residuals:

$$\hat{\phi} = N^{-1}\sum_i \exp(\hat{\epsilon}_i), \quad \left(\hat{\epsilon}_i = \ln y_i - x_i\hat{\beta}\right)$$

from a standard linear regression on log-costs. ϕ is termed Duan's smearing factor and typically lies between 1.5 and 4.0 in empirical applications to health data.

Marginal effects can be calculated analogously to the case where the errors are assumed to be normally distributed.

Implement the linear regression estimator for log-costs using the following set of commands (without showing the output for the regression itself):

```
quietly regress lny $xvars, robust
predict lyhat, xb
estat ovtest
```

```
Ramsey RESET test using powers of the fitted values of lny
        Ho: model has no omitted variables
                F(3, 2944) =    9.04
                    Prob > F =    0.0000
```

```
linktest
```

Source	SS	df	MS		
				Number of obs =	2955
				F(2, 2952)	= 454.81
Model	1301.41696	2	650.708481	Prob > F	= 0.0000
Residual	4223.47242	2952	1.43071559	R-squared	= 0.2356
				Adj R-squared	= 0.2350
Total	5524.88938	2954	1.87030785	Root MSE	= 1.1961

y	Coef.	Std. Err.	t	P>|t|	[95% Conf. Interval]	
_hat	4.429216	.6779517	6.53	0.000	3.09991	5.758522
_hatsq	-.2084091	.0411515	-5.06	0.000	-.2890976	-.1277206
_cons	-14.01127	2.779936	-5.04	0.000	-19.46208	-8.56046

While the logarithmic transformation produces a more symmetric distribution of costs, the RESET test and link test both cast doubt on the specification of the model (on the transformed scale). Duan's smearing estimator is computed as follows:

```
/* Duan' s smearing estimator */
generate expr = exp(lny - lyhat)
quietly summarize expr
scalar duan = _result(3)
generate yhatduan = exp(lyhat) * duan
```

We can return the scalar value of Duan's smearing estimate for these data:

```
display duan
```

```
1.999155
```

The correlation between the predictions after applying Duan's smearing estimator and the observed costs is slightly worse than for the linear regression on untransformed expenditures, while the rank correlation is greater than the corresponding untransformed regression.

```
correlate y yhatduan

(obs=2955)
             |    y        yhatduan
-----------|---------------------
         y |   1.0000
  yhatduan |   0.2974    1.0000

spearman y yhatduan

 Number of obs =    2955
Spearman's rho =     0.4902

Test of Ho: y and yhatduan are independent
     Prob > |t| =    0.0000
```

In practice, assuming homoskedastic errors is unlikely to be tenable, even on the log-scale, and where the errors are heteroskedastic then Duan's smearing estimator will be biased. If the form of heteroskedasticity, as a function of regressors x is known then in the general case unbiased predictions of cost can be obtained as:

$$E[y_i|x_i] = \rho(x_i) \times \exp(x_i\beta)$$

where $\rho(x)$ is a heteroskedastic smearing estimator. This shows that eliminating bias requires knowledge of the form of heteroskedasticity. This added complexity extends to computing marginal effects from the log-transformed coefficients,

$$\frac{\partial E[y_i|x_i]}{\partial x_{ki}} = \beta_k E[y_i|x_i] + \exp(x_i\beta)\frac{\partial \rho(x_i)}{\partial x_{ki}}$$

Computing the expected conditional mean and marginal effects is manageable if there are a limited number of binary regressors. For example, if the residual variance is a function of a binary regressor, x_k, then a smearing factor can be computed for each value that x takes ($\rho(x_k^{|x_k=0}$)) and ($\rho(x_k^{|x_k=1}$)). The average incremental effect can then be computed as

$$\frac{\Delta E[y_i|x_i]}{\Delta x_{ki}} = \exp(x_i\beta^{|x_k=1})\rho(x_k^{|x_k=1}) - \exp(x_i\beta^{|x_k=0})\rho(x_k^{|x_k=0})$$

where the variance is a function of multiple regressors, and where regressors take cardinal rather than discrete values, specifying the form of heteroskedasticity becomes difficult. In such cases, it can be useful to compute a smearing estimator for percentiles of the range of fitted values from the estimated model (for example, based on percentiles of $\exp(x\hat{\beta})$). For cost data, heteroskedasticity might be more pronounced in the right-hand tail of the distribution and as such, separate smearing estimators might be computed for a limited number of deciles at the top of the fitted distribution. Alternatively, we can exploit the fact that $\rho(x) = E[\exp(\epsilon) \mid x]$, which suggests running a regression of the exponentiated residuals on the set of covariates x and using the predictions from this auxiliary regression as the smearing factor. In the absence of knowledge of the form of heteroskedasticity, this is an approximation, but we follow this approach for our application to the MEPS data below.

```
/* Heteroskedastic case - form unknown */
regress expr $xvars
```

This produces the results reported in Table 3.5. We can see from the regression output that heteroskedasticity appears to be mainly a function of age, supplementary insurance status and the number of chronic conditions. The smearing estimator for the heteroskedastic case varies across individuals ranging from 0.99 to 3.04 and has a mean equivalent to Duan's estimator.

The marginal effect of income is $9.87, which contrasts to $6.47 for simple OLS and $20.9 assuming normally distributed errors on the log scale and $20.4 for Duan's smearing estimator. Similarly, for the incremental effect of supplemental health insurance assuming heteroskedastic errors leads to an estimate of $847 contrasted against $725 for OLS, $2,044 for normally distributed and homoskedastic errors and $1,987 for Duan's estimator. The marginal effects estimated assuming homoskedastic errors differ substantially from those assuming heteroskedastic errors and estimates for the latter are closer to OLS. It is emphasised, however, that these estimates are an approximation as the functional form of heteroskedasticity is not known.

Square-root transformation

There may be circumstances where a square root transformation is preferred over a logarithmic transformation, such that we estimate

$$\sqrt{y_i} = x_i\beta + \epsilon_i , \quad i = 1,\dots, N$$

For example, in a two-part model, Ettner *et al.* (1998) found that the square-root transformation provided a better fit to data on psychiatric services than a log-transformation, reflecting data on psychiatric services being less skewed than that on total health care costs. However, similarly to the log transformation, we cannot simply estimate a model of the square root of expenditures and square the fitted values to back transform to the original cost scale: $E[y \mid x]$ is not equivalent to $[E(\sqrt{(y \mid x)})]^2$. The smearing estimators, however, can be adapted to square-root

Table 3.5 Heteroskedasticity on log-scale

```
-------------------------------------------------------------------
  Source |       SS      df         MS      Number of obs =    2955
---------|--------------------------------   F( 7, 2947)   =    4.06
   Model | 291.023052      7  41.5747216     Prob > F      = 0.0002
Residual | 30207.0793   2947  10.2501117     R-squared     = 0.0095
---------|--------------------------------   Adj R-squared = 0.0072
   Total | 30498.1023   2954  10.3243407     Root MSE      = 3.2016
-------------------------------------------------------------------


-------------------------------------------------------------------
    expr |     Coef. Std. Err.      t  P>|t|   [95% Conf. Interval]
-------------------------------------------------------------------
     age | -.0205247  .0097356  -2.11  0.035   -.039614   -.0014355
  female | -.1820937  .1212758  -1.50  0.133   -.4198875   .0557002
  income | -.0023125  .0027145  -0.85  0.394   -.0076349   .0030099
 suppins | -.2707465  .1230924  -2.20  0.028   -.5121023  -.0293907
  phylim |  .2002335   .151703   1.32  0.187   -.0972211   .4976881
  actlim |   .179024  .1653922   1.08  0.279   -.1452718   .5033199
  totchr | -.1961736  .0490563  -4.00  0.000   -.2923617  -.0999855
   _cons |  4.057932  .7369607   5.51  0.000    2.612922   5.502942
-------------------------------------------------------------------
```

```
predict smearhat, xb
generate yhathetro = exp(lyhat) * smearhat
summarize smearhat
```

```
    Variable |     Obs      Mean   Std. Dev.      Min       Max
-------------|-------------------------------------------------
    smearhat |    2955  1.999155   .3138762   .9892805   3.04122
```

Use this to compute marginal effects for income:

```
quietly regress lny $xvars, robust
generate minc=_b[income]
quietly regress expr $xvars
generate pinc=_b[income]
generate margin = (minc*yhathetro) + (exp(lyhat)*pinc)
summarize margin
```

```
    Variable |     Obs      Mean   Std. Dev.      Min       Max
-------------|-------------------------------------------------
      margin |    2955  9.873228   6.286285   1.885871  45.76725
```

transformed models of expenditures. In this case, the correction term is additive rather than multiplicative. For the homoskedastic case:

$$E[y_i|x_i] = (x_i\beta)^2 + \phi$$

where the smearing factor, ϕ, can be consistently estimated as the average of the squared residuals: $N^{-1}\sum_i\hat{\epsilon}_i^2$. The marginal effect for a continuous regressor, x_k, can be computed as

$$\frac{\partial E[y_i|x_i]}{\partial x_{ki}} = 2(x_i\beta)\beta_k$$

For a discrete regressor, the average incremental effect is given by

$$\frac{\Delta E[y_i|x_i]}{\Delta x_{ki}} = \left(x_i\beta^{|x_k=1}\right)^2 - \left(x_i\beta^{|x_k=0}\right)^2$$

Estimate the square root transformed model of costs as follows:

```
regress sqrty $xvars, robust
```

This produces the results reported in Table 3.6. A RESET and link test that follows the regression output suggests that the square root transformation offers a reasonable specification of the model.

For heteroskedastic errors (the commonly encountered situation), the relevant smearing factor for a square root transformed regression, $\rho(x)$, can be estimated by running an auxiliary regression of the squared residuals on functions of x, for example, the fitted values of the linear index.

Comparison of approaches

A useful way to summarise the various approaches to modelling transformed health care cost data using linear models is to consider a simple model of expenditures regressed on supplementary insurance status and a constant. The example is contrived to illustrate how the various smearing factors improve on a naive retransformation (without applying a smearing factor). Since only a discrete variable is specified in the model, including a smearing factor when retransforming predictions to the original cost scale should lead to fitted values that equate to the sample means of costs. In the absence of heteroskedasticity, then the smearing factor should be sufficient; where heteroskedasticity is a function of the discrete variable, then the smearing factor should take this into account.

The first row of Table 3.7 provides the mean costs for the two values of suppins. The following rows summarise predictions of costs for insurance status for square root transformed and log-transformed regressions. The naive estimator represents either the square of predictions (for the square root models) or

Table 3.6 Square root transformed linear regression

```
-----------------------------------------------------------------
Linear regression                        Number of obs =    2955
                                         F( 7, 2947)   =   86.71
                                         Prob > F      =  0.0000
                                         R-squared     =  0.1893
                                         Root MSE      =  44.065


             -----------------------------------------------------
             |          Robust
     sqrty |    Coef. Std. Err.      t  P>|t|  [95% Conf. Interval]
-----------------------------------------------------------------
       age |-.1311046   .1409585  -0.93  0.352  -.4074917   .1452826
    female |-5.276307   1.689172  -3.12  0.002  -8.588382  -1.964231
    income | .0557385   .0347503   1.60  0.109  -.0123989   .1238759
   suppins | 5.703147   1.691982   3.37  0.001   2.385561   9.020733
    phylim | 11.87169   2.163689   5.49  0.000     7.6292   16.11419
    actlim | 16.08803   2.641183   6.09  0.000   10.90928   21.26678
    totchr | 10.83763   .7068999  15.33  0.000   9.451566    12.2237
     _cons | 48.77443   10.66255   4.57  0.000   27.86764   69.68123
-----------------------------------------------------------------
```

estat ovtest

```
Ramsey RESET test using powers of the fitted values of sqrty
        Ho: model has no omitted variables
            F(3, 2944) =    1.26
               Prob > F =   0.2875
```

linktest

```
    Source |        SS      df       MS      Number of obs =    2955
---------|---------------------------       F( 2, 2952)   = 344.73
    Model | 1336425         2 668212.501    Prob > F      =  0.0000
 Residual | 5721990.17   2952 1938.34355    R-squared     =  0.1893
---------|---------------------------       Adj R-squared =  0.1888
    Total | 7058415.17   2954 2389.44319    Root MSE      =  44.027


-----------------------------------------------------------------
     sqrty |    Coef. Std. Err.      t  P>|t|  [95% Conf. Interval]
-----------------------------------------------------------------
      _hat | 1.090201   .2307615   4.72  0.000    .637731   1.542671
    _hatsq | -.0005954   .0015023  -0.40  0.692  -.0035411   .0023503
     _cons | -3.127451   8.368906  -0.37  0.709  -19.53693   13.28203
-----------------------------------------------------------------
```

The smearing estimator and retransformed costs are computed as

```
predict sqrtyhat, xb
generate sqrr = (sqrty - sqrtyhat)^2
quietly summarize sqrr
scalar s_sqrt = _result(3)
generate yhatsqrt = sqrtyhat^2 + s_sqrt
display s_sqrt
```

1936.4787

The retransformed costs are investigated below:

```
summarize yhatsqrt, detail
```

```
                    yhatsqrt
-------------------------------------------------------------
      Percentiles       Smallest
 1%    3135.777       3007.828
 5%    3561.352       3018.235
10%    3944.347       3028.845      Obs                 2955
25%    4748.121       3060.595      Sum of Wgt.         2955

50%    6429.097                     Mean            7290.235
                       Largest      Std. Dev.       3266.748
75%    9075.197       21190.35
90%    11943.75       21236.92      Variance        1.07e+07
95%    14001.65        21335.7      Skewness        1.164404
99%    17027.46       24458.18      Kurtosis        4.270064
```

```
correlate y yhatsqrt
```

```
(obs=2955)

             |   y         yhatsqrt
-------------|-------------------------------
          y  |  1.0000
    yhatsqrt |  0.3371      1.0000
```

```
spearman y yhatsqrt
```

```
 Number of obs =   2955
Spearman's rho =     0.4834

Test of Ho: y and yhatsqrt are independent
     Prob > |t| =        0.0000
```

Table 3.7 Comparison of approaches for a binary regressor

Estimation of $E[y_i \mid x_i]$	Suppins = 0 N = 1207	Suppins = 1 N = 1748
Observed scale		
Total cost	6824.3	7612.0
Square root transformed		
Naive (no smearing correction)	4425.7	5244.4
Homoskedastic smearing estimator	6806.0	7624.6
Heteroskedastic smearing estimator	6824.3	7612.0
Log-transformed		
Naïve (no smearing correction)	2710.8	3522.1
Assuming log-normality	6847.0	8896.0
Homoskedastic smearing estimator	6253.1	8124.4
Heteroskedastic smearing estimator	6824.3	7612.0

exponentiated predictions (for the log transformed regressions). As can be seen, the naive estimates of the mean cost by insurance status deviate dramatically from the observed cost data. Applying the smearing estimator improves the predictions of costs in both the square root model and the log-transformed model. However, there is still a notable departure from observed costs for the retransformed log predictions compared to the square root retransformed predictions.

Applying the heteroskedastic smearing estimator produces predictions equivalent to the sample data on the original cost scale. Since insurance status is a binary indicator (and the sole regressor in the model) the correction for heteroskedasticity is simply Duan's smearing estimator applied separately to each of the two insurance groups. This illustrates that where the form of heteroskedasticity is known, and the model has a simple specification, consisting of a limited number of discrete variables, the smearing correction works well and inference from the model will be preferred to OLS on the linear specification on the original cost scale. In general, regression models of health care expenditures will typically consist of many variables, often a mixture of both discrete and continuous regressors and possible interactions. The ability to model heteroskedasticity in such models is far more challenging.

Table 3.8 summarises mean predictions against observed costs for the various models of health care expenditures using the full set of regressors. Predictions from regressions on a transformed scale and applying a smearing correction again perform far better than the naive estimate (without a smearing factor). The means of the predictions are closer to untransformed costs, and with the exception of the non-normal homoskedastic square root model, have greater variability. They also have the desirable property of producing positive predictions and do better than OLS on untransformed costs at predicting high-cost patients. The latter is

Table 3.8 Comparison of predictions following retransformation

Health care costs: actual and predictions

	Actual	OLS	Log transformed regressions			Square root transformed regressions		
			Naive	*Normality Homosked.*	*Non-normal Homosked.*	*Non-normal Heterosked.*	*Non-normal Homosked.*	*Non-normal Heterosked.*
Mean	7290.2	7290.2	4004.5	8233.8	8005.5	7503.9	7290.2	7290.2
s.d.	11990.8	4089.6	3303.6	6792.6	6604.3	5196.8	3266.7	4128.7
Median	3334	6464.7	2961.9	6090.1	5921.2	5731.7	6429.1	6144.1
Min.	3	−236.4	959.6	1973.1	1918.4	2228.6	3007.8	24458.2
Max.	125610	22559	37726.2	77571.2	75420.6	51649.3	24458.2	27488.8
Corr.								
Spearman		0.3411	0.2974	0.2974	0.2974	0.3264	0.3371	0.3409
Rank corr.		0.4666	0.4902	0.4902	0.4902	0.4757	0.4834	0.4684

particularly true for the log-transformed regressions compared to the square root transformations. While OLS on the untransformed scale performs best on the correlation between predictions and actual costs, the transformed models outperform OLS on the original scale when considering the rank correlation.

Box–Cox models

An alternative to imposing specific functional forms, such as a logarithmic or square root, is the Box–Cox transformation (see Box and Cox 1964):

$$
y_i^{(\theta)} = \begin{cases} \dfrac{y_i^{\theta} - 1}{\theta} & \text{if } \theta \neq 0 \\ \log(y_i) & \text{if } \theta \neq 0 \end{cases},
$$

The approach was developed to produce a conditional distribution of the transformed outcome, y, more closely resembling normality and exhibiting less heteroskedasticity. The transformation embeds several popular functional forms including: levels ($\theta = 1$), square root ($\theta = \frac{1}{2}$) and logs ($\theta = 0$) as special cases. The transformation can be applied to cost data in a similar way to the transformations previously considered. The parameters of Box–Cox transformed models can be estimated via maximum likelihood assuming the error, ϵ, has a normal distribution. This is illustrated below for the default case where a transformation is applied only to the dependent variable (the more general model that applies the Box–Cox transformation to the covariates as well as the dependent variable is encompassed by the Stata command). Table 3.9 reports the results.

```
boxcox y $xvars, nolog vce(robust)
```

It is evident from the results in Table 3.9 that standard errors are not provided for the coefficient estimates of the set of regressors, but a standard error is provided for the estimate of the transformation parameter, $\hat{\theta}$. This is due to a result by Spitzer (1984) who showed that Wald tests of the significance of regression parameters in a Box–Cox transformed regression are not invariant to the scale of y (in a linear regression, the scale of y has no impact on a Wald test of significance of any particular regressor). Accordingly, the significance of a given regressor can be manipulated by changing the scale of y. However, this result does not hold for estimates of the transformation parameter, θ, and its variance and Stata only reports standard errors for this parameter. Drukker (2000) provides an intuitive exposition of this issue. Accordingly, boxcox is not supported by the post estimation command margins and hence computing marginal effects and their significance is not straightforward. A solution to testing for the significance of individual regressors (on the transformed scale) is obtained using likelihood ratio tests, which are invariant to the scale of the dependent variable. This can be implemented using the lrtest option.

Table 3.9 Box–Cox transformed regression

```
-------------------------------------------------------------------

Fitting comparison model


Fitting full model


                                    Number of obs  =     2955
                                    LR chi2(7)     =   773.02
Log likelihood = -28518.267         Prob > chi2    =    0.000
-------------------------------------------------------------------
        y |   Coef.    Std. Err.    z  P>|z|  [95% Conf. Interval]
----------|--------------------------------------------------------
  /theta |  .0758956  .0069066  10.99  0.000  .0623588  .0894323
-------------------------------------------------------------------


Estimates of scale-variant parameters
-----------------------
          |      Coef.
----------|--------------
Notrans   |
      age |   .0051321
   female |  -.1767976
   income |   .0044039
  suppins |   .4459618
   phylim |    .577317
   actlim |   .6905939
   totchr |   .6754338
    _cons |   8.930566
----------|--------------
   /sigma |   2.189679
-----------------------



---------------------------------------------------------
    Test       Restricted    LR statistic    P-value
    H0:       log likelihood     chi2      Prob > chi2
---------------------------------------------------------
theta = -1    -37454.643       17872.75       0.000
theta = 0     -28550.353          64.17       0.000
theta = 1     -31762.809        6489.08       0.000
---------------------------------------------------------
```

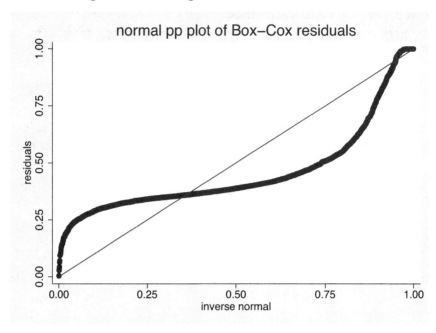

Figure 3.7 Normal probability plot for Box–Cox residuals.

Table 3.10 Summary of residuals from Box–Cox transformed regression

```
----------------------------------------------------------------
Summary of residuals
----------------------------------------------------------------

      Percentiles      Smallest
 1%     -8863.253      -26722.74
 5%     -4659.561      -18680.06
10%     -3227.277      -18589.85     Obs               2955
25%     -1551.531      -17251.83     Sum of Wgt.       2955

50%     -116.4847                    Mean          3131.093
                         Largest     Std. Dev.        11418
75%      3373.265       101658.3
90%     12392.22        103741.4     Variance      1.30e+08
95%     22825.68        115842.1     Skewness      4.213149
99%     56017.36         116985     Kurtosis      27.44099
----------------------------------------------------------------
```

From the output in Table 3.9, the Box–Cox parameter, θ, is estimated as 0.076 and independent tests of the hypothesis that this takes one of the three discrete values (−1 (inverse), 0 (log), 1 (levels)) are firmly rejected. Figure 3.7 and Table 3.10 show that the residuals from the Box–Cox regression exhibit substantial departures from normality and are heavily skewed, implying caution is warranted in deriving inference from the model results.

Retransformation of the predictions to the cost scale (and hence marginal effects) is not straightforward using the Box–Cox transformation, especially in the presence of heteroskedasticity (estimation assumes homoskedastic errors). A more satisfactory use of the transformation is provided by the extended estimating equations (EEE) approach discussed in Chapter 12, where the model explicitly allows for heteroskedasticity through a flexible specification of the variance as a function of the conditional mean. We will see that once we relax the assumption of normality, the Box–Cox parameter estimate of 0.076 is misleading in this application to the MEPS data.

3.5 OVERVIEW

By using data on the medical expenditures of elderly individuals in the United States, this chapter has described the challenges that modelling health care costs present. Individual level data on medical expenditures typically feature a spike at zero, are heavily right-skewed, have heavy tails and exhibit heteroskedasticity. Linear regression of untransformed costs leads to negative predictions and inefficient parameter estimates. Transformations of costs, aimed at producing a more symmetrical distribution, are appealing but do not easily recover predictions and marginal effects on the original cost scale. Smearing factors are required to retransform fitted values to the scale of observation, but these can be challenging where heteroskedasticity is a function of the regressors. Chapter 12 extends the analysis set out here to model nonlinear models, which avoid the retransformation problem and offer greater flexibility in modelling cost data.

Part II
Categorical data

4 Reporting heterogeneity in health

SYNOPSIS

This chapter describes methods to deal with bias in subjective and self-reported measures of health. It uses data for France from the Survey of Health, Ageing and Retirement in Europe (SHARE). The standard ordered probit model is extended to include applications of the generalised ordered model and the 'HOPIT'. These exploit hypothetical 'vignettes' to deal with reporting bias.

4.1 INTRODUCTION

Self-assessed health (SAH) is often included in general socioeconomic surveys. It is a popular measure of health, which has been widely used in applied health economics studies. Despite the popularity and recognised value of this type of subjective measure, there are concerns about its validity. As a self-reported subjective measure of health, SAH may be prone to measurement error. General evidence of non-random measurement error in self-reported health is reviewed in Currie and Madrian (1999) and Lindeboom (2006). Crossley and Kennedy (2002) report evidence of measurement error in a five-category SAH question. They exploit the fact that a random sub-sample of respondents to the 1995 Australian National Health Survey were asked the same version of the SAH question twice, before and after other morbidity questions. The first question was administered as part of the SF-36 questionnaire on a self-completion form, and the second as part of a face-to-face interview on the main questionnaire. They find a statistically significant difference in the distribution of SAH between the two questions and evidence that these differences are related to age, income and occupation. This measurement error could be explained by a *mode of administration effect*, due to the use of self-completion and face-to-face interviews (Grootendorst *et al.*, 1997, find evidence that self-completion questions reveal more morbidity); or a *framing or learning effect* by which SAH responses are influenced by the intervening morbidity questions.

It is sometimes argued that the mapping of 'true health' into SAH categories may vary with respondent characteristics. This is the source of measurement error that we focus on in this chapter. It occurs if sub-groups of the population use systematically different cut-point levels when reporting their SAH, which can for example result in different self-reports for individuals who have the same level of 'true health', and generally will bias analyses that rely on interpersonal comparability of SAH (Butler *et al.*, 1987; Bound, 1991). In the remainder of this chapter, we use the terminologies 'response category cut-point shift' and 'reporting heterogeneity', which have been most commonly used in recent health economics literature.

SAH is usually modelled through an ordered regression model – such as the ordered probit or logit – which rules out reporting heterogeneity. In this context, reporting heterogeneity can be introduced by making the cut-points dependent on covariates – i.e. through a generalised ordered regression model. This requires however strong *a priori* restrictions on which variables affect health and which affect reporting, as it is not possible to separately identify effects of the same variable on both (Terza, 1985; Pudney and Shields, 2000).

Attempts to surmount this fundamental identification problem include conditioning on additional information on true health, namely a set of more 'objective' health indicators (Kerkhofs and Lindeboom, 1995; Kreider, 1999; Lindeboom and Van Doorslaer, 2004). Lindeboom and Van Doorslaer (2004) analyse SAH in the Canadian National Population Health Survey and use the McMaster Health Utility Index (HUI-3) as their objective measure of health, conditional on which all remaining variation with respect to respondent characteristics is attributed to cut-point shift. They find evidence of cut-point shift with respect to age and gender, but not income, education or linguistic group.

An alternative approach is to use additional information on reporting behaviour itself, in particular, to examine variation in the evaluation of given health states represented by hypothetical vignettes (Tandon *et al.*, 2003; King *et al.*, 2004). The vignettes are fixed and so all variation in the rating of them can be attributed to reporting heterogeneity, which can in turn be purged from the individual's own health assessment.

Murray *et al.* (2003) evaluate the vignette approach to the measurement of health, in the domain of mobility, using data from 55 countries from the World Health Organization Multi-Country Survey Study on Health and Responsiveness (WHO-MCS, 2000–2001). Their main goal is to obtain measures of population health that are comparable across countries and so use the vignettes to purge self-reports of cross-country reporting differences (and also with respect to age, sex and education). Bago d'Uva *et al.* (2008a) apply the vignettes approach with the goal of measuring socioeconomic-related health inequalities in China, Indonesia and India, using WHO-MCS data. They find significant reporting differences by education and income, in addition to age, gender and rural/urban residence. This leads to overestimated inequalities by education, and underestimated by income, but in general the corrections are not large. Using data from the Survey on Health, Ageing and Retirement in Europe – SHARE – Bago d'Uva *et al.* (2008b) find that the more highly educated rate the health of vignettes more severely in six of the eight countries considered, which leads to underestimation of education-related health inequalities if no account is taken of those reporting differences. Kapteyn *et al.* (2007) find that about half of the difference in rates of self-reported work disability between the Netherlands and the United States can be attributed to reporting behaviour, as identified by vignettes.

Vignettes are being fielded in a growing number of other surveys including the WHO World Health Surveys (WHS), English Longitudinal Study of Ageing (ELSA) and the Health and Retirement Study (HRS). This chapter illustrates the use of vignettes for identification and correction of reporting heterogeneity in self-reported health across sociodemographic group. The application is to health in the domain of breathing and to one country, France, and is based on Bago d'Uva *et al.* (2008b), who cover seven other countries and five other health domains.

4.2 DATA

In this chapter, we use data taken from the first wave of the Survey of Health, Ageing and Retirement in Europe (SHARE), collected in 2004–2005. Vignettes and self-reported health on six domains were collected from supplementary probability samples, who also completed the core SHARE questionnaire, in 8 of the 12 countries that participated in the first wave. For illustrative purposes, we consider only one country (France) and one health domain (breathing). Self-reported health in this domain is obtained from the question: 'Overall in the last 30 days, how much of a problem did you have because of shortness of breath?' and the five response categories are Extreme, Severe, Moderate, Mild, None.

The vignette ratings are stored in the variables vig1–vig3. The descriptions of these vignettes are:

Vignette 1: Marc/Karine has no problems with walking slowly. He/She gets out of breath easily when climbing uphill for 20 metres or a flight of stairs.

Vignette 2: Paul/Karine suffers from respiratory infections about once every year. He/She is short of breath 3 or 4 times a week and had to be admitted in hospital twice in the past month with a bad cough that required treatment with antibiotics.

Vignette 3:Henri/Marie has been a heavy smoker for 30 years and wakes up with a cough every morning. He/She gets short of breath even while resting and does not leave the house anymore. He/She often needs to be put on oxygen.

Preparation of the dataset used here involved merging three of the original SHARE data files, selection of observations and variables, and construction of variables in a convenient form. Observations with missing values in at least one covariate or own health are dropped, as well as those with missing values in all breathing vignettes. Stata code for these preparations can be found in the Appendix. The resulting dataset includes the measure of self-reported health in the domain of breathing, y, vignette ratings `vig1-vig3` (recoded so as to become increasing in good health, from 1 – extreme problems – to 5 – no problems) and respondent characteristics. In particular, we test for reporting heterogeneity in relation to age (in years, variable `age`), sex (dummy `female`) and education. Education is measured according to the International Standard Classification of Education (ISCED97) as: (i) finished at most primary education or first stage of basic education (ISCED 0–1, reference category), (ii) lower secondary or second stage of basic education (ISCED 2, dummy `isced2`), (iii) upper secondary education (ISCED 3–4, dummy `isced34`) and (iv) recognised third level education, which includes higher vocational education and university degree (ISCED 5–6, dummy `isced56`) (UNESCO, 1997). Before moving on with the analysis, create a list of covariates to be used throughout:

```
global xvars "female age isced2 isced34 isced56"
```

4.3 STANDARD ANALYSIS

Standard regression analyses of SAH use ordered regression models, such as the ordered probit or logit. We opt for the ordered probit as this is the specification that has been generalised to deal with reporting heterogeneity (Terza, 1985; Pudney and Shields, 2000; King *et al.*, 2004).

Let h_i^s be a self-reported categorical health measure, for individual i. It is assumed that h_i^s is generated by a corresponding latent true health variable h_i^{s*}. The ordered probit model assumes the following specification:

$$h_i^{s*} = x_i \beta + \epsilon_i^s, \quad \epsilon_i^s \sim N(0,1) \tag{4.1}$$

where x_i is a vector of observed respondent characteristics, and ϵ_i^s is a random error term that is independent of x_i. Since the latent variable is unobserved and its observed counterpart is categorical, neither scale nor location is identified. For this reason, the variance of the error term is normalised to 1 and the constant term to 0. Specifically, we exclude a constant from the vector x_i throughout this chapter and will explicitly include constant terms in later specifications, where identifiable. The observed categorical response h_i^s relates to h_i^{s*} as follows:

$$h_i^s = k \Leftrightarrow \mu^{k-1} \leq h_i^{s*} < \mu^k, \quad k = 1,\dots,5 \tag{4.2}$$

where $\mu^0 < \mu^1 < \dots < \mu^4 < \mu^5$, and $\mu^0 = -\infty$ and $\mu^5 = \infty$. The assumption of homogeneous reporting inherent to the ordered probit model arises from the assumption that cut-points μ^k are constant. If this does not hold, in particular, if the cut-points vary according to some of the covariates x_i, then imposing this restriction will lead to biased estimates of the coefficients β in the latent health index. This is because they will reflect both health and reporting effects, the latter being effects of x_i on the cut-points.

Combining equations (4.1) and (4.2) results in the following probability of observing each response category k, conditional on x_i:

$$P_{ik}^s = \Pr\left[h_i^s = k \mid x_i\right] = \Phi\left(\mu^k - x_i\beta\right) - \Phi\left(\mu^{k-1} - x_i\beta\right), \quad k = 1,\ldots,5 \quad (4.3)$$

where $\Phi(.)$ denotes the distribution function of the standard normal.

We start by estimating a standard ordered probit as a baseline model with which to compare the more flexible specifications that do not impose the assumption of reporting homogeneity, to assess the extent to which this assumption biases the estimated health effects. The following commands estimate the ordered probit model (Table 4.1) and save results for later comparison with the specifications that accommodate reporting heterogeneity:

```
oprobit y $xvars
estimates store OPROBIT
```

Table 4.1 Ordered probit for self-reported health in the domain of breathing

```
Ordered probit regression                        Number of obs =     837
                                                  LR chi2(5)    =   27.20
                                                  Prob > chi2   = 0.0001
Log likelihood = -858.23464                       Pseudo R2     = 0.0156
```

y	Coef.	Std. Err.	z	P>|z|	[95% Conf. Interval]	
female	-.0395535	.0832709	-0.47	0.635	-.2027614	.1236545
age	-.0173939	.0041571	-4.18	0.000	-.0255416	-.0092461
isced2	.0940107	.1627129	0.58	0.563	-.2249008	.4129221
isced34	.0492632	.1023685	0.48	0.630	-.1513753	.2499017
isced56	.1800551	.1180077	1.53	0.127	-.0512358	.4113459
/cut1	-3.970806	.3797361			-4.715075	-3.226537
/cut2	-2.934572	.3129412			-3.547925	-2.321218
/cut3	-2.041952	.3034121			-2.636629	-1.447275
/cut4	-1.356767	.3004287			-1.945597	-.767938

The coefficients of the covariates have a qualitative interpretation: a positive coefficient means a positive effect on the latent health index, thus a higher probability of reporting a higher category of self-reported health. The results indicate a significant negative relationship between health and age, while no significant relationships are found with gender and education.

The latent health index and the coefficients are not measured in natural units. It is however possible to estimate quantitative effects of the covariates on the probabilities of reporting each health category, for each individual (equation (4.3)). Here, we illustrate with the partial effect of each covariate on the probability of reporting the best category in the domain of breathing ($k = 5$, no problem because of shortness of breath) for a reference individual. We consider as reference individual throughout this chapter a male, aged 64 with at most primary education. Keeping the rest constant, we consider: a unit change in age; a change from male to female; and from the lowest education level ISCED 0–1 to ISCED 2, ISCED 3–4 and ISCED 5–6, respectively. The following commands obtain these partial effects and save them for later comparison with other specifications:

```
#delimit ;
nlcom (PE_5_female: normal(b[/cut4] -b[age]*64)
                   -normal(b[/cut4] -b[age]*64-b[female]))
      (PE_5_age:     normal(b[/cut4] -b[age]*64)
                   -normal(b[/cut4] -b[age]*65))
      (PE_5_isced2: normal(b[/cut4] -b[age]*64)
                   -normal(b[/cut4] -b[age]*64-b[isced2]))
      (PE_5_isced34:normal(b[/cut4] -b[age]*64)
                   -normal(b[/cut4] -b[age]*64-b[isced34]))
      (PE_5_isced56:normal(b[/cut4] -b[age]*64)
                   -normal(b[/cut4] -b[age]*64-b[isced56])),
                   post;
#delimit cr
estimates store PE_5_OPROBIT
```

This returns not only partial effects but also standard errors, test statistics and confidence intervals (Table 4.2). In accordance with the estimated coefficients, the only significant partial effect on the probability of reporting the top health category is that of age. For a 64-year-old male with at most primary education, an additional year of age decreases that probability by –0.0068.

Table 4.2 Partial effects on the probability of reporting no problems with breathing for reference individual, with homogeneous reporting

y	Coef.	Std. Err.	z	P>|z|	[95% Conf.Interval]	
PE_5_female	-.0153884	.0323559	-0.48	0.634	-.0788047	.0480279
PE_5_age	-.0067503	.0015857	-4.26	0.000	-.0098582	-.0036424
PE_5_isced2	.0359424	.0615867	0.58	0.559	-.0847654	.1566502
PE_5_isced34	.0189572	.0393731	0.48	0.630	-.0582126	.0961269
PE_5_isced56	.0678625	.0440385	1.54	0.123	-.0184513	.1541763

We opt for the `nlcom` command here as this is the one that will be used for the models below, not accommodated by the postestimation command `margins`. It should however be noted that the same results would be obtained with the commands below. Note that `isced_cat` is a variable with categories ISCED 0–1, ISCED 2, ISCED 3–4, and ISCED 5–6. This variable, as well as the gender indicator, should be flagged in the `oprobit` estimation as factor variables, `i.isced_cat` and `i.female`, so that Stata appropriately computes discrete changes from the base level, ISCED 0–1 and male, respectively:

```
quietly oprobit oprobit y i.female age i.isced_cat
margins, dydx(*) predict(outcome(5)) at(age=64 female=0 ///
   i.isced_cat=1)
```

(*Results not shown*)

4.4 USING VIGNETTES

Vignettes describe hypothetical cases and individuals are asked to rate them in the same way as they evaluate their own health. As they represent fixed levels of health, individual variation in vignette ratings must be due to reporting heterogeneity. This means that the external vignette information can be used to model the cut-points (assumed fixed in the ordered probit model) as functions of the respondent's characteristics. These cut-points can then be imposed on the model for self-reported health, making it possible to identify health effects (β in the latent health index) rather than a mixture of health effects and reporting effects. This can be done using the hierarchical ordered probit – HOPIT (Tandon *et al.*, 2003; King *et al.*, 2004).

The HOPIT model has two components: the vignette component reflects reporting behaviour (i.e. it models the cut-points as functions of covariates, thus allowing for reporting heterogeneity) and the health component represents the relationship between the individual's own health and covariates (with cut-points determined by the vignette component). The use of vignettes to identify the cut-points that individuals use when reporting their own health relies on two assumptions. First, *vignette equivalence* requires that all individuals perceive the vignette description as corresponding to a level of functioning on the same unidimensional scale. If this did not hold, then one could not attribute variation in rating of a given vignette to reporting heterogeneity. Second, there must be *response consistency*: individuals use the same response scales to classify the hypothetical cases represented by the vignettes and own health. That is, the mapping used to translate the perceived latent health of others to reported categories is the same as that governing the correspondence between own health and reported health. There has been little formal testing of these assumptions (on vignette equivalence, see Murray *et al.*, 2003; Kristensen and Johansson, 2008; Datta Gupta *et al.*, 2010; Bago d'Uva *et al.*, 2011; and on response consistency, see Van Soest *et al.*, 2011; Bago d'Uva *et al.*, 2011).

The two components of the HOPIT model are linked through the cut-points, so the model does not factorise into two independent parts. Joint estimation of the two parts of the model is more efficient than a two-step procedure (Kapteyn *et al.*, 2007). In this chapter, we start by presenting the two-step procedure as this enables a better understanding of how the model works. Additionally, under the assumption that the covariates have the same effect on all cut-points (parallel cut-point shift) the two-step procedure can be implemented using built-in Stata commands (oprobit for the vignette model and intreg for own health, as will be shown below). When either parallel cut-point shift is relaxed in the two-step procedure or the one-step estimation procedure is adopted, it becomes necessary to define specific programs, which we will do in the remainder of this chapter.

4.4.1 Reporting behaviour: modelling vignette ratings

We use the ratings of vignettes j, $j = 1,2,3$, (variables vig1 to vig3) to model individual reporting behaviour. From the frequencies below, we can see that, despite representing fixed levels of distress, the vignette ratings show considerable variation. This is the variation that can be exploited to test for systematic reporting heterogeneity in relation to demographic and socioeconomic characteristics and to purge health disparities across such characteristics of reporting heterogeneity. The number of observations for each vignette varies slightly reflecting the fact that we have decided to keep in the dataset, and use in the analysis, some individuals who rate some vignettes but not others.

```
tab1 vig1-vig3

-> tabulation of vig1
```

Breathing vignette 1	Freq.	Percent	Cum.
extreme	4	0.48	0.48
severe	47	5.70	6.18
moderate	203	24.61	30.79
mild	266	32.24	63.03
none	305	36.97	100.00
Total	825	100.00	

```
-> tabulation of vig2
```

Breathing vignette 2	Freq.	Percent	Cum.
extreme	84	10.19	10.19
severe	543	65.90	76.09

| moderate | 154 | 18.69 | 94.78 |
| mild | 19 | 2.31 | 97.09 |
none	24	2.91	100.00
Total	824	100.00	

-> tabulation of vig3

Breathing vignette 3	Freq.	Percent	Cum.
extreme	231	27.86	27.86
severe	508	61.28	89.14
moderate	45	5.43	94.57
mild	16	1.93	96.50
none	29	3.50	100.00
Total	829	100.00	

The vignette component of the HOPIT is specified in the spirit of the generalised ordered probit proposed by Terza (1985) by extending the ordered probit model so as to allow the cut-points to be functions of x_i. When applied to self-reported health, this model requires that one cut-point is normalised to a constant and cut-point shift is then measured relative to that (i.e. for each covariate, what is identifiable is the difference between the impact on each cut-point and the impact on the fixed one). Alternatively, identification can be achieved by assuming that each covariate can be excluded from either the cut-points or the health index (Pudney and Shields, 2000). While it is difficult to maintain such assumptions in the context of self-reported health, this framework becomes more attractive for modelling vignettes. Under the assumption of vignette equivalence, all systematic variation in vignette ratings can be attributed to reporting heterogeneity. In this way, the covariates are naturally excluded from the latent vignette health index and included only in the cut-points. Despite this, we refer to the vignette component of the HOPIT as a generalised ordered probit.

More formally, apart from measurement error, all individuals perceive each particular vignette $j, j = 1,2,3$, to be consistent with the same latent health level, ruling out any association between h_{ij}^{v*} and an individual's characteristics. Consequently, the latent health of each vignette j as perceived by individual i can be specified as an intercept (α_j) plus random measurement error (ϵ_{ij}^{v}):

$$h_{ij}^{v*} = \alpha_j + \epsilon_{ij}^{v}, \quad \epsilon_{ij}^{v} \sim N(0,1) \tag{4.4}$$

with the normalisation $\alpha_1 = 0$, and ϵ_{ij}^{v} independent of each other and of x_i.

The respective observed categorical rating h_{ij}^v is related to h_{ij}^{v*} through the following mechanism:

$$h_{ij}^v = k \ \text{if} \ \mu_i^{k-1} \leqslant h_{ij}^{v*} < \mu_i^k, \quad k = 1,\ldots,5 \tag{4.5}$$

where $\mu_i^1 < \mu_i^2 < \ldots < \mu_i^5$, and $\mu_i^0 = -\infty$, $\mu_i^5 = \infty$, $\forall \ i$. The exclusion restriction in (4.4) permits identification of cut-points as functions of covariates:

$$\mu_i^k = \gamma_0^k + x_i \gamma^k, \quad k = 1,\ldots,4 \tag{4.6}$$

As explained above, x_i does not include a constant and so γ_0^k are the intercepts in the respective cut-points. With evaluations of multiple vignettes, it would also be possible to allow for unobserved heterogeneity in the response scale (Kapteyn *et al.*, 2007), although identification of such random individual effect may be weak with a small number of vignettes like here.

The probabilities of rating vignettes in each of the five categories are given by

$$P_{ijk}^v = \Pr\left[h_{ij}^v = k \mid x_i\right] = \Phi\left(\mu_i^k - \alpha_j\right) - \Phi\left(\mu_i^{k-1} - \alpha_j\right), \quad k = 1,\ldots,5 \tag{4.7}$$

where $\Phi(.)$ is the cumulative standard normal distribution.

We now proceed with preparations for estimation of the vignette component of the HOPIT model separately, that is, with the first step of the two-step estimation procedure. In order to model the vignette ratings using a built-in Stata command, it is necessary to reshape the dataset from the original (wide) form, where each row represents one individual (identified by variable `mergeid`) and there are three columns containing vignette ratings `vig1-vig3`, to a 'long form', with three rows per individual and vignette ratings combined in a single column/variable (`vig`). All other variables in the dataset will simply appear repeated across each of the individual's three rows. The new variable `vignum` represents the vignette j, $j = 1,\ldots,3$, to which the observation corresponds:

```
reshape long vig, i(mergeid) j(vignum)
```

The output displayed after `reshape` describes the transformations that occur:

```
(note: j = 1 2 3)

Data                             wide  ->    long
------------------------------------------------------
Number of obs.                    837  ->    2511
Number of variables                14  ->      13
j variable (3 values)                  ->   vignum
xij variables:
                        vig1 vig2 vig3  ->     vig
------------------------------------------------------
```

Parallel cut-point shift

Suppose one is willing to impose the restriction that the covariates affect all cut-points by the same magnitude, i.e. that there is *parallel cut-point shift*. In this case, the vignettes model is equivalent to a standard ordered probit for the vignette ratings (vig). This can be seen through a simple transformation of equation (4.7), for $k = 2,...,4$, with cut-points defined as in equation (4.6) and with $\gamma^1 = ... = \gamma^4 = \gamma$:

$$\Pr\left[h_{ij}^v = k \mid x_i\right] = \Phi\left(\gamma_0^k + x_i\gamma - \alpha_j\right) - \Phi\left(\gamma_0^{k-1} + x_i\gamma - \alpha_j\right)$$

$$= \Phi\left(\gamma_0^k - (\alpha_j - x_i\gamma)\right) - \Phi\left(\gamma_0^{k-1} - (\alpha_j - x_i\gamma)\right) \qquad (4.8)$$

$$= \Phi\left(\gamma_0^k - (\alpha_j + x_i\beta^v)\right) - \Phi\left(\gamma_0^{k-1} - (\alpha_j + x_i\beta^v)\right)$$

The covariates in this ordered probit model are those in x_i and dummy variables indicating to which vignette each observation corresponds, except for one (as α_1 is normalised to 0). The vector of coefficients of the variables in x_i is equal to $-\gamma$, and so each coefficient represents 'minus (parallel) cut-point shift' according to the respective variable. The dummy variables vigdum2-vigdum3 can be obtained as follows:

```
tabulate vignum, generate(vigdum)
drop vigdum1
```

Now estimate the model:

```
oprobit vig $xvars vigdum*
```

Table 4.3 shows the results of the ordered probit model for vignette ratings. Before making an explicit correspondence between these results and the generalised ordered probit specified by equations (4.1) to (4.3), it is already possible to get an impression of reporting heterogeneity. We can see that the coefficient of isced56 is significantly negative, showing that individuals in the top education category are less likely to evaluate the vignettes positively than those in the bottom category. This model shows no other significant effects.

   To interpret these results explicitly in terms of (parallel) cut-point shift, we just have to bear in mind that the coefficients of x_i in this model, β^v, represent minus (parallel) cut-point shift, that is, $\mu_i^k = \gamma_0^k + x_i\gamma = \gamma_0^k - x_i\beta^v$. So, for example, the coefficient of isced56 in cut-points 1 to 4 is 0.188 ($z = 2.96$). This means that individuals in the top education category, due to higher standards in the domain of breathing, place their cut-points higher and are thus more likely to classify a given level of breathing problems negatively, than those in the bottom education category. Individual cut-points (mu1par-mu4par) can be obtained as follows (note that the vignette dummies are first set equal to zero to enable the prediction of minus cut-point shift, $x_i\beta^v$, directly using `predict, xb`, which have otherwise returned estimates of $\alpha_j + x_i\beta^v$):

```
replace vigdum2=0
replace vigdum3=0
predict minuscutptshift, xb
generate mu1par=_b[/cut1]-minuscutptshift
generate mu2par=_b[/cut2]-minuscutptshift
generate mu3par=_b[/cut3]-minuscutptshift
generate mu4par=_b[/cut4]-minuscutptshift
```

Now save the uppermost cut-point for the reference individual (`ref_mu4par`) for later use and restore vignette dummies to their original values:

```
generate minuscutptshift_ref=_b[age]*64
scalar ref_mu4par=_b[/cut4]-minuscutptshift_ref

drop vigdum*
tabulate vignum, generate(vigdum)
drop vigdum1
```

Table 4.3 Ordered probit for vignette ratings in the domain of *breathing*

```
--------------------------------------------------------------------
Ordered probit regression                     Number of obs =     2478
                                               LR chi2(7)    =  1628.07
                                               Prob > chi2   =   0.0000
Log likelihood = -2791.9384                    Pseudo R2     =   0.2257
--------------------------------------------------------------------
     vig |    Coef.    Std. Err.     z    P>|z|   [95% Conf. Interval]
---------|----------------------------------------------------------
  female |  .0585425   .0454105    1.29   0.197   -.0304603   .1475454
     age | -.0023562   .0022967   -1.03   0.305   -.0068577   .0021453
  isced2 | -.0051707   .0888405   -0.06   0.954   -.1792949   .1689534
 isced34 | -.0720406   .0560023   -1.29   0.198    -.181803   .0377219
 isced56 | -.1879341   .0635664   -2.96   0.003   -.3125219  -.0633463
 vigdum2 | -1.907149   .0623004  -30.61   0.000   -2.029255  -1.785042
 vigdum3 | -2.430886   .0667261  -36.43   0.000   -2.561667  -2.300106
---------|----------------------------------------------------------
   /cut1 | -3.258166   .1758325                   -3.602791   -2.91354
   /cut2 | -1.433763   .1712613                   -1.769429  -1.098097
   /cut3 |  -.622642   .1687902                   -.9534647  -.2918193
   /cut4 |  .0363809   .1680424                   -.2929762   .3657379
--------------------------------------------------------------------
```

Non-parallel cut-point shift

If reporting heterogeneity is stronger at some levels of health than others, then cut-point shift is not parallel and so the vignette component of the HOPIT model does not reduce to a standard ordered probit. In this case, we need to define a program to estimate a generalised ordered probit model, as this is not available as a built-in Stata command. This program, which we call gop, defined here specifically for the case of three vignettes and five response categories, is shown in the appendix. This program is to be used for estimation of a generalised ordered probit on a dataset in long form. Save it in a separate Stata .do file called 'gop.do', and call it using the following command:

```
run "gop.do"
```

From here on, we refer to the models where the hypothesis of parallel shift is not imposed, as models with *non-parallel shift*. It should however be understood that this does not necessarily mean that cut-point shift is non-parallel but only that the models accommodate this feature.

Program gop is called to estimate the generalised ordered probit model for vignette ratings with vignette dummies, except for one, in the latent health index (xb, equation (4.4)) and covariates in the cut-points (mu3 to mu4, equation (4.6)):

```
ml model lf gop (xb: vigdum*, nocons)                    ///
    (mu1: $xvars) (mu2: $xvars) (mu3: $xvars) (mu4: $xvars)  ///
    if vig!=.
ml search
ml maximize
```

Note that the expression if vig!=. is not strictly necessary since observations with missing vignette ratings do not contribute to the likelihood, and so are not being used in the estimation, but we opt for using it here so that the output returns the correct number of used observations. Table 4.4 shows the results for the generalised ordered probit model for vignette ratings. All variables have at least one significant coefficient in the cut-points. Higher health standards or expectations are represented by positive shifts in the cut-points. For example, isced56 has positive and significant coefficients across cut-points 2 to 4, so higher educated individuals have higher standards in this health domain, except regarding the distinction between extreme versus less than extreme problems (mu1). It is noticeable that the coefficients vary considerably across cut-points, which was ruled out in the model with parallel shift. In some cases, the effects are not even monotonic. Males and older individuals tend to place their cut-points higher but only towards the top end of the health distribution: males are less likely to consider that a given vignette corresponds to no, mu4, and at most mild breathing problems, mu3, while age decreases the probability of classifying a given vignette as no breathing problems, mu4. Imposing parallel shift (Table 4.3) hides significant

Table 4.4 Generalised ordered probit for vignette ratings in the domain of *breathing*

```
-------------------------------------------------------------------
                                  Number of obs   =      2478
                                  Wald chi2(2)    =   1414.33
Log likelihood = -2770.9716       Prob > chi2     =    0.0000
-------------------------------------------------------------------
            |    Coef.  Std. Err.     z   P>|z|  [95% Conf. Interval]
---------|---------------------------------------------------------
xb          |
  vigdum2   | -1.911462  .0628471 -30.41  0.000   -2.03464  -1.788284
  vigdum3   |   -2.4398  .0673243 -36.24  0.000  -2.571753  -2.307846
---------|---------------------------------------------------------
mu1         |
   female   | -.0196504  .0725302  -0.27  0.786   -.161807   .1225061
      age   |  -.004002  .0037456  -1.07  0.285  -.0113433   .0033392
   isced2   | -.3112466  .1502143  -2.07  0.038  -.6056612   -.016832
  isced34   | -.1411833  .0901736  -1.57  0.117  -.3179203   .0355536
  isced56   |  .0138055  .0977951   0.14  0.888  -.1778694   .2054803
    _cons   | -2.756122  .2710394 -10.17  0.000   -3.28735  -2.224895
---------|---------------------------------------------------------
mu2         |
   female   |  .0462445  .0630271   0.73  0.463  -.0772863   .1697753
      age   |  .0002361   .003137   0.08  0.940  -.0059124   .0063846
   isced2   |   .061723   .124746   0.49  0.621  -.1827747   .3062207
  isced34   |  .0567552  .0768592   0.74  0.460  -.0938861   .2073966
  isced56   |  .1826049  .0890043   2.05  0.040   .0081598    .35705
    _cons   | -1.358312  .2288616  -5.94  0.000  -1.806873  -.9097515
---------|---------------------------------------------------------
mu3         |
   female   | -.1570787  .0687964  -2.28  0.022  -.2919171  -.0222403
      age   |  .0054948  .0034292   1.60  0.109  -.0012262   .0122159
   isced2   |  .1674885  .1365011   1.23  0.220  -.1000487   .4350257
  isced34   |  .3032337  .0842541   3.60  0.000   .1380987   .4683686
  isced56   |  .3567829  .0989701   3.60  0.000   .1628051   .5507607
    _cons   | -.8762722  .2463317  -3.56  0.000  -1.359073  -.3934709
---------|---------------------------------------------------------
mu4         |
   female   | -.2173922  .0766302  -2.84  0.005  -.3675847  -.0671998
      age   |  .0139093  .0039129   3.55  0.000   .0062401   .0215785
   isced2   |  .2257577  .1482252   1.52  0.128  -.0647584   .5162738
  isced34   |  .2634366  .0942687   2.79  0.005   .0786733   .4481998
  isced56   |  .3582365  .1094243   3.27  0.001   .1437689   .5727042
    _cons   | -.7201745  .2768797  -2.60  0.009  -1.262849  -.1775002
-------------------------------------------------------------------
```

cut-point shifts by age and gender, which are revealed only in this more flexible specification.

We can test for reporting homogeneity across all cut-points for all covariates by means of a test of joint significance of all variables in all cut-points. The null hypothesis of homogeneity is strongly rejected:

```
test ([mu1]) ([mu2]) ([mu3]) ([mu4])

 ( 1)   [mu1]female = 0
 ( 2)   [mu1]age = 0
 ( 3)   [mu1]isced2 = 0
 ( 4)   [mu1]isced34 = 0
 ( 5)   [mu1]isced56 = 0
 ( 6)   [mu2]female = 0
 ( 7)   [mu2]age = 0
 ( 8)   [mu2]isced2 = 0
 ( 9)   [mu2]isced34 = 0
 (10)   [mu2]isced56 = 0
 (11)   [mu3]female = 0
 (12)   [mu3]age = 0
 (13)   [mu3]isced2 = 0
 (14)   [mu3]isced34 = 0
 (15)   [mu3]isced56 = 0
 (16)   [mu4]female = 0
 (17)   [mu4]age = 0
 (18)   [mu4]isced2 = 0
 (19)   [mu4]isced34 = 0
 (20)   [mu4]isced56 = 0

       chi2( 20) =   53.16
     Prob > chi2 =   0.0001
```

Tests of significance of individual covariates in all cut-points show evidence of heterogeneity by all factors considered:

```
test [mu1]female [mu2]female [mu3]female [mu4]female

 ( 1)   [mu1]female = 0
 ( 2)   [mu2]female = 0
 ( 3)   [mu3]female = 0
 ( 4)   [mu4]female = 0

         chi2(  4) =    12.47
       Prob > chi2 =    0.0142
```

```
test [mu1]age [mu2]age [mu3]age [mu4]age
```

```
 ( 1)   [mu1]age = 0
 ( 2)   [mu2]age = 0
 ( 3)   [mu3]age = 0
 ( 4)   [mu4]age = 0
```

```
        chi2(  4) =    14.48
      Prob > chi2 =    0.0059
```

```
test [mu1]isced2 [mu2]isced2 [mu3]isced2 [mu4]isced2       ///
     [mu1]isced34 [mu2]isced34 [mu3]isced34 [mu4]isced34   ///
     [mu1]isced56 [mu2]isced56 [mu3]isced56 [mu4]isced56
```

```
 ( 1)   [mu1]isced2 = 0
 ( 2)   [mu2]isced2 = 0
 ( 3)   [mu3]isced2 = 0
 ( 4)   [mu4]isced2 = 0
 ( 5)   [mu1]isced34 = 0
 ( 6)   [mu2]isced34 = 0
 ( 7)   [mu3]isced34 = 0
 ( 8)   [mu4]isced34 = 0
 ( 9)   [mu1]isced56 = 0
 (10)   [mu2]isced56 = 0
 (11)   [mu3]isced56 = 0
 (12)   [mu4]isced56 = 0
```

```
        chi2( 12) =    30.31
      Prob > chi2 =    0.0025
```

We also test the hypotheses of parallel shift, by all covariates and by each individual variable. As suspected from inspection of generalised ordered probit estimation results (Table 4.4), there is evidence of non-parallel shift by all variables:

```
test [mu1=mu2=mu3=mu4]
```

```
 ( 1)   [mu1]female - [mu2]female = 0
 ( 2)   [mu1]age - [mu2]age = 0
 ( 3)   [mu1]isced2 - [mu2]isced2 = 0
 ( 4)   [mu1]isced34 - [mu2]isced34 = 0
 ( 5)   [mu1]isced56 - [mu2]isced56 = 0
 ( 6)   [mu1]female - [mu3]female = 0
 ( 7)   [mu1]age - [mu3]age = 0
 ( 8)   [mu1]isced2 - [mu3]isced2 = 0
```

```
( 9)   [mu1]isced34 - [mu3]isced34 = 0
(10)   [mu1]isced56 - [mu3]isced56 = 0
(11)   [mu1]female - [mu4]female = 0
(12)   [mu1]age - [mu4]age = 0
(13)   [mu1]isced2 - [mu4]isced2 = 0
(14)   [mu1]isced34 - [mu4]isced34 = 0
(15)   [mu1]isced56 - [mu4]isced56 = 0

        chi2( 15) =    41.74
       Prob > chi2 =     0.0002
```

```
test [mu1]female=[mu2]female=[mu3]female=[mu4]female
```

```
( 1)   [mu1]female - [mu2]female = 0
( 2)   [mu1]female - [mu3]female = 0
( 3)   [mu1]female - [mu4]female = 0

        chi2( 3) =    10.72
       Prob > chi2 =     0.0133
```

```
test [mu1]age=[mu2]age=[mu3]age=[mu4]age
```

```
( 1)   [mu1]age - [mu2]age = 0
( 2)   [mu1]age - [mu3]age = 0
( 3)   [mu1]age - [mu4]age = 0

        chi2( 3) =    13.33
       Prob > chi2 =     0.0040
```

```
test ([mu1]isced2=[mu2]isced2=[mu3]isced2=[mu4]isced2)     ///
     ([mu1]isced34=[mu2]isced34=[mu3]isced34=[mu4]          ///
     isced34)                                               ///
     ([mu1]isced56=[mu2]isced56=[mu3]isced56=[mu4]isced56)
```

```
( 1)   [mu1]isced2 - [mu2]isced2 = 0
( 2)   [mu1]isced2 - [mu3]isced2 = 0
( 3)   [mu1]isced2 - [mu4]isced2 = 0
( 4)   [mu1]isced34 - [mu2]isced34 = 0
( 5)   [mu1]isced34 - [mu3]isced34 = 0
( 6)   [mu1]isced34 - [mu4]isced34 = 0
( 7)   [mu1]isced56 - [mu2]isced56 = 0
( 8)   [mu1]isced56 - [mu3]isced56 = 0
( 9)   [mu1]isced56 - [mu4]isced56 = 0

        chi2( 9) =    20.84
       Prob > chi2 =     0.0134
```

Prediction of individual cut-points from the generalised ordered probit is straightforward:

```
predict mu1, equation(mu1)
predict mu2, equation(mu2)
predict mu3, equation(mu3)
predict mu4, equation(mu4)
```

We will also need later the estimated uppermost cut-point for our reference individual:

```
scalar ref_mu4=_b[mu4:_cons]+_b[mu4:age]*64
```

4.4.2 Health equation adjusted for reporting heterogeneity

As in the ordered probit, the second component of the HOPIT defines the latent level of individual own health, h_i^{s*} and the observation mechanism that relates this latent variable to the observed categorical variable, h_i^s. The difference is that the cut-points are no longer constant parameters but can vary across individuals, and are determined by the vignette component of the model. The possibility of fixing the cut-points leads to the specification of the model for individual own health as an interval regression. It should however be noted that, unlike in traditional applications of interval regression, here the parameter estimates and the linear health index are not measured on a meaningful scale. This is because the cut-points, and consequently location and scale parameters in this interval regression regression, are only identifiable up to normalisation of scale and location parameters in the vignette component (equation 4.4).

Similar to the ordered probit, the second component of the HOPIT defines the latent level of individual own health, h_i^{s*}, as:

$$h_i^{s*} = \beta_0 + x_i\beta + \epsilon_i^s , \quad \epsilon_i^s \sim N(0,\sigma^2)$$ (4.9)

where ϵ_i^s is independent x_i and of $\epsilon_{ij}^v, j = 1,2,3$; and the observation mechanism that relates this variable to the observed health categories as:

$$h_i^s = k \Leftrightarrow \mu_i^{k-1} \leqslant h_i^{s*} < \mu_i^k,$$ (4.10)

where $\mu_i^1 < \mu_i^2 < ... < \mu_i^5$, $\mu_i^0 = -\infty$, $\mu_i^5 = \infty$. Reflecting the response consistency assumption, μ_i^k are set equal to those in equation (4.6) of the vignette component. As noted above, rather than being measured in natural units as in the standard interval regression, the cut-points μ_i^k, β_0, β and σ are measured relative to the normalisations of scale and location parameters in the ordered probit for the vignettes. Note also that because the variance of the error term is normalised to 1 in the ordered probit model, the vectors of coefficients in the two models (equations (4.1) and (4.9)) are not directly comparable.

It follows that the probabilities associated with each of the five categories are defined as follows:

$$P_{ik}^s = \Pr\left[h_i^s = k\right]$$

$$= \Phi\left[\frac{\left(\mu_i^k - \beta_0 - x_i\beta\right)}{\sigma}\right] - \Phi\left[\frac{\left(\mu_i^{k-1} - \beta_0 - x_i\beta\right)}{\sigma}\right], \quad k = 1,...,5 \qquad (4.11)$$

where $\Phi[.]$ is the cumulative standard normal distribution.

The remainder of this sub-section is devoted to the second step in the estimation of the HOPIT model (equations 4.9 and 4.10), using interval regression. For this purpose, return to the original form of the dataset (wide format, in terms of the vignette variables):

```
drop vigdum*
reshape wide vig, i(mergeid) j(vignum)

(note: j = 1 2 3)

Data                          long    ->    wide
-----------------------------------------------------------------
Number of obs.                2511    ->     837
Number of variables             23    ->      24
j variable (3 values)       vignum    ->  (dropped)
xij variables:
                               vig    ->  vig1 vig2 vig3
-----------------------------------------------------------------
```

Adjusting for parallel cut-point shift

In order to estimate the health equation using an interval regression, we need to create variables containing individual limits for the intervals, which are obtained directly from the individual cut-points predicted in the reporting behaviour model (vignette component). We start with the cut-points obtained in the model with *parallel shift*. Following equation (4.10), for a given observed category k for own health, the lower limit of the interval is μ_i^{k-1} and the upper limit is μ_i^k. Upper (lower) limits for the highest (lowest) categories are set as missing values:

```
generate y1par = mu1par* (y==2)+mu2par* (y==3)+mu3par* (y==4) ///
                             +mu4par* (y==5) if y>1
generate y2par = mu1par* (y==1)+mu2par* (y==2)+mu3par* (y==3) ///
                             +mu4par* (y==4) if y<5
```

Then estimate an interval regression for own health with cut-points adjusted by parallel shift and save the results:

```
intreg y1par y2par $xvars
estimates store TwoS_par
```

The results are shown in Table 4.5. Under the assumption of parallel cut-point shift (and response consistency and vignette equivalence, the estimated coefficients represent health effects purged from reporting heterogeneity. We leave a more careful comparison for later but for now just note that the education gradient has become clearer and significant with this adjustment. Note also that care should be taken in using these results (as well as those of partial effects below) for inference since estimation of this second step does not take into account sampling variability of cut-points estimated in the first step.

Table 4.5 Interval regression for self-reported health in the domain of breathing with parallel cut-point shift

```
---------------------------------------------------------------------
Interval regression                      Number of obs  =       837
                                         LR chi2(5)     =     34.67
Log likelihood = -862.42907              Prob > chi2    =    0.0000
---------------------------------------------------------------------
             |     Coef. Std. Err.     z   P>|z|    [95% Conf.Interval]
-------------|-------------------------------------------------------
      female | -.0966278  .0819426 -1.18   0.238  -.2572325   .0639768
         age | -.0146566  .0041197 -3.56   0.000  -.0227311  -.0065821
      isced2 |  .0986726  .1601731  0.62   0.538  -.2152608    .412606
     isced34 |  .1224812   .100683  1.22   0.224  -.0748539   .3198163
     isced56 |  .3589818  .1161237  3.09   0.002   .1313836   .5865801
        _cons|  1.371079   .302558  4.53   0.000   .7780764   1.964082
-------------|-------------------------------------------------------
    /lnsigma | -.0171241  .0482659 -0.35   0.723  -.1117236   .0774754
-------------|-------------------------------------------------------
       sigma |  .9830217  .0474465                .8942914   1.080556
---------------------------------------------------------------------
  Observation summary:     2  left-censored observations
                           0     uncensored observations
                         505 right-censored observations
                         330       interval observations
```

As done above for the ordered probit model, we can calculate partial effects of the covariates on the probabilities of being in each health category (equation (4.11)). As above, we exemplify here with the probability of being in the best health category, for the reference individual. In order to correct for reporting heterogeneity, so that the partial effects reflect pure health effects, the cut-points should be fixed. Set them as those of the same reference individual, estimated in Section 4.4.1:

```
#delimit ;
nlcom
(PE_5_female: normal((ref_mu4par-_b[_cons]-_b[age]*64)
                                /exp([lnsigma]_b[_cons]))
        -normal((ref_mu4par-_b[_cons]-_b[age]*64-_b[female])
                                /exp([lnsigma]_b[_cons])))
(PE_5_age:  normal((ref_mu4par-_b[_cons]-_b[age]*64)
                                /exp([lnsigma]_b[_cons]))
        -normal((ref_mu4par-_b[_cons]-_b[age]*65)
                                /exp([lnsigma]_b[_cons])))
(PE_5_isced2: normal((ref_mu4par-_b[_cons]-_b[age]*64)
                                /exp([lnsigma]_b[_cons]))
        -normal((ref_mu4par-_b[_cons]-_b[age]*64-_b[isced2])
                                /exp([lnsigma]_b[_cons])))
(PE_5_isced34:normal((ref_mu4par-_b[_cons]-_b[age]*64)
                                /exp([lnsigma]_b[_cons]))
        -normal((ref_mu4par-_b[_cons]-_b[age]*64-_b[isced34])
                                /exp([lnsigma]_b[_cons])))
(PE_5_isced56:normal((ref_mu4par-_b[_cons]-_b[age]*64)
                                /exp([lnsigma]_b[_cons]))
        -normal((ref_mu4par-_b[_cons]-_b[age]*64-_b[isced56])
                                /exp([lnsigma]_b[_cons]))),post;
#delimit cr
estimates store PE_5_2S_par
```

Table 4.6 Partial effects on the probability of having no problems with breathing for reference individual, with parallel cut-point shift

	Coef.	Std. Err.	z	P>|z|	[95% Conf.Interval]	
PE_5_female	-.0384159	.0324914	-1.18	0.237	-.1020979	.0252662
PE_5_age	-.0057755	.0015839	-3.65	0.000	-.0088799	-.0026711
PE_5_isced2	.0382643	.0614315	0.62	0.533	-.0821392	.1586678
PE_5_isced34	.0473116	.0388924	1.22	0.224	-.028916	.1235392
PE_5_isced56	.1320694	.0418705	3.15	0.002	.0500048	.214134

The partial effect of `female` increases in absolute value but does not reach statistical significance (see Table 4.5). The most important change is that of the effect of the top education category, reflecting the only observed statistically significant parallel shift (Table 4.3). Allowing for parallel cut-point shift, it is estimated that the probability of having no problems with shortness of breath of 64-year-old males with recognised third level education is 0.13 higher than that of 64-year-old males with at most primary education (see Table 4.5).

Adjusting for non-parallel cut-point shift

The procedure required to estimate an equation for own health adjusted by *non-parallel cut-point shift* involves the same steps as the case of parallel shift. Start by defining the interval limits implied by the reporting model with non-parallel cut-point shift (generalised ordered probit in Table 4.4):

```
gen y1 = mu1*(y==2)+mu2*(y==3)+mu3*(y==4)+mu4*(y==5) if y>1
gen y2 = mu1*(y==1)+mu2*(y==2)+mu3*(y==3)+mu4*(y==4) if y<5
```

Then repeat estimation of model and implied partial effects of covariates on the probability of having no breathing problems, for our reference individual:

```
intreg y1 y2 $xvars
estimates store TwoS
#delimit ;
nlcom
(PE_5_female:  normal((ref_mu4-_b[_cons]-_b[age]*64)
                             /exp([lnsigma]_b[_cons]))
           - normal((ref_mu4-_b[_cons]-_b[age]*64-_b[female])
                             /exp([lnsigma]_b[_cons])))
(PE_5_age:    normal((ref_mu4-_b[_cons]-_b[age]*64)
                             /exp([lnsigma]_b[_cons]))
           - normal((ref_mu4-_b[_cons]-_b[age]*65)
                             /exp([lnsigma]_b[_cons])))
(PE_5_isced2:  normal((ref_mu4-_b[_cons]-_b[age]*64)
                             /exp([lnsigma]_b[_cons]))
           - normal((ref_mu4-_b[_cons]-_b[age]*64-_b[isced2])
                             /exp([lnsigma]_b[_cons])))
(PE_5_isced34: normal((ref_mu4-_b[_cons]-_b[age]*64)
                             /exp([lnsigma]_b[_cons]))
           - normal((ref_mu4-_b[_cons]-_b[age]*64-_b[isced34])
                             /exp([lnsigma]_b[_cons])))
(PE_5_isced56: normal((ref_mu4-_b[_cons]-_b[age]*64)
                             /exp([lnsigma]_b[_cons]))
           - normal((ref_mu4-_b[_cons]-_b[age]*64-_b[isced56])
                             /exp([lnsigma]_b[_cons]))),post;
#delimit cr
estimates store PE_5_2S
```

Table 4.7 Interval regression for self-reported health in the domain of breathing with non-parallel cut-point shift

```
------------------------------------------------------------------
Interval regression              Number of obs    =         837
                                 LR chi2(5)       =       41.59
Log likelihood = -865.79157      Prob > chi2      =      0.0000
------------------------------------------------------------------
           |      Coef.  Std. Err.      z   P>|z|   [95% Conf. Interval]
---------- |------------------------------------------------------
    female |  -.2098007   .0829273   -2.53   0.011   -.3723352   -.0472662
       age |  -.0074343   .0041765   -1.78   0.075   -.0156202    .0007515
    isced2 |   .2759791   .1619065    1.70   0.088   -.0413518      .59331
   isced34 |   .3046212    .101998    2.99   0.003    .1047088    .5045336
   isced56 |    .504592   .1175284    4.29   0.000    .2742406    .7349435
     _cons |    .882951   .3069107    2.88   0.004    .2814171    1.484485
---------- |------------------------------------------------------
  /lnsigma |  -.0057971   .0481819   -0.12   0.904   -.1002319    .0886377
---------- |------------------------------------------------------
     sigma |   .9942197   .0479034                    .9046276    1.092685
------------------------------------------------------------------
   Observation summary:     2  left-censored observations
                            0     uncensored observations
                          505 right-censored observations
                          330    interval observations
```

Table 4.8 Partial effects on the probability of having no problems with breathing for reference individual, with non-parallel cut-point shift – two-step estimation

```
------------------------------------------------------------------
              |     Coef.  Std. Err.      z   P>|z|   [95% Conf.Interval]
------------- |----------------------------------------------------
 PE_5_female  | -.0832919   .0329139  -2.53   0.011   -.147802   -.0187818
    PE_5_age  |  -.002902   .0016015  -1.81   0.070  -.0060409    .0002369
 PE_5_isced2  |  .1028483    .058117   1.77   0.077  -.0110589    .2167555
PE_5_isced34  |  .1128324   .0379962   2.97   0.003   .0383611    .1873037
PE_5_isced56  |  .1779199   .0405113   4.39   0.000   .0985191    .2573206
------------------------------------------------------------------
```

As a consequence of adjusting for mostly positive cut-point shift (Table 4.4), the estimated effect of education on health is larger than in the homogeneous reporting model. This is even clearer now that the restriction of parallel cut-point shift is relaxed; the partial effects of education on the probability of having no breathing problems are: 0.10 (isced2, significant at 10 per cent), 0.11 (isced34, significant at 1 per cent), and 0.18 (isced56, significant at 1 per cent) (Table 4.8). Allowing for non-parallel shift uncovers a negative and significant shift by gender of only the two top cut-points (Table 4.4). Correcting for this leads to an increase, in absolute value, in the effect of female on individual's own health, which now becomes significantly negative (Table 4.7). This means that the insignificant female effect on health found in the homogeneous reporting model (Table 4.1) was a mixture of a true negative health effect and a tendency for women to report better health. The adjustment of the health effect for parallel shift is smaller than what is obtained in the non-parallel shift model, indicating the importance of the more flexible version of cut-point shift.

4.4.3 One-step estimation of HOPIT model

Joint estimation of the two components of the HOPIT model (equations (4.4)–(4.6) and (4.9) and (4.10)) in a one-step procedure is more efficient than the two-step procedure illustrated in the two previous sub-sections (Kapteyn *et al.*, 2007). The log-likelihood function of the model is composed of the sum of the log-likelihoods of the two components:

$$\ln L = \sum_{i=1}^{n}\sum_{k=1}^{5} h_{ik}^{s}\, \ln P_{ik}^{s} + \sum_{i=1}^{n}\sum_{j=1}^{3}\sum_{k=1}^{5} h_{ijk}^{v}\, \ln P_{ijk}^{v}, \tag{4.12}$$

where h_{ik}^{s} and h_{ijk}^{v} are binary variables that equal 1 if $h_{i}^{s} = k$ and $h_{ij}^{v} = k$, respectively; and P_{ik}^{s} and P_{ijk}^{v} are as defined in equations (4.11) and (4.7), respectively. The two components are linked through the cut-points and so do not factorise into two independent models.

The program required to define the joint likelihood in (4.12) is shown in the Appendix, for the specific case of three vignettes and five response categories, in a dataset in wide format. Save it in a separate Stata .do file 'hopit.do' and call it:

```
run "hopit.do"
```

Estimation of the HOPIT is performed with the syntax below, that specifies that the variables contained in xvars enter the own health index (xb, equation 4.9) and the cut-points (mu1–mu4, equation 4.6). The first two arguments are from the latent index equation in the own health component; constant terms of vig2–vig3 are the coefficients of vignette dummies in the latent index of the vignette component; and cut-points mu1–mu4 belong to the two components, being identified by the latter. Results are stored after the estimation:

```
ml model lf hopit (xb: $xvars) (sig:) (vigdum2:)          ///
  (vigdum3:) (mu1: $xvars) (mu2: $xvars)                  ///
  mu3: $xvars) (mu4: $xvars)
ml search
ml maximize
estimates store OneS_HOPIT
```

The estimation results for the HOPIT are shown in Table 4.9.

Table 4.9 HOPIT for self-reported health in the domain of breathing with cut-point
shift – one-step estimation

```
------------------------------------------------------------------
                                   Number of obs   =       837
                                   Wald chi2(5)    =     27.77
Log likelihood = -3634.7704        Prob > chi2     =    0.0000
------------------------------------------------------------------
           |    Coef.  Std. Err.     z   P>|z|   [95% Conf. Interval]
-----------+------------------------------------------------------
xb         |
    female | -.1844584  .1032868  -1.79  0.074  -.3868967    .01798
       age |  -.008625  .0051603  -1.67  0.095  -.0187391  .0014891
    isced2 |  .2827502  .2017781   1.40  0.161  -.1127276  .6782279
   isced34 |  .3282516  .1275763   2.57  0.010   .0782067  .5782965
   isced56 |  .4989591  .1478399   3.37  0.001   .2091983  .7887199
     _cons |  .9452477  .3791769   2.49  0.013   .2020747  1.688421
-----------+------------------------------------------------------
sig        |
     _cons | 1.001175  .0575901  17.38  0.000   .8883003  1.114049
-----------+------------------------------------------------------
vigdum2    |
     _cons | -1.922725 .0627321 -30.65  0.000  -2.045678 -1.799772
-----------+------------------------------------------------------
vigdum3    |
     _cons | -2.447348 .0671653 -36.44  0.000  -2.578989 -2.315706
-----------+------------------------------------------------------
mu1        |
    female | -.0263219 .0720843  -0.37  0.715  -.1676045  .1149607
       age | -.0036747  .003721   -0.99  0.323  -.0109677  .0036183
    isced2 | -.3160598 .1498562  -2.11  0.035  -.6097726 -.0223471
   isced34 | -.1502848 .0897993  -1.67  0.094  -.3262882  .0257185
   isced56 |  .0288165 .0970061   0.30  0.766   -.161312   .218945
     _cons | -2.776558 .2694212 -10.31  0.000  -3.304614 -2.248503
-----------+------------------------------------------------------
mu2        |
    female |  .0227952 .0612015   0.37  0.710  -.0971576   .142748
       age |  .0012157 .0030404   0.40  0.689  -.0047433  .0071747
```

Table 4.9 continued

```
 isced2 |  .0713954   .1210574    0.59  0.555  -.1658727    .3086635
isced34 |   .049268   .0748781    0.66  0.511  -.0974904    .1960263
isced56 |  .1834019   .0864845    2.12  0.034   .0138954    .3529084
  _cons | -1.426112   .2223961   -6.41  0.000     -1.862   -.9902235
--------|------------------------------------------------------------
mu3     |
 female | -.1548368   .0653561   -2.37  0.018  -.2829325   -.0267411
    age |  .0055808   .0032519    1.72  0.086  -.0007928    .0119544
------------------------------------------------------------------
 isced2 |  .1575193   .1293036    1.22  0.223  -.0959111    .4109496
isced34 |  .2844983   .0806487    3.53  0.000   .1264299    .4425668
isced56 |  .3121997   .0939722    3.32  0.001   .1280176    .4963817
  _cons | -.8725979   .2348272   -3.72  0.000  -1.332851   -.4123451
--------|------------------------------------------------------------
mu4     |
 female | -.1740052   .0707205   -2.46  0.014  -.3126149   -.0353956
    age |  .0117797   .0035841    3.29  0.001    .004755    .0188045
 isced2 |  .2334455   .1373437    1.70  0.089  -.0357433    .5026342
isced34 |  .3076885   .0875215    3.52  0.000   .1361496    .4792274
isced56 |   .360722   .1013544    3.56  0.000   .1620711    .5593729
  _cons | -.6160956   .2553143   -2.41  0.016  -1.116502   -.1156887
------------------------------------------------------------------
```

Tests of significance of coefficients in the cut-points and of parallel cut-point shift can be performed in the same way as done above for the generalised ordered probit model:

```
test ([mu1]) ([mu2]) ([mu3]) ([mu4])

( 1)  [mu1]female = 0
( 2)  [mu1]age = 0
( 3)  [mu1]isced2 = 0
( 4)  [mu1]isced34 = 0
( 5)  [mu1]isced56 = 0
( 6)  [mu2]female = 0
( 7)  [mu2]age = 0
( 8)  [mu2]isced2 = 0
( 9)  [mu2]isced34 = 0
(10)  [mu2]isced56 = 0
(11)  [mu3]female = 0
(12)  [mu3]age = 0
(13)  [mu3]isced2 = 0
```

```
(14)    [mu3]isced34 = 0
(15)    [mu3]isced56 = 0
(16)    [mu4]female = 0
(17)    [mu4]age = 0
(18)    [mu4]isced2 = 0
(19)    [mu4]isced34 = 0
(20)    [mu4]isced56 = 0

            chi2( 20) =    49.87
          Prob > chi2 =     0.0002

test [mu1]female [mu2]female [mu3]female [mu4]female

( 1)    [mu1]female = 0
( 2)    [mu2]female = 0
( 3)    [mu3]female = 0
( 4)    [mu4]female = 0

            chi2( 4)  =    10.19
          Prob > chi2 =     0.0373

test [mu1]age [mu2]age [mu3]age [mu4]age

( 1)    [mu1]age = 0
( 2)    [mu2]age = 0
( 3)    [mu3]age = 0
( 4)    [mu4]age = 0

              chi2( 4) =    12.70
          Prob > chi2 =     0.0128

test [mu1]isced2 [mu2]isced2 [mu3]isced2 [mu4]isced2        ///
    [mu1]isced34 [mu2]isced34 [mu3]isced34 [mu4]isced34     ///
    [mu1]isced56 [mu2]isced56 [mu3]isced56 [mu4]isced56

( 1)    [mu1]isced2 = 0
( 2)    [mu2]isced2 = 0
( 3)    [mu3]isced2 = 0
( 4)    [mu4]isced2 = 0
( 5)    [mu1]isced34 = 0
( 6)    [mu2]isced34 = 0
( 7)    [mu3]isced34 = 0
( 8)    [mu4]isced34 = 0
( 9)    [mu1]isced56 = 0
(10)    [mu2]isced56 = 0
(11)    [mu3]isced56 = 0
(12)    [mu4]isced56 = 0
```

```
        chi2( 12) =    31.85
      Prob > chi2 =    0.0015
```

test [mu1=mu2=mu3=mu4]

```
 ( 1)  [mu1]female - [mu2]female = 0
 ( 2)  [mu1]age - [mu2]age = 0
 ( 3)  [mu1]isced2 - [mu2]isced2 = 0
 ( 4)  [mu1]isced34 - [mu2]isced34 = 0
 ( 5)  [mu1]isced56 - [mu2]isced56 = 0
 ( 6)  [mu1]female - [mu3]female = 0
 ( 7)  [mu1]age - [mu3]age = 0
 ( 8)  [mu1]isced2 - [mu3]isced2 = 0
 ( 9)  [mu1]isced34 - [mu3]isced34 = 0
 (10)  [mu1]isced56 - [mu3]isced56 = 0
 (11)  [mu1]female - [mu4]female = 0
 (12)  [mu1]age - [mu4]age = 0
 (13)  [mu1]isced2 - [mu4]isced2 = 0
 (14)  [mu1]isced34 - [mu4]isced34 = 0
 (15)  [mu1]isced56 - [mu4]isced56 = 0

        chi2( 15) =    38.34
      Prob > chi2 =    0.0008
```

test [mu1]female=[mu2]female=[mu3]female=[mu4]female

```
 ( 1)  [mu1]female - [mu2]female = 0
 ( 2)  [mu1]female - [mu3]female = 0
 ( 3)  [mu1]female - [mu4]female = 0

        chi2( 3) =     8.40
      Prob > chi2 =    0.0385
```

test [mu1]age=[mu2]age=[mu3]age=[mu4]age

```
 ( 1)  [mu1]age - [mu2]age = 0
 ( 2)  [mu1]age - [mu3]age = 0
 ( 3)  [mu1]age - [mu4]age = 0

        chi2( 3) =    11.52
      Prob > chi2 =    0.0092
```

test ([mu1]isced2=[mu2]isced2=[mu3]isced2=[mu4]isced2)   ///
     ([mu1]isced34=[mu2]isced34=[mu3]isced34=[mu4]isced34)///
     ([mu1]isced56=[mu2]isced56=[mu3]isced56=[mu4]isced56)

```
( 1)  [mu1]isced2 - [mu2]isced2 = 0
( 2)  [mu1]isced2 - [mu3]isced2 = 0
( 3)  [mu1]isced2 - [mu4]isced2 = 0
( 4)  [mu1]isced34 - [mu2]isced34 = 0
( 5)  [mu1]isced34 - [mu3]isced34 = 0
( 6)  [mu1]isced34 - [mu4]isced34 = 0
( 7)  [mu1]isced56 - [mu2]isced56 = 0
( 8)  [mu1]isced56 - [mu3]isced56 = 0
( 9)  [mu1]isced56 - [mu4]isced56 = 0

        chi2( 9) =    22.42
     Prob > chi2 =    0.0076
```

We calculate adjusted partial effects on the probability of having no breathing problems in the much the same way as done above after intreg estimations. The difference is that here we can enter explicitly the expression for the cut-point 4 for the reference individual, parameters that are estimated jointly in this one-step procedure. This means that standard errors of the estimated partial effects take into consideration sampling variation in estimation of cut-points, neglected in the two-step procedure presented above.

```
#delimit ;
nlcom (PE_5_female: normal((_b[mu4:_cons]+_b[mu4:age]*64
    -_b[xb:_cons]-_b[xb:age]*64)/_b[sig:_cons])
                -normal((_b[mu4:_cons]+_b[mu4:age]*64
    -_b[xb:_cons]-_b[xb:age]*64-_b[xb:female])/_b[sig:_cons]))
(PE_5_age:          normal((_b[mu4:_cons]+_b[mu4:age]*64
    -_b[xb:_cons]-_b[xb:age]*64)/_b[sig:_cons])
                -normal((_b[mu4:_cons]+_b[mu4:age]*64
    -_b[xb:_cons]-_b[xb:age]*65)/_b[sig:_cons]))
(PE_5_isced2:       normal((_b[mu4:_cons]+_b[mu4:age]*64
    -_b[xb:_cons]-_b[xb:age]*64)/_b[sig:_cons])
                -normal((_b[mu4:_cons]+_b[mu4:age]*64
    -_b[xb:_cons]-_b[xb:age]*64-_b[xb:isced2])/_b[sig:_cons]))
(PE_5_isced34:      normal((_b[mu4:_cons]+_b[mu4:age]*64
    -_b[xb:_cons]-_b[xb:age]*64)/_b[sig:_cons])
                -normal((_b[mu4:_cons]+_b[mu4:age]*64
    -_b[xb:_cons]-_b[xb:age]*64-_b[xb:isced34])/_b[sig:_cons]))
(PE_5_isced56:      normal((_b[mu4:_cons]+_b[mu4:age]*64
    -_b[xb:_cons]-_b[xb:age]*64)/_b[sig:_cons])
                -normal((_b[mu4:_cons]+_b[mu4:age]*64
    -_b[xb:_cons]-_b[xb:age]*64-_b[xb:isced56])/_b[sig:_cons]))
,post;
#delimit cr
estimates store PE_5_HOPIT
```

Table 4.10 Partial effects on the probability of having no problems with breathing for reference individual in model with non-parallel cut-point shift – one-step HOPIT estimation

```
--------------------------------------------------------------------
              |   Coef. Std. Err.    z   P>|z| [95% Conf.Interval]
--------------|-----------------------------------------------------
PE_5_female   | -.072432   .0406842 -1.78  0.075 -.1521716   .0073077
   PE_5_age   | -.0033304  .0019673 -1.69  0.090 -.0071862   .0005254
PE_5_isced2   |  .1038665  .0706179  1.47  0.141 -.0345421   .2422751
PE_5_isced34  |   .119363  .0453443  2.63  0.008  .0304898   .2082362
PE_5_isced56  |  .1737368   .047996  3.62  0.000  .0796664   .2678073
--------------------------------------------------------------------
```

The results of the one-step estimation of the HOPIT model (Table 4.9) are in line with the ones obtained in the two-step procedure (Tables 4.3 and 4.4) and essentially the same comments apply.

The health effects on the own latent health index as well as corresponding partial effects on the probability of being in the top health category appear less precisely estimated in the latter but that is because the former takes the first-step estimates of the cut-points as fixed, as noted above.

4.5 OVERVIEW

We finish with a short comparison of the main results obtained in this chapter. To this end, it is useful to show the results of the different specifications and estimation procedures in the same table. Do this for both estimated coefficients on the own latent health index (coefficients β in equations (4.1) in the ordered probit model and (4.9) in the HOPIT) and partial effects on the probability of having no problems in the domain of breathing, using the following commands:

```
esttab OPROBIT TwoS_par TwoS OneS_HOPIT, b(%10.4f)        ///
t(%10.4f) mtitles star(* 0.10 ** 0.05 *** 0.01) keep(main:)

esttab PE_5_OPROBIT PE_5_2S_par PE_5_2S PE_5_HOPIT,       ///
b(%10.4f) t(%10.4f) mtitles star(* 0.10 ** 0.05 *** 0.01)
```

This results in the output tables (Tables 4.11 and 4.12).

Note first that the magnitudes of the coefficients reported in Table 4.11 are generally not comparable across specifications because the scale in the ordered probit is normalised to 1, while it is estimated (up to normalisation of scale in the vignette component) in the other three models. However, since the estimated σ always turns out very close to 1 (Tables 4.5, 4.7 and 4.9), we can compare them in this specific case. The sets of estimates TwoS (PE_5_2S) and OneS_HOPIT

Table 4.11 Estimated coefficients in latent health index in all models

	(1) OPROBIT	(2) TwoS_par	(3) TwoS	(4) OneS_HOPIT
main				
female	-0.0396	-0.0966	-0.2098**	-0.1845*
	(-0.4750)	(-1.1792)	(-2.5299)	(-1.7859)
age	-0.0174***	-0.0147***	-0.0074*	-0.0086*
	(-4.1841)	(-3.5577)	(-1.7800)	(-1.6714)
isced2	0.0940	0.0987	0.2760*	0.2828
	(0.5778)	(0.6160)	(1.7046)	(1.4013)
isced34	0.0493	0.1225	0.3046***	0.3283**
	(0.4812)	(1.2165)	(2.9865)	(2.5730)
isced56	0.1801	0.3590***	0.5046***	0.4990***
	(1.5258)	(3.0914)	(4.2934)	(3.3750)
_cons		1.3711***	0.8830***	0.9452**
		(4.5316)	(2.8769)	(2.4929)
N	837	837	837	837

t statistics in parentheses
* p<0.10, ** p<0.05, *** p<0.01

(PE_5_HOPIT) result from the two-step and one-step estimations of the HOPIT model, respectively, and are therefore similar. As explained above the apparent lower precision of the one-step estimates is misleading.

The most restricted specification ruling out any reporting heterogeneity, that is, the standard ordered probit model for self-reported health in the domain of breathing shows no other significant effects than older individuals being less likely to be in good health (OPROBIT). The estimated health effect of being a male increases when moving from the homogeneous reporting model to one allowing for parallel cut-point shift and further in the most flexible specification, where eventually it reaches statistical significance at 10 per cent. In particular, letting our reference individual age one year is associated with a decrease in the probability that he has no problems in the domain of breathing (OPROBIT). Allowing for parallel (TwoS_par) and then non-parallel cut-point shift (TwoS and OneS_HOPIT)

Table 4.12 Partial effects on the probability of reporting no problems with breathing for reference individual in all models

	(1) PE_5_OPROBIT	(2) PE_5_2S_par	(3) PE_5_2S	(4) PE_5_HOPIT
PE_5_female	-0.0154	-0.0384	-0.0833**	-0.0724*
	(-0.4756)	(-1.1823)	(-2.5306)	(-1.7803)
PE_5_age	-0.0068***	-0.0058***	-0.0029*	-0.0033*
	(-4.2570)	(-3.6464)	(-1.8121)	(-1.6929)
PE_5_isced2	0.0359	0.0383	0.1028*	0.1039
	(0.5836)	(0.6229)	(1.7697)	(1.4708)
PE_5_isced34	0.0190	0.0473	0.1128***	0.1194***
	(0.4815)	(1.2165)	(2.9696)	(2.6324)
PE_5_isced56	0.0679	0.1321***	0.1779***	0.1737***
	(1.5410)	(3.1542)	(4.3919)	(3.6198)
N	837	837	837	837

t statistics in parentheses
* p<0.10, ** p<0.05, *** p<0.01

decreases the point estimate and respective significance gradually. The reverse occurs with the health effect of education, which increases and becomes more significant as we move to a more flexible specification. This example illustrates the importance of allowing for cut-point shift, and in a flexible way. In sum, under the assumptions of the vignette methodology, and in this particular application, we conclude that ignoring reporting heterogeneity would mask a positive health effect of being a male and better educated, whilst overestimating the detrimental effect of age. In the context of the study on which this example is based, we show some evidence that measured health inequalities by education can go undetected if no account is taken of reporting heterogeneity, in particular, a tendency for the better educated to rate a given health state more negatively.

APPENDIX

STATA CODE FOR PREPARATION OF DATASET

```
clear all

* Merge the files for modules that will be used in this
* case study: i) cover screen, ii) generated variables on
* educational achievement and iii) vignettes and own health
use  "sharew1_rel2-5-0_cv_r.dta", clear
merge mergeid using "sharew1_rel2-5-0_gv_isced.dta"        ///
   "sharew1_rel2-5-0_vignettes.dta"

* Keep only variables which will be used in this case study
keep mergeid _merge2 gender v5 v20 v22 v24 country         ///
   isced_r  int_year yrbirth

* Consider only French data and disregard individuals who do
* not appear in vignettes file.
keep if _merge2*(country==17)
drop _merge2 country

* Information on own self-reported health and vignettes in the
* domain of breathing, from vignettes questionnaire
rename v5 y
rename v20 vig1
rename v22 vig2
rename v24 vig3
label variable vig1 "Breathing vignette 1"
label variable vig2 "Breathing vignette 2"
label variable vig3 "Breathing vignette 3"

* Recode vignettes and own health to be increasing in good
* health                                              *
label define labels_health 5 "none" 4 "mild" 3 "moderate"  ///
   2 "severe" 1 "extreme"
foreach var in y vig1 vig2 vig3 {
   replace `var' = 6-`var'
   label values `var' labels_health
}

* Education: categorical variable and respective dummies
generate isced01=(isced_r==0)+(isced_r==1)                 ///
```

```
   if (isced_r!=.)*(isced_r<90)
generate isced2 =(isced_r==2) if (isced_r!=.)*(isced_r<90)
generate isced34 =(isced_r==3)+(isced_r==4)                    ///
   if (isced_r!=.)*(isced_r<90)
generate isced56 =(isced_r==5)+(isced_r==6)                    ///
   if (isced_r!=.)*(isced_r<90)
drop isced_r

gen isced_categ = isced01*1 + isced2*2 + isced34*3 + isced56*4
label define labels_isced 1 "isced 01" 2 "isced 2"            ///
   3 "isced 34" 4 "isced 56"
label values isced_categ labels_isced

* Age
generate age = int_year - yrbirth                             ///
   if (int_year!=.)*(yrbirth!=.)*(yrbirth>0)
drop  int_year yrbirth

* Gender
generate female = gender -1
drop gender

* Drop observations with missings:
* - in all vignette ratings:
drop if (vig1==.)&(vig2==.)&(vig3==.)
* - at least covariate or own health:
drop if (y==.)|(age==.)|(female==.)|(isced2==.)|             ///
   (isced34==.)|(isced56==.)
```

PROGRAM FOR GENERALISED ORDERED PROBIT IN LONG FORM

The program gop defines the log-likelihood in the same way that it would be defined for the ordered probit model. In the oprobit, however, the only argument (args) modelled as a function of the covariates would be the latent health linear index b, while in the generalised ordered probit model with vignettes, we will instead include the covariates in the cut-points m1-m4. Note that this program is defined for estimation in a dataset in long form in terms of the vignette ratings (i.e. these are contained in a single variable, here vig, and there are as many observations per individual as vignettes, in this case three). This is done for simplicity and for ease of presentation as in this chapter the respective estimation follows that of an ordered probit model using the built-in Stata command (necessarily in long form).

```
program define gop
    args lnf b m1 m2 m3 m4
    tempvar p1 p2 p3 p4 p5
    quietly {
      gen double `p1' = 0
      gen double `p2' = 0
      gen double `p3'= 0
      gen double `p4' = 0
      gen double `p5' = 0

      replace `p1' = norm(`m1'-`b')
      replace `p2' = norm(`m2'-`b') - norm(`m1'-`b')
      replace `p3' = norm(`m3'-`b') - norm(`m2'-`b')
      replace `p4' = norm(`m4'-`b') - norm(`m3'-`b')
      replace `p5' = 1 - norm(`m4'-`b')

      replace `lnf' = (vig==1)*ln(`p1')+(vig==2)*ln(`p2')    ///
        +(vig==3)*ln(`p3')+(vig==4)*ln(`p4')+ (vig==5)*ln(`p5')
          }
end
```

PROGRAM FOR HOPIT MODEL IN WIDE FORM

The program `hopit` specifies the joint log-likelihood of the model with cut-points determined by the vignette component. It should be noted that, in order to use this program for estimation, the dataset should be in wide form in terms of the vignette ratings (that is, contained in three different variables, here `vig1-vig3`, and with a single observation per individual). The individual contribution to the log-likelihood (`lnf`) is composed by the sum of the log-likelihoods of the own health component (interval regression with cut-points `m1-m4` and dependent variable `y`) and of the vignette component (generalised ordered probit for vignettes `vig1-vig4`, with cut-points `m1-m4` and health index depending on the corresponding vignette):

```
#delimit ;
cap program drop hopit;
program define hopit;
args lnf b s
        b_2 b_3
        m1 m2 m3 m4;

tempvar b_1  p1_1 p2_1 p3_1 p4_1 p5_1
             p1_2 p2_2 p3_2 p4_2 p5_2
             p1_3 p2_3 p3_3 p4_3 p5_3

             p1 p2 p3 p4 p5;
```

```
quietly {;
 gen double `p1_1'=0; gen double `p2_1'=0; gen double `p3_1'=0;
 gen double `p4_1'=0; gen double `p5_1'=0;
 gen double `p1_2'=0; gen double `p2_2'=0; gen double `p3_2'=0;
 gen double `p4_2'=0; gen double `p5_2'=0;
 gen double `p1_3'=0; gen double `p2_3'=0; gen double `p3_3'=0;
 gen double `p4_3'=0; gen double `p5_3'=0;

 gen double `p1'=0  ; gen double `p2'=0;   gen double `p3'=0;
 gen double `p4' = 0; gen double `p5'=0;
 gen double `b_1'= 0;

   replace `p1_1' = normal(`m1'-`b_1');
   replace `p2_1' = normal(`m2'-`b_1') - normal(`m1'-`b_1');
   replace `p3_1' = normal(`m3'-`b_1') - normal(`m2'-`b_1');
   replace `p4_1' = normal(`m4'-`b_1') - normal(`m3'-`b_1');
   replace `p5_1' = 1 - normal(`m4'-`b_1');

   replace `p1_2' = normal(`m1'-`b_2');
   replace `p2_2' = normal(`m2'-`b_2') - normal(`m1'-`b_2');
   replace `p3_2' = normal(`m3'-`b_2') - normal(`m2'-`b_2');
   replace `p4_2' = normal(`m4'-`b_2') - normal(`m3'-`b_2');
   replace `p5_2' = 1 - normal(`m4'-`b_2');

   replace `p1_3' = normal(`m1'-`b_3');
   replace `p2_3' = normal(`m2'-`b_3') - normal(`m1'-`b_3');
   replace `p3_3' = normal(`m3'-`b_3') - normal(`m2'-`b_3');
   replace `p4_3' = normal(`m4'-`b_3') - normal(`m3'-`b_3');
   replace `p5_3' = 1 - normal(`m4'-`b_3');

   replace `p1' = normal((`m1'-`b')/`s');
   replace `p2' = normal((`m2'-`b')/`s')
                               - normal((`m1'-`b')/`s');
   replace `p3' = normal((`m3'-`b')/`s')
                               - normal((`m2'-`b')/`s');
   replace `p4' = normal((`m4'-`b')/`s')
                               - normal((`m3'-`b')/`s');
   replace `p5' = 1 - normal((`m4'-`b')/`s');

   replace `lnf' = (vig1==1)*ln(`p1_1')+(vig1==2)*ln(`p2_1')
                +(vig1==3)*ln(`p3_1')+(vig1==4)*ln(`p4_1')
                +(vig1==5)*ln(`p5_1')
                +(vig2==1)*ln(`p1_2')+(vig2==2)*ln(`p2_2')
                +(vig2==3)*ln(`p3_2')+(vig2==4)*ln(`p4_2')
                +(vig2==5)*ln(`p5_2')
```

```
+(vig3==1)*ln(`p1_3')+(vig3==2)*ln(`p2_3')
+(vig3==3)*ln(`p3_3')+(vig3==4)*ln(`p4_3')
+(vig3==5)*ln(`p5_3')

+(y==1)*ln(`p1')+ (y==2)*ln(`p2')
+(y==3)*ln(`p3')+(y==4)*ln(`p4')
+(y==5)*ln(`p5');


    };
end;
#delimit cr
```

5 Health and lifestyles

SYNOPSIS

This chapter uses a sub-sample of the HALS 1984–85 and the deaths data released in 2003. It shows how to estimate a triangular recursive system of equations using a multivariate probit model, dealing with unobservable individual heterogeneity. It also shows how to calculate average partial effects. The outcomes of interest are binary measures of mortality, health status and lifestyles. The focus of the analysis is on socioeconomic and lifestyle gradients in mortality.

5.1 INTRODUCTION

It is widely accepted that lifestyle has an effect on individual health and that variations in health across individuals may depend upon differences in health-related behaviours. Disparities in health, for example across socioeconomic groups, are partly explained by differences in lifestyle and living conditions, and lifestyle choices are dependent on many factors including socioeconomic conditions.

Multivariate analysis allows a deeper investigation of the association between health-related behaviours and health, and the correlation among different lifestyles. An economic approach to the health production function has the advantage of relying on structural equations and accounting for methodological problems, such as unobservable heterogeneity, omitted variables bias and endogeneity. Contoyannis and Jones (2004) propose a model of health and lifestyle that controls for individual heterogeneity. This model is developed further in Balia and Jones (2008) and their paper is the basis for the case study presented in this chapter. For illustrative purposes, we consider only two health-related behaviours, namely smoking and drinking.

Balia and Jones (2008) propose a behavioural model for health, which contains socioeconomic characteristics as well as individual health-related behaviours.

The main health outcome is mortality and investments in health are assumed to be endogenous and to influence longevity. The relationship between individual socioeconomic characteristics and mortality is investigated, emphasising the role of lifestyle choices. These choices are influenced by socioeconomic characteristics but, to some extent, socioeconomic characteristics themselves have a direct effect on health outcomes. Furthermore, unobservable individual heterogeneity can influence both health outcomes and health-related behaviours.

The model assumes that individuals choose the optimal level of the demand for health given a time and budget constraint and given the trade-off with other consumption goods that enhance their utility. The individual is a rational and forward-looking economic agent who maximises lifetime utility and knows the marginal productivity of investing in health-related behaviours as well as all the parameters of the decision process. Future utility at each point in time depends on the probability of surviving until the next period and on past consumption and investment decisions. The idea is that individuals face a trade-off between choices that maximise their direct satisfaction and other choices that improve health. If individuals decide to improve their health, they can reduce the consumption of goods believed to be detrimental for health, and consume more goods which have beneficial effects. As an example, cigarettes, alcohol and high-calorie foods produce an intrinsic pleasure, but also might have a long-term negative impact on health. Individual tastes, the rate of time preference and expectations about the probability of survival should influence the pattern of intertemporal consumption. These elements are typically hidden from the researcher.

The behavioural model described above motivates an econometric model for mortality that takes the form of a recursive system of equations for mortality, self-assessed health and lifestyles. The model consists of structural form equations for mortality (m) and health (h) and reduced-form equations for lifestyles (c):

$$\begin{aligned} m &= \pi(c, h, x, \mu_m) \\ h &= h(c, x, \mu_h) \\ c &= f(x, \mu) \end{aligned} \qquad (5.1)$$

where x is the vector of all observable exogenous variables in the model; and μ includes unobservable factors which influence both the individual utility function (μ_U), the health outcome (μ_h) and the risk of mortality (μ_m). Heterogeneity is modelled by assuming that the error terms are correlated.

5.2 HALS DATA AND SAMPLE

To estimate the structural model for mortality we use data from the first wave of the Health and Lifestyle Survey (HALS) from 1984–85. We do not use the second wave of the HALS (1991–92) because of attrition problems. Mortality information is provided by the follow-up deaths data that was released in May 2003

(Chapter 6 uses a subsequent follow-up from 2005, but here we use the same data as Balia and Jones, 2008). Most of the 9,003 individuals interviewed in 1984 have been traced on the NHS Central Register, where all causes of death are notified. The flagging process was quite lengthy because it required several checks in order to be sure that flagging was related to the person that had been interviewed. About 97.8 per cent of the sample had been flagged in 2003. At that time deaths account for some 24 per cent of the original sample.

The variable `flagcode` in the data file enables the current status of the respondent to be identified. Respondents can be:

- `on file` – currently alive and flagged on the NHS register
- `not nhs regist` – not currently registered with the NHS – but not known to be dead
- `deceased` – known dead and death certificate information recorded on file
- `rep dead not id` – reported dead to HALS not on NHS register (may be alive)
- `embarked-abroad` – identified on NHS register but currently out of country
- `not yet flagged` – not currently flagged for various reasons (no name etc.)

Use the command:

```
tabulate flagcode
```

```
current flagging |
   status Feb 03 |      Freq.      Percent        Cum.
-----------------|------------------------------------
         on file |      6,506        72.26       72.26
 not nhs regist. |         86         0.96       73.22
        deceased |      2,171        24.11       97.33
 rep.dead not id |          1         0.01       97.35
 embarked -abroad|         43         0.48       97.82
 no flag yet rec.|        196         2.18      100.00
-----------------|------------------------------------
           Total |      9,003       100.00
```

The mortality data allows us to measure health outcomes up to 2003, thus covering a relatively long follow-up period so that increased risk of mortality may reflect the cumulative effect of poor health. In this framework, the risk of mortality is defined as a function of observed characteristics, health-related behaviours and self-reported health at the time of the HALS.

The sample

For the statistical analysis in this study, the original sample size has been reduced to 3,655 individuals: only individuals who answered all the questions relevant to the analysis and who were 40 years of age and older at the time of the first survey are included in the sample. To describe the flagging status in the target sample, the reader can execute again the command `tabulate flagcode`.

The main variables used from the HALS sample are indicators of health (`death, sah`) and lifestyle (`nsmoker alqprud`) indicators; socioeconomic indicators (`sc12 sc3 sc45 lhqdg lhqhndA lhq0 lhqnone lhqoth full part unemp sick retd keephse wkshft1`); geographical and area indicators (`wales north nwest yorks wmids emids anglia swest london scot rural suburb`); marital status (`married widow divorce seprd single`); ethnicity (`ethwheur`); demographic characteristics (`male height age age2 housown hou`) and parental smoking and drinking behaviours (`smother mothsmo fathsmo bothsmo alpa alma`). These variables are listed as a global:

```
global xvars  "death sah nsmoker alqprud sc12 sc3 sc45 lhqdg
    lhqhndA lhq0 lhqnone lhqoth married widow divorce seprd
    single full part unemp sick retd keephse wkshft1 wales
    north nwest yorks wmids emids anglia swest london scot
    rural suburb ethwheur male height age age2 housown hou
    smother mothsmo fathsmo bothsmo alpa alma"
```

First describe the information available and summarise the variables of interest:

```
describe $xvars
```

variable name	storage type	display format	value label	variable label
death	float	%9.0g		1 if has died at May 2003, 0 alive
sah	float	%9.0g		1 if self-assessed health is excellent or good, 0 if fair or poor
nsmoker	float	%9.0g		1 if does not smoke, 0 if current smoker
alqprud	float	%9.0g		1 if consume alcohol prudently
sc12	float	%9.0g		1 if professional/student or managerial/intermediate
sc3	float	%9.0g		1 if skilled or armed service
sc45	float	%9.0g		1 if partly skilled, unskilled, unclass. or never occupied
lhqdg	byte	%9.0g		1 if University degree

lhqhndA	float	%9.0g	1 if higher vocational qualifications or A level or equivalent
lhqO	byte	%9.0g	1 if O level/CSE
lhqnone	byte	%9.0g	1 if no qualification
lhqoth	byte	%9.0g	1 if other vocational/professional qualifications
married	byte	%8.0g	1 if married
widow	byte	%8.0g	1 if widow
divorce	byte	%8.0g	1 if divorced
seprd	byte	%8.0g	1 if separated
single	byte	%8.0g	1 if single
full	byte	%8.0g	1 if full time worker or student
part	byte	%8.0g	1 if part time worker
unemp	byte	%9.0g	1 if the individual unemployed
sick	byte	%9.0g	1 if absent from work due to sickness
retd	byte	%8.0g	1 if retired
keephse	byte	%8.0g	1 if housekeeper
wkshft1	float	%9.0g	1 if shift worker
wales	byte	%8.0g	1 if lives in Wales
north	byte	%8.0g	1 if lives in North
nwest	byte	%8.0g	1 if lives in North West
yorks	byte	%8.0g	1 if lives in Yorkshire
wmids	byte	%8.0g	1 if lives in West Midlands
emids	byte	%8.0g	1 if lives in East Midlands
anglia	byte	%8.0g	1 if lives in East Anglia
swest	byte	%8.0g	1 if lives in South West
london	byte	%8.0g	1 if lives in London
scot	byte	%8.0g	1 if lives in Scotland
rural	byte	%8.0g	1 if lives in the countryside
suburb	byte	%8.0g	1 if lives in the suburbs of the city
ethwheur	byte	%8.0g	1 if White European
male	byte	%9.0g	1 if male
height	byte	%9.0g	height in inches
age	double	%10.0g	age in years
age2	float	%9.0g	age /100
housown	byte	%9.0g	1 if own or rent house
hou	byte	%9.0g	number of other people in the house
smother	byte	%4.0g	1 if anyone else in house smoked
mothsmo	float	%9.0g	1 if only mother smoked
fathsmo	float	%9.0g	1 if only father smoked
bothsmo	float	%9.0g	1 if both parents smoked
alpa	byte	%9.0g	father, non to heavy drinker (0-4)
alma	byte	%9.0g	mother, non to heavy drinker (0-4)

```
summarize $xvars
```

Variable	Obs	Mean	Std. Dev.	Min	Max
death	3655	.3592339	.4798415	0	1
sah	3655	.7025992	.4571769	0	1
nsmoker	3655	.6995896	.4584992	0	1
alqprud	3655	.8798906	.3251339	0	1
sc12	3655	.3154583	.4647617	0	1
sc3	3655	.4667579	.498962	0	1
sc45	3655	.2177839	.4127962	0	1
lhqdg	3655	.1250342	.3308029	0	1
lhqhndA	3655	.1247606	.3304925	0	1
lhqO	3655	.0943912	.2924123	0	1
lhqnone	3655	.6082079	.4882174	0	1
lhqoth	3655	.047606	.2129603	0	1
married	3655	.7606019	.4267745	0	1
widow	3655	.1277702	.3338794	0	1
divorce	3655	.0383037	.1919547	0	1
seprd	3655	.0166895	.1281227	0	1
single	3655	.0566347	.231175	0	1
full	3655	.3641587	.4812593	0	1
part	3655	.1318741	.3384002	0	1
unemp	3655	.0303694	.1716249	0	1
sick	3655	.0331053	.1789361	0	1
retd	3655	.3387141	.4733373	0	1
keephse	3655	.1017784	.302398	0	1
wkshft1	3655	.0574555	.2327428	0	1
wales	3655	.0577291	.2332625	0	1
north	3655	.0651163	.2467647	0	1
nwest	3655	.1277702	.3338794	0	1
yorks	3655	.0861833	.2806729	0	1
wmids	3655	.0801642	.2715843	0	1
emids	3655	.0766074	.2660039	0	1
anglia	3655	.0399453	.1958575	0	1
swest	3655	.0883721	.2838741	0	1
london	3655	.0943912	.2924123	0	1
scot	3655	.09658	.2954255	0	1
rural	3655	.2183311	.4131698	0	1

```
------------|-----------------------------------------------------------
     suburb |    3655      .471409     .4992502          0            1
   ethwheur |    3655     .978933     .1436275          0            1
       male |    3655    .4552668     .4980631          0            1
     height |    3655    65.95021     3.703241         54           79
        age |    3655    57.46802     11.67334         40         96.8
------------|-----------------------------------------------------------
       age2 |    3655    34.38802     14.07611         16      93.7024
    housown |    3655    .9658003     .1817667          0            1
        hou |    3655    1.650889      1.27226          0           10
    smother |    3655    .3507524     .4772709          0            1
    mothsmo |    3655    .0309166     .1731153          0            1
------------|-----------------------------------------------------------
    fathsmo |    3655    .5950752     .4909446          0            1
    bothsmo |    3655    .2456908      .430555          0            1
       alpa |    3655    1.891382      1.20047          0            4
       alma |    3655    .9119015     .9811625          0            4
```

tabulate death

```
    death |      Freq.     Percent        Cum.
----------|-----------------------------------
        0 |      2,342       64.08       64.08
        1 |      1,313       35.92      100.00
----------|-----------------------------------
    Total |      3,655      100.00
```

Around 70 per cent of the individuals interviewed in 1984 reported having good or excellent health status relative to people of their own age. The sample comprises 46 per cent men and 54 per cent women and is made up of individuals whose behaviours are mostly healthy. A high proportion of the sample is prudent in the consumption of alcohol (88 per cent) and only 30 per cent of individuals are smokers. As for the socioeconomic characteristics, individuals are largely concentrated in skilled occupations (sc3), about 47 per cent of the sample, while only 32 per cent of the sample belongs to professional and managerial occupations (sc12) and 22 per cent to semi- and non-skilled occupations (sc45). Around 61 per cent of the respondents do not have formal educational qualifications, and only 13 per cent has a university degree.

5.3 DESCRIPTIVE ANALYSIS

Lifestyle and socioeconomic status

We are interested in the response of different socioeconomic groups to risky behaviours. Define a list of the two lifestyle indicators:

```
global lifestyles "nsmoker alqprud"
```

A simple way of investigating the relationship between individual lifestyle and socioeconomic characteristics consists of computing the partial correlation of each lifestyle with different social classes and education level. We use a foreach command to loop over each lifestyle while executing the command pcorr. The command pcorr calculates the partial correlation coefficients of lifestyles with the top and bottom social class, holding sc3 constant:

```
foreach x of global lifestyles{
        pcorr `x' sc12 sc45
        }
```

```
Partial and semipartial correlations of nsmoker with
```

Variable	Partial Corr.	Semipartial Corr.	Partial Corr.^2	Semipartial Corr.^2	Significance Value
sc12	0.1006	0.1002	0.0101	0.0100	0.0000
sc45	-0.0467	-0.0463	0.0022	0.0021	0.0048

```
Partial and semipartial correlations of alqprud with
```

Variable	Partial Corr.	Semipartial Corr.	Partial Corr.^2	Semipartial Corr.^2	Significance Value
sc12	-0.0425	-0.0425	0.0018	0.0018	0.0102
sc45	-0.0312	-0.0312	0.0010	0.0010	0.0592

The variable nsmoker is correlated with the occupational social class variables, the correlation is positive for sc12 and negative for sc45. alqprud is negatively correlated with both the top and the bottom social class.

Compute correlation coefficients by education levels, holding lhq0 constant:

```
foreach x of global lifestyles{
      pcorr `x' lhqdg lhqhndA lhqoth lhqnone
      }
```

Partial and semipartial correlations of nsmoker with

Variable	Partial Corr.	Semipartial Corr.	Partial Corr.^2	Semipartial Corr.^2	Significance Value
lhqdg	0.0441	0.0438	0.0019	0.0019	0.0077
lhqhndA	0.0137	0.0136	0.0002	0.0002	0.4067
lhqoth	-0.0452	-0.0448	0.0020	0.0020	0.0063
lhqnone	-0.0468	-0.0465	0.0022	0.0022	0.0047

Partial and semipartial correlations of alqprud with

Variable	Partial Corr.	Semipartial Corr.	Partial Corr.^2	Semipartial Corr.^2	Significance Value
lhqdg	-0.0027	-0.0027	0.0000	0.0000	0.8713
lhqhndA	-0.0076	-0.0076	0.0001	0.0001	0.6470
lhqoth	-0.0183	-0.0183	0.0003	0.0003	0.2694
lhqnone	0.0156	0.0156	0.0002	0.0002	0.3446

In order to see how lifestyles are distributed across socioeconomic groups, divide the sample into groups according to the number of 'healthy' behaviours adopted:

```
generate ls1=nsmoker
generate ls2=alqprud
summaruze ls1-ls2
egen sumls=rsum(ls1-ls2)
summarize sumls
global zero "sumls==0"
global one "sumls==1"
global two "sumls==2"
```

Compare the sample means of socioeconomic and demographic variables between the three sub-samples that are defined according to the number of healthy behaviours: 0, 1 or 2:

```
global subvars "death sah sc12 sc3 sc45 lhqdg lhqhndA lhq0
   lhqnone lhqoth full part unemp sick retd keephse wkshft1
   male age"
```

```
summarize $subvars if $zero
summarize $subvars if $one
summarize $subvars if $two
```

Results are displayed in the following summary table:

	Full sample	0	1	2
death	0.359	0.356	0.376	0.351
sah	0.703	0.639	0.660	0.729
sc12	0.315	0.277	0.259	0.346
sc3	0.467	0.396	0.500	0.456
sc45	0.218	0.327	0.240	0.197
lhqdg	0.125	0.084	0.094	0.144
lhqhndA	0.125	0.109	0.112	0.132
lhqO	0.094	0.089	0.087	0.098
lhqnone	0.608	0.649	0.648	0.585
lhqoth	0.048	0.069	0.058	0.041
full	0.364	0.624	0.384	0.332
part	0.132	0.074	0.130	0.138
unemp	0.030	0.084	0.047	0.018
sick	0.033	0.040	0.045	0.027
retd	0.339	0.109	0.288	0.384
keephse	0.102	0.069	0.107	0.102
wkshftl	0.057	0.114	0.076	0.044
male	0.455	0.762	0.476	0.419
age	57.468	51.491	55.763	58.821
N	3655	202	1133	2320

The number of deaths decreases moving from the group with the fewest healthy behaviours to the group with the healthiest lifestyle. The more healthy behaviours there are, the bigger the proportion of persons belonging to the higher occupational social classes. The number of individuals in the bottom classes decreases moving from the most unhealthy lifestyles to the healthiest. The general result is that smoking and drinking are not randomly distributed but cluster together in certain groups of the population, suggesting that the relationship between lifestyles and the socioeconomic environment must be taken into account. However, this does not say whether, and to what extent, health is affected by the propensities to undertake behaviours. Further analysis is needed.

Health and lifestyle

Use pcorr to compute partial correlations between lifestyles and the health indicators:

```
pcorr sah $lifestyles
pcorr death $lifestyles
```

```
Partial and semipartial correlations of death with
```

Variable	Partial Corr.	Semipartial Corr.	Partial Corr.^2	Semipartial Corr.^2	Significance Value
nsmoker	-0.0368	-0.0368	0.0014	0.0014	0.0262
alqprud	0.0216	0.0216	0.0005	0.0005	0.1912

```
Partial and semipartial correlations of sah with
```

Variable	Partial Corr.	Semipartial Corr.	Partial Corr.^2	Semipartial Corr.^2	Significance Value
nsmoker	0.1137	0.1137	0.0129	0.0129	0.0000
alqprud	-0.0341	-0.0339	0.0012	0.0012	0.0391

As expected, mortality and health are negatively and positively correlated with nsmoker respectively. Correlations go in the opposite directions in the case of alqprud. Use a Pearson Chi-squared test to further investigate the relationship between health, mortality and lifestyles represented in two-way tables:

```
foreach x of global lifestyles{
          tabulate `x' sah, chi2
          }
foreach x of global lifestyles{
          tabulate `x' death , chi2
          }
```

1 if does not smoke,0 if current smoker	1 if has died at May 2003, 0 alive 0	1	Total
0	676	422	1,098
1	1,666	891	2,557

```
       Total |     2,342       1,313 |      3,655


         Pearson chi2(1) =   4.2961  Pr = 0.038


       1 if |
     consume | 1 if has died at May
     alcohol |     2003, 0 alive
   prudently |          0          1 |      Total
   ----------|---------------------|-----------
           0 |        291        148 |        439
           1 |      2,051      1,165 |      3,216
   ----------|---------------------|-----------
       Total |      2,342      1,313 |      3,655


         Pearson chi2(1) =   1.0590  Pr = 0.303
```

The tests confirm the existence of a strong correlation between death and nsmoker.

Mortality and socioeconomic status

HALS provides information about the cause of death. Causes of death are coded using the ICD-9-CM diagnostic and procedure code system. Stata has a built-in command (icd9) to decode each specific cause of death. Generate 19 dummy variables for types of disease-specific mortality:

```
icd9  clean ucause, d p
icd9  generate u1=ucause, range(001/139)
label variable u1 "infectious and parasitic dis"
icd9  generate u2=ucause, range(140/239)
label variable u2 "neoplasms"
icd9  generate u3=ucause, range(240/279)
label variable u3 "endocrine, nutritional and metabolic dis ///
      and immunity disorders"
icd9  generate u4=ucause, range(280/289)
label variable u4 "dis of the blood and blood-forming organs"
icd9  generate u5=ucause, range(290/319)
label variable u5 " mental disorder"
icd9  generate u6=ucause, range(320/389)
label variable u6 "dis of the nervous system and sense organs"
icd9  generate u7=ucause, range(390/459)
label variable u7 "dis of the circulatory system"
icd9  generate u8=ucause, range(460/519)
label variable u8 "dis of the respiratory system"
icd9  generate u9=ucause, range(520/579)
```

```
label variable u9 "dis of the digestive system"
icd9  generate u10=ucause, range(580/629)
label variable u10 "dis of the genitourinary system"
icd9  generate u11=ucause, range(630/679)
label variable u11 "complications of pregnancy, childbirth  ///
      and the puerperium"
icd9  generate u12=ucause, range(680/709)
label variable u12 "dis of the skin and subcutaneous tissue"
icd9  generate u13=ucause, range(710/739)
label variable u13 "dis of the musculoskeletal system and   ///
      connective tissue"
icd9  generate u14=ucause, range(740/759)
label variable u14 "congenital anomalies"
icd9  generate u15=ucause, range(760/779)
label variable u15 "certain conditions originating in the   ///
      perinatal period"
icd9  generate u16=ucause, range(780/799)
label variable u16 "symptoms, signs, and ill-defined         ///
      conditions"
icd9  generate u17=ucause, range(800/999)
label variable u17 "injury and poisoning"
icd9  generate u18=ucause, range(E800/E999)
label variable u18 "supplementary classification of          ///
      external causes of injury and poisoning"
icd9  generate u19=ucause, range(V01/V83)
label variable u19 "supplementary classification of factors ///
 influencing health status and contact with health services"

generate cd=0                    /* cd=0 if missing cause*/
replace cd=1 if u1==1
  ... ... ...
replace cd=19 if u19==1
```

Then explore the distribution of causes of death in the sample as a whole and split by social class (scgr equals 1 for sc12, 2 for sc3 and 3 for sc45):

```
describe u1-u19
tabulate cd if death==1
```

cd	Freq.	Percent	Cum.
0	27	2.06	2.06
1	9	0.69	2.74
2	367	27.95	30.69
3	17	1.29	31.99

```
     4 |          2         0.15        32.14
     5 |         20         1.52        33.66
     6 |         15         1.14        34.81
     7 |        597        45.47        80.27
     8 |        162        12.34        92.61
     9 |         43         3.27        95.89
    10 |         15         1.14        97.03
    13 |          4         0.30        97.33
    16 |         13         0.99        98.32
    17 |          6         0.46        98.78
    18 |         16         1.22       100.00
--------|---------------------------------
 Total |      1,313       100.00
```

```
sort scgr. by scgr: tabulate cd if death==1
```

```
-> scgr = 1
```

```
    cd |      Freq.      Percent         Cum.
--------|---------------------------------
     0 |          7         2.26         2.26
     1 |          4         1.29         3.55
     2 |         89        28.71        32.26
     3 |          5         1.61        33.87
     4 |          2         0.65        34.52
     5 |         10         3.23        37.74
     6 |          3         0.97        38.71
     7 |        126        40.65        79.35
     8 |         35        11.29        90.65
     9 |          9         2.90        93.55
    10 |          6         1.94        95.48
    16 |          5         1.61        97.10
    17 |          3         0.97        98.06
    18 |          6         1.94       100.00
--------|---------------------------------
 Total |        310       100.00
```

```
-> scgr = 2
```

```
    cd |      Freq.      Percent         Cum.
--------|---------------------------------
     0 |         15         2.26         2.26
     1 |          3         0.45         2.71
     2 |        191        28.81        31.52
     3 |          5         0.75        32.28
```

```
    5 |          6        0.90       33.18
    6 |         10        1.51       34.69
    7 |        319       48.11       82.81
    8 |         72       10.86       93.67
    9 |         17        2.56       96.23
   10 |          8        1.21       97.44
   13 |          4        0.60       98.04
   16 |          5        0.75       98.79
   17 |          3        0.45       99.25
   18 |          5        0.75      100.00
--------|------------------------------------
 Total |        663     100.00
```

-> scgr - 3

```
   cd |       Freq.     Percent        Cum.
--------|------------------------------------
    0 |          5        1.47        1.47
    1 |          2        0.59        2.06
    2 |         87       25.59       27.65
    3 |          7        2.06       29.71
    5 |          4        1.18       30.88
    6 |          2        0.59       31.47
    7 |        152       44.71       76.18
    8 |         55       16.18       92.35
    9 |         17        5.00       97.35
   10 |          1        0.29       97.65
   16 |          3        0.88       98.53
   18 |          5        1.47      100.00
--------|------------------------------------
 Total |        340     100.00
```

The most frequent causes of death are diseases of the circulatory system (u7), neoplasms (u2) and diseases of the respiratory system (u8). Deaths in the three classes are mainly due to diseases of the respiratory system, with a maximum of 48 per cent of deaths due to this cause among those in skilled occupations (sc3). The incidence of respiratory diseases is higher for semi- and non-skilled occupations (sc45).

A crude way to see if mortality varies with the characteristics of the population is to look at the simple death rate. Stata has a built-in command called proportion, which produces estimates of proportion of deaths by any covariate. Instead this can be calculated directly:

```
global varlist "sc12 sc3 sc45 lhqdg lhqhndA lhqO lhqnone
    male sah"
```

```
foreach x of global varlist{
     quietly{
            count if `x'==1&death==1
            scalar d`x'=r(N)
            quietly count if `x'==1
            scalar n`x'=r(N)
            scalar drate`x'=(d`x'/n`x')*100
            }
     display "death rate `x' : " drate`x'
     }
```

	Death rate
sc12	26.89
sc3	38.86
sc45	42.71
hqdg	24.73
lhqhnda	22.59
lhqo	22.32
lhqnone	43.10
male	42.91
sah	31.09

The death rate increases from the highest social class to the lowest. Such a clear gradient is not found across education levels. The mortality rate is higher for men and for individuals in fair or poor health status.

5.4 ESTIMATION STRATEGY AND RESULTS

This section illustrates our estimation strategy and describes the econometric approach adopted to obtain estimates of the effect of the lifestyle variables on health. We estimate a model that allows us to control for unobservable individual heterogeneity, which is a common methodological problem in the empirical estimation of the health production function.

The econometric model

The model described in (5.1) is a recursive triangular system of equations for lifestyles, morbidity and mortality. We assume that the random components of the lifestyle equations are correlated with the random components of the mortality and health equations. This means that potentially there are factors, unobservable to the researchers, which influence individual health-related behaviours as well as health status and the risk of mortality. Hence, the issue is to take into account this unobservable individual-specific heterogeneity in the estimation procedure in order to recover consistent estimates of the coefficients. Potential endogeneity of self-assessed health and the lifestyle variables in the recursive model is reflected in the correlation between the error terms. If endogeneity is a problem, then coefficient estimates from a univariate probit model for mortality will be inconsistent.

We estimate a triangular recursive system, which consists of structural equations for the health production functions and two reduced-form equations for lifestyles. The dependent variables in the recursive model are binary variables: y_{id}, y_{ih} and y_{ic} denote death, sah and the set of lifestyles (nsmoker alqprud), respectively. The latent variables underlying each observed variable define the following system of equations:

$$y_{id}^* = \delta_d' y_{ic} + \vartheta_d' y_{ih} + \alpha_d' w_i + \epsilon_{id}$$
$$y_{ih}^* = \delta_h' y_{ic} + \alpha_h' w_i + \beta_h' z_i + \epsilon_{ih} \qquad (5.2)$$
$$y_{ic}^* = \alpha_c' w_i + \beta_c' z_i + \gamma_c v_i + \epsilon_{ic}$$

such that

$$y_{id} = 1\left(y_{id}^* \geq 0\right)$$
$$y_{ih} = 1\left(y_{ih}^* \geq 0\right)$$
$$y_{ic} = 1\left(y_{ic}^* \geq 0\right)$$

where $y_{ic} = \{y_{i1} y_{i2}\}$ is a vector of two lifestyles, and w_i, z_i and v_i are individual-specific exogenous vectors that explain respectively, mortality, health and lifestyle, health and lifestyle and lifestyle only. These variables are chosen following an approach to identification that will be illustrated later.

We assume that the error terms of the latent equations in (5.2) have a multivariate normal distribution. Therefore the log-likelihood depends on a multivariate standard normal distribution, ϕ_M, where M is the number of equations in the system. Full information maximum likelihood (FIML) estimation cannot be performed directly as the integrals in the likelihood function have no closed-form. For this reason, we estimate the model using the user-written command mvprobit; the algorithm is fully described in Cappellari and Jenkins (2003). The module can be installed by typing:

```
ssc install mvprobit
```

The mvprobit uses the GHK (Geweke-Hajivassilou-Keane) simulator for probabilities and a Maximum Simulated Likelihood (MSL) procedure. Further statistical details on the estimation of the multivariate probit model described in equations (5.2) are provided in Balia and Jones (2008).

The GHK simulator exploits the Choleski decomposition of the covariance matrix, so that the joint probability originally based on unobservables can be written as the product of univariate conditional probabilities where the errors in the *M* equations are substituted by disturbances that are independent from each other by construction. A maximum likelihood procedure using the GHK simulator at each iteration is numerically intensive and simulation bias may arise: the researcher has to choose the appropriate number of random draws for a given sample size. For further details about MSL see Contoyannis *et al.* (2004a) and Train (2003).

Estimation

Systems of binary dependent variables with endogenous binary regressors typically require exclusion restrictions for robust identification of the parameters. This would imply finding a set of variables which are instrumental to identify the effect of y_{ih} on mortality risk, and the effect of y_{il} on health and mortality risk, as shown in (5.2). However, given the assumptions of joint normality and recursivity, the model is in principle identified by functional form, meaning that exclusion restrictions are not required and that exogenous covariates for all the *M* equations can be identical (see Wilde, 2000). We compare results for models with and without exclusion restrictions.

We choose the best set of exclusion restrictions looking at the statistical fit of different specifications. In particular, both in the univariate mortality equation probit and in the multivariate probit model, the Akaike information criterion (AIC) and the Bayesian information criterion (BIC), support the exclusion of wales, north, nwest, yorks, wmids, emids, anglia, swest, london, scot, widow, divorce, seprd, single, housown, hou, smother, mothsmo, fathsmo, bothsmo, alpa and alma from the mortality equations. The same test is used to compare this model with a model estimated without exclusion restrictions.

We first define alternative global macros (xvar1 and xvar2) for the exogenous regressors in the right hand sides of our equations. We include a squared term for age, which allows the probability of death to be a smooth and flexible function of age. Separate global macros for variables describing parental smoking and drinking behaviour (smiv and driv) are defined as well.

```
global xvar1 "sc12 sc45 lhqdg lhqhndA lhqnone lhqoth part
    unemp sick retd keephse wkshft1 rural suburb ethwheur
    height male age age2"

global xvar2 "sc12 sc45 lhqdg lhqhndA lhqnone lhqoth widow
    divorce seprd single part unemp sick retd keephse
    wkshft1 wales north nwest yorks wmids emids anglia swest
    london scot rural suburb ethwheur housown hou height
    male age age2"

global smiv "smother mothsmo fathsmo bothsmo"

global driv "alpa alma"
```

Table 5.1 Probit model for mortality – without exclusion restrictions

```
----------------------------------------------------------------
Probit regression                       Number of obs =    3655
                                        LR chi2(44)   = 1624.33
                                        Prob > chi2   =  0.0000
Log likelihood = -1574.4619             Pseudo R2     =  0.3403
----------------------------------------------------------------
```

death	Coef.	Std. Err.	z	P>|z|	[95% Conf. Interval]	
sah	-.3179813	.0570215	-5.58	0.000	-.4297413	-.2062213
nsmoker	-.3335308	.0594839	-5.61	0.000	-.450117	-.2169446
alqprud	-.1103899	.081432	-1.36	0.175	-.2699936	.0492138
sc12	-.1235674	.0670384	-1.84	0.065	-.2549602	.0078254
sc45	-.0214667	.0653072	-0.33	0.742	-.1494665	.106533
lhqdg	.0508621	.123517	0.41	0.680	-.1912267	.292951
lhqhndA	-.0576475	.1205907	-0.48	0.633	-.294001	.1787061
lhqnone	.1210006	.0992769	1.22	0.223	-.0735785	.3155796
lhqoth	-.0707609	.1498875	-0.47	0.637	-.3645349	.2230131
widow	.112275	.0882363	1.27	0.203	-.0606649	.285215
divorce	.0522788	.1428293	0.37	0.714	-.2276615	.3322192
seprd	.1676799	.2139065	0.78	0.433	-.2515691	.5869289
single	.1422949	.1180581	1.21	0.228	-.0890947	.3736846
part	.1372722	.1017277	1.35	0.177	-.0621105	.3366548
unemp	.2631324	.1429041	1.84	0.066	-.0169546	.5432194
sick	.5985598	.1410771	4.24	0.000	.3220538	.8750657
retd	.0523245	.093042	0.56	0.574	-.1300344	.2346834
keephse	.2688326	.1088021	2.47	0.013	.0555843	.4820809
wkshft1	-.2339265	.1298302	-1.80	0.072	-.4883889	.020536
wales	.1468177	.1264935	1.16	0.246	-.101105	.3947403
north	.2914888	.1173529	2.48	0.013	.0614814	.5214961
nwest	.2042567	.0950052	2.15	0.032	.0180498	.3904635
yorks	.0928741	.1094636	0.85	0.396	-.1216707	.307418
wmids	.2608396	.1091491	2.39	0.017	.0469113	.4747679
emids	.1384053	.1117852	1.24	0.216	-.0806898	.3575003
anglia	-.0285042	.1439493	-0.20	0.843	-.3106398	.2536313
swest	.2235278	.1088436	2.05	0.040	.0101982	.4368574
london	.1788563	.1056406	1.69	0.090	-.0281955	.3859081
scot	.2534408	.103502	2.45	0.014	.0505806	.4563011
rural	-.1253628	.0772217	-1.62	0.105	-.2767145	.0259889
suburb	-.0576427	.0603113	-0.96	0.339	-.1758506	.0605653
ethwheur	.3030231	.2068341	1.47	0.143	-.1023642	.7084104
housown	.0427828	.1538341	0.28	0.781	-.2587265	.344292
hou	.0143918	.0298877	0.48	0.630	-.0441869	.0729705
height	.0131609	.0096902	1.36	0.174	-.0058316	.0321533
male	.4098419	.0802539	5.11	0.000	.2525471	.5671367

Table 5.1 continued

```
      age |  .0409883   .0278213    1.47  0.141  -.0135404    .0955171
     age2 |  .0363769   .0227806    1.60  0.110  -.0082723    .0810261
  smother |    .08787   .0611921    1.44  0.151  -.0320644    .2078044
  mothsmo | -.0155907   .1711016   -0.09  0.927  -.3509436    .3197622
  fathsmo |  .0901155   .0813916    1.11  0.268  -.0694092    .2496402
  bothsmo |  .1077702   .0969624    1.11  0.266  -.0822725    .2978129
     alpa |  .0166751   .0230257    0.72  0.469  -.0284544    .0618046
     alma | -.0039824   .0284652   -0.14  0.889  -.0597731    .0518083
    _cons | -5.341181   1.109316   -4.81  0.000  -7.515401   -3.166962
```

/*RESET test*/
(1) [death]yhat2 = 0
         chi2(1) = 1.00
       Prob > chi2 = 0.3169

Table 5.2 Probit model for mortality – with exclusion restrictions

```
------------------------------------------------------------------
Probit regression                        Number of obs =    3655
                                         LR chi2(22)   = 1603.20
                                         Prob > chi2   =  0.0000
Log likelihood = -1585.026               Pseudo R2     =  0.3359
------------------------------------------------------------------
   death |   Coef. Std. Err.    z  P>|z|   [95% Conf. Interval]
---------|--------------------------------------------------------
     sah | -.3220497  .0565242  -5.70  0.000  -.4328351  -.2112644
 nsmoker | -.3672686  .0572446  -6.42  0.000  -.4794661  -.2550712
  alqprud| -.1362186  .0799651  -1.70  0.088  -.2929472   .0205101
    sc12 | -.1383619  .0665248  -2.08  0.038  -.2687481  -.0079757
    sc45 | -.0125873  .0646587  -0.19  0.846  -.139316    .1141414
   lhqdg |  .0314484  .1217418   0.26  0.796  -.2071611   .2700579
 lhqhndA | -.0784501  .1191228  -0.66  0.510  -.3119265   .1550263
 lhqnone |  .1133078  .0978815   1.16  0.247  -.0785364   .3051519
  lhqoth | -.0737711  .1483012  -0.50  0.619  -.3644361   .2168939
    part |  .1243422  .1004507   1.24  0.216  -.0725376   .3212219
   unemp |  .3007517  .1411966   2.13  0.033   .0240115   .577492
    sick |  .6329989  .1396152   4.53  0.000   .3593581   .9066398
    retd |  .0515816  .0919922   0.56  0.575  -.1287197   .231883
  keephse|  .2545123  .1070106   2.38  0.017   .0447754   .4642492
 wkshft1 | -.2314675  .1287503  -1.80  0.072  -.4838135   .0208784
   rural | -.1742009  .0732617  -2.38  0.017  -.3177913  -.0306106
  suburb | -.0902304  .0585737  -1.54  0.123  -.2050327   .024572
 ethwheur|  .3595832  .2023639   1.78  0.076  -.0370428   .7562092
```

Table 5.2 continued

```
   height |  .0091417   .0095645    0.96   0.339   -.0096045    .0278878
     male |  .4046066   .0781588    5.18   0.000    .2514183    .557795
      age |  .0345884   .0260525    1.33   0.184   -.0164735    .0856502
     age2 |  .0404307   .0216342    1.87   0.062   -.0019716    .082833
    _cons | -4.423958   1.008396   -4.39   0.000   -6.400378   -2.447537
```

/* RESET test*/

```
( 1)   [death]yhat2 = 0
           chi2( 1)  =   0.91
         Prob > chi2 =   0.3414
```

We estimate univariate probit models for mortality using the command `probit`, and compare the two identification approaches using the post-estimation commands `estimates store` and `estimates stats`. As an alternative one can use the user-written command `fitstat` (Long and Freese, 2006), which computes fit statistics for single equation regression models and can be downloaded by typing `findit fitstat` in Stata. We also test misspecification of the models by means of the RESET test. Tables 5.1–5.2 report the estimation results.

```
probit death sah nsmoker alqprud $xvar2 $smiv $driv, nolog
estimates store m1
/* RESET test*/
predict yhat, xb
generate yhat2=yhat^2
quietly probit death sah nsmoker alqprud $xvar2 $smiv      ///
   $driv yhat2
test yhat2=0
drop yhat yhat2

probit death sah nsmoker alqprud $xvar2, nolog
estimates store m2
/* RESET test*/
predict yhat, xb
generate yhat2=yhat^2
quietly probit death sah nsmoker alqprud $xvar2 yhat2
test yhat2=0
drop yhat yhat2

probit death sah nsmoker alqprud $xvar1, nolog
estimates store m3
/* RESET test*/
```

```
predict yhat, xb
generate yhat2=yhat^2
quietly probit death sah nsmoker alqprud $xvar1 yhat2
test yhat2=0
drop yhat yhat2
```

Comparing the two probit models above we get:

```
estimates stats m1 m2
----------------------------------------------------------------------
  Model |   Obs     ll(null)    ll(model)   df        AIC         BIC
--------|-------------------------------------------------------------
    m1 |  3655    -2386.628    -1574.462    45    3238.924    3518.097
    m2 |  3655    -2386.628    -1585.026    23    3216.052    3358.741
----------------------------------------------------------------------
```

Note that in Stata the AIC and BIC are calculated as $AIC = -2 \ln L + 2q$ and $BIC = -2 \ln L + \ln(N)q$ where q is the number of parameters estimated. The smaller the value of the information criteria, the better the fit of the model. Here they both favour the model with exclusion restrictions. The RESET test suggests that the mortality model is not misspecified in all three cases.

Likewise, we estimate and compare two different specifications of the four-dimensional multivariate probit model. Estimation of the mvprobit requires the option `draws(#)` indicating the number of random draws in the simulation procedure (a higher # increases accuracy but is more time-consuming). `memory` and `matsize` need to be set accordingly: a good rule of thumb is to `set memory` at least equal to the value (#)*M, and increase `matsize` for models with many covariates:

```
set memory 400
set matsize 10000

mvprobit (death=sah nsmoker alqprud $xvar2 $smiv $driv)   ///
    (sah= nsmoker alqprud $xvar2 $smiv $driv)             ///
    (nsmoker=$xvar2 $smiv $driv)                          ///
    (alqprud=$xvar2 $smiv $driv), dr(50)
```

Table 5.3 reports results for the first equation and a selection of the correlation coefficients from the Stata output. The `rho` parameters are the estimated correlation coefficients. Stata reports the asymptotic z-test for significance. This can be used to test the null hypothesis of exogeneity of the dummy regressors (see Knapp and Seaks, 1998). Note that the `rho` for `death-nsmoker` is statistically significant at a 10 per cent significance level and that the correlation for `nsmoker` and `alqprud` is also highly statistically significant.

Table 5.3 Multivariate probit model – without exclusion restrictions

```
----------------------------------------------------------------
Multivariate probit (SML, # draws = 50)   Number of obs  =    3655
                                           Wald chi2(169) = 2586.23
Log likelihood = -6702.0152                Prob > chi2    =  0.0000
----------------------------------------------------------------
```

death	Coef.	Std. Err.	z	P>|z|	[95% Conf.	Interval]
sah	-.9128022	.3135803	-2.91	0.004	-1.527408	-.298196
nsmoker	-.8253812	.3400228	-2.43	0.015	-1.491814	-.1589488
alqprud	-.290108	.3496682	-0.83	0.407	-.975445	.3952291
sc12	-.0649878	.0699653	-0.93	0.353	-.2021172	.0721417
sc45	-.0738689	.0656328	-1.13	0.260	-.2025068	.0547689
lhqdg	.0686881	.1185564	0.58	0.562	-.1636782	.3010544
lhqhndA	-.0603501	.1157762	-0.52	0.602	-.2872672	.1665671
lhqnone	.0346588	.100069	0.35	0.729	-.1614728	.2307903
lhqoth	-.1524212	.1477408	-1.03	0.302	-.4419879	.1371454
widow	.0235294	.0905871	0.26	0.795	-.154018	.2010768
divorce	-.0466194	.1430949	-0.33	0.745	-.3270802	.2338413
seprd	.0976899	.2075058	0.47	0.638	-.3090139	.5043937
single	.0994084	.1153932	0.86	0.389	-.1267581	.325575
part	.1181936	.1001439	1.18	0.238	-.0780848	.314472
unemp	.1206702	.1489783	0.81	0.418	-.1713218	.4126622
sick	.1836968	.2282765	0.80	0.421	-.263717	.6311105
retd	-.0284638	.0957587	-0.30	0.766	-.2161474	.1592199
keephse	.1800797	.1108468	1.62	0.104	-.037176	.3973354
wkshft1	-.2646154	.1253741	-2.11	0.035	-.5103441	-.0188867
wales	.0442916	.127158	0.35	0.728	-.2049335	.2935166
north	.2161172	.1217844	1.77	0.076	-.0225758	.4548102
nwest	.1014478	.099295	1.02	0.307	-.0931668	.2960625
yorks	.0193049	.1093267	0.18	0.860	-.1949715	.2335814
wmids	.187365	.1092006	1.72	0.086	-.0266642	.4013941
emids	.1017023	.1094978	0.93	0.353	-.1129095	.3163141
anglia	-.0721503	.1390248	-0.52	0.604	-.3446339	.2003333
swest	.1621182	.1086589	1.49	0.136	-.0508493	.3750857
london	.1363692	.1033231	1.32	0.187	-.0661404	.3388788
scot	.1291943	.1097053	1.18	0.239	-.085824	.3442127
rural	-.060937	.0783605	-0.78	0.437	-.2145207	.0926468
suburb	-.0290625	.0594906	-0.49	0.625	-.145662	.087537
ethwheur	.4010516	.2037826	1.97	0.049	.001645	.8004582
housown	-.0172502	.1497231	-0.12	0.908	-.310702	.2762016
hou	.0267543	.0296583	0.90	0.367	-.0313749	.0848834
height	.01323	.0093611	1.41	0.158	-.0051175	.0315775
male	.323805	.0937387	3.45	0.001	.1400805	.5075295
age	.0255325	.0275037	0.93	0.353	-.0283737	.0794386

Table 5.3 continued

```
    age2 |  .0481237   .022286   2.16  0.031   .0044439   .0918034
 smother | -.061669   .0983432  -0.63  0.531  -.2544181   .1310801
 mothsmo | -.1445689  .1697951  -0.85  0.395  -.4773612   .1882235
 fathsmo |  .0336035  .0811452   0.41  0.679  -.1254382   .1926451
 bothsmo |  .0283181   .097456   0.29  0.771  -.1626922   .2193284
    alpa |  .0003959  .0243699   0.02  0.987  -.0473681   .0481599
    alma | -.0043713  .0286569  -0.15  0.879  -.0605379   .0517952
   _cons | -3.627174  1.260352  -2.88  0.004   -6.09742  -1.156929
---------|-----------------------------------------------------------
(omissis)
---------|-----------------------------------------------------------
   rho21 |  .4195476  .1712584   2.45  0.014   .0397571    .693417
---------|-----------------------------------------------------------
   rho31 |  .3384867  .1969604   1.72  0.086  -.0834113   .6574849
---------|-----------------------------------------------------------
   rho41 |  .1317494  .1838756   0.72  0.474   -.230044   .4615471
---------|-----------------------------------------------------------
   rho32 |  .3337173  .2106374   1.58  0.113  -.1170363   .6704645
---------|-----------------------------------------------------------
   rho42 |  .2732985  .1563618   1.75  0.080   -.050733   .5452713
---------|-----------------------------------------------------------
   rho43 |    .18097  .0378715   4.78  0.000   .1058473   .2540387
-------------------------------------------------------------------
Likelihood ratio test of rho21 = rho31 = rho41 = rho32 = rho42 =
rho43 = 0:
          chi2(6) = 29.9878  Prob > chi2 = 0.0000
```

Results are stored in m3 and the values of the log-likelihood and the number of parameters are saved as scalars and displayed:

```
estimates store m3
scalar logLmvp0=e(ll)
display "logL= " logLmvp0

logL= -6702.0152

scalar q0=e(k)
display "q= " q0

q= 179
```

Now estimate the multivariate probit model using a different set of exclusion restrictions:

```
mvprobit (death=sah nsmoker alqprud $xvar1)               ///
    (sah= nsmoker alqprud $xvar2)                         ///
    (nsmoker=$xvar2 $smiv)                                ///
    (alqprud=$xvar2 $driv), dr(50)

estimates store m4
scalar logLmvp2=e(ll)
display "logL= " logLmvp2
scalar q2=e(k)
display "q= " q2
```

Results are reported in Table 5.4. Calculate the likelihood ratio (LR) test as $LR = -2(\log L_{unrestr} - \log L_{restr})$ and display the information criteria calculated by estimates stats:

```
scalar testLR =2* (logLmvp0- logLmvp2)
display testLR

51.207981

scalar qLR= q0-q2
display "q= " qLR

q= 34

display chi2tail(qLR, testLR)

.02937049

estimates stats m3 m4
```

```
----------------------------------------------------------------------
  Model |   Obs  ll(null)    ll(model)     df      AIC        BIC
--------|-------------------------------------------------------------
    m3  |  3655         .    -6702.015    179  13762.03   14872.52
    m4  |  3655         .    -6727.619    145  13745.24   14644.8
----------------------------------------------------------------------
```

The model with exclusion restrictions, reported in Table 5.4, is favoured by the penalised likelihood criteria.

The z-tests reported in Table 5.4 show that the null of exogeneity (H_0: $\rho_{jk} = 0$) is rejected for all the lifestyle variables included in the model. We interpret this

Table 5.4 Multivariate probit model – with exclusion restrictions

```
--------------------------------------------------------------------
Multivariate probit (SML, #draws = 50)     Number of obs   =     3655
                                            Wald chi2(135)  = 2596.56
Log likelihood = -6727.6192                 Prob > chi2     =  0.0000
--------------------------------------------------------------------
     death |     Coef. Std. Err.      z  P>|z|   [95% Conf. Interval]
---------|----------------------------------------------------------
       sah | -1.048801  .2306954  -4.55  0.000  -1.500956  -.5966467
   nsmoker | -.6092642  .1940785  -3.14  0.002   -.989651  -.2288774
    alqprud | -.5402866  .2652184  -2.04  0.042  -1.060105   -.020468
       sc12 | -.0799067   .067134  -1.19  0.234   -.211487   .0516735
       sc45 | -.0803742   .063564  -1.26  0.206  -.2049572   .0442089
      lhqdg |  .0690006  .1167208   0.59  0.554   -.159768   .2977693
    lhqhndA |  -.067561  .1140233  -0.59  0.554  -.2910425   .1559205
    lhqnone |   .032463  .0956292   0.34  0.734  -.1549668   .2198928
     lhqoth | -.1352757  .1429558  -0.95  0.344  -.4154638   .1449125
       part |  .1402982   .096442   1.45  0.146  -.0487246    .329321
      unemp |  .1513976  .1410807   1.07  0.283  -.1251156   .4279107
       sick |  .1601284  .1974569   0.81  0.417  -.2268799   .5471368
       retd | -.0060198  .0910537  -0.07  0.947  -.1844818   .1724421
    keephse |  .1900613  .1052572   1.81  0.071  -.0162389   .3963616
    wkshft1 | -.2508464  .1233516  -2.03  0.042   -.492611  -.0090817
      rural | -.0849008  .0733635  -1.16  0.247  -.2286906    .058889
     suburb | -.0437849  .0573299  -0.76  0.445  -.1561495   .0685796
    ethwheur |  .3860987  .1970589   1.96  0.050  -.0001296   .7723271
     height |  .0108151  .0092213   1.17  0.241  -.0072583   .0288884
       male |  .3218315  .0823158   3.91  0.000   .1604956   .4831675
        age |  .0210809  .0249658   0.84  0.398  -.0278511    .070013
       age2 |  .0495004  .0207668   2.38  0.017   .0087982   .0902027
      _cons | -2.942098  1.033758  -2.85  0.004  -4.968226  -.9159698
---------|----------------------------------------------------------
sah        |
   nsmoker |  .2280292  .1722706   1.32  0.186   -.109615   .5656734
    alqprud | -.4601436  .2403573  -1.91  0.056  -.9312353   .0109481
       sc12 |  .1794563  .0613956   2.92  0.003   .0591232   .2997894
       sc45 | -.1588097  .0577325  -2.75  0.006  -.2719634  -.0456561
      lhqdg |  .1302982  .1076352   1.21  0.226   -.080663   .3412594
    lhqhndA |  .0446903  .1030174   0.43  0.664  -.1572201   .2466006
    lhqnone | -.1898973  .0853028  -2.23  0.026  -.3570877  -.0227068
     lhqoth | -.1028049  .1326014  -0.78  0.438  -.3626989   .1570891
      widow | -.2002126  .0756392  -2.65  0.008  -.3484626  -.0519625
    divorce | -.1074065  .1207147  -0.89  0.374   -.344003   .1291899
      seprd | -.0331659  .1790871  -0.19  0.853  -.3841701   .3178383
     single | -.0465762  .1050416  -0.44  0.657   -.252454   .1593016
       part |  .0062398  .0847814   0.07  0.941  -.1599288   .1724084
      unemp | -.2089962  .1356546  -1.54  0.123  -.4748743    .056882
```

Table 5.4 continued

```
     sick |  -1.567092    .1537515  -10.19   0.000    -1.86844   -1.265745
     retd |  -.1934811     .087528   -2.21   0.027   -.3650328   -.0219294
  keephse |  -.2592148    .0906308   -2.86   0.004    -.436848   -.0815817
  wkshft1 |  -.0432045    .1035438   -0.42   0.676   -.2461466    .1597376
    wales |  -.3010022    .1040993   -2.89   0.004   -.5050331   -.0969712
    north |  -.0641213    .1064013   -0.60   0.547    -.272664    .1444214
    nwest |  -.2117348    .0825238   -2.57   0.010   -.3734785   -.0499912
    yorks |  -.1299591    .0938928   -1.38   0.166   -.3139856    .0540675
    wmids |  -.1519413    .0955343   -1.59   0.112   -.3391852    .0353026
    emids |  -.0689948    .0995894   -0.69   0.488   -.2641864    .1261968
   anglia |  -.1623524    .1231503   -1.32   0.187   -.4037226    .0790178
    swest |  -.2100924     .093284   -2.25   0.024   -.3929257   -.0272591
   london |  -.0886984    .0945442   -0.94   0.348   -.2740017    .0966048
     scot |  -.2538354    .0899765   -2.82   0.005   -.4301861   -.0774847
    rural |   .1487211    .0684385    2.17   0.030     .014584    .2828582
   suburb |    .087598    .0534646    1.64   0.101   -.0171908    .1923867
 ethwheur |   .4923654    .1581663    3.11   0.002    .1823652    .8023655
  housown |  -.1845441    .1302443   -1.42   0.157   -.4398183    .0707301
      hou |  -.0039876     .024668   -0.16   0.872    -.052336    .0443607
   height |  -.0024506    .0086856   -0.28   0.778   -.0194741     .014573
     male |  -.0240377    .0770057   -0.31   0.755    -.174966    .1268907
      age |  -.0538851    .0206079   -2.61   0.009   -.0942759   -.0134943
     age2 |   .0450618    .0168059    2.68   0.007    .0121228    .0780009
    _cons |   2.552172    .8856496    2.88   0.004    .8163305    4.288013
---------|------------------------------------------------------------------
nsmoker  |
     sc12 |   .1366833    .0601404    2.27   0.023    .0188103    .2545564
     sc45 |  -.0868663    .0587902   -1.48   0.140    -.202093    .0283604
    lhqdg |   .1105428    .1079553    1.02   0.306   -.1010456    .3221313
  lhqhndA |  -.0398684    .1021549   -0.39   0.696   -.2400883    .1603514
  lhqnone |  -.2292742    .0844988   -2.71   0.007   -.3948887   -.0636596
   lhqoth |  -.3675581    .1280615   -2.87   0.004   -.6185539   -.1165623
    widow |  -.2153161    .0847606   -2.54   0.011   -.3814438   -.0491884
  divorce |  -.3740346    .1203129   -3.11   0.002   -.6098435   -.1382257
    seprd |  -.2450616    .1757032   -1.39   0.163   -.5894336    .0993103
   single |  -.1360022     .111454   -1.22   0.222   -.3544481    .0824437
     part |  -.0954671    .0826254   -1.16   0.248     -.25741    .0664758
    unemp |  -.3733972     .132239   -2.82   0.005   -.6325808   -.1142136
     sick |  -.2517569    .1308805   -1.92   0.054    -.508278    .0047642
     retd |  -.2579629    .0895942   -2.88   0.004   -.4335642   -.0823616
  keephse |  -.1050377    .0912189   -1.15   0.250   -.2838234    .0737479
  wkshft1 |  -.1798741    .0995079   -1.81   0.071    -.374906    .0151577
    wales |   -.178826    .1108768   -1.61   0.107   -.3961406    .0384886
    north |  -.3160399    .1047872   -3.02   0.003    -.521419   -.1106607
```

Table 5.4 continued

```
  nwest |  -.3130866   .0845132    -3.70   0.000   -.4787294   -.1474437
  yorks |  -.2346819   .0958231    -2.45   0.014   -.4224916   -.0468721
  wmids |  -.2584206   .0989932    -2.61   0.009   -.4524437   -.0643974
  emids |  -.0900868   .1031871    -0.87   0.383   -.2923299    .1121562
 anglia |  -.0905583   .1289481    -0.70   0.483   -.3432918    .1621753
  swest |  -.0719345   .0989572    -0.73   0.467    -.265887    .1220179
 london |  -.1708737   .0970994    -1.76   0.078    -.361185    .0194376
   scot |  -.3457907   .0926104    -3.73   0.000   -.5273038   -.1642776
  rural |   .102918    .0695223     1.48   0.139   -.0333432    .2391791
 suburb |   .0175555   .0545181     0.32   0.747    -.089298    .124409
ethwheur |  .0199722   .1656433     0.12   0.904   -.3046826    .3446271
housown |  -.125296    .1375935    -0.91   0.362   -.3949743    .1443824
    hou |   .0564712   .0251854     2.24   0.025    .0071087    .1058337
 height |   .0090446   .0088356     1.02   0.306    -.008273    .0263621
   male |  -.2327984   .0724164    -3.21   0.001   -.3747321   -.0908648
    age |  -.0467656   .0225389    -2.07   0.038   -.0909411   -.0025902
   age2 |   .0599429   .0190538     3.15   0.002    .0225981    .0972877
smother |  -.6912594   .0511818   -13.51   0.000   -.7915738   -.5909449
mothsmo |  -.4812859   .1461884    -3.29   0.001   -.7678098   -.1947619
fathsmo |  -.2412699   .0768893    -3.14   0.002   -.3919701   -.0905697
bothsmo |  -.3484599   .0858407    -4.06   0.000   -.5167047   -.1802152
  _cons |  1.689552    .9147875     1.85   0.065   -.1033987   3.482503
--------|-------------------------------------------------------------
alqprud |
   sc12 |  -.2367453   .075169     -3.15   0.002   -.3840738   -.0894168
   sc45 |  -.1946469   .0765796    -2.54   0.011   -.3447402   -.0445535
  lhqdg |   .0058167   .1264058     0.05   0.963   -.2419341    .2535675
lhqhndA |  -.1140583   .1223894    -0.93   0.351   -.3539371    .1258205
lhqnone |  -.005493    .1047576    -0.05   0.958   -.2108141    .1998282
 lhqoth |  -.0721799   .1556397    -0.46   0.643   -.3772281    .2328683
  widow |   .0242835   .1156598     0.21   0.834   -.2024055    .2509725
 divorce |  .1422075   .1575356     0.90   0.367   -.1665567    .4509716
  seprd |  -.0689465   .2103849    -0.33   0.743   -.4812933    .3434004
 single |  -.0102039   .1356942    -0.08   0.940   -.2761597    .2557519
   part |   .242529    .1130262     2.15   0.032    .0210018    .4640563
  unemp |  -.2056043   .1453482    -1.41   0.157   -.4904815    .0792729
   sick |   .4091209   .173581      2.36   0.018    .0689084    .7493333
   retd |   .2328533   .1124441     2.07   0.038    .012467     .4532397
keephse |   .153532    .1283524     1.20   0.232   -.0980341    .4050981
wkshft1 |  -.0890784   .1148833    -0.78   0.438   -.3142455    .1360887
  wales |  -.1876087   .1437141    -1.31   0.192   -.4692831    .0940657
  north |  -.548535    .1318742    -4.16   0.000   -.8070036   -.2900664
  nwest |  -.2435645   .1103392    -2.21   0.027   -.4598254   -.0273036
  yorks |  -.364351    .1198032    -3.04   0.002   -.5991609   -.1295412
```

Table 5.4 continued

```
   wmids | -.1343016    .1287426   -1.04   0.297   -.3866325    .1180293
   emids | -.2698415    .1248925   -2.16   0.031   -.5146263   -.0250566
  anglia | -.0947033    .1676922   -0.56   0.572   -.4233739    .2339674
   swest | -.3061339    .1207188   -2.54   0.011   -.5427383   -.0695294
  london | -.2195679    .1220615   -1.80   0.072   -.4588041    .0196683
    scot | -.3168476    .1212047   -2.61   0.009   -.5544045   -.0792907
   rural |  .1957657    .0878253    2.23   0.026    .0236312    .3679001
  suburb |  .1029285    .0683155    1.51   0.132   -.0309675    .2368245
ethwheur | -.6508731    .2925393   -2.22   0.026    -1.22424   -.0775066
 housown |  .2077856    .1609547    1.29   0.197   -.1076798    .5232509
     hou |  .0896561    .0311205    2.88   0.004     .028661    .1506513
  height | -.0016927    .0110231   -0.15   0.878   -.0232976    .0199121
    male | -.6576322    .0920044   -7.15   0.000   -.8379576   -.4773068
     age |  .0292894    .0269235    1.09   0.277   -.0234796    .0820584
    age2 | -.0099189    .0228797   -0.43   0.665   -.0547622    .0349244
    alpa | -.1648389    .0268469   -6.14   0.000   -.2174578     -.11222
    alma | -.1175973    .0296386   -3.97   0.000    -.175688   -.0595067
   _cons |  1.256597    1.123751    1.12   0.263   -.9459158    3.459109
---------|------------------------------------------------------------------
/atrho21 |  .5022248    .1758401    2.86   0.004    .1575844    .8468651
---------|------------------------------------------------------------------
/atrho31 |  .2290019    .1200994    1.91   0.057   -.0063885    .4643924
---------|------------------------------------------------------------------
/atrho41 |  .2583195    .1504741    1.72   0.086   -.0366042    .5532432
---------|------------------------------------------------------------------
/atrho32 |   .020785    .1045378    0.20   0.842   -.1841054    .2256753
---------|------------------------------------------------------------------
/atrho42 |  .2466392    .1407373    1.75   0.080   -.0292008    .5224791
---------|------------------------------------------------------------------
/atrho43 |   .181739    .0389084    4.67   0.000     .10548     .257998
---------|------------------------------------------------------------------
   rho21 |   .463865    .1380045    3.36   0.001    .1562928    .6894282
---------|------------------------------------------------------------------
   rho31 |  .2250811     .114015    1.97   0.048   -.0063885    .4336574
---------|------------------------------------------------------------------
   rho41 |   .252723    .1408634    1.79   0.073   -.0365879     .502947
---------|------------------------------------------------------------------
   rho32 |   .020782    .1044927    0.20   0.842   -.1820531    .2219206
---------|------------------------------------------------------------------
   rho42 |  .2417568    .1325117    1.82   0.068   -.0291925    .4796111
---------|------------------------------------------------------------------
   rho43 |  .1797642     .037651    4.77   0.000    .1050906    .2524221
----------------------------------------------------------------------------
Likelihood ratio test of rho21 = rho31 = rho41 = rho32 = rho42 =
rho43 = 0:
        chi2(6) = 35.8144  Prob > chi2 = 0.0000
```

evidence to suggest that unobservable factors that influence the probability of being a non-smoker and drinking prudently also influence the probability of dying. The correlation between the mortality equations and the error terms of the nsmoker and alqprud equations is positive, meaning that unobserved factors that increase the probability of being a non-smoker and drinking prudently, also increase the mortality risk. This suggests that assuming lifestyles are exogenous would lead to downward biased estimates of the effects of these behaviours. Accounting for endogeneity of the regressors allows us to capture a statistically significant effect of unobserved factors both on the mortality risk and the probability of some of the health-related behaviours.

Now calculate a LR-test that replicates the one computed by mvprobit:

```
scalar nrho= e(nrho)
quietly probit death sah nsmoker alqprud $xvar1
scalar logL1=e(ll)
quietly probit sah nsmoker alqprud $xvar2
scalar logL2=e(ll)
quietly probit nsmoker $xvar2 $smiv
scalar logL3=e(ll)
quietly probit alqprud $xvar2 $driv
scalar logL4=e(ll)

scalar logL_restr=logL1+logL2+logL3+logL4
display logL_restr
scalar testLR =2*(logLmvp2 - logL_restr)
display testLR
display chi2tail(nrho, testLR)
```

The LR test compares the log-likelihood of the multivariate probit model to the sum of the log-likelihoods of the marginal probit models, estimated separately. These should be equal in the case of independent errors across the marginal distributions, ergo the LR test compares an unrestricted model to a restricted one, considering the separate probit estimates as a multivariate probit in which all correlations are restricted to zero. In this case, the null is rejected, which confirms the previous findings on endogeneity.

We calculate the average partial effects (APE) of covariates on the probability of death using the finite difference method as in Wooldridge (2002b). Partial effects are computed for each individual as the change in the probability that death equals 1 when a covariate changes, then averaged across individuals, so that they refer to the entire population. The finite difference methods allow us to calculate APEs when sets of dummy variables are included in the model. The command margins could be used to calculate APEs: however, this is not compatible with mvprobit because it does not use a standard predict programme. As an alternative, we show how to calculate APEs using the commands preserve and restore, which are of help when the programmer wants to temporarily change the data in use. We report, as an example, the code used to calculate partial effects of sc12 and sc45:

```
preserve
      quietly{
            replace sc12=0
            replace sc45=0
            mvppred xb_ref
            drop xb_ref2 xb_ref3 xb_ref4
            replace sc12=1
            replace sc45=0
            mvppred xb_sc12
            drop xb_sc122 xb_sc123 xb_sc124
            replace sc12=0
            replace sc45=1
            mvppred xb_sc45
            drop xb_sc452 xb_sc453 xb_sc454

      generate PE_sc12=normal(xb_sc121)-normal(xb_ref1)
      generate PE_sc45=normal(xb_sc451)-normal(xb_ref1)
      }
      summarize PE_sc12 PE_sc45
restore
```

Note that the post-estimation command mvppred is used to calculate the linear index for the mortality equation (option xb is the default). Linear predictions for the other equations are dropped.

The following code calculates the incremental effect of an extra year of age considering that a quadratic term is included in the model:

```
preserve
      quietly{
            mvppred xb_ref
            drop xb_ref2 xb_ref3 xb_ref4
            replace age=age+1
            replace age2=(age^2)/100
            mvppred xb_age
            drop xb_age2 xb_age3 xb_age4
            generate PE_age=normal(xb_age1)-normal(xb_ref1)
      }
      summarize PE_age
restore
```

Table 5.5 Average partial effects from alternative models for mortality

	Probit model without sah and lifestyle variables		Probit model with sah and lifestyle variables		Multivariate Probit model	
	APE	s.d.	APE	s.d.	APE	s.d.
sah			-0.081	0.037	-0.281	0.105
nsmoker			-0.090	0.043	-0.150	0.071
alqprud			-0.034	0.016	-0.134	0.064
sc12	-0.045	0.021	-0.034	0.017	-0.019	0.010
sc45	0.006	0.003	-0.003	0.002	-0.019	0.010
lhqdg	0.001	0.000	0.008	0.004	0.017	0.009
lhqhndA	-0.020	0.010	-0.019	0.010	-0.016	0.008
lhqnone	0.040	0.018	0.028	0.014	0.008	0.004
lhqoth	-0.005	0.002	-0.018	0.009	-0.032	0.017
part	0.033	0.015	0.030	0.015	0.034	0.017
unemp	0.101	0.043	0.075	0.035	0.036	0.019
sick	0.225	0.085	0.163	0.071	0.039	0.020
retd	0.022	0.010	0.012	0.006	-0.001	0.001
keephse	0.078	0.034	0.063	0.030	0.046	0.024
wkshft1	-0.045	0.023	-0.053	0.029	-0.057	0.032
rural	-0.054	0.025	-0.042	0.021	-0.020	0.011
suburb	-0.026	0.012	-0.022	0.011	-0.011	0.005
ethwheur	0.078	0.040	0.083	0.045	0.088	0.049
height	0.001	0.001	0.002	0.001	0.003	0.001
male	0.111	0.049	0.100	0.048	0.078	0.039
age	0.020	0.010	0.020	0.011	0.019	0.011

We compare the APEs on mortality risk from the recursive multivariate probit model with those from two univariate probit models, one that includes health and lifestyles and another one that excludes them, in order to assess the advantages of estimating a model that controls for endogeneity. The way we calculate the partial effects is different from the post-estimation command dprobit (as of Stata 11 this is no longer an official part of Stata), since the latter calculates the partial effects at specific regressor values. Partial effects after probit use predict to obtain the linear index (option xb needs to be specified in this case).

The results are summarised in Table 5.5, which reports the average of the partial effects (APE) and standard deviations from summarize. Notice that standard deviation reflects heterogeneity across the point estimates for each individual in the sample (unlike the standard error which reflects sampling variation around a particular point estimate).

Table 5.5 shows that including lifestyles and health even under the restrictive assumption of exogeneity has a strong impact on the APE of the socioeconomic variables. Controlling for endogeneity in the multivariate probit model we find that lifestyles have a high impact on the risk of mortality relative to socioeconomic characteristics. The risk of mortality for a non-smoker is about 15 per cent lower than for a current smoker.

5.5 OVERVIEW

In this case study, we investigated the extent to which differences in the risk of mortality depend on lifestyle and individual socioeconomic characteristics, focusing mainly on social class and education differences in the sample.

We relate the risk of mortality to a set of observable and unobservable factors. Observable factors influencing mortality are perceived health, socioeconomic and demographic characteristics, ethnicity, type of area and individual health-related behaviours. Individuals' choices about their lifestyle may induce variations in health status and affect mortality. We assume that the relationship between the socioeconomic environment and mortality risk is mediated by lifestyles. In order to assess the impact of lifestyles, we estimate probit models and compare models without lifestyles and models which include them.

The main econometric issue arising here is unobservable individual hetero-geneity and endogeneity of the discrete explanatory variables, which is taken into account by estimating a multivariate probit model for a recursive system of equations for deaths, health and lifestyles. We find that lifestyles have a high impact on the risk of mortality relative to socioeconomic characteristics.

Part III
Duration data

6 Smoking and mortality

SYNOPSIS

This chapter uses the same sub-sample of the HALS used in Chapter 5 and a more recent release of the deaths data (2005) for a duration analysis of smoking behaviour and mortality rates. It shows how to build survival time indicators and how to estimate failure, survivor, hazard and cumulative hazard functions using non-parametric procedures. It goes on to estimate the hazard of starting and quitting smoking and the mortality hazard using continuous time parametric duration models with right-censoring and left-truncation.

6.1 INTRODUCTION

This chapter is about the use of survival analysis in health economics. The aim is to give the reader an insight into the modelling of continuous-time duration data, the use of non-parametric and parametric procedures and estimation methods that are commonly employed to analyse survival times. We present an application of these techniques to smoking initiation and cessation and the hazard of mortality, using data from the Health and Lifestyle Survey (HALS), that draws on Forster and Jones (2001) and Balia and Jones (2011). The analysis focuses on the socioeconomic gradient in smoking duration and survival probability and the impact of smoking behaviour on survival probability.

6.2 BASIC CONCEPTS OF DURATION ANALYSIS

In health economics, as in other fields of economics, many outcomes of interest indicate the time elapsed before an event occurs. Therefore these variables are in the form of a duration. Time to death, time to starting using a drug and time to quitting are typical examples. Survival time data give additional information relative to binary variables describing the occurrence of an event (death) or the choice of participation (starting or quitting).

In this chapter we focus on continuous time data assuming that the transition event may occur at any instant in time, while Chapter 7 covers discrete time models. In particular, we define the length of a spell for an individual in the sample as the realisation of a continuous random variable, T, that has the following CDF:

$$F(t) = P(T \leq t)$$

The CDF is known as the *failure function*, it is the complement of the *survivor function*, which indicates the probability of surviving up a specific point in time t:

$$S(t) = 1 - F(t) = P(T > t) \quad \text{where } 0 \leq S(t) \leq 1$$

The probability of survival is equal to 1 at entry in the state of interest. The density function, which is the slope of the failure function, indicates the concentration of failure times along the time axis, and is expressed by:

$$f(t) = \frac{\partial F(t)}{\partial t} = -\frac{\partial S(t)}{\partial t}$$

The hazard function is the instantaneous rate of failing per unit of time, conditional on individual survival up to that instant and can be expressed as:

$$h(t) = \lim_{\Delta t \to 0} \frac{F(t + \Delta t) - F(t)}{\Delta t} \cdot \frac{1}{1 - F(t)} = \frac{f(t)}{1 - F(t)} = \frac{f(t)}{S(t)}$$

Integrating the hazard rate we obtain the *cumulative hazard function*, which sums up the hazard at each instant in time:

$$H(t) = \int_0^t h(u) \, du$$

Survival analysis constructs variables indicating the length of time a person stays in the state of interest. Usually respondents in population samples are asked about the date of entry and exit from the state, as in the case of HALS.

Individuals are assumed to enter the state at time 0 and leave it at some time t, when the failure occurs. If entry and failure are observed, it will be possible to measure a complete spell, while, if only entry is observed and exit will eventually occur at some time in the future, the spell will be incomplete. Such incomplete durations are known as *right-censored* spells, where censoring is at the time of observation, and we only know that the complete duration will be greater than the observed time, $T > t$. When the date of entry is not known we cannot measure the exact length of the spell and the survival time is said to be *left-censored*.

Depending on the state of interest, only those individuals who have survived for a minimum amount of time in the state are included in the sample or, putting the problem another way, individuals who fail before the time of observation will not be included in the observed sample. Hence, the remaining observed survival times are said to be *left-truncated* (to describe left-truncation Stata refers to the concept of *delayed entry*). In the analysis we use, at most, one completed spell per individual. *Right-truncation* can be forced by the researcher who wants to restrict the population sample to those individuals who failed by the observation time, thus eliminating all longer survival times. More complete readings on survival analysis are available in Wooldridge (2002b) and Cameron and Trivedi (2005).

6.3 THE HALS DATA

The HALS data describe the British population as in 1984 and provide information about individual mortality by tracking each respondent on the NHS registers on a regular basis. The deaths data used here were released in June 2005. This allows us to investigate survival up to April 2005. More recent deaths data are available from the UK Data Archive.

As shown in Chapter 5, the status of the respondent at the latest update of the survey can be explored in Stata generating a one-way table of frequencies using the command `tabulate flagcode`. This shows that up to April 2005, 97.8 per cent of the original sample had been flagged and 27 per cent of the respondents had died.

```
current flagging |
status April 05 |      Freq.    Percent       Cum.
-----------------|-------------------------------------
       on file |      6,248      69.40      69.40
not nhs regist. |         85       0.94      70.34
       deceased |      2,431      27.00      97.35
rep.dead not id |          1       0.01      97.36
embarked -abroad |        42       0.47      97.82
no flag yet rec. |       196       2.18     100.00
-----------------|-------------------------------------
          Total |      9,003     100.00
```

For the purpose of our analysis, the target sample has been reduced according to item non-response in the variables of interest. Furthermore, since only 1 per cent of the sample died before age 40 we restrict the analysis to individuals older than 40 years old. To describe the flagging status in the target sample, the reader can execute again the command `tabulate flagcode`.

Now define a global list of variables:

```
global xvars "birthmth birthday birthyr seenmth seenday seenyr
    age death deathage agestrt exfag exfagan regfag sc12 sc3
    sc45 lhqdg lhqoth lhqnone lhqO lhqA lhqhnd rural married
    widow sepdiv single part unemp sick retd keephse wkshft1
    housown hou suburb mothsmo fathsmo bothsmo smother male"
```

Then describe these variables:

```
describe $xvars
```

variable name	storage type	display format	value label	variable label
birthmth	byte	%8.0g		month of birth
birthday	byte	%8.0g		birth day of month
birthyr	byte	%8.0g		year of birth
seenmth	byte	%8.0g		SEENMTH
seenday	byte	%8.0g		SEENDAY
seenyr	byte	%8.0g		SEENYR
age	float	%9.0g		age at HALS1
death	float	%9.0g		
deathage	double	%10.0g		age at death
agestrt	float	%9.0g		age at starting smoking
exfag	byte	%9.0g		if ex-smoker
exfagan	byte	%4.0g		how long ago stopped smoking
regfag	byte	%9.0g		1 if smokes regularly at least one fag a day
sc12	float	%9.0g		1 if professional/student or managerial/intermediate
sc3	float	%9.0g		1 if skilled or armed service
sc45	float	%9.0g		1 if partly skilled, unskilled, unclass. or never occupied
lhqdg	byte	%9.0g		1 if University degree
lhqoth	byte	%9.0g		1 if other vocational/ professional qualifications
lhqnone	byte	%9.0g		1 if no qualification
lhqO	byte	%9.0g		1 if O level/CSE
lhqA	byte	%9.0g		
lhqhnd	byte	%9.0g		
rural	byte	%8.0g		1 if lives in the countryside
married	byte	%8.0g		1 if married
widow	byte	%8.0g		1 if widow
sepdiv	float	%9.0g		1 if separated or divorced

single	byte	%8.0g	1 if single
part	byte	%8.0g	1 if part time worker
unemp	byte	%9.0g	1 if the individual unemployed
sick	byte	%9.0g	1 if absent from work due to sickness
retd	byte	%8.0g	1 if retired
keephse	byte	%8.0g	1 if housekeeper
wkshft1	float	%9.0g	1 if shift worker
housown	byte	%9.0g	1 if own or rent house
hou	byte	%9.0g	number of other people in the house
suburb	byte	%8.0g	1 if lives in the suburbs of the city
mothsmo	float	%9.0g	1 if only mother smoked
fathsmo	float	%9.0g	1 if only father smoked
bothsmo	float	%9.0g	1 if both parents smoked
smother	byte	%4.0g	1 if anyone else in house smoked
male	byte	%9.0g	1 if male

6.4 DURATION DATA IN HALS

The HALS questionnaire is designed to provide comprehensive information about risky behaviours. In particular, the survey data contain retrospective information on smoking. The age at the onset of smoking is known as well as whether they are regular smokers or stopped completely, and, if so, how long ago. The self-reported variables agestrt, exfag, exfagan, regfag are used to derive two time variables which can be used to study the hazard of starting smoking and the hazard of quitting smoking. This follows Forster and Jones (2001) who use the HALS data to investigate the role of tobacco taxes in starting and quitting smoking.

Smoking initiation

Define starting as the number of years elapsed before someone starts smoking. First, adjust the variable agestrt to measure the true age in years at starting:

```
generate agestart = .
replace agestart = agestrt*10
```

Then eliminate individuals who claimed to be current smokers but whose age at starting was zero and generate the binary indicator start that indicates whether an individual started smoking at some point in their life prior to HALS:

```
drop if regfag==1 & agestart==0
generate start=.
```

```
replace start = 1 if agestart>0
replace start = 0 if start==.
label variable start "eversmoker"
```

The time variable `starting` measures a complete duration if an individual had started smoking and an incomplete, or censored, duration if they had not:

```
generate starting=agestart if start==1
replace starting =age if start==0
label variable starting "number of years non-smoking"
```

For those who started smoking, `starting` is equal to the age at starting (`agestart`), and it is censored at the age at the time of the interview for those who had not started by then.

Smoking cessation

The variable `exfagan` provides information about how long ago an ex-smoker stopped smoking. This can be used to build a time variable indicating the number of years a person smoked. In order to derive the survival time variable for smoking we also need to exploit the information available about the onset of smoking. First, generate the binary indicator `quit` that takes value 1 if a smoker had stopped smoking completely and zero otherwise:

```
generate quit=.
replace quit=1 if exfag==1&exfagan<98
replace quit=0 if regfag==1
```

The definition of the dummy variable `quit` requires consistent information from the variables `regfag`, `exfag` and `exfagan`, in particular only values of `exfagan` smaller than 98 can be used, because higher values identify a missing record.

Generate each individual's date of interview using the `mdy(m,d,y)` date function, which returns the elapsed date corresponding to the numeric arguments of month, day, and year, and use the command `format`, which specifies that the variable will be displayed in default numeric elapsed date format:

```
generate seenmdy=mdy(seenmth,seenday,seenyr+1900)
format seenmdy %d
```

Then use the variables `birthmth`, `birthday`, `birthyr` to generate the exact date of birth.

```
generate birthmdy = mdy(birthmth,birthday,birthyr+1800) if ///
    birthyr>=87
format birthmdy %d
```

```
replace birthmdy =mdy(birthmth,birthday,birthyr+1900) if ///
    birthyr<87
format birthmdy %d
```

Cross-checking with the variable age in the original sample shows that there cannot be individuals born before 1887 or after 1986. For this reason, we use the if qualifier, which allows us to recover the true year of birth. The new variable birthmdy can be listed with the command list, which is used here to display the first ten observations in the data:

```
list birthmdy in 1/10

-----|-----------|-
     |  birthmdy |
-----|-----------|-
  1. | 18jun1930 |
  2. | 29mar1932 |
  3. | 25aug1918 |
  4. | 03mar1904 |
  5. | 07may1909 |
-----|-----------|-
  6. | 11oct1937 |
  7. | 02jul1922 |
  8. | 28mar1932 |
  9. | 06feb1913 |
 10. | 31jul1922 |
-----|-----------|-
```

Now define the date of the onset of smoking:

```
summarize agestart if start==1,d
generate startmdy = birthmdy+(agestart*365.25) if start==1
replace startmdy = birthmdy+(17*365.25) if start==0
format startmdy %d
```

For those who did not start smoking before the survey, the date of starting is rescaled using the median age at starting, 17 years old, found by summarising agestart, which is the age at which individuals are potentially at risk of starting. Recover the year of starting using the function year() and, for the purpose of including the variable as a control variable in the econometric model, rescale it relative to the earliest year, 1904, and take the logarithm:

```
generate strtyear=year(startmdy)
summarize strtyear
generate year=strtyear-1904
generate lnyear=ln(year)
```

Now generate the time variable `sm_years` according to the smoking status of the respondent:

```
generate sm_years=(seenmdy-startmdy)/365.25 if quit==0
replace sm_years=(seenmdy-startmdy-(exfagan*365.25))/365.25 ///
    if quit==1
generate sm_years2=round(sm_years,1)
drop sm_years
rename sm_years2 sm_years
```

For current smokers, i.e. `quit==0`, smoking duration is censored at the time of the interview; for quitters, i.e. `quit==1`, the true duration is recovered using `exfagan`.

Lifespan

The HALS data give us the scope to investigate the hazard of death. A complete duration is observed for those who died before the follow-up period, while an incomplete duration is observed for individuals who are still alive in April 2005. First generate the age at censoring and use that variable to create the time variable `lifespan`:

```
gen ageATcens=( mdy(4,1,2005) - birthmdy)/365.25 if death==0
generate lifespan = .
replace lifespan = deathage if death==1
replace lifespan = ageATcens if death==0
label var lifespan "Survival time: censoring at April 2005"
```

The variable `lifespan` is simply equal to the age at death, `deathage`, for those who died, and to the age at censoring, `ageATcens`, for those who are still alive. Our time variable `lifespan` assumes that the measure of duration begins at birth and measures the full lifespan. As an alternative one could assume that individuals enter the initial state only when they participate in the survey process, so that the entry date would be the seen date at HALS. The advantage of defining lifespan in the way that we do is that we are able to measure length of survival from birth, conditional on survival up to the time of the survey, in which case the distribution of the survival time is said to be *left-truncated*.

Data cleaning

Having created the relevant time variables for the analysis, we test the data for consistency and drop those individuals who report negative or nil value for `sm_years`. We also drop those who are ex-smokers but either do not have a record for `exfagan` or do not report their age of starting smoking:

```
list serno sm_years regfag exfag exfagan birthmdy        ///
   agestart start startmdy
drop if sm_years<=0
drop if exfag==1&exfagan==.
drop if exfag==1 & agestart==0
```

6.5 DESCRIPTIVE STATISTICS

Our sample consists of 4,646 observations; 43 per cent of the respondents had died by April 2005 and the mean `lifespan` is 74 years. Those who started smoking at some point in their life account for the 62 per cent of the sample among whom about 50 per cent had stopped smoking at the time of HALS. On average, smokers (current and ex-smokers) in the sample smoked for 32 years. For some variables, we need to restrict the sample according to the values of `death` to calculate sample means:

```
summarize age if death==0
```

Variable	Obs	Mean	Std. Dev.	Min	Max
age	2659	51.98514	8.669153	40	90.6

```
summarize deathage if death==1,d
```

```
                     age at death
```

	Percentiles	Smallest		
1%	52	41.5		
5%	58.8	43.9		
10%	62.3	44.4	Obs	1987
25%	69.6	45.4	Sum of Wgt.	1987
50%	77.4		Mean	76.55702
		Largest	Std. Dev.	10.22046
75%	84.1	100.5		
90%	89.2	100.6	Variance	104.4577
95%	92	101.2	Skewness	-.2947964
99%	97.1	101.6	Kurtosis	2.759138

The mean age is about 52 and half of the respondents died before age 77. The mean age at death is around 76.

6.6 DURATION MODELS

Smoking initiation

We start investigating the onset of smoking using the binary outcome `start` and the duration variable `starting`:

```
tabulate start
```

eversmoker	Freq.	Percent	Cum.
0	1,745	37.56	37.56
1	2,901	62.44	100.00
Total	4,646	100.00	

```
summarize starting, d
```

number of years non-smoking

	Percentiles	Smallest		
1%	8	4		
5%	12	4		
10%	14	5	Obs	4646
25%	16	5	Sum of Wgt.	4646
50%	21		Mean	33.18405
		Largest	Std. Dev.	21.54336
75%	50.6	92.7		
90%	67.1	93.9	Variance	464.1165
95%	74.2	94.9	Skewness	.7810813
99%	83.1	96.8	Kurtosis	2.243695

In our sample, 2,901 individuals started smoking and, on average, the length of time elapsed before smoking smoking is about 33 years, with half of the sample surviving for at least 21 years.

Stata has a built-in command that allows us to declare that a variable contains survival time data. Use `stset` to check the consistency of the time data and ensure that they make sense:

```
stset starting, failure(start) /*id(serno)*/
```

The command `stset` requires us to specify options that help identify the duration of interest. We specify `failure(start)` because the duration `starting` is complete for those who start smoking or, in other words, the onset of smoking represents the failure event. The option id(serno) can be specified if there are repeated observations for each individual, as there would be with time varying covariates. In our case, this option does not affect stset because we only have one record per individual. Stata provides the following output:

```
    failure event:  start != 0 & start < .
obs. time interval:  (0, starting]
 exit on or before:  failure
----------------------------------------------------------------
    4646  total obs.
       0  exclusions
----------------------------------------------------------------
    4646  obs. remaining, representing
    2901  failures in single record/single failure data
  154173.1  total analysis time at risk, at risk from t =        0
                              earliest observed entry t =        0
                                last observed exit t =    96.8
```

The full sample size is used because no exclusion has been specified using the if qualifier.

Explore the data by summarising individual survival time:

```
stsum

        failure _d: start
  analysis time _t: starting

        |                    incidence    no. of  |----Survival time ----|
        | time at risk          rate    subjects    25%    50%    75%
--------|-------------------------------------------------------------
  total |    154173.1     .0188165        4646     16     21      .
```

This shows total time at risk and the incidence rate calculated as the ratio between the number of failures and total time at risk (2901/154173.1).

```
stdescribe

        failure _d: start
  analysis time _t: starting

                       |-------------- per subject --------------|
Category                  total     mean     min    median     max
----------------------------------------------------------------
no. of subjects           4646
no. of records            4646        1       1         1        1
```

```
(first) entry time                          0        0          0         0
(final) exit time            33.18405                4         21      96.8

subjects with gap        0
time on gap if gap       0
time at risk       154173.1   33.18405      4         21      96.8

failures               2901   .6244081      0    1    1
```

This shows that subjects enter the state at time 0 (i.e. there is no left-censoring) and that data contains a record for each subject at risk. Mean, median, minimum and maximum values of time at risk are reported.

The command sts graph produces graphs of the estimated failure, survivor, hazard and cumulative hazard functions obtained with non-parametric procedures. The functions $f(t)$, $S(t)$ and $h(t)$ are estimated using the Kaplan–Meier (or product-limit) estimator. The observation period is divided in k survival times $t_1 < t_2 < \ldots < t_j < \ldots t_k$ such that the beginning of each survival time corresponds to the previous failure. If there is no censoring, the empirical survivor function is:

$$\hat{S}(t) = \prod_{j=1}^{k} \frac{n_j - d_j}{n_j}$$

where n_j is the number of persons at risk of making a transition and d_j is the number of persons for which exit is observed. Therefore, the estimated survivor function is the product for each time j of the ratio between those who survive and the total number of persons at risk; it has the shape of a step function with origin in $t = 0$ and at each t_j the height is equal to $S(t_j)$. From the estimated survivor function, one can derive the estimated failure function and the integrated hazard function.

The graph for sts graph produces a smooth hazard function (usually kernel smoothers are used) and the option na allows to graph the estimated Nelson–Aalen cumulative hazard function that behaves better than the Kaplan–Meier estimator in small samples:

$$\hat{H}(t) = \sum_{j=1}^{k} \frac{d_j}{n_j}$$

Use the following commands:

```
sts graph, title("Kaplan-Meier Survival")                        ///
      saving(KMsurv_start, replace)
sts graph, hazard title("Kaplan-Meier Hazard")                   ///
      saving(KMhaz_start, replace)
```

```
sts graph, na title("Nelson-Aalen cumulative Hazard")        ///
    saving(NAcumhaz_start, replace)
graph combine "KMsurv_start" "KMhaz_start"                   ///
    "NAcumhaz_start", iscale(0.6) saving(startingNP, replace)
```

Graphs can be modified by starting the Graph Editor. In this case we have selected the *y*-axis in each graph and set the label angle as horizontal.

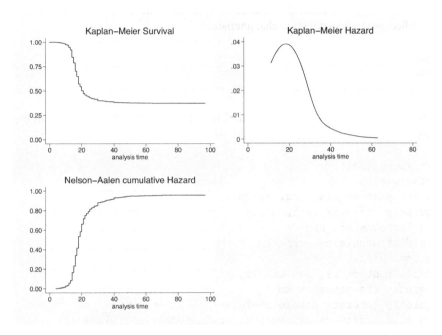

Figure 6.1 Non-parametric functions for smoking initiation.

Figure 6.1 shows the shape of the survivor function with survival diminishing faster between 15 and 20 years and then less than proportionally. The hazard of starting smoking increases up to age 20 and than falls close to 0 for durations longer than 35 years.

The estimation of a parametric model for the onset of smoking is informed by tests for the distribution that best represents the duration variable `starting`. We use both the cumulative Cox–Snell residuals and information criteria to choose the best fitting distribution. In particular we compare the exponential, Weibull, log-normal and log-logistic distributions.

The exponential is the most basic model, because it assumes a flat baseline hazard function, that is the hazard function is constant over time, and requires no additional parameter to be estimated (the 'shape parameter' is set equal to one). The Weibull has a more general form of the hazard function, which can be monotonically increasing or decreasing depending on the shape parameter. If the shape parameter equals 1, then the Weibull reduces to the exponential distribution. The log-logistic and the log-normal represent the logarithm of time using a logistic and a normal distribution respectively.

We define a list of variables that we want to include as regressors. We want our duration model to be a function of age and here age is expressed in logarithms. We also assume that the onset of smoking depends on socioeconomic variables (social class and education), the environment, and smoking behaviour of the household. Social class and education level at the observation time are assumed to reflect past socioeconomic characteristics.

```
generate lnage=ln(age)
global xstart "sc12 sc45 lhqdg lhqhndA lhqnone lhqoth rural
suburb mothsmo fathsmo bothsmo smother male lnage"
```

Use the option `clear` to ask Stata to forget the `st` markers generated with the previous `stset` command and then `stset` the data again:

```
/*Exponential*/
stset, clear
quietly stset starting, failure(start) id(serno)
quietly streg $xstart, d(exp) time
estimates store exp
predict double cs, csnell
stset, clear
quietly stset cs, failure (start)
quietly sts generate km=s
quietly generate double H=-ln(km)
quietly line H cs cs, sort title("Exponential") leg(off)    ///
    ylabel(0 (0.5)3) ytitle("Cumulative Hazard",            ///
    size(small) margin(medsmall))                           ///
    xtitle(Cox-Snell Residuals, size(small)                 ///
    margin(medsmall))saving("ExpCSstart",replace)

/*Weibull*/
stset, clear
quietly stset starting, failure(start)
quietly streg $xstart, d(w) time
estimates store weibull
predict double cs2, csnell
stset, clear
quietly stset cs2, failure (start)
quietly sts gen km2=s
quietly generate double H2=-ln(km2)
quietly line H2 cs2 cs2, sort title("Weibull") leg(off)     ///
    ylabel(0 (0.5)3)ytitle("Cumulative Hazard",             ///
```

```
   size(small) margin(medsmall))                              ///
   xtitle(Cox-Snell Residuals, size(small)                    ///
   margin(medsmall)) saving("WeibCSstart",replace)

/*Log-normal*/
stset, clear
quietly stset starting, failure(start)
quietly streg $xstart, d(lognormal)
estimates store logN
predict double cs3, csnell
stset, clear
quietly stset cs3, failure (start)
quietly sts generate km3=s
quietly generate double H3=-ln(km3)
quietly line H3 cs3 cs3, sort title("logNormal")leg(off)    ///
   ylabel(0 (0.5)3) ytitle("Cumulative Hazard",             ///
   size(small) margin(medsmall))                            ///
   xtitle(Cox-Snell Residuals, size(small)                  ///
   margin(medsmall)) saving("LogNormalCSstart", replace)

/*Log-logistic*/
stset, clear
quietly stset starting, failure(start)
quietly streg $xstart, d(loglogistic)
estimates store logL
predict double cs4, csnell
stset, clear
quietly stset cs4, failure (start)
quietly sts generate km4=s
quietly generate double H4=-ln(km4)
quietly line H4 cs4 cs4, sort title("logLogistic")          ///
   ylabel(0 (0.5)3) legend( off)                            ///
   ytitle("Cumulative Hazard", size(small)                  ///
   margin(medsmall)) xtitle(Cox-Snell Residuals,            ///
   size(small) margin(medsmall))                            ///
   saving("LogLogisticCSstart", replace)

drop cs km H cs2 km2 H2 cs3 km3 H3 cs4 km4 H4

graph combine "ExpCSstart" "WeibCSstart" "LogNormalCSstart"///
   "LogLogisticCSstart", iscale(0.6) imargin(1 10 1 10)     ///
   graphregion(margin(l=2 r=2))                             ///
   saving("CoxSnell_start", replace)

estimates stats exp weibull logN logL
drop _est*
```

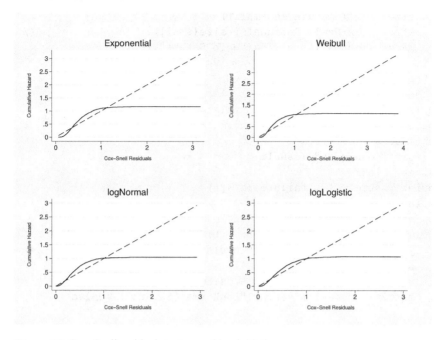

Figure 6.2 Cox–Snell residuals test – smoking initiation.

For each distribution we `quietly` estimate the regression model by maximum likelihood using `streg`. The option `d()` is used to specify the distribution. All models are estimated in the accelerated failure time (AFT) metric specifying the option `time` for the models that do not have a priori an AFT parameterisation. The `csnell` option in `predict` generates the Cox–Snell residuals. For observation j at time t_j the residuals are defined as the cumulative hazard from the fitted model, $CS_j = -\ln \hat{S}_j(t_j)$, and are saved in `cs`. If the model fits the data well the residuals are distributed as a standard exponential distribution with ancillary parameter equal to one. To verify this, it is sufficient to estimate the Kaplan–Meier or the Nelson–Aalen cumulative hazard. We save the Kaplan–Meier survival estimate in `km` and the cumulative hazard in `H`. Then `H` is plotted against `cs`. A comparison between the four graphs show that the distributions that fit the data better are the log-normal and the log-logistic (Figure 6.2).

Table 6.1 Information criteria – smoking initiation

Model	Obs	ll(null)	ll(model)	df	AIC	BIC
exp	4646	-6175.839	-5802.74	15	11635.48	11732.14
weibull	4646	-6152.564	-5712.719	16	11457.44	11560.54
logN	4646	-5588.572	-5208.542	16	10449.08	10552.18
logL	4646	-5695.691	-5285.974	16	10603.95	10707.05

We use the post-estimation command `estimates store` followed by the name of the model to store the statistics of the fitted model. The command `estat ic` could be used as well after each regression model but it does not allow us to store results. This command produces the information criteria AIC and BIC. Table 6.1 summarises the results.

The information criteria confirm that the models with the best fit are the log-normal and the log-logistic. We present results from the estimation of the log-logistic model that was favoured by Forster and Jones (2001). In the log-logistic model the hazard, the survival and the density function are as follows:

$$h(t_i \mid x_i; \beta) = \frac{\varphi_i^{1/\gamma} t_i^{(1/\gamma - 1)}}{\gamma \left[1 + (\varphi_i t_i)^{1/\gamma} \right]}$$

$$S(t_i \mid x_i; \beta) = \left[1 + (\varphi_i t_i)^{1/\gamma} \right]^{-1}$$

$$f(t_i \mid x_i; \beta) = \frac{\varphi_i^{1/\gamma} t_i^{(1/\gamma - 1)}}{\gamma \left[1 + (\varphi_i t_i)^{1/\gamma} \right]^2}$$

where $\varphi_i = \exp(-x_i \beta)$ is a non-negative function that depends on observed characteristics. The shape of the hazard depends on the ancillary parameter γ: if $\gamma \geq 1$ the hazard rate is monotonically increasing, if $\gamma < 1$ then the hazard first rises and then decreases monotonically.

For a duration model with right censoring, the contribution to the likelihood of individual i is:

$$L_i = f(t_i \mid x_i; \beta)^{d_i} \cdot \left[S(t_i \mid x_i; \beta) \right]^{(1 - d_i)}$$

where d_i is the failure, or censoring, indicator. Individuals who start smoking (i.e. they fail) have a complete spell for starting, and those who never start have a censored spell. Hence, in this case, if `start==1` the contribution to the likelihood function is the duration density function; if `start==0` the likelihood is the survivor function. For the log-logistic distribution the likelihood function becomes:

$$L_i = \left(\frac{\varphi_i^{1/\gamma} t_i^{(1/\gamma - 1)}}{\gamma \left[1 + (\varphi_i t_i)^{1/\gamma} \right]^2} \right)^{\text{start}} \cdot \left(\left[1 + (\varphi_i t_i)^{1/\gamma} \right]^{-1} \right)^{(1 - \text{start})}$$

The log-logistic model has an AFT metric. Hence, the model can be written as $\ln(t_i) = x_i \beta^* + \alpha u_i$ where α is the inverse of the ancillary parameter and u_i is an error term. The AFT metric assumes a linear relationship between the log of survival time t_i and characteristics x_i.

Estimate the model with `streg`. There is no need to specify the option `time`:

```
stset, clear
quietly stset starting, failure(start)
streg $xstart , d(loglogistic) nolog
```

As shown in Table 6.2, time to starting smoking is predicted to be shorter ('accelerated') for men, individuals in the lowest socioeconomic groups and those with no formal qualifications. The presence of smokers in the family also accelerates time to failure, meaning that the age of starting is lower for these individuals. As expected, survival time is longer for older individuals. `gamma` is the shape parameter and is estimated to be positive and smaller than 1, thus indicating that the hazard first rises with survival time and then falls monotonically. It must be noted that the option `time` after `streg` produces coefficients that are equal to the coefficients estimated from the proportional hazard (PH) model divided by the ancillary parameter. In the case of the log-logistic, which has only an AFT metric, the option `nohr` and the option `time` give the same coefficients.

Next calculate the predicted mean and median survival using the post-estimation command predict:

```
predict median_start, median time
predict mean_start, mean time
summarize mean_start median_start
```

Variable	Obs	Mean	Std. Dev.	Min	Max
mean_start	4646	57.00607	24.00365	19.65003	168.7198
median_start	4646	34.40472	14.48686	11.85933	101.827

Use `stcurve` to graph the survivor, the hazard and the cumulative hazard functions of the fitted model:

```
stcurve, survival title("LogLog Survivor")              ///
     saving(logLsurv_start, replace)
stcurve, hazard title("LogLog Hazard")                 ///
     saving(logLhaz_start, replace)
stcurve, cumhaz title("LogLogCumulative Hazard")       ///
     saving(logLcumhaz_start, replace)
graph combine "logLsurv_start" "logLhaz_start"         ///
    "logLcumhaz_start", iscale(0.6) saving(startingP, replace)
```

Figure 6.3 shows that the hazard of starting is higher for young individuals (lower duration) and decreases dramatically for survival times higher than 35 years, as the empirical hazard function in Figure 6.1 suggested.

Table 6.2 Smoking initiation – coefficients from log-logistic model (AFT)

```
-----------------------------------------------------------------
Log-logistic regression - accelerated failure-time form

No. of subjects =         4646              Number of obs =      4646
No. of failures =         2901
Time at risk    =      154173.1
                                            LR chi2(14)   =   819.43
Log likelihood  =   -5285.9735              Prob > chi2   =   0.0000
-----------------------------------------------------------------
```

_t	Coef.	Std. Err.	z	P>|z|	[95% Conf.	Interval]
scl2	.0997876	.0363994	2.74	0.006	.0284461	.1711292
sc45	-.079418	.0348648	-2.28	0.023	-.1477517	-.0110844
lhqdg	.121542	.0649816	1.87	0.061	-.0058196	.2489036
lhqhndA	-.0084562	.0620451	-0.14	0.892	-.1300623	.1131499
lhqnone	-.133598	.0505779	-2.64	0.008	-.2327288	-.0344672
lhqoth	-.0788673	.0755278	-1.04	0.296	-.2268991	.0691644
rural	.1165216	.0396693	2.94	0.003	.0387712	.1942721
suburb	.0519555	.0316588	1.64	0.101	-.0100945	.1140056
mothsmo	-.4478221	.0748388	-5.98	0.000	-.5945034	-.3011408
fathsmo	-.3740176	.0442889	-8.44	0.000	-.4608223	-.287213
bothsmo	-.5199595	.0506314	-10.27	0.000	-.6191953	-.4207237
smother	-.2308891	.0296456	-7.79	0.000	-.2889934	-.1727848
male	-.6421316	.0280485	-22.89	0.000	-.6971056	-.5871576
lnage	.3321544	.0764499	4.34	0.000	.1823153	.4819935
_cons	2.851352	.3175137	8.98	0.000	2.229036	3.473667
/ln_gam	-.6430285	.0157277	-40.88	0.000	-.6738543	-.6122027
gamma	.525698	.008268			.5097401	.5421554

Table 6.2 and Figure 6.3 suggest that, as it stands, the model is inadequate. The predicted age of starting is far too high when compared to the actual age of starting among smokers. Standard duration models, like the log-logistic model used here, assume that eventually everyone fails – in this case everyone would eventually start smoking. This seems to be an implausible assumption, and models based on it do not do a good job of fitting the observed data. An alternative is to use a so-called split population model. This augments the standard duration analysis by adding a splitting mechanism. So, for example, a probit specification could be added to model the probability that somebody will eventually start smoking. When this splitting mechanism is added to the duration model, it does a far better job of explaining the observed data on age of starting than models that omit a splitting mechanism (see Forster and Jones, 2001).

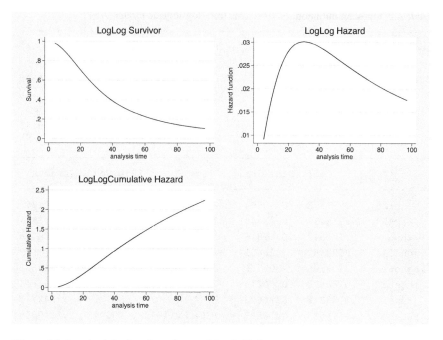

Figure 6.3 Log-logistic functions for smoking initiation.

The results of Forster and Jones (2001) suggest that a simplified version of the split population model will work well with the HALS data. This uses a standard binary choice model, such as a logit or probit, for the indicator of whether an individual has started (start) and then applies the duration model only to the starters in the sample. This can be viewed as a two-part specification of the duration model.

Again we can compare different distributions for the sub-sample of 'starters' using both the graphical test of Cox–Snell residuals and the information criteria. This implies specifying the option if in the stset commands as reported in the case of the exponential below:

```
stset, clear
qui stset starting if start==1, failure(start)
qui streg $xstart, d(exp) time
estimates store exp
predict double cs, csnell
stset,clear
quietly stset cs if start==1, failure(start)
quietly sts generate km=s
quietly generate double H=-ln(km)
quietly line H cs cs,sort title("Exponential" )leg(off)   ///
    ytitle("Cumulative Hazard", size(small)                ///
```

```
       margin(medsmall)) xtitle(Cox-Snell REsiduals,         ///
       size(small) margin(medsmall))                          ///
       saving("ExpCSstart1",replace)
estimates stats exp
```

Replicating this for each distribution we obtain Figure 6.4 and Table 6.3.

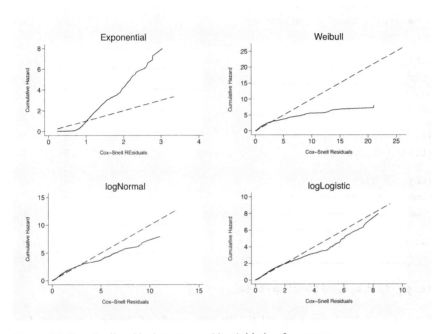

Figure 6.4 Cox–Snell residuals test – smoking initiation for starters.

Table 6.3 Information criteria – smoking initiation for starters

```
----------|-----------------------------------------------------------
    Model |   Obs   ll(null)   ll(model)   df        AIC         BIC
----------|-----------------------------------------------------------
      exp |  2901  -3042.621  -3019.219   15   6068.437    6158.029
  weibull |  2901  -1208.255  -853.0659   16   1738.132    1833.697
     logN |  2901  -672.9196  -443.9794   16   919.9588    1015.524
     logL |  2901  -498.6487  -291.3713   16   614.7426    710.3076
----------------------------------------------------------------------
```

The graphical test and the information criteria again favour the log-logistic distribution, which we use to estimate the final parametric model for smoking initiation:

```
stset, clear
quietly stset starting if start==1, failure(start)
stdescribe
```

The `stdescribe` command produces the following table, which shows that the mean and median survival times are 18 and 17, respectively.

```
        failure _d: start
  analysis time _t: starting

                            |---------- per subject ----------|
Category             total      mean      min    median     max
---------------------------------------------------------------
no. of subjects       2901
no. of records        2901         1        1         1       1

(first) entry time                 0        0         0       0
(final) exit time          18.04688        4        17      70

subjects with gap        0
time on gap if gap       0
time at risk         52354 18.04688        4        17      70

failures              2901         1        1         1       1
---------------------------------------------------------------
```

```
streg $xstart, d(loglogistic) nolog
```

Estimates of the duration model for the sub-sample of starters are reported in Table 6.4. Time to failure is predicted to be accelerated for men, individuals from the lowest social group and with no education, and individuals whose relatives smoke. The variables `lnage` and `suburb` slow down time to starting smoking. The parameter `gamma` still indicates that the hazard rises before declining monotonically with survival time. Calculate the predicted survival times using:

```
predict median_start, median time
predict mean_start, mean time
summarize mean_start median_start
drop mean_start median_start
```

```
    Variable |   Obs     Mean   Std. Dev.      Min       Max
-------------|-------------------------------------------------
  mean_start |  2901   17.6986   1.715094   14.29607   23.5218
median_start |  2901  17.08602   1.655731   13.80125  22.70767
```

The predicted survival is very close to the observed value and that the model fits much better for the data on the sub-sample of starters.

Table 6.4 Smoking initiation for starters – coefficients from log-logistic model (AFT)

```
-----------------------------------------------------------------
Log-logistic regression — accelerated failure-time form

No. of subjects =      2901               Number of obs =     2901
No. of failures =      2901
Time at risk     =     52354
                                          LR chi2(14)   =   414.55
Log likelihood = -291.37131               Prob > chi2   =   0.0000
-----------------------------------------------------------------
     _t |      Coef.  Std. Err.      z   P>|z|  [95% Conf. Interval]
--------|--------------------------------------------------------
   sc12 |   .0038026   .0121417   0.31   0.754  -.0199947   .0275999
   sc45 |  -.0259335   .0115498  -2.25   0.025  -.0485707  -.0032962
  lhqdg |   .0240003   .0216664   1.11   0.268  -.0184651   .0664657
lhqhndA |   .0131455    .020759   0.63   0.527  -.0275414   .0538325
lhqnone |  -.0619486   .0171223  -3.62   0.000  -.0955076  -.0283895
 lhqoth |  -.0223088   .0253117  -0.88   0.378  -.0719188   .0273011
  rural |   .0145314   .0131891   1.10   0.271  -.0113187   .0403815
 suburb |   .0177562   .0105353   1.69   0.092  -.0028926   .0384051
mothsmo |  -.0577735   .0251914  -2.29   0.022  -.1071478  -.0083992
fathsmo |  -.0597182   .0156403  -3.82   0.000  -.0903727  -.0290637
bothsmo |    -.08849   .0175068  -5.05   0.000  -.1228027  -.0541773
smother |  -.0142472   .0097939  -1.45   0.146  -.0334429   .0049485
   male |  -.1707894   .0094643 -18.05   0.000  -.1893391  -.1522396
  lnage |   .1123013   .0263235   4.27   0.000   .0607082   .1638944
  _cons |   2.571063   .1089259  23.60   0.000   2.357572   2.784554
--------|--------------------------------------------------------
/ln_gam |  -1.925379   .0158796 -121.25   0.000  -1.956502  -1.894255
--------|--------------------------------------------------------
  gamma |   .1458205   .0023156                   .141352   .1504303
-----------------------------------------------------------------
```

The following commands are used to produce the graphical analysis from the fitted model:

```
stcurve, survival title("LogLog Survivor ")
saving(logLsurv_start1, replace)
stcurve, hazard title("LogLog Hazard ")                        ///
   saving(logLhaz_start1, replace)
stcurve, cumhaz title("LogLogCumulative Hazard ")              ///
   saving(logLcumhaz_start1, replace)
graph combine "logLsurv_start1" "logLhaz_start1"              ///
  "logLcumhaz_start1", iscale(0.6) saving(startingP1, replace)
```

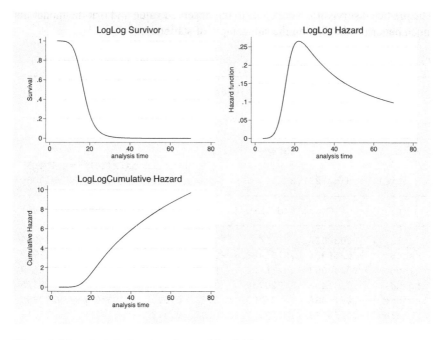

Figure 6.5 Log-logistic functions for smoking initiation.

Figure 6.5 shows that survival declines rapidly from ages 17–18. The hazard is predicted to rise and then fall monotonically.

Smoking cessation

As for the onset of smoking, use some basic commands to investigate smoking duration:

```
tabulate quit
```

```
    quit |      Freq.    Percent        Cum.
---------|---------------------------------
       0 |      1,443      49.74       49.74
       1 |      1,458      50.26      100.00
---------|---------------------------------
   Total |      2,901     100.00
```

```
summarize sm_years,d
```

```
                                sm_years
-----------------------------------------------------------------
        Percentiles        Smallest
  1%             3                 1
  5%             8                 1
 10%            13                 1   Obs                   2901
 25%            23                 1   Sum of Wgt.           2901

 50%            32                     Mean              32.23716
                            Largest    Std. Dev.         14.00826
 75%            42                70
 90%            50                71   Variance          196.2313
 95%            55                72   Skewness          .0175091
 99%            64                72   Kurtosis          2.599601
```

```
stset, clear
stset sm_year, failure(quit)

   failure event:  quit != 0 & quit < .
obs. time interval: (0, sm_years]
 exit on or before: failure
-----------------------------------------------------------------
    4646  total obs.
    1745  event time missing (sm_years>=.)        PROBABLE ERROR
-----------------------------------------------------------------
    2901 obs. remaining, representing
    1458 failures in single record/single failure data
   93520 total analysis time at risk, at risk from t =      0
                             earliest observed entry t =    0
                                 last observed exit t =    72
```

```
stsum

        failure _d: quit
   analysis time _t: sm_years

        |   time  incidence   no. of |----- Survival time -----|
        | at risk      rate  subjects    25%     50%      75%
--------|--------------------------------------------------------
  total |  93520  .0155902      2901     26      43       59
```

```
stdescribe
```

```
        failure _d: quit
  analysis time _t: sm_years
```

| | |-------------- per subject ---------------| | | |
Category	total	mean	min	median	max
no. of subjects	2901				
no. of records	2901	1	1	1	1
(first) entry time		0	0	0	0
(final) exit time		32.23716	1	32	72
subjects with gap	0				
time on gap if gap	0				
time at risk	93520	32.23716	1	32	72
failures	1458	.5025853	0	1	1

The first table shows that 50 per cent of the 2,901 individuals who had started smoking at some time had quit by the time of the HALS. For this reason the use of stset needs to be conditional on the sub-sample of starters. The failure event is indicated by the dummy variable quit. The stsum command shows the cumulative distribution of total time at risk: 25 per cent of the sample quit after 26 years, 50 per cent after 43 years and 75 per cent after 59 years of smoking. The stdescribe output shows that both mean and median time at risk is about 32 years, indicating a symmetric distribution, and the longest smoking duration is 72 years.

Use the non-parametric approach to explore survival time and the hazard function:

```
sts graph, title("Kaplan-Meier Survival")                    ///
    saving(KMsurv_quit,replace)
sts graph, hazard title("Kaplan-Meier Hazard")               ///
    saving(KMhazard_quit,replace)
sts graph, na ylab(0(1)3) title("Nelson-Aalen Cum. Hazard") ///
    saving(NAcumhaz_quit, replace)
graph combine "KMsurv_quit" "KMhazard_quit" "NAcumhaz_quit",///
    iscale(0.6) saving(quittingNP,replace)
```

This graphs the Kaplan–Meier survivor and hazard function and the Nelson–Aalen cumulative hazard (Figure 6.6).

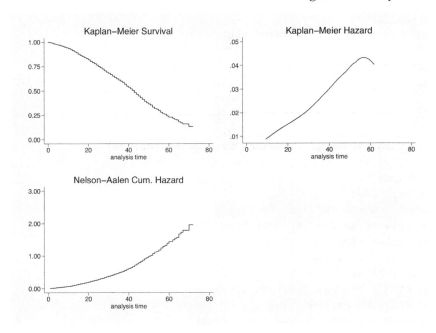

Figure 6.6 Non-parametric functions for smoking cessation.

The survivor function diminishes less than proportionally for the first 40 years of the analysis time. In fact, the survival probability is still very high (between 1 and 0.50) for durations as long as 40 years and than decreases faster. The shape of the hazard function is increasing and shows a peak between 50 and 60 years of smoking, and then decreases.

The parametric model includes a list of regressors defined as:

```
global xquit "sc12 sc45 lhqdg lhqhndA lhqnone lhqoth widow
    sepdiv single part unemp sick retd keephse wkshft1 rural
    suburb housown hou mothsmo fathsmo bothsmo smother male
    lnage lnyear"
```

The hazard of quitting is assumed to depend on a large set of socioeconomic characteristics, demographics and family smoking behaviour. The logarithm of year at starting is used as a control. The parametric distribution that best fits the data is chosen using the Cox–Snell residuals test and the information criteria:

```
/*Exponential*/
stset, clear
qui stset sm_year, failure(quit)
qui streg $xquit, d(exp) time
estimates store exp
predict double cs, csnell
```

```
stset, clear
quietly stset cs, failure(quit)
quietly sts gen km=s
quietly gen double H=-ln(km)
quietly line H cs cs, sort title("Exponential") leg(off)    ///
    ylabel(0 (0.5)3) ytitle("Cumulative Hazard",            ///
    size(small) margin(medsmall))                           ///
    xtitle(Cox-Snell Residuals, size(small)                 ///
    margin(medsmall))saving("ExpCSquit",replace)

/*Weibull*/
stset, clear
quietly stset sm_year, failure(quit) id(serno)
quietly streg $xquit, d(w) time
estimates store weibull
predict double cs2, csnell
stset, clear
quietly stset cs2, failure (quit)
quietly sts generate km2=s
quietly generate double H2=-ln(km2)
quietly line H2 cs2 cs2, sort title("Weibull") leg(off)    ///
    ylabel(0 (0.5)3)ytitle("Cumulative Hazard",            ///
    size(small) margin(medsmall))                          ///
    xtitle(Cox-Snell Residuals, size(small)                ///
    margin(medsmall)) saving("WeibCSquit",replace)

/*Log-Normal*/
stset, clear
quietly stset sm_year, failure(quit)
quietly streg $xquit, d(lognormal)
estimates store logN
predict double cs3, csnell
stset, clear
quietly stset cs3, failure (quit)
quietly sts generate km3=s
quietly generate double H3=-ln(km3)
quietly line H3 cs3 cs3, sort title("logNormal")leg(off)   ///
    ylabel(0 (0.5)3)  ytitle("Cumulative Hazard",          ///
    size(small) margin(medsmall))                          ///
    xtitle(Cox-Snell Residuals, size(small)                ///
    margin(medsmall)) saving("LogNormalCSquit", replace)

/*Log-Logistic*/
stset, clear
quietly stset sm_year, failure(quit)
```

```
quietly streg $xquit, d(loglogistic)
estimates store logL
predict double cs4, csnell
stset, clear
quietly stset cs4, failure (quit)
quietly sts generate km4=s
quietly generate double H4=-ln(km4)
quietly line H4 cs4 cs4, sort title("logLogistic")          ///
    ylabel(0 (0.5)3) legend( off)                           ///
    ytitle("Cumulative Hazard", size(small)                 ///
    margin(medsmall)) xtitle(Cox-Snell Residuals,           ///
    size(small) margin(medsmall))                           ///
    saving("LogLogisticCSquit", replace)

drop cs km H cs2 km2 H2 cs3 km3 H3 cs4 km4 H4

graph combine "ExpCSquit" "WeibCSquit" "LogNormalCSquit"    ///
    "LogLogisticCSquit", iscale(0.6) imargin(1 10 1 10)     ///
    graphregion(margin(l=2 r=2))                            ///
    saving("CoxSnell_quit", replace)

estimates stats exp weibull logN logL
drop  _est_*
```

Figure 6.7 and Table 6.5 compare the exponential, Weibull, log-normal and log-logistic distributions.

Table 6.5 Information criteria – smoking cessation

Model	Obs	ll(null)	ll(model)	df	AIC	BIC
exponential	2901	-3012.043	-2874.715	27	5803.43	5964.696
weibull	2901	-2781.768	-2560.507	28	5177.013	5344.252
logN	2901	-2911.074	-2738.088	28	5532.176	5699.414
logL	2901	-2828.102	-2621.761	28	5299.522	5466.76

The graphical analysis shows that, except for the exponential, all the distributions fit the data quite well. The penalised log-likelihood criteria calculated by estat favour the Weibull distribution. The Weibull model is characterised by the following expressions for the hazard, the survivor and the density function:

$$h(t_i \mid x_i; \beta) = \lambda_i p t_i^{p-1}$$
$$S(t_i \mid x_i; \beta) = \exp(-\lambda_i t_i^p)$$
$$f(t_i \mid x_i; \beta) = \lambda_i p t_i^{p-1} \exp(-\lambda_i t_i^p)$$

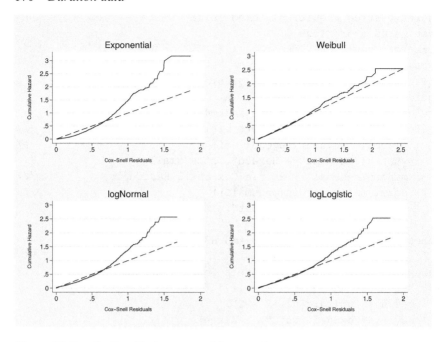

Figure 6.7 Cox–Snell residuals test – smoking cessation.

where λ_i is a non-negative function that depends on the observed characteristics, $\lambda_i = \exp(-px_i\beta)$; pt_i^{p-1} is the baseline hazard whose shape depends on the ancillary parameter p. The Weibull model can yield a monotonic increasing or decreasing hazard of quitting. Regarding this, the sign of the shape parameters needs to be interpreted. If $p = 1$ the Weibull equals the exponential, with $h(t) = \lambda$. If $p > 1$ the hazard function is monotonically increasing; if $p < 1$ the hazard function is monotonically decreasing. The last two cases are known as positive and negative duration dependence.

For the Weibull model, the likelihood is:

$$L_t = \left(\lambda_i p t_i^{p-1} \exp\left(-\lambda_i t_i^p\right)\right)^{\text{quit}} \cdot \left(\exp\left(-\lambda_i t_i^p\right)\right)^{(1-\text{quit})}$$

This expression is maximised in Stata with the command `streg`. Estimate a Weibull model for quitting smoking in accelerated failure time metric and save the predicted mean and median survival time:

```
stset, clear
quietly stset sm_year, failure(quit)
streg $xquit, d(weibull) time nolog

predict median_quit1, median time
predict mean_quit1, mean time
```

```
summarize mean_quit1 median_quit1
drop mean_quit1 median_quit1
```

```
     Variable |      Obs        Mean    Std. Dev.         Min         Max
--------------|----------------------------------------------------------
   mean_quit1 |     2901    44.85645    13.66769    18.69054    125.2251
 median_quit1 |     2901    41.98409    12.79249     17.4937    117.2064
```

Table 6.6 reports the estimated coefficients. The coefficients for sc12 and male are negative, meaning that time to quitting smoking accelerates for individuals in the top social group and men. It also accelerates with lnage and lnyear, meaning that older individuals as well as individuals who started smoking later have a shorter survival time. Survival in the state of smoking is also shorter for individuals from rural areas. The socioeconomic gradient in quitting is confirmed by the coefficient of the variables lhqnone lhqoth unemp and sick, which suggest that for less educated individuals and persons who do not work time to quitting decelerates, hence the decision to quit is postponed. The ancillary parameter p is positive suggesting that the hazard is monotonically increasing.

The graphical analysis allows comparison of the fitted survivor and hazard functions with the non-parametric functions and shows that the Weibull survivor function is a good match with the Kaplan–Meier survivor function. The Weibull hazard function (Figure 6.8) moves away the empirical hazard function only for the right tail of the survival time distribution (Stata code shown on page 173).

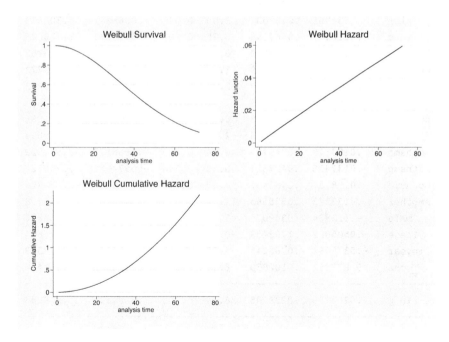

Figure 6.8 Weibull estimated functions for smoking cessation.

Table 6.6 Smoking cessation – coefficients from Weibull model (AFT)

```
----------------------------------------------------------------
Weibull regression — accelerated failure-time form

No. of subjects =        2901              Number of obs =     2901
No. of failures =        1458
Time at risk     =       93520
                                           LR chi2(26)   =   442.52
Log likelihood  = -2560.5066               Prob > chi2   =   0.0000
----------------------------------------------------------------
     _t |      Coef. Std. Err.      z  P>|z|   [95% Conf. Interval]
---------|------------------------------------------------------
    sc12 | -.0867281  .0347142  -2.50  0.012  -.1547668  -.0186895
    sc45 |  .0357743  .0349416   1.02  0.306    -.03271   .1042586
   lhqdg | -.0773818  .0613357  -1.26  0.207  -.1975976   .0428341
 lhqhndA |  .0428267  .0603626   0.71  0.478  -.0754817   .1611352
 lhqnone |  .1259208  .0503522   2.50  0.012   .0272324   .2246092
  lhqoth |   .154064  .0748662   2.06  0.040    .007329    .300799
   widow |  .0452093  .0470219   0.96  0.336   -.046952   .1373706
  sepdiv |  .2991298  .0783928   3.82  0.000   .1454827   .4527768
  single |  .1302167   .063006   2.07  0.039   .0067272   .2537062
    part | -.0353926  .0523524  -0.68  0.499  -.1380014   .0672163
   unemp |  .2480242  .0880589   2.82  0.005   .0754319   .4206164
    sick |  .1551065  .0758037   2.05  0.041   .0065341    .303679
    retd |  .0116477  .0464198   0.25  0.802  -.0793334   .1026288
 keephse |  .0464702  .0640859   0.73  0.468  -.0791358   .1720762
 wkshft1 |  .1080792  .0643879   1.68  0.093  -.0181188   .2342772
   rural | -.0716918  .0380537  -1.88  0.060  -.1462756    .002892
  suburb | -.0566373   .031345  -1.81  0.071  -.1180723   .0047978
 housown |  .0445485   .053348   0.84  0.404  -.0600116   .1491086
     hou | -.0386157  .0151083  -2.56  0.011  -.0682274   -.009004
 mothsmo |  .0103378  .0749785   0.14  0.890  -.1366173   .1572929
 fathsmo | -.0137415  .0427324  -0.32  0.748  -.0974955   .0700124
 bothsmo |  .0198731  .0498491   0.40  0.690  -.0778293   .1175756
 smother |  .4133573  .0335065  12.34  0.000   .3476858   .4790288
    male |  -.113804  .0348075  -3.27  0.001  -.1820253  -.0455826
   lnage | -.0505022  .1702438  -0.30  0.767  -.3841738   .2831694
  lnyear | -.5379062  .0768245  -7.00  0.000  -.6884795  -.3873329
   _cons |  5.877322  .9102839   6.46  0.000   4.093199   7.661446
---------|------------------------------------------------------
   /ln_p |  .6751269  .0238205  28.34  0.000   .6284395   .7218143
---------|------------------------------------------------------
       p |  1.964282  .0467903                 1.874683   2.058164
     1/p |  .5090918  .0121268                   .48587   .5334236
```

```
stcurve, survival title("Weibull Survival")                ///
    saving(wsurv_quit1, replace)
stcurve, hazard title("Weibull Hazard")                    ///
    saving(wH_quit1, replace)
stcurve, cumhaz title("Weibull Cumulative Hazard")         ///
    saving(wcumH_quit1, replace)
graph combine "wsurv_quit1" "wH_quit1" "wcumH_quit1",      ///
    iscale(0.6) saving("quittingP", replace)
```

Lifespan

To study the hazard of dying in the HALS sample we use the same approach used so far with smoking durations. Deaths account for about 43 per cent of the sample of those aged over 40 at HALS. First calculate some statistics for the survival time variable lifespan:

```
summarize lifespan, d
```

```
        Survivor time: censoring at April 2005
-------------------------------------------------------------------

        Percentiles      Smallest
  1%          55.1           41.5
  5%      60.55852           43.9
 10%      61.82615           44.4      Obs                4646
 25%          66.2           45.4      Sum of Wgt.        4646

 50%          73.3                     Mean            73.99948
                            Largest    Std. Dev.        9.62414
 75%          81.2          101.6
 90%          86.8       106.1602      Variance        92.62407
 95%          90.1       106.2834      Skewness        .2362737
 99%      96.47365       110.976       Kurtosis        2.523947
```

This shows that 1 per cent of the sample survived to age 55 and a half of the sample up to 73. The mean survival time is about 74.

The pnorm command produces a graph of a standardised normal probability (normal probability plot) and suggests that lifespan is approximately distributed as a Gaussian random variable. Using the Graph Editor one can modify the size and colour of the lines in the plot region (Figure 6.9).

```
pnorm lifespan, saving("pnorm", replace)
```

Use the stset command to explore the survival time for lifespan. Failure is indicated by death and age is used to indicate left-truncation:

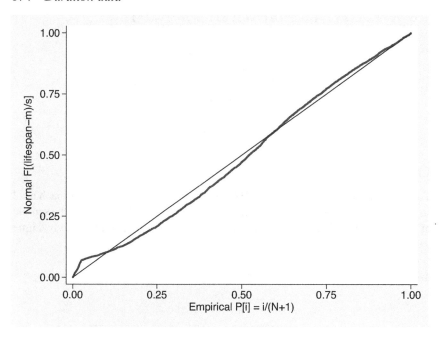

Figure 6.9 Normal probability plot for lifespan.

```
stset, clear
stset lifespan, failure(death) enter(age)

      failure event:  death != 0 & death < .
obs. time interval:  (0, lifespan]
 enter on or after:  time age
 exit on or before:  failure
------------------------------------------------------------------
      4646  total obs.
         0  exclusions
------------------------------------------------------------------
      4646  obs. remaining, representing
      1987  failures in single record/single failure data
   74121.4  total analysis time at risk, at risk from t =          0
                              earliest observed entry t =         40
                                 last observed exit t = 110.976
```

Here the key concept is that individuals who died before 1984 (the observation time in HALS) are not surveyed but are excluded from the sample: the HALS sample is the result of a selection process, conditional on the event of death having not occurred prior to the survey time. Hence, the remaining sample has a lower hazard relative to the truncated part of the population. The option `enter` allows us to account for left truncation and should not be confused with options `origin` and `time0`. The Stata manual [ST] illustrates the main differences between options in `stset`.

```
stsum

        failure _d: death
   analysis time _t: lifespan
  enter on or after: time age

         |         time  incidence    no. of  |--- Survival time ---|
         |      at risk        rate  subjects     25%      50%      75%
---------|-----------------------------------------------------------------
   total | 74121.40066    .0268074      4646    71.6     80.2     87.3

stdescribe

        failure _d: death
   analysis time _t: lifespan
  enter on or after: time age

                      |--------------- per subject ---------------|
Category              total       mean       min    median       max
---------------------------------------------------------------------
no. of subjects        4646
no. of records         4646          1         1         1         1

(first) entry time             58.04567        40      57.2      96.8
(final) exit time              73.99948      41.5      73.3   110.976

subjects with gap         0
time on gap if gap        0
time at risk      74121.401   15.95381  .0999985  19.79925  20.53997

failures               1987  .4276797         0         0         1
---------------------------------------------------------------------
```

Notice the difference between the command used here and those used for the smoking data in the line `(first) entry time`, because here summary statistics are calculated also for survival time at entry. On average, survival time is 58 at entry and 74 at exit. Statistics for survival time at entry can be verified with the following command:

```
summ age

Variable |     Obs        Mean    Std. Dev.        Min        Max
---------|-------------------------------------------------------------
     age |    4646    58.04567     11.75395         40       96.8
```

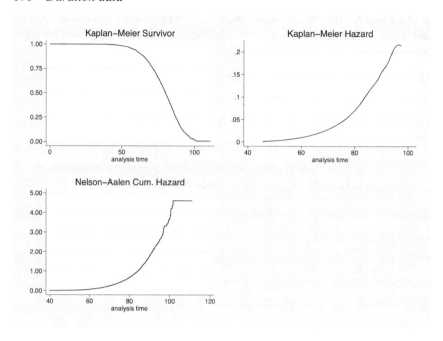

Figure 6.10 Non-parametric functions for lifespan.

The usual non-parametric procedures are used to generate the combined graph shown in Figure 6.10. Figure 6.10 shows that the hazard function is increasing and is steeper for durations longer than 80 years and shows a decreasing pattern after the peak around age 95 where the cumulative hazard function appears to be flat.

For the parametric analysis define a `global` for the regressors:

```
replace quit=0 if quit==.

global xls "sc12 sc45 lhqdg lhqhndA lhqnone lhqoth part unemp
    sick retd keephse wkshft1 rural suburb male lnage start
    quit"
```

The hazard of dying is assumed to be a function of socioeconomic characteristics and demographics. Smoking behaviour is considered an important determinant of the hazard so the variables `start` and `quit` are included as regressors. In order to estimate the model for `lifespan` on the full sample, missing values for `quit` are set equal to zero. We do not attempt to deal with potential endogeneity of these variables, so the estimates should be treated with caution if they are to be interpreted as causal effects of smoking on lifespan.

We calculate the Cox–Snell residual test and the information criteria to compare five alternative distributions. We follow the same procedure shown for smoking

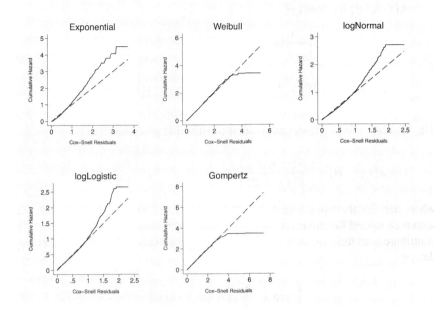

Figure 6.11 Cox–Snell residuals test – lifespan.

Table 6.7 Information criteria – lifespan

Model	Obs	ll(null)	ll(model)	df	AIC	BIC
exp	4646	-577.0944	487.887	19	-937.7741	-815.3426
weibull	4646	521.9582	710.9347	20	-1381.869	-1252.994
logN	4646	440.1666	620.3466	20	-1200.693	-1071.818
logL	4646	461.7225	643.5775	20	-1247.155	-1118.28
gomp	4646	510.0126	709.284	20	-1378.568	-1249.693

initiation and cessation but include the Gompertz distribution (the law of human mortality was first described by Benjamin Gompertz in 1825; the Gompertz mortality model has been used in biology and medical modelling) (Figure 6.11 and Table 6.7).

Note that the error message 'convergence not achieved' appears when estimating streg with option d(w) for lifespan. Stata returns this message when it first attempts fitting the constant-only model, as can be seen by running the command without quietly switched on.

Both the Cox–Snell residuals test and the information criteria favour the Gompertz distribution for lifespan. The Gompertz model is parameterised as follows:

$$h(t_i \mid x_i; \beta) = \lambda_i \, \exp(\gamma t_i)$$

$$S(t_i \mid x_i; \beta) = \exp\left\{-\frac{\lambda_i}{\gamma}\left[\exp(\gamma t_i) - 1\right]\right\}$$

$$f(t_i \mid x_i; \beta) = \lambda_i \, \exp(\gamma t_i) \cdot \exp\left\{-\frac{\lambda_i}{\gamma}\left[\exp(\gamma t_i) - 1\right]\right\}$$

The likelihood for a left-truncated duration model is given by:

$$L_i = h(t_i \mid x_i; \beta)^{d_i} \cdot \left(\frac{S(t_i \mid x_i; \beta)}{S(\tau_i \mid x_i; \beta)}\right)$$

where individuals with a complete spell (death==1) contribute to the likelihood with their hazard function and individuals with right-censored spells (death==0) contribute with their survivor function conditional on survival up to the interview date, τ_i.

$$L_i = \left(\lambda_i \, \exp(\gamma t_i)\right)^{d_i} \cdot \left(\frac{\exp\left\{-\dfrac{\lambda_i}{\gamma}\left[\exp(\gamma t_i) - 1\right]\right\}}{\exp\left\{-\dfrac{\lambda_i}{\gamma}\left[\exp(\gamma \tau_i) - 1\right]\right\}}\right)$$

The Gompertz model (Table 6.8) is parameterised as a proportional hazard model or log-relative hazard form:

$$h(t_i \mid x_i; \beta) = h_0(t) \cdot \exp(x_i \beta)$$

where the baseline hazard is $h_0(t) = \exp(\gamma t_i)$ and $\exp(x_i \beta) = \lambda_i$ scales the baseline hazard multiplicatively by the same amount at each instant t. The ancillary parameter γ is estimated by Stata. If $\gamma > 0$ the hazard function increases with time, if $\gamma < 0$ the hazard function decreases with time. The exponential hazard function is a special case of the Gompertz hazard when $\gamma = 0$.

Use streg to maximise the log-likelihood function with options nohr and hr to get both the coefficients β_k and the hazard ratios $\exp(\beta_k) = [h(\tilde{t}, x_i)/h(\tilde{t}, x_j)]$:

```
stset, clear
stset lifespan, failure(death) enter(age)
streg $xls , d(gompertz) nohr nolog

streg, hr

predict median_ls, median time
summarize median_ls
drop median_ls
```

Variable	Obs	Mean	Std. Dev.	Min	Max
median_ls	4646	81.23831	5.72825	62.4798	96.35618

The coefficients of sc45, unemp, sick and keephse are positive (Table 6.8), meaning that for individuals in these groups the hazard of dying is higher. For example, the hazard of dying for sc45 is about 11 per cent higher than in the other social classes. Also the coefficient of sc12 is statistically significant and, as expected, it has negative sign. The result for male indicates that, for men, the hazard of dying is 51 per cent higher than for women.

Smoking decisions affect the risk of mortality. The choice variable start is statistically significant with a positive coefficient, meaning that the decision of

Table 6.8 Lifespan – coefficients from Gompertz model

Gompertz regression – log relative-hazard form

No. of subjects = 4646   Number of obs   =   4646
No. of failures = 1987
Time at risk = 74121.40066

                                LR chi2(18)   =   398.54
Log likelihood = 709.28401   Prob > chi2   =   0.0000

_t	Coef.	Std. Err.	z	P>|z|	[95% Conf.	Interval]
sc12	-.1530234	.0625764	-2.45	0.014	-.2756709	-.030376
sc45	.1032688	.0540068	1.91	0.056	-.0025826	.2091202
lhqdg	-.0569884	.1220213	-0.47	0.640	-.2961457	.1821689
lhqhndA	-.1958631	.1234852	-1.59	0.113	-.4378897	.0461634
lhqnone	.1045263	.0961881	1.09	0.277	-.0839989	.2930516
lhqoth	.1157708	.1332891	0.87	0.385	-.145471	.3770126
part	.0273555	.1041368	0.26	0.793	-.1767489	.23146
unemp	.4617398	.1428298	3.23	0.001	.1817986	.7416811
sick	.7548937	.1163245	6.49	0.000	.5269019	.9828854
retd	.0303732	.0859395	0.35	0.724	-.1380651	.1988115
keephse	.2416043	.1226376	1.97	0.049	.001239	.4819696
wkshft1	-.1831301	.147969	-1.24	0.216	-.4731439	.1068838
rural	-.0867819	.064179	-1.35	0.176	-.2125705	.0390066
suburb	-.0672467	.0506829	-1.33	0.185	-.1665834	.03209
male	.4090663	.0518999	7.88	0.000	.3073444	.5107882
lnage	.971717	.2983871	3.26	0.001	.3868891	1.556545
start	.6437472	.0594012	10.84	0.000	.527323	.7601713
quit	-.3777534	.0563624	-6.70	0.000	-.4882218	-.2672851
_cons	-14.30188	1.011103	-14.14	0.000	-16.28361	-12.32016
gamma	.0869282	.0041305	21.05	0.000	.0788326	.0950238

Table 6.9 Lifespan – hazard ratio from Gompertz model

```
--------------------------------------------------------------------
Gompertz regression - log relative-hazard form

No. of subjects =         4646              Number of obs   =     4646
No. of failures =         1987
Time at risk     = 74121.40066
                                           LR chi2(18)     =   398.54
Log likelihood   =    709.28401            Prob > chi2     =   0.0000
--------------------------------------------------------------------
```

_t	Haz. Ratio	Std. Err.	z	P>|z|	[95% Conf. Interval]	
sc12	.8581096	.0536974	-2.45	0.014	.7590627	.9700807
sc45	1.108789	.0598822	1.91	0.056	.9974207	1.232593
lhqdg	.944605	.1152619	-0.47	0.640	.743679	1.199817
lhqhndA	.8221247	.1015202	-1.59	0.113	.645397	1.047246
lhqnone	1.110185	.1067866	1.09	0.277	.9194322	1.340512
lhqoth	1.122739	.1496488	0.87	0.385	.864615	1.457923
part	1.027733	.1070249	0.26	0.793	.8379902	1.260439
unemp	1.586832	.226647	3.23	0.001	1.199373	2.099462
sick	2.127385	.247467	6.49	0.000	1.693677	2.672155
retd	1.030839	.0885898	0.35	0.724	.871042	1.219952
keephse	1.27329	.1561533	1.97	0.049	1.00124	1.619261
wkshft1	.8326599	.1232078	-1.24	0.216	.6230404	1.112805
rural	.916877	.0588443	-1.35	0.176	.8085033	1.039777
suburb	.9349645	.0473867	-1.33	0.185	.8465522	1.03261
male	1.505412	.0781307	7.88	0.000	1.359809	1.666604
lnage	2.642478	.7884812	3.26	0.001	1.472393	4.742408
start	1.903601	.1130761	10.84	0.000	1.69439	2.138643
quit	.6853995	.0386308	-6.70	0.000	.6137168	.7654548
gamma	.0869282	.0041305	21.05	0.000	.0788326	.0950238

starting smoking increases the hazard of dying. The variable quit is statistically significant with negative coefficient, meaning that the decision of quitting slows down the hazard of dying: at each time the hazard rate of quitters is 69 per cent of the hazard rate of those who do not quit. For a more meaningful interpretation of the coefficients, we can divide the sample of respondents into current smokers, ex-smokers and never smokers, depending on the value of start and quit. For current smokers (start==1 and quit==0) the coefficient of interest is 0.644. For ex-smokers (start==1 and quit==1) we sum the coefficients of start and quit and obtain that 0.266 is the effect on lifespan. Both current and ex-smokers have shorter lifespan than never smokers, but the effect on the hazard of dying is bigger for those individuals who had not quit yet.

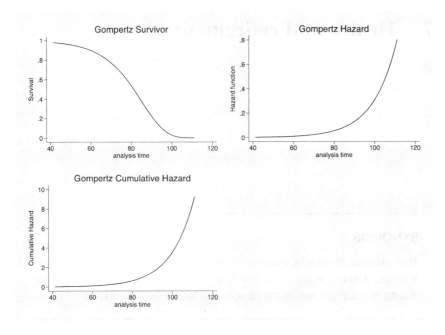

Figure 6.12 Gompertz estimated functions for lifespan.

For the variable `ln_age` the model in `nohr` gives the elasticity of the hazard with respect to `age`, which is around 97 per cent. The ancillary parameter `gamma` is positive; thus suggesting that the hazard function is increasing with time. Predicted mean survival time cannot be calculated for the Gompertz, because there is no closed-form expression for it, but the predicted median time is about 81 years.

The survivor, hazard and cumulative hazard functions are produced by the commands already shown for smoking initiation and cessation, and then combined in a single graph. The Gompertz model produces estimated functions that mimic very well the empirical functions reported in Figure 6.10. The shape of the hazard function is increasing with time (Figure 6.12).

6.7 OVERVIEW

There are two types of duration data: continuous and discrete time. This chapter focuses on continuous time duration models while the next covers discrete time models. The chapter takes the analysis of the HALS data on health and mortality from Chapter 5 a step further by estimating parametric models for initiation and cessation of smoking and for the age of death (this draws on work by Forster and Jones (2001) and Balia and Jones (2011)).

7   Health and retirement

SYNOPSIS

This chapter illustrates convenient methods for discrete-time duration analysis. A sub-sample of the BHPS is used to investigate the extent that 'health shocks' are one of the factors that lead to early retirement.

7.1 INTRODUCTION

This chapter illustrates the use of discrete-time duration models by analysing the impact of health on early retirement decisions. Health is undoubtedly an important factor in the decision to retire, however, the relationship between health and retirement is complex. It is difficult to estimate the impact because health and work are jointly determined and there are problems finding an appropriate measure of health for use in this context. In order to usefully investigate the relationship, it is necessary to use longitudinal data to enable us to track individuals from work into retirement.

The case study presented follows Jones *et al.* (2010) where attention is paid to the problem of potential measurement error in using self-reported measures of health status and to the question of whether a change in labour market status is best identified by a 'shock' to an individual's health or by a levels effect (for example, a slow deterioration in health status).

7.2 PREPARING AND SUMMARISING THE DATA

We use data from the first 12 waves (1991–2002) of the British Household Panel Survey (BHPS). The main variables used in the analysis are reported below.

Retirement and labour market status

The definition of retirement used here is a self-reported classification based on the answer to the question on job status (jbstat) in the BHPS. Individuals are asked to classify their status as one of the following: self-employed, employed, unemployed, retired, on maternity leave, caring for the family, in full-time education, long-term sick or disabled, or on a government training scheme. The following commands recode the job status variable into a series of dummy variables, including one representing individuals who have reported themselves as retired (retired):

```
/* Job status */
recode jbstat -9 -8 -7 -1 =. /* remove missing data */
tabulate jbstat, gen(jobdm)
```

jbstat	Freq.	Percent	Cum.
self-employed	1341	12.66	12.66
employed	4766	45.01	57.67
unemployed	402	3.80	61.47
retired	3487	32.93	94.40
maternity leave	1	0.01	94.41
family care	210	1.98	96.39
ft studt, school	6	0.06	96.45
lt sick, disabld	347	3.28	99.73
gvt trng scheme	3	0.03	99.75
other	26	0.25	100.00
Total	10589	100.00	

```
rename jobdm1 selfemp
rename jobdm2 emp
rename jobdm3 unemp
rename jobdm4 retired
rename jobdm5 matleave
rename jobdm6 famcare
rename jobdm7 student
rename jobdm8 ltsick
rename jobdm9 govtrain
rename jobdm10 jobothr
```

For the duration analysis reported in Section 7.4, we follow individuals from work to the time when they first report retirement. Any subsequent transitions back to work are ignored. The focus is on early retirement and hence we limit the sample to those who retire prior to reaching state retirement age.

Health variables

As discussed in Chapter 2, the BHPS includes a number of health and health-related variables. Of particular interest is the measure of general self-assessed health (SAH) status as well as an alternative measure of health that refers to limitations in daily activities.

The simple five-point SAH variable (hlstat) available in the BHPS is a subjective measure of general health based on answers to the question: 'Please think back over the last 12 months about how your health has been. Compared to people of your own age, would you say that your health has on the whole been excellent/ good/ fair/ poor/ very poor?'

As mentioned in Chapter 2, a problem arises with using this variable because in wave 9 (only) of the BHPS there was a change in the question together with a modification to the available response categories. The wave 9 question (hlfs1) asks respondents about their 'general state of health' (without the age benchmark used in the original version) on the scale: excellent, very good, good, fair, poor. Both versions of the variable are coded such that 1 represents the best possible health and 5 represents worst health. Recode the variables to be increasing in good health:

```
/* Self-assessed health */
recode hlstat -9 -8 -7 -6 -2 -1 = .  /* remove missing data */
recode hlstat 1 = 5 2 = 4 4 = 2 5 = 1 /* recode variable */

/* Change labelling of variable */
label define health 1 "very poor" 2 "poor" 3 "fair"        ///
    4 "good" 5 "excellent"
label values hlstat health

/* General state of health */
recode hlsf1 -9 -8 -7 -1 = .
recode hlsf1 1 = 5 2 = 4 4 = 2 5 = 1

/* Change labelling of variable */
label define health2 1 "poor" 2 "fair" 3 "good"            ///
    4 "very good" 5 "excellent"
label values hlsf1 health2
```

In order to maximise the span of data available and to achieve consistency over all 12 waves, we follow the method of Hernandez-Quevedo *et al.* (2004) and collapse SAH into the following 4-category scale where 1 represents *very poor or poor health*, 2 *fair health*, 3 *good or very good health* and 4 *excellent health* (hlstatc4). In this way, both the original SAH question asked of respondents in waves 1 to 8 and 10 to 12 and the wave 9 version of the SAH question can be used.

```
/* Recode general health into a 4 category variable */
generate hlstatc4 = hlstat
replace hlstatc4 = hlsf1 if wavenum == 9
recode hlstatc4 2 = 1 if wavenum ~= 9
recode hlstatc4 3 = 2 if wavenum ~= 9
recode hlstatc4 4 = 3 if wavenum ~= 9
recode hlstatc4 5 = 4 if wavenum ~= 9
recode hlstatc4 4 = 3 if wavenum == 9
recode hlstatc4 5 = 4 if wavenum == 9

label define healthc4 1 "vpoor or poor" 2 "fair"              ///
    3 "good or vgood" 4 "excellent"
label values hlstatc4 healthc4
```

Create dummy variables representing each health state as follows:

```
tabulate hlstatc4, gen(hlc4dm)
rename hlc4dm1 sah4vpp
rename hlc4dm2 sah4fair
rename hlc4dm3 sah4gvg
rename hlc4dm4 sah4ex
```

An alternative health measure is self-reported functional limitations, based on the question 'Does your health in any way limit your daily activities compared to most people of your age?' This is arguably more objective than the general SAH question, and more directly related to ability to work and accordingly is a useful alternative to the self-assessed health variable. The question was not asked in wave 9 and given that health limitations are likely to consist of chronic problems, we assume that wave 8 values hold for wave 9. Create a variable coded 1 if an individual reports a health limitation and 0 otherwise (hlltyes):

```
/* Health limits daily activities */

recode hllt -9/-1 = .

sort pid wavenum
replace hllt = hllt[_n-1] if wavenum == 9
tabulate hllt, gen(hlltdm)
rename hlltdm1 hlltyes
```

Finally, we make use of questions on specific health problems. These are used to construct a latent health stock (see Section 7.3). Individuals are asked whether or not they have any of a list of specific health problems from the following: arms, legs or hands (hlparms), sight (hlpsee), hearing (hlphear), skin conditions or allergies (hlpskin), chest/breathing (hlpchest), heart/blood pressure (hlpheart), stomach or digestion (hlpstom), diabetes (hlpdiab), anxiety or depression (hlpanx), alcohol or drugs (hlpalch), epilepsy or migraine (hlpanx), or other (hlpothr). We create a binary dummy variable for the presence or not of each specific problem.

Spousal/partner variables

We focus on modelling the impact of health on the timing of retirement for men only and include a variable representing the health status of the individual's spouse or partner (should they have one – shlltyes, slatsah). This allows us to investigate the interaction between spousal or partner's health and an individual's decision to retire. We also include a variable representing whether a spouse or partner is employed (lspjb). To reduce concerns over endogeneity bias, this variable is lagged one period (the variable label has the prefix, l, to denote a lag).

Income and wealth

The main income variable used is the log of household income across all waves in which an individual is observed. Household income consists of labour and non-labour income (fihhyr), adjusted using the Retail Price Index and equivalised by the McClement's scale (fieqfca) to adjust for household size and composition. In the models reported here, we adapt this to represent the mean across all waves prior to retirement. This is to reduce concerns over endogeneity, as income is expected to reduce significantly at retirement (m2lnhinc) and is computed as follows:

```
generate fihhyr2 = fihhyr
replace fihhyr2 = fihhyr* (133.5/138.5) if wavenum == 2
replace fihhyr2 = fihhyr* (133.5/140.7) if wavenum == 3
replace fihhyr2 = fihhyr* (133.5/144.1) if wavenum == 4
replace fihhyr2 = fihhyr* (133.5/149.1) if wavenum == 5
replace fihhyr2 = fihhyr* (133.5/152.7) if wavenum == 6
replace fihhyr2 = fihhyr* (133.5/157.5) if wavenum == 7
replace fihhyr2 = fihhyr* (133.5/162.9) if wavenum == 8
replace fihhyr2 = fihhyr* (133.5/165.4) if wavenum == 9
replace fihhyr2 = fihhyr* (133.5/170.3) if wavenum == 10
replace fihhyr2 = fihhyr* (133.5/173.3) if wavenum == 11
replace fihhyr2 = fihhyr* (133.5/176.2) if wavenum == 12
sort pid wavenum
quietly by pid: generate increeq=fihhyr2/fieqfca
quietly by pid: generate lninc=ln(increeq)
by pid: egen m2lnhinc = mean(lninc) if retired == 0
replace m2lnhinc = m2lnhinc[_n-1] if retired == 1
```

Table 7.1 Variable names and definitions

Variable	Description
retired	Binary dependent variable; 1 if respondent states he/she is retired, 0 otherwise
hlltyes	Self-assessed health limitations; 1 if health limits daily activities, 0 otherwise
sah	Self-assessed health; 1: very poor or poor, 2: fair, 3: good or very good, 4: excellent
sah4ex	Self-assessed health: 1 if excellent, 0 otherwise
sah4gvg	Self-assessed health: 1 if good or very good, 0 otherwise
sah4fair	Self-assessed health: 1 if fair, 0 otherwise
sah4vpp	Self-assessed health: 1 if poor or very poor, 0 otherwise (baseline category)
m2lnhinc	Individual-specific mean of log equivalised real household labour and non-labour income
HseOwn	1 if house owned outright, 0 otherwise (baseline category)
HseMort	1 if house has outstanding mortgage, 0 otherwise
HseRent	1 if house is rented, 0 otherwise
HseAuthAss	1 if house is owned by housing authority/association, 0 otherwise
marcoup	1 if married or living as a couple, 0 otherwise
deghdeg	1 if highest educational attainment is degree or higher degree, 0 otherwise
hndalev	1 if highest educational attainment is HND or A level, 0 otherwise
ocse	1 if highest educational attainment is O level or CSE, 0 otherwise
noqual	1 if no qualifications, 0 otherwise (baseline category)
everppenr	1 if respondent has made contributions to a private pension plan during observation period, 0 otherwise
everemppr	1 if respondent has been a member of an employers pension plan during observation period, 0 otherwise
privcomp0	1 if respondent's sector of employment is within the private sector, 0 otherwise
civlocgov0	1 if respondent's sector of employment is within civic or local government, 0 otherwise
jbsecto0	1 if respondent's sector of employment is other to above, 0 otherwise
selfemp	1 if respondent is self-employed, 0 otherwise (baseline category)
job	1 if respondent's spouse/partner has a job, 0 otherwise
age5054	1 if respondent is aged 50 to 54 (inclusive), 0 otherwise

Table 7.1 continued

Variable	Description
age5559	1 if respondent is aged 55 to 59 (inclusive), 0 otherwise
age6064	1 if respondent is aged 60 to 64 (inclusive), 0 otherwise
age6569	1 if respondent is aged 65 to 69 (inclusive), 0 otherwise
NorthW	1 if respondent resides in North West, Merseyside or Greater Manchester, 0 otherwise
NorthE	1 if respondent resides in North, South Yorkshire, West Yorkshire, North Yorkshire, Humberside or Tyne & Wear, 0 otherwise
SouthE	1 if respondent resides in South East or East Anglia, 0 otherwise (baseline category)
SouthW	1 if respondent resides in South West, 0 otherwise
London	1 if respondent resides in Inner or Outer London, 0 otherwise
Midland	1 if respondent resides in East or West Midlands, 0 otherwise
Scot	1 if respondent resides in Scotland, 0 otherwise
Wales	1 if respondents resides in Wales, 0 otherwise
hlthprb	Self-reported health problems: 1 if problem reported, 0 otherwise. There are also individual dummies for problems with: arms, legs or hands (arms), sight (see), hearing (hear), skin conditions or allergies (skin) chest/breathing (chest), heart/blood pressure (heart), stomach or digestion (stomach), diabetes (diabetes), anxiety or depression (anxiety), alcohol or drugs (alcohol), epilepsy (epilepsy), migraine (migraine) or Other (other)

We also have information on pension entitlement, which distinguishes between people who have no occupational or private pension, an occupational pension, or a private pension. From these, we construct a variable representing whether an individual has ever, over the course of BHPS observations, made contributions to a private pension plan (everppenr) and whether an individual has been a member of an employer's pension plan (everemppr). Data on housing tenure are also available, which distinguish between people who own their home outright (HseOwn), own with a mortgage (HseMort), or live in privately rented (HseRent) or local authority rented housing (HseAuthAss).

Other socio-demographic variables

Other variables we are interested in using include age, sex, marital status (marcoup), educational attainment (deghdeg, hndalev, ocse), and regional dummies (NorthW - Wales). We also include variables that indicate the employment sector of the individual in the first wave of observation (privcomp0, `civlocgov0, jbsecto0)`. The latter variables carry the postfix 0 to indicate that they represent initial values. These variables have been constructed from their respective source variables in the BHPS. Variable names and definitions are summarised in Table 7.1.

Stock sample

Our interest lies on the role of health in determining the timing of the decision to retire. As such we wish to observe individuals who at the beginning of the BHPS survey can be considered to be at risk of retirement. Jenkins (1995) defines such a sample as a stock sample. For our purposes, the stock sample consists of those individuals who were original BHPS sample members aged 50 or older *and* had provided a full interview (BHPS variable: `ivfio=1`) *and* were in work (defined here as employed or self-employed) in the *first wave* of the survey. This sample consists of $n = 1,135$ individuals, 494 women and 641 men. 661 individuals are present for all 12 waves, but others are lost due to sample attrition and death. Our models of retirement are estimated on complete sequences of observations such that should an individual leave the panel but then return at a later date, we only make use of information up to the wave of first exit. The Stata code for the selection of the stock sample is as follows:

```
/* 1. Select if provided full interview in wave 1 */
drop if (ivfio ~= 1 & wavenum == 1)

/* 2. Select if aged 50 or over in wave 1 */
drop if (age <= 49 & wavenum == 1)

/* 3. Select iff employed or self-employed in wave 1 */
drop if ((jbstat < 1 | jbstat > 2) & wavenum == 1)

/* 4. Select only individuals interviewed at wave 1 */
sort pid wavenum
by pid: egen minwave = min(wavenum)
drop if minwave ~= 1

/* 5. Select complete sequences of responses - i.e. stop at */
/* first unit non-response */
drop if (ivfio < 1 | ivfio > 3)
generate const = 1
by pid: generate sumcon = sum(const)
by pid: generate diff = wavenum - sumcon
drop if diff ~= 0
```

For the duration analysis we consider the decision to take early retirement and accordingly, remove individuals over state retirement age (see Section 7.4).

However, for the descriptive analysis presented in this section we consider complete sequences of transitions from work to retirement including that consistent with reaching state retirement age. For illustrative purposes, this chapter only considers the retirement behaviour of men so remove women from the sample of interest:

```
drop if male ~= 1
```

Analogous results for women can be found in Jones *et al.* (2010).

Labour market transitions

The stock sample consists of individuals in work at the first wave of the BHPS. At subsequent waves, transitions to other labour market states, including retirement, may be made. We can summarise information on labour market transitions in each wave by using the tabulate command. For example, at wave 2:

```
table jbstat if wavenum==2
---------------------------
          jbstat |    Freq.
-----------------|----------
   self-employed |      138
        employed |      349
      unemployed |       19
         retired |       50
lt sick, disabld |       11
           other |        2
---------------------------
```

An efficient way to summarise transitions across all waves is provided as follows:

```
forvalues j=1(1)12 {
  table jbstat if wavenum == `j'
  }
```

Table 7.2 summarises the transitions across the 12 waves and further includes individuals lost to attrition and death (where this is known in the BHPS). Our sample consists of 641 men reporting employment or self-employment status in wave 1 and this figure gradually decreases to 100 by the twelfth wave. Fifty individuals classify themselves as retired in wave 2 and this increases to 241 in wave 12, representing a near five-fold increase. Some caution is required, however, in interpreting the retirement figures. For example, while at wave 2, 50 individuals and at wave 3, 80 individuals are reported to have retired it does not follow that 30 (80 – 50) individuals retired between waves 2 and 3. The number retired will

Table 7.2 Labour market status by wave

	1	2	3	4	5	6	7	8	9	10	11	12
Attrition		68	116	146	176	199	209	222	235	248	262	278
Self-employed	162	138	124	105	97	89	76	68	53	46	49	38
Employed	479	349	270	228	193	169	147	129	104	93	78	62
Unemployed		19	20	23	13	10	9	5	6	5	0	2
Retired		50	80	105	125	141	168	187	214	226	233	241
LT sick, disabled		11	23	25	27	28	25	22	19	13	14	10
Other		2	2	2	1	1	3	1	4	5	1	1
Deaths		4	6	7	9	4	4	7	6	5	4	9
Total	641	641	641	641	641	641	641	641	641	641	641	641
In work*	641	487	394	333	290	258	223	197	157	139	127	100

* Employed and self-employed.

Table 7.3 Descriptive statistics

	All	*Pre-Retirement*	*Post-Retirement*
Retired	.324	0	1
Own Health			
hlltyes	.156	.127	.216
sah4ex	.238	.257	.197
sah4gvg	.486	.485	.488
sah4fair	.213	.200	.240
sah4vpp	.064	.058	.075
Spousal Health			
shlltyes	.180	.166	.207
ssah4ex	.156	.171	.126
ssah4gvg	.431	.437	.419
ssah4fair	.191	.192	.191
ssah4vpp	.085	.084	.088
Covariates			
m2lnhinc	9.76	9.76	9.76
HseOwn	.522	.421	.732
HseMort	.320	.415	.122
HseRent	.046	.054	.027
HseAuthAss	.112	.109	.118
marcoup	.867	.886	.827
deghdeg	.084	.087	.078
hndalev	.180	.188	.164
ocse	.217	.214	.223
everppenr	.402	.454	.274
everemppr	.539	.527	.563
privcomp0	.503	.488	.534
civlocgov0	.137	.123	.167
jbsecto0	.100	.098	.105
lspjb	.429	.551	.219

be greater than 30 due to some retirees being lost to follow-up between the two waves. Accordingly, by wave 12 more than 241 men will have made the transition to retirement.

Descriptive statistics for our stock sample of men are summarised in Table 7.3 for the sample as a whole and broken down by retirement status. These were obtained using the following commands:

```
global summvars "retired hlltyes sah4ex sah4gvg sah4fair
 sah4vpp shlltyes ssah4ex ssah4gvg ssah4fair ssah4vpp
 m2lnhinc HseOwn HseMort HseRent HseAuthAss marcoup deghdeg
 hndalev ocse
```

```
everppenr everemppr privcomp0 civlocgov jbsecto0 lspjb"

summarize $summvars
bysort retired: summarize $summvars
```

The majority of individuals report SAH status as good or very good. It is notable that the reporting of fair and poor/very poor health increases from pre- to post-retirement while the reporting of excellent health is lower post-retirement. Similarly, the reporting of heath limitations increases post-retirement. Interestingly, the proportion of men whose partner, should they have one, reported fair or poor/very poor SAH is roughly the same pre- and post-retirement. The reporting of health limitations by a partner increases post- compared to pre-retirement.

Of the other variables, the majority of individuals own their house outright (HseOwn); this proportion increases after retirement and is accompanied by a decrease in the proportion of people with an outstanding mortgage. In the rental sector, the proportion living in Local Authority rented accommodation (HseAuthAss) increases after retirement. The majority of individuals sampled do not have an educational qualification (52 per cent). Men are likely to have paid into either a private or employee pension scheme (94 per cent). Fifty per cent of individuals report working within the private sector, and approximately 41 per cent of men have a spouse or partner who is in employment.

7.3 DEALING WITH SELF-REPORTED HEALTH

Subjective measures of health have been a focus in the literature attempting to quantify the impact of health on retirement. There are, however, problems in relying on self-reported measures of health status. First, self-reported measures are based on subjective judgements and there is no reason to believe that these judgements are comparable across individuals (see Chapter 4 for further discussion of this issue). Second, self-reported health may not be independent of labour market status. Third, citing health problems may be a way to rationalise behaviour for individuals outside the labour market given that ill-health is a legitimate reason for not working. In addition, there may exist financial incentives to report ill-health as means of obtaining disability benefits for individuals for whom the financial rewards of continuing in the labour force are low – often cited as the 'disability route into retirement' (Riphahn, 1997; Blundell *et al.*, 2002). For example, in a study of social security benefit programmes in the Netherlands, Kerkhofs and Lindeboom (1995) show that recipients of disability insurance systematically overstated their health problems. However, in general, empirical studies on the role of health on retirement provide mixed conclusions about the endogeneity of SAH and the extent of the bias provided through measurement error.

To attempt to deal with the difficulties noted above from using a self-reported measure of health, we estimate a model of SAH as a function of more objective measures of health to define a latent 'health stock' variable. This health stock variable is then used as an indicator of health in the model of retirement. This follows the approach set-out in Bound (1991) and Bound *et al.* (1999) and subsequently adopted by Disney *et al.* (2006) and Au *et al.* (2005). The idea of constructing a health stock is analogous to using objective measures of health to instrument the endogenous and potentially error-ridden SAH variable.

Consider the aspect of health that affects an individual's decision to retire, h_{it}^R, to be a function of objective and specific measures of health, z_{it}, such that:

$$h_{it}^R = z_{it}\beta + \epsilon_{it} \,, \quad i = 1,2,...n; \ t = 1,2,...T_i \qquad (7.1)$$

where ϵ_{it} is a time varying error term uncorrelated with z_{it}.

We do not directly observe h_{it}^R but instead observe a measure of SAH, h_{it}^S. We can specify the latent counterpart to h_{it}^S as h_{it}^* such that:

$$h_{it}^* = h_{it}^R + \eta_{it} \,, \quad i = 1,2,...n; \ t = 1,2,...T_i \qquad (7.2)$$

where η_{it} represents measurement error in the mapping of h_{it}^* to h_{it}^R and is uncorrelated with h_{it}^R. Substituting (7.1) into (7.2) gives:

$$h_{it}^* = z_{it}\beta + \epsilon_{it} + \eta_{it} = z_{it}\beta + \nu_{it} \,, \quad i = 1,2,...n; \ t = 1,2,...T_i \qquad (7.3)$$

The presence of η_{it} in (7.3) represents measurement error, which may be related to labour market status of the individual, and is the source of the bias that would be obtained if we were to use h_{it}^* directly when estimating the impact of health on retirement behaviour. To avoid such bias we use the predicted health stock, $\hat{h}_{it}^*$, which is purged of measurement error.

We combine (7.3) with an observation mechanism linking the categorical or dichotomous indicator (h_{it}) to the latent measure of health, h_{it}^* expressed as follows:

$$h_{it} = k \quad \text{if } \mu_{k-1} < h_{it}^* \le \mu_k \,, \quad k = 1,2,...m$$

where, $\mu_0 = -\infty$, $\mu_k \le \mu_{k+1}$, $\mu_m = \infty$. By imposing normality on the error, ν_{it}, model (7.3) can then be estimated as a standard ordered probit using maximum likelihood. The predicted values for the health stock can then be used in our retirement model.

Computing the health stock

We construct our health stock variable using a pooled ordered probit model by regressing our measure of self-assessed health (hlstatc4) onto a set of 'objective' health measures (Table 7.4). For the latter we use the set of variables on health problems (hlparms to hlpothr). The following command is used:

```
oprobit hlstatc4 hlparms hlpsee hlphear hlpskin hlpchest ///
    hlpheart hlpstom hlpdiab hlpanx hlpalch              ///
    hlpepil hlpmigr hlpothr
```

To obtain the latent health stock variable, termed, `sahlat`, we use the `predict` command with the `xb` option to specify that we require the linear index. Predict the health stock for individuals for whom we have the relevant set of health variables by specifying `e(sample)`:

```
predict sahlat if e(sample), xb
```

The estimated coefficients display the expected negative sign – health problems are associated with lower reporting of self-assessed health. All effects are highly statistically significant. The dominant effect (in terms of the size of coefficient) is health problems associated with the use of alcohol or drugs, but problems with arms, legs or hands, chest and breathing, heart or blood pressure, stomach or

Table 7.4 Ordered probits for self-assessed health

```
-----------------------------------------------------------------
Ordered probit estimates              Number of obs =      5449
                                      LR chi2(13)   = 1731.05
                                      Prob > chi2   =  0.0000
Log likelihood =  -5656.06            Pseudo R2     =  0.1327
-----------------------------------------------------------------
hlstatc4 |   Coef.   Std. Err.     z   P>|z|  [95% Conf. Interval]
---------|-------------------------------------------------------
 hlparms | -.5818711  .0328725 -17.70  0.000  -.6463001  -.5174421
  hlpsee | -.4033917  .0700121  -5.76  0.000  -.5406128  -.2661705
 hlphear | -.0902711  .0392977  -2.30  0.022  -.1672931  -.0132491
 hlpskin | -.2482158  .055881   -4.44  0.000  -.3577406   -.138691
hlpchest | -.6621975  .0483275 -13.70  0.000  -.7569175  -.5674774
hlpheart | -.6228053  .0348666 -17.86  0.000  -.6911426  -.5544679
 hlpstom | -.6267968  .0627513  -9.99  0.000   -.749787  -.5038065
 hlpdiab | -.7773897  .0747391 -10.40  0.000  -.9238756  -.6309039
  hlpanx | -.6515209  .0763856  -8.53  0.000  -.8012339  -.5018079
 hlpalch | -1.286594  .3272145  -3.93  0.000  -1.927922  -.6452649
 hlpepil | -.3914404  .1728269  -2.26  0.024  -.7301749  -.0527059
 hlpmigr | -.2186143  .0866258  -2.52  0.012  -.3883978  -.0488308
 hlpothr | -.8190626  .069569  -11.77  0.000  -.9554153  -.6827098
---------|-------------------------------------------------------
   _cut1 |  -2.54126  .0417798        (Ancillary parameters)
   _cut2 | -1.339949  .0287601
   _cut3 |  .2179189  .0242035
-----------------------------------------------------------------
```

digestion, diabetes, anxiety or depression, and problems reported as other are also notable.

From the ordered probit model, we also construct a latent health stock of an individual's spouse or partner, should they have one – slatsah. This allows us to investigate the effect of their spouse's health on an individual's retirement decision.

Defining a health shock

Of further relevance is whether the transition to retirement is best identified by a 'shock' to an individual's health or by a levels effect, through a slow deterioration in health status. It is often argued that modelling health 'shocks' is a convenient way to eliminate one source of potential endogeneity bias caused through correlation between individual-specific unobserved factors and health (see for example, Disney *et al.*, 2006).

To identify a health shock, we include a measure of health lagged one period together with initial period health. By conditioning on initial health we can interpret the estimated coefficient on lagged health as representing a deviation from some underlying health stock and accordingly, the approach has the advantage of controlling for person-specific unobserved health-related heterogeneity. Lagged health may be more informative about the decision to retire than contemporaneous health simply because transitions take time. That is, it may take time to adjust fully to a health limitation to enable an individual to assess his/her ability to work or to learn whether an employer can or will accommodate a health limitation.

Compute initial period health and health lagged one period as follows:

```
sort pid wavenum
by pid: generate hlltyes0 = hlltyes[1]
by pid: generate sahlat0 = sahlat[1]
by pid: generate lhlltyes = hlltyes[_n-1]
by pid: generate lsahlat = sahlat[_n-1]
```

7.4 EMPIRICAL APPROACH TO DURATION MODELLING

Descriptive analysis

Before proceeding to estimating duration models, we describe the pattern of responses using xtdes. To invoke this command we must first define the individual identifier, pid, and the cross-section identifier, wavenum, using the command xtset as follows:

```
xtset pid wavenum
xtdes, patterns(20)
```

which produces:

```
    pid: 10014608, 10020179, ..., 19130392              n =    641
wavenum: 1, 2, ..., 12                                  T =     12
         Delta(wavenum) = 1; (12-1)+1 = 12
         (pid*wavenum uniquely identifies each observation)

Distribution of T_i:  min    5%    25%    50%    75%    95%    max
                        1     1      4     12     12     12     12


    Freq.      Percent      Cum. |  Pattern
---------------------------------------------------------------------
     354        55.23       55.23 |  111111111111
      72        11.23       66.46 |  1...........
      50         7.80       74.26 |  11..........
      32         4.99       79.25 |  1111........
      31         4.84       84.09 |  111.........
      21         3.28       87.36 |  11111111111.
      18         2.81       90.17 |  11111.......
      16         2.50       92.67 |  1111111.....
      13         2.03       94.70 |  1111111111..
      12         1.87       96.57 |  ·11111111....
      12         1.87       98.44 |  111111111...
      10         1.56      100.00 |  111111......
---------------------------------------------------------------------
     641       100.00             |  XXXXXXXXXXXX
```

This clearly shows that we observe only full sequences of responses. That is, the sequences are not interrupted by missing data at a particular wave. Individuals may or may not have retired during the course of a sequence.

Stata's survival time commands

Before proceeding to estimate discrete-time hazard models, first prepare the dataset in a manner suitable to implement the suite of Stata commands for the analysis of survival time data. This is achieved using Stata's st (survival time) commands.

In general, we assume that the dataset is organised in such a way that, for each individual, there are as many rows as there are intervals at risk of retirement (or in more general applications events such as death), and accordingly each individual contributes T_i rows of data, where T_i is the number of waves the individual is observed up to and including the wave of retirement, or the wave in which the individual is censored. This corresponds to an unbalanced panel data format.

Since our interest lies in modelling durations to age at early retirement (defined by the state pension age of 65 years for men) the duration stock sample of interest consists of men who were original sample members and aged between 50 and 65 years at the start of the BHPS. Accordingly we restrict the risk set to those individuals aged between 50 and state retirement age, implying that the baseline hazard of retirement is zero for individuals aged below 50 years, and that individuals leave the risk set on reaching 65 years.

We construct a variable to represent duration time (age) to retirement as follows:

```
sort pid wavenum
by pid: gen age0=age[1]
generate time = age0+wavenum-1
```

The variable `time` is constructed as the age at which an individual entered the stock sample plus the number of waves the individual has been observed in the sample. This provides a more appropriate duration measure of the age at retirement than simply using the variable `age`, since in the dataset the latter is time invariant across adjacent waves for some individual-wave combinations due to the exact timing of the administration of the survey (for example, just after a birthday one year, and just before a birthday in the following year). An alternative specification is to consider duration as the number of years or time elapsed from entering the panel to retirement. However, this is not an appropriate measure of duration dependence when age of retirement is the outcome of interest and individuals enter the panel at different ages. Remove individuals over state retirement age as follows:

```
drop if time >= 65 | age >= 65
```

In addition to having a unique identifier for each individual (`pid`), we require an identifier for each discrete age interval at which the person is at risk of retirement. This can be generated from our age identifier, `time`. We further require a binary variable to indicate whether between waves of observation an individual is observed to retire. For an individual who is observed to be at risk over a number of discrete-time points and is then observed to retire, this variable will be equal to 0 for all points up to retirement (wave 1, ..., T_i-1) and equal to 1 for the final observation period (wave T_i). If an individual is censored at time T_i, 0 would be recorded for all time-periods (waves: 1, ..., T_i). The variable, `retired`, is coded in the manner described. Generate a variable to represent the age at which individuals first become at risk of retirement, which in this study is 50 years:

```
generate risk50 = 50
```

We are now able to prepare the data for analysis by ensuring the data are sorted and invoking the `stset` command as follows:

```
sort pid time
stset time , id(pid) failure(retired == 1) origin(risk50)
```

The option, `origin`, specifies the age at which individuals first become at risk of retiring. These commands return the following:

```
id:  pid
       failure event: retired == 1
obs. time interval: (time[_n-1], time]
 enter on or after: time age0
 exit on or before: failure
     t for analysis: (time-origin)
             origin: time risk50
------------------------------------------------------------------
   3747  total obs.
    581  obs. end on or before enter()
    530  obs. begin on or after (first) failure
------------------------------------------------------------------
   2636  obs. remaining, representing
    499  subjects
    166  failures in single failure-per-subject data
   2636  total analysis time at risk, at risk from t =      0
                          earliest observed entry t =       0
                             last observed exit t =        14
```

Stata internally creates a binary variable, _d, indicating retirement status, and a second variable, _t, to represent the number of age periods (years above the base age of 50) a person is at risk of early retirement. The results show that the last observed exit is at $t=14$, corresponding to an age of 64 years, that is, just prior to reaching state retirement age for men. We can tabulate the number of retirement events by age as follows: `table _t _d`, providing:

```
          |          _d
      _t  |      0          1  |      Total
----------|-------------------|----------------------------------
       1  |     51          1  |         52
       2  |     87          2  |         89
       3  |    133          3  |        136
       4  |    171          4  |        175
       5  |    190          2  |        192
       6  |    203         14  |        217
       7  |    215         10  |        225
       8  |    224         16  |        240
       9  |    232          8  |        240
      10  |    232         27  |        259
      11  |    215         20  |        235
      12  |    194         11  |        205
```

```
13 |        172       29 |         201
14 |        151       19 |         170
----------|-------------------|-----------------------------------
 Total |     2,470      166 |       2,636
```

Similarly, retirement events can be tabulated by health limitations using, table _d lhlltyes, to return:

```
          |      lhlltyes
    _d |        0          1 |      Total
----------|-------------------|-----------------------------------
     0 |     2,190      279 |       2,469
     1 |       125       41 |         166
----------|-------------------|-----------------------------------
 Total |     2,315      320 |       2,635
```

The table shows that while 13 per cent of men reporting health limitations take early retirement over the observation period, only 5 per cent reporting no health limitations retire.

Life tables

Further descriptive analysis of the impact of health on the decision to retire can be achieved using life table methods. Life tables provide an estimate of the survival, failure or hazard function associated with a categorical variable (in our example, hlltyes). These are obtained using the ltable command. By default, the corresponding output is provided in table form, but can also be displayed graphically.

An important consideration in the use of ltable is the underlying process leading to the observations of the events of interest. In our example, although we only observe retirement at the end of each observation period (that is, when a BHPS sample member is interviewed) we assume that the underlying survival time (duration to age at retirement) is continuous, but we are unable to observe the exact age of retirement. In such circumstances, estimates of the underlying hazard rate are derived from assumptions about the shape of the hazard within each time interval and it is common to assume that events occur at a uniform rate between intervals (years). This is often termed an *actuarial adjustment* and ltable applies this adjustment by default.

The life table estimate of survival is obtained as follows. Assume that in the age interval, t_j to t_{j+1} we observe d_j transitions to early retirement, while c_j individuals are censored. Further assume that there are n_j individuals at risk at the beginning of the age interval. By assuming that the censoring process is such that the censored survival times occur at a uniform rate across the age interval, the average number of individuals who are at risk during the interval is: $n_j^r = n_j - c_j/2$. Accordingly in the *j*-th interval, the probability of retirement becomes: d_j/n_j^r.

The probability that an individual survives (does not retire) beyond age t_k, that is until sometime after the start of the k-th age interval, is:

$$S(t) = \prod_{j=1}^{k} \frac{\left(n_j^r - d_j\right)}{n_j^r}$$

This is the life table or actuarial estimate. The estimated probability of survival to the *beginning* of the first age interval at risk (age 50 years) is unity, and the probability of survival *within* any age interval is assumed constant.

The following command is used to produce the life table for early retirement by health limitations (defined at baseline). The test option produces chi-squared tests of the difference between the groups (health limitations versus no health limitations when entering the sample), failure indicates that a cumulative failure table is required (1 – survival).

```
ltable _t (_d) , by(hlltyes0) test tvid(pid) failure
```

This produces the output shown in Table 7.5.

The likelihood ratio test of homogeneity fails to reject the null hypothesis that the failure function is equivalent across men who do and do not report health limitations; similarly the log-rank test for equality fails to reject the null at the 5 per cent significance level.

We can graph the output of ltable using the graph option, shown below for survival estimates (proportion not retired):

```
sts graph, by(hlltyes0) l1title("Proportion not retired") ///
    plot1(lpattern(dash)) noshow
```

This produces the estimates displayed as Figure 7.1.

While we cannot reject the null hypothesis that the retirement functions are equivalent, the figure indicates that men reporting health limitations appear to be associated with a greater probability of early retirement compared to those not reporting limitations.

7.5 STOCK SAMPLING AND DISCRETE-TIME HAZARD ANALYSIS

The starting point for our analysis is the duration model stock-sampling approach of Jenkins (1995). This method represents the transition to retirement as a discrete-time hazard model enabling us to estimate the effect of covariates on the probability of retirement. The Jenkins (1995) approach relies on organising the data so that there are multiple rows of observations for each individual with as many rows are periods at risk. Accordingly, the dataset has an unbalanced panel data format.

Table 7.5 Life-table for retirement by health limitations

Interval		Beg. Total	Deaths	Lost	Cum. Failure	Std. Error	[95% Conf.Int.]	
hlltyes0	0							
1	2	459	1	4	0.0022	0.0022	0.0003	0.0154
2	3	454	1	6	0.0044	0.0031	0.0011	0.0175
3	4	447	3	8	0.0111	0.0050	0.0047	0.0266
4	5	436	3	12	0.0180	0.0063	0.0091	0.0358
5	6	421	2	10	0.0228	0.0071	0.0123	0.0419
6	7	409	11	12	0.0494	0.0105	0.0325	0.0749
7	8	386	9	10	0.0719	0.0127	0.0508	0.1013
8	9	367	15	10	0.1103	0.0156	0.0835	0.1451
9	10	342	6	10	0.1262	0.0166	0.0973	0.1628
10	11	326	25	19	0.1952	0.0202	0.1590	0.2385
11	12	282	19	27	0.2522	0.0226	0.2110	0.2997
12	13	236	11	23	0.2888	0.0240	0.2446	0.3390
13	14	202	27	21	0.3891	0.0273	0.3380	0.4450
14	15	154	17	137	0.5105	0.0343	0.4454	0.5793
hlltyes0	1							
2	3	40	1	0	0.0250	0.0247	0.0036	0.1645
4	5	39	1	0	0.0500	0.0345	0.0127	0.1855
5	6	38	0	1	0.0500	0.0345	0.0127	0.1855
6	7	37	3	2	0.1292	0.0540	0.0558	0.2831
7	8	32	1	0	0.1564	0.0587	0.0734	0.3158
8	9	31	1	1	0.1840	0.0630	0.0921	0.3482
9	10	29	2	1	0.2413	0.0704	0.1332	0.4135
10	11	26	2	0	0.2997	0.0761	0.1779	0.4768
11	12	24	1	3	0.3308	0.0788	0.2023	0.5102
12	13	20	0	1	0.3308	0.0788	0.2023	0.5102
13	14	19	2	1	0.4031	0.0853	0.2591	0.5886
14	15	16	2	14	0.5358	0.1060	0.3483	0.7472

```
Likelihood-ratio test statistic of homogeneity (group=hlltyes0):
chi2( 1 ) = .54504395,   P = .46034984

Logrank test of homogeneity (group=hlltyes0):

Log-rank test for equality of survivor functions
```

hlltyes0	Events observed	Events expected
0	150	152.29
1	16	13.71
Total	166	166.00

```
              chi2(1) =      0.43
              Pr>chi2 =    0.5100
```

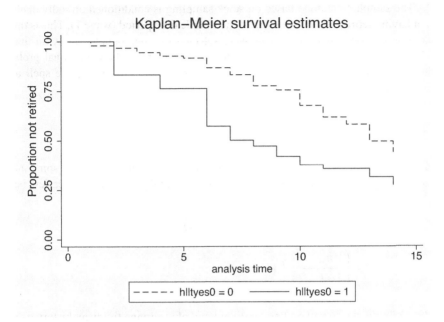

Figure 7.1 Life table estimates of the proportion not retired by health limitations.

By arranging the data in such a manner and conditioning on stock sampling –
so that time periods prior to selection into the stock sample can be ignored – the
estimation of a discrete-time hazard model is simplified to such an extent that
estimation methods suitable for a binary outcome (retired versus not retired) may
be used. The longitudinal nature of the BHPS dataset together with the use of the
stset command has ensured our data is organised appropriately.

Adopting the notation of Jenkins (1995), we use data for a stock sample of all
individuals who are aged between 50 and state retirement age and working at wave
1 ($t = \tau$). At the end of the time period for which we have data, each individual
will either still be working (censored duration data, $\delta_i = 0$), or will have retired
(complete duration data, $\delta_i = 1$). $t = \tau + s_i$ is the age when retirement occurs
if $\delta_i = 1$ and the age corresponding to the final year of observation if $\delta_i = 0$.
Accordingly, each respondent, i, contributes s_i years of employment spell data in
the interval between the start of the first period and the final wave of observation.

The probability of retiring at each age, t, provides information on the duration
distribution and we define the discrete time hazard rate as:

$$h_{it} = P[T_i = t \mid T_i \geqslant t; x_{it}]$$

where x_{it} is a vector of covariates which may vary across time and T_i is a discrete
random variable representing the age at which the end of the spell occurs.

The sample likelihood based on stock sampling is conditioned on individuals not having retired at the beginning of the sample time period (wave 1). This is the condition upon which individuals were selected into our sample, implying that all periods prior to the selection period can be ignored. The conditional probability of observing the event history of someone with an incomplete spell at interview is:

$$\text{prob} (T_i > t \mid \tau - 1) = \prod_{t=\tau}^{\tau+s_i}(1 - h_{it})$$

and the conditional probability of observing the event history of someone completing a spell between the initial period, τ, and the time of the interview is:

$$\text{prob} (T_i = t \mid T_i > \tau - 1) = h_{i\tau+s_i} \prod_{t=\tau}^{\tau+s_i-1} (1 - h_{it})$$

$$= \left(\frac{h_{i\tau+s_i}}{1 - h_{i\tau+s_i}} \right) \prod_{t=\tau}^{\tau+s_i}(1 - h_{it})$$

Accordingly, the corresponding log-likelihood of observing the event history data for the whole sample is:

$$\log L = \sum_{i=1}^{n} \delta_i \, \log \left(\frac{h_{i\tau+s_i}}{1 - h_{i\tau+s_i}} \right) + \sum_{i=1}^{n} \sum_{t=\tau}^{\tau+s_i} \log (1 - h_{it})$$

The log-likelihood can be simplified by defining:

$$y_{it} = 1 \quad \text{if} \quad t = \tau + s_i \quad \text{and} \quad \delta_i = 1, \, y_{it} = 0 \text{ otherwise.}$$

Accordingly, for stayers, $y_{it} = 0$, for *all* spell periods, while for exiters, $y_{it} = 0$, for *all* periods *except* the exit period. At exit, $y_{it} = 1$.

The likelihood can then be expressed as:

$$\log L = \sum_{i=1}^{n} \sum_{t=\tau}^{\tau+s_i} y_{it} \, \log \left(\frac{h_{it}}{1 - h_{it}} \right) + \sum_{i=1}^{n} \sum_{t=\tau}^{\tau+s_i} \log (1 - h_{it})$$

To complete the specification of the likelihood, an expression for the hazard rate, h_{it}, is required. We specify a complementary log-log hazard rate which is the discrete-time counterpart of the hazard for an underlying continuous-time proportional hazards model (Prentice and Gloeckler, 1978):

$$h_{it} = 1 - \exp \left(- \exp \left(x_{it} \beta + \theta(t) \right) \right)$$

where $\theta(t)$ is an appropriately specified baseline hazard. For our application we are interested in modelling the duration to age at early retirement, hence we complete the model by specifying $\theta(t)$ flexibly as a piecewise-constant function, by using dummy variables for each year of age. This represents a semi-parametric specification of the discrete-time duration model.

The model can be generalised to account for unobserved heterogeneity uncorrelated with the explanatory variables (Narendranathan and Stewart, 1993). Monte Carlo evidence suggests that discrete-time hazard models are robust to misspecification of the form of unobserved heterogeneity, particularly when considering the estimated effects of covariates (Nicoletti and Rondinelli, 2010) and we compare across a range of specifications of heterogeneity.

Estimation in Stata

Stata does not have a suite of built-in commands to estimate directly discrete-time hazard models. However, these models can be easily estimated using existing commands. Before applying any of the commands described, the data must be arranged in the panel data form described for the estimation of life tables. The reader is referred to Jenkins (1995) for details on how to transform discrete-time survival data collected on individuals and stored in wide format (one row per individual) to data stored in long format (multiple rows per individual, one for each discrete-time at which observations are made).

There are a number of ways to estimate discrete-time hazard models using either existing Stata commands or, alternatively, by downloading the stb program, pgmhaz8 developed by Jenkins (1997). Estimation is via maximum likelihood and follows the form of ML estimation of a binary dependent variable since at any discrete point in time we observe whether an individual has retired or not. Accordingly, models for binary dependent variables, for example probit, logistic and complementary log-log models, can be used to model discrete-time hazard functions. Jenkins (1995) provides an intuitive overview of these methods.

For models without frailty (unobserved heterogeneity) we use the complementary log-log command, cloglog. Prior to estimating the model we need to define variables to summarise the pattern of duration dependence. These variables will be a function of age. A commonly used form in continuous-time duration analysis is the Weibull baseline hazard, $\theta(t) = \log(t)$, which can be computed as: gen lnt = ln(_t). Greater flexibility in duration dependence can be achieved using a piece-wise constant specification where a dummy variable is included in the hazard model to represent each of the discrete ages between 50 and 64 years under observation. Within each age period duration dependence is assumed constant. This leads to a semi-parametric form for the hazard model analogous to Cox's model for continuous-time duration analysis and can be computed using the following routine:

```
tabulate age, gen(aged)
forvalues i=1(1)15 {
```

```
local k = 49 + `i'
rename aged`i' age`k'
}
```

Before proceeding to estimate hazard functions it is useful to remove missing observations on the binary retirement variable _d:

```
drop if _d == .
```

After defining the global macro for the set of regressors in addition to the health variables estimate the hazard function as follows:

```
global xvars "lspjb marcoup deghdeg hndalev ocse lHseMort
  lHseAuthAss lHseRent m2lnhinc everppenr everemppr privcomp0
  civlocgov0 jbsecto0 NorthE NorthW SouthW London Midland Scot
  Wales"
cloglog _d lhlltyes hlltyes0 shlltyes $xvars age53-age64, ///
  nolog eform
```

where _d is the `stset` variable representing the retirement event. Notice that we have only specified dummy variables for age 53 to age 64. This is due to the model containing a constant and there being very few retirements between ages 50 to 51, and ages 51 to 52 and so we combine these age groups with the constant in the baseline hazard. The option, `eform`, request results to be expressed as hazard ratios, which show the proportional effect on the underlying (instantaneous) hazard of retiring early, for a unit change in the variable of interest.

The complementary log-log model is within the class of generalised linear models and alternatively can be estimated using Stata's `glm` command by specifying a complementary log-log link function together with a binomial density: `glm _d lhlltyes hlltyes0 shlltyes $xvars age53-age64, f(bin) l(cloglog) eform`. Using either the `cloglog` or `glm` command produces the results in Table 7.6.

We will assess the fit of the model against other specifications using the Akaike information criterion. This can be computed as follows:

```
estat ic
```

Model	Obs	ll(null)	ll(model)	df	AIC	BIC
.	2510	−545.7593	−458.3129	37	990.6257	1206.263

Note: N=Obs used in calculating BIC; see [R] BIC note

As would be expected the hazard of early retirement increases across the age dummies and is significant for ages close to state retirement age. There is also an

Table 7.6 Discrete-time hazard model – no heterogeneity

```
--------------------------------------------------------------------
Complementary log-log regression        Number of obs      =     2510
                                         Zero outcomes      =     2368
                                         Nonzero outcomes   =      142
                                         LR chi2(36)        =   174.89
Log likelihood = -458.31287             Prob > chi2        =   0.0000
--------------------------------------------------------------------
        _d |   exp(b)  Std. Err.      z   P>|z|  [95% Conf.Interval]
-----------|--------------------------------------------------------
   lhlltyes | 3.908468  .9392519   5.67  0.000   2.440352   6.259801
   hlltyes0 | .3456942   .118424  -3.10  0.002   .1766434   .6765299
   shlltyes | 1.164629   .255584   0.69  0.487   .7575074   1.790557
      lspjb | .6026734  .1195533  -2.55  0.011   .4085336   .8890706
    marcoup | .8729224  .2678918  -0.44  0.658   .4783544   1.592948
    deghdeg | .7633023  .2623176  -0.79  0.432   .3891987      1.497
    hndalev | .8897567  .2127297  -0.49  0.625   .5568774   1.421618
       ocse | .8578886  .2115264  -0.62  0.534   .5291189    1.39094
   lHseMort | .9622258  .1862859  -0.20  0.842   .6583932    1.40627
lHseAuthAss | .9835358  .3244659  -0.05  0.960   .5152061   1.877584
   lHseRent | .4609044  .2847139  -1.25  0.210   .1373406   1.546759
   m2lnhinc | 2.379288  .5014744   4.11  0.000   1.574136   3.596267
   everppenr | .5393677  .1023167  -3.25  0.001   .3718897   .7822684
   everemppr | 1.429803   .403069   1.27  0.205   .8228454   2.484474
   privcomp0 | 1.614053  .5929242   1.30  0.192   .7856478   3.315947
   civlocgov0 | 3.935778  1.661856   3.24  0.001   1.720349    9.00419
   jbsecto0 | 1.644896  .7469522   1.10  0.273   .6754687   4.005637
     NorthE | 1.453913  .4078429   1.33  0.182    .839005   2.519488
     NorthW | .9253589  .3058939  -0.23  0.814   .4840946   1.768846
     SouthW | 1.031736  .3431993   0.09  0.925   .5375544   1.980224
     London | .6311702  .2330594  -1.25  0.213    .306084   1.301524
    Midland | 1.191968  .3306774   0.63  0.527   .6920269   2.053081
       Scot | .8491164  .3739374  -0.37  0.710   .3581885   2.012903
      Wales | 2.573396  .8126241   2.99  0.003   1.385847   4.778572
      age53 | 1.103675  1.104645   0.10  0.921   .1552002   7.848571
      age54 | 1.224149  1.119358   0.22  0.825   .2039382   7.348019
      age55 | 1.013426  .9276519   0.01  0.988   .1685134   6.094664
      age56 | 4.155101  3.171151   1.87  0.062   .9309987   18.54445
      age57 | 2.372454  1.884013   1.09  0.277   .5003128   11.25004
      age58 | 4.084406  3.092327   1.86  0.063   .9261458   18.01268
      age59 | 2.489098  1.956918   1.16  0.246   .5331277   11.62125
      age60 | 6.113743  4.557162   2.43  0.015   1.418485   26.35055
      age61 | 5.684641  4.296406   2.30  0.021   1.292325   25.00543
      age62 |  3.76345  2.947472   1.69  0.091   .8108472    17.4676
      age63 | 10.35622  7.752779   3.12  0.002   2.387717   44.91795
      age64 | 9.554741  7.267931   2.97  0.003   2.151503   42.43223
--------------------------------------------------------------------
```

indication of a gradient across educational attainment such that higher levels of education are associated with a decreasing hazard of early retirement. The effects, which are compared to the baseline category of no qualifications, however, are not significant. The employment sector variables (measured at the first wave) indicate a larger hazard of retirement compared to the self-employed (the baseline category). This is particularly the case for individuals employed within civil and local government (`civlocgov0`), which is large and highly significant.

We also observe a significant effect of pension entitlements. These variables represent whether an individual has made a contribution into a private pension plan (or an employer has made a contribution on behalf of the individual) during the observation period (`everppenr`) and whether an individual has been a member of an employer pension scheme during the observation period (`everemppr`). The estimated effect of the former variable is less than unity and highly significant, while the latter is greater than unity and not significant. The combined effect of these variables suggests that men with access to private pension entitlements are more likely to delay early retirement compared to individuals either without a pension or those within an employee pension scheme.

Individuals with a greater mean logged household income (`m2lnhinc`) have a greater hazard of early retirement. Men for whom their partner or spouse is employed (`lspjb`) have a lower hazard of retirement. The effects of housing tenure (`lHseMort`, `lHseAuthAss`, and `lHseRent`) and marital status (`marcoup`) are not significant at conventional levels.

Our primary focus is the impact of health on the decision to retire. The results clearly show that men with health limitations (`lhlltyes`) have a greater hazard of retirement than men not reporting health limitations. The effect is large and significant at the 1 per cent level. For men, the health status of a spouse or partner (`shlltyes`) does not appear to be a significant predictor of the decision to take early retirement. This may reflect offsetting effects of pressure to provide personal care and to maintain household income when a partner becomes ill.

The alternative to estimating discrete-time hazard models is provided by `pgmhaz8` (Jenkins, 1997). This command is not built-in to Stata and has to be downloaded as an `stb` file. This is very much recommended as a useful feature of this command is that the estimation procedure automatically incorporates frailty (unobserved heterogeneity). The `pgmhaz8` routine for models without frailty is essentially the `glm` command with a complementary log-log link function and a binomial density function for `_d`. This is estimated using iterative, reweighted least squares (using the `irls` option) to maximise the deviance rather than the default of maximisation of the log likelihood. `pgmhaz8` is implemented as follows:

```
pgmhaz8 lhlltyes hlltyes0 shlltyes $xvars age53-age64,   ///
   i(pid) d(_d) s(_t) eform
```

In many health economics applications, it is desirable to fit models that take into account unobserved heterogeneity. For ordinary linear regression analysis the consequences of ignoring unobserved heterogeneity is not serious if the heterogeneity is independent of the sets of regressors. In that case, the conditional mean is unchanged and unobserved heterogeneity is absorbed into the error term. In duration models, which are nonlinear, the treatment of unobserved heterogeneity – often referred to as frailty – causes more concern. Evidence on the effects of ignoring frailty (where it exists) relates mainly to experience with continuous time duration models where it has been suggested that this leads to: (i) over-estimation of negative duration dependence and under-estimation of positive duration dependence. This has the effect of exaggerating the rate of failure for individuals with a high unobserved heterogeneity effect and underestimating the rate for failure of individuals with a low effect; (ii) under-estimation of the 'true' effects of positive relationships between regressors and duration and an over-estimation of the effect of negative relationships. This is due to the proportionality assumption (that the regressors act proportionally on the underlying hazard function) being attenuated by unobserved heterogeneity. Monte Carlo evidence on discrete hazard models suggests that estimation is robust to misspecification of the form of unobserved heterogeneity (Nicoletti and Rondinelli, 2010). This holds for parametric or semi-parametric specifications and is particularly the case for estimated effects of model covariates.

We investigate the impact of heterogeneity by comparing across a range of specifications and assess model fit using information criteria. We can incorporate unobserved heterogeneity into our discrete-time hazard model by using either the panel data command: xtcloglog or the pgmhaz8 command. xtcloglog is the panel data equivalent of the cloglog command and estimates models with unobserved heterogeneity assumed to be normally distributed and constant over time. The results are shown in Table 7.7.

```
xtcloglog _d lhlltyes hlltyes0 shlltyes $xvars           ///
     age53-age64 , re nolog eform
```

The final two rows of Table 7.7 report the standard deviation of the hetero-geneity variance (sigma_u) and the proportion of total unexplained variation due to heterogeneity (rho). If the hypothesis that unobserved heterogeneity is zero (rho = 0) cannot be rejected, then we may conclude that frailty is unimportant. The likelihood ratio test fails to reject the null hypothesis at the 5 per cent level and a comparison of the coefficient estimates to those of Table 7.6 indicates that, apart from lhlltyes coefficient estimates do not change dramatically. Interestingly, the magnitudes of the estimated coefficients on the set of age dummies are consistently larger compared to those presented in Table 7.6, implying slightly greater duration dependence in the model with unobserved heterogeneity. The AIC for this model is 990.9, slightly worse than the model without heterogeneity.

Frailty is also incorporated into the pgmhaz8 routine, which assumes gamma distributed unobservable heterogeneity (Meyer, 1990). The routine estimates a model with frailty automatically after the non-frailty model results are returned and no additional statement or option is required. Accordingly, one can estimate

Table 7.7 Complementary log-log model with frailty

```
------------------------------------------------------------------
Random-effects complementary          Number of obs      =    2510
    log-log model
Group variable: pid                   Number of groups   =     465
Random effects u_i ~ Gaussian         Obs per group: min =       1
                                                       avg =     5.4
                                                       max =      11
                                      Wald chi2(36)      =   66.66
Log likelihood = -457.47778           Prob > chi2        =  0.0014
------------------------------------------------------------------
```

_d	exp(b)	Std. Err.	z	P>|z|	[95% Conf.Interval]	
lhlltyes	4.781554	1.507393	4.96	0.000	2.577664	8.869759
hlltyes0	.3522049	.1418208	-2.59	0.010	.1599727	.7754343
shlltyes	1.16632	.2834626	0.63	0.527	.7243388	1.877993
lspjb	.5735072	.1273804	-2.50	0.012	.371091	.8863339
marcoup	.8348636	.2925953	-0.51	0.607	.4200435	1.659345
deghdeg	.7318331	.2944058	-0.78	0.438	.3326489	1.610045
hndalev	.9302457	.2622416	-0.26	0.798	.5353515	1.616428
ocse	.8735969	.2488215	-0.47	0.635	.499883	1.5267
lHseMort	.9898314	.2167783	-0.05	0.963	.6443823	1.520474
lHseAuthAss	.9135218	.3478996	-0.24	0.812	.4330648	1.927014
lHseRent	.3706187	.257663	-1.43	0.153	.094875	1.447781
m2lnhinc	2.640488	.6876252	3.73	0.000	1.584958	4.398967
everppenr	.4786477	.1120359	-3.15	0.002	.3025362	.7572767
everemppr	1.548177	.5055755	1.34	0.181	.8163014	2.936233
privcomp0	1.70362	.6960266	1.30	0.192	.7649059	3.79435
civlocgov0	4.691536	2.366059	3.07	0.002	1.745955	12.60658
jbsecto0	1.782132	.9168309	1.12	0.261	.6501788	4.8848
NorthE	1.558006	.5172081	1.34	0.182	.8128261	2.986351
NorthW	.8839174	.3396982	-0.32	0.748	.4161851	1.877314
SouthW	1.024838	.3891618	0.06	0.948	.4868872	2.157158
London	.5695146	.2446045	-1.31	0.190	.2454239	1.321578
Midland	1.238832	.3960732	0.67	0.503	.6620191	2.318219
Scot	.776191	.3901915	-0.50	0.614	.2897805	2.079065
Wales	2.915711	1.147664	2.72	0.007	1.348031	6.306511
age53	1.116699	1.122277	0.11	0.913	.1557694	8.005521
age54	1.344545	1.242301	0.32	0.749	.2198376	8.223345
age55	1.085965	1.006431	0.09	0.929	.1765855	6.67847
age56	4.735284	3.703402	1.99	0.047	1.022428	21.93104
age57	2.816221	2.304972	1.27	0.206	.566226	14.00695
age58	5.107168	4.052608	2.05	0.040	1.078301	24.18913
age59	3.109229	2.553366	1.38	0.167	.6217671	15.54812
age60	8.237485	6.621208	2.62	0.009	1.70454	39.80906

Table 7.7 continued

```
    age61 | 7.632045  6.213005   2.50  0.013  1.547765   37.6337
    age62 | 5.092405  4.293399   1.93  0.054  .9756095  26.58091
    age63 |  14.7815  12.24006   3.25  0.001  2.916534  74.91517
    age64 | 14.56087  12.53595   3.11  0.002  2.693761  78.70741
----------+---------------------------------------------------------
 /lnsig2u | -.529768  .8967939                -2.287452  1.227916
----------+---------------------------------------------------------
  sigma_u |  .767295  .3440527                 .3186296   1.84773
      rho | .2635752  .1740707                 .0581318  .6748526
----------------------------------------------------------------------
Likelihood-ratio test of rho=0:
chibar2(01) =    1.67 Prob >= chibar2 = 0.098
```

a model with gamma frailty by invoking the command for pgmhaz8 as specified above. Note that an option (nobeta0) exists to switch off the reporting of the non-frailty model estimates if this is desired.

Table 7.8 reports the results from implementing pgmhaz8. The non-frailty model results have been suppressed to conserve space (using the nobeta0 option) but are equivalent to those reported in Table 7.6. Again, the likelihood ratio test statistic once again fails to reject the null hypothesis of no frailty at the conventional 5 per cent level and the AIC is marginally larger than that for the model with no frailty. Incorporating gamma frailty results in a similar estimate of the impact of health limitations as the model with Gaussian frailty.

```
pgmhaz8 lhlltyes hlltyes0 shlltyes $xvars age53-age64,    ///
     i(pid) d(_d) s(_t) nobeta0 nolog eform

estat ic

----------------------------------------------------------------------
  Model |   Obs  ll(null)   ll(model)   df       AIC        BIC
--------+-------------------------------------------------------------
      . |  2510        .     -457.398   38   990.7959  1212.261
----------------------------------------------------------------------
     Note: N=Obs used in calculating BIC; see [R] BIC note
```

A further approach to incorporating unobserved heterogeneity in discrete-time duration models is via the finite density estimator: in which the distribution of unobserved heterogeneity is approximated by a set of discrete mass points (Heckman and Singer, 1984). The attraction of this approach is that it leads to a flexible parameterisation of heterogeneity; the drawback is that estimation may be fragile and checks to ensure models have converged to global maxima should be undertaken, for example by using different starting values. Cameron and Trivedi (2005) provide a thorough treatment of finite mixture models in the

Table 7.8 Discrete-time duration model with gamma distributed frailty

```
-------------------------------------------------------------------
PGM hazard model with gamma frailty        Number of obs  =    2510
                                           LR chi2()      =       .
Log likelihood = -457.39796                Prob > chi2    =       .
-------------------------------------------------------------------
        _d |    exp(b)  Std. Err.      z   P>|z|  [95% Conf.Interval]
-----------|-------------------------------------------------------
hazard     |
  lhlltyes |   4.95279   1.650062    4.80  0.000   2.577895  9.515566
  hlltyes0 |  .3793118   .1661924   -2.21  0.027   .1607123   .895248
  shlltyes |   1.15579   .2865176    0.58  0.559   .7109975   1.87884
     lspjb |  .5684979   .1285538   -2.50  0.013    .364962   .885544
   marcoup |  .8366317    .300423   -0.50  0.619   .4138848  1.691177
   deghdeg |  .7013234   .2942765   -0.85  0.398   .3081433  1.596188
   hndalev |  .9322795   .2719695   -0.24  0.810   .5262949  1.651441
      ocse |  .8785146   .2572455   -0.44  0.658   .4948815  1.559541
  lHseMort |  1.008107    .227717    0.04  0.971   .6474888  1.569571
lHseAuthAss|  .8842528   .3496296   -0.31  0.756   .4073945  1.919277
  lHseRent |  .3556107   .2514719   -1.46  0.144    .088929  1.422022
  m2lnhinc |  2.657138   .7072468    3.67  0.000    1.57707  4.476899
  everppenr|  .4637324   .1147352   -3.11  0.002   .2855393   .7531282
  everemppr|  1.595267   .5422152    1.37  0.169    .819443  3.105619
  privcomp0|  1.688175   .6931738    1.28  0.202    .754935  3.775074
 civlocgov0|  4.766831   2.444832    3.04  0.002   1.744464  13.02559
   jbsecto0|  1.806966   .9467078    1.13  0.259   .6471236  5.045596
     NorthE|  1.613659   .5634848    1.37  0.171   .8139067  3.199254
     NorthW|  .8911821   .3514093   -0.29  0.770   .4114549  1.930237
     SouthW|  1.034493   .4009529    0.09  0.930   .4839671  2.211259
     London|  .5573473    .245882   -1.33  0.185   .2347501  1.323263
    Midland|  1.270495   .4179856    0.73  0.467   .6667028  2.421104
       Scot|  .7405568   .3829456   -0.58  0.561   .2687805  2.040417
      Wales|  2.958974   1.219021    2.63  0.008   1.319678  6.634594
      age53|  1.113313   1.118142    0.11  0.915   .1554974  7.970971
      age54|  1.348084   1.242905    0.32  0.746   .2212725  8.213091
      age55|  1.086083   1.003902    0.09  0.929   .1774475  6.647467
      age56|  4.748817   3.694709    2.00  0.045   1.033541  21.81943
      age57|  2.848004   2.320255    1.28  0.199   .5768603  14.06081
      age58|  5.177618   4.079315    2.09  0.037   1.105324  24.25327
      age59|  3.152826   2.572488    1.41  0.159   .6370574  15.60348
      age60|  8.457857   6.766773    2.67  0.008   1.762991  40.57613
      age61|  7.847392   6.370716    2.54  0.011   1.598445   38.5259
      age62|  5.211951   4.370417    1.97  0.049   1.007478  26.96279
      age63|   15.2817   12.61615    3.30  0.001   3.030004   77.0726
      age64|  15.29726   13.22049    3.16  0.002   2.811719  83.22528
-----------|-------------------------------------------------------
```

Table 7.8 continued

```
 ln_varg   |
-----------|---------------------------------------------------------
 Gamma var. | .6676388   .5501152   1.21   0.225   .1327932   3.356658
-----------|---------------------------------------------------------
LR test of Gamma var. = 0: chibar2(01) =   1.82983
Prob.>=chibar2 = .088074
```

context of duration analysis and Chapter 11 discusses their use with count data. We implement this version of the model using the downloadable program, hshaz written by Jenkins (1997). The option, nmp(2), specifies two classes (note that in this case the option is redundant as two classes is the default). The results are presented in Table 7.9.

```
hshaz lhlltyes hlltyes0 shlltyes $xvars age53-age64,        ///
      i(pid) d(_d) s(_t) nmp(2) nobeta0 nolog eform
```

The results of applying the finite mixture discrete-time duration model leads to estimates of the impact of health limitations that are much larger than those obtained using normally distributed or gamma frailty. This suggests that estimates are more sensitive to this specification of unobserved heterogeneity than the previous approaches. The AIC for this specification of unobserved heterogeneity is, once again, slightly greater than for the corresponding model without frailty (Table 7.6):

```
estat ic
```

```
-----------------------------------------------------------------------
   Model |    Obs   ll(null)   ll(model)    df        AIC        BIC
---------|-------------------------------------------------------------
       . |    2510          .   -456.3554    39   990.7107   1218.004
-----------------------------------------------------------------------
       Note: N=Obs used in calculating BIC; see [R] BIC note
```

In the models presented above we have conditioned on initial period health at wave 1 using the variable hlltyes0. This allows us to interpret the estimated coefficient on lagged health as the effect of an adverse health shock occurring between the first wave and the current wave of data. An alternative way of modelling the impact of a health shock is by selecting the sample of men who had not experienced a health limitation on entry to the panel (wave 1). This is easily achieved using the commands: drop if hlltyes0 == 1, which results in 185 observations being removed.

By conditioning the analysis on individuals without health limitations and repeating the above estimations the results summarised in Table 7.10 can be

Table 7.9 Discrete-time duration model with Heckman–Singer frailty

```
--------------------------------------------------------------------
Discrete time PH model, with                    Number of obs = 2510
discrete mixture
                                                LR chi2()     =    .
Log likelihood = -456.35537                     Prob > chi2   =    .
--------------------------------------------------------------------
         _d |   exp(b)   Std. Err.     z   P>|z|  [95% Conf.Interval]
------------|-------------------------------------------------------
hazard      |
   lhlltyes | 6.836885  3.142565   4.18  0.000  2.777184  16.83108
   hlltyes0 | .3342713  .1635163  -2.24  0.025  .1281488  .8719335
   shlltyes | 1.231453  .3305591   0.78  0.438  .7276624   2.08404
      lspjb | .5720013  .1348487  -2.37  0.018  .3603521  .9079604
    marcoup | .7771016  .3337012  -0.59  0.557  .3349321  1.803013
    deghdeg | .7248437  .3308832  -0.70  0.481  .2962649  1.773407
    hndalev | 1.035592  .3378387   0.11  0.915  .5463911  1.962792
       ocse | .8927979  .2935352  -0.34  0.730   .468699  1.700639
   lHseMort | .9474335   .232984  -0.22  0.826  .5850988  1.534151
lHseAuthAss |  .760486  .4089239  -0.51  0.611  .2650869  2.181696
   lHseRent | .2627984  .2075188  -1.69  0.091  .0559076  1.235305
   m2lnhinc | 2.788338  .7956975   3.59  0.000  1.593827  4.878088
   everppenr| .4067538  .1155247  -3.17  0.002  .2331184  .7097196
   everemppr| 1.651676  .6298041   1.32  0.188  .7822607  3.487372
   privcomp0| 1.997293  .9399705   1.47  0.142  .7940492  5.023844
  civlocgov0| 5.737278  3.361151   2.98  0.003  1.819845  18.08745
   jbsecto0 | 1.855995  1.042638   1.10  0.271  .6171627  5.581541
     NorthE | 1.568706  .5973991   1.18  0.237  .7436774  3.309014
     NorthW | .8326086  .3606854  -0.42  0.672  .3562058   1.94617
     SouthW | .9553483  .4060714  -0.11  0.914  .4152962  2.197685
     London | .4644533  .2512296  -1.42  0.156  .1608847  1.340817
    Midland | 1.11487   .4070592   0.30  0.766  .5450483  2.280412
       Scot | .7800125  .6186601  -0.31  0.754  .1648081  3.691684
      Wales | 3.373778  1.612997   2.54  0.011  1.321778  8.611413
      age53 | 1.12699    1.13283   0.12  0.905  .1571473   8.08226
      age54 | 1.417087  1.306217   0.38  0.705  .2326973  8.629821
      age55 | 1.109905   1.02737   0.11  0.910  .1808762   6.81067
      age56 | 5.104428  3.983121   2.09  0.037  1.105941  23.55929
      age57 | 3.148945  2.567773   1.41  0.160  .6368867  15.56926
      age58 | 6.042833  4.788378   2.27  0.023  1.278625  28.55867
      age59 | 3.710839  3.071373   1.58  0.113  .7327449  18.79279
      age60 | 10.90528  8.919735   2.92  0.003  2.194904  54.18242
      age61 | 10.1802   8.439175   2.80  0.005   2.00506  51.68743
      age62 | 6.85057   5.982513   2.20  0.028  1.237039   37.9376
      age63 | 21.73387  19.53215   3.43  0.001  3.733926  126.5053
      age64 | 22.94866  21.17149   3.40  0.001  3.762477  139.9719
------------|-------------------------------------------------------
         m2 |
------------|-------------------------------------------------------
```

Table 7.9 continued

```
   logitp2   |
------------|--------------------------------------------------------
Prob.Type 1 | .5996791   .1470997   4.08  0.000  .3107011  .8327299
Prob.Type 2 | .4003209   .1470997   2.72  0.007  .1672701  .6892989
------------|--------------------------------------------------------
Note: m1 = 0
```

obtained. As can be seen the information criteria and χ^2 tests of the null of no heterogeneity, once again, offer no compelling support for models with frailty. The effects of health limitations are quantitatively the same as those estimated using the full sample with no heterogeneity. Models with heterogeneity exhibit smaller effects of health limitations in the conditional sample than for corresponding estimates from the full sample.

We are also interested in the impact on retirement of our measure of latent health stock constructed from the pooled ordered probit regressions reported above. Replacing the health limitation variables by our constructed latent health variables (lsahlat and slatsah) and estimating assuming gamma distributed heterogeneity results in the estimates provided in Table 7.11:

```
pgmhaz8 lsahlat sahlat0 slatsah $xvars age53-age64,       ///
        i(pid) d(_d) s(_t) nobeta0 nolog eform
```

Qualitatively, the results of the non-health variables are the same as the corresponding model with health limitations. Again, health is shown to have a statistically significant impact on the timing of retirement. The coefficient is less than unity due to the measure of latent health stock being increasing in good health. As with models with health limitations, we fail to reject the null hypothesis of no unobserved heterogeneity at the 5 per cent level.

Table 7.10 Discrete-time duration model with Heckman–Singer frailty

Conditioned sample (n = 2328)	Log L	AIC	BIC	χ^2 (p-value)		Health limitations (s.e.)	
Cloglog: no hetero.	−405.21	882.42	1089.52			3.424	(.876)
Xtcloglog: Gaussian hetero.	−405.19	884.37	1097.23	0.05	(.415)	3.530	(1.054)
pgmhaz8: Gamma hetero.	−405.19	884.39	1097.24	0.03	(.428)	3.502	(1.014)
hshaz: H-Singer hetero.	−405.09	886.17	1104.78	0.24	(.887)	3.842	(1.420)

Table 7.11 Discrete-time duration models with latent self-assessed health

```
--------------------------------------------------------------------
PGM hazard model with gamma frailty          Number of obs =   2485
                                             LR chi2()     =      .
Log likelihood = -466.64337                  Prob > chi2   =      .
--------------------------------------------------------------------
```

_d	exp(b)	Std. Err.	z	P>|z|	[95% Conf.	Interval]
hazard						
lsahlat	.5248343	.1167074	-2.90	0.004	.3394225	.8115286
sahlat0	1.20075	.301093	0.73	0.466	.7345313	1.962885
slatsah	.9359441	.1431996	-0.43	0.665	.6934513	1.263234
lspjb	.4983859	.1188671	-2.92	0.004	.3122846	.7953913
marcoup	.8801319	.3468812	-0.32	0.746	.4065076	1.905578
deghdeg	.7021457	.3053437	-0.81	0.416	.2994079	1.646611
hndalev	.9241587	.2850816	-0.26	0.798	.5048595	1.691697
ocse	.9004641	.28118	-0.34	0.737	.4882803	1.660594
lHseMort	1.06302	.2497333	0.26	0.795	.6707651	1.684662
lHseAuthAss	.890187	.3611904	-0.29	0.774	.4018917	1.971757
lHseRent	.3139577	.2289853	-1.59	0.112	.0751704	1.311281
m2lnhinc	2.446169	.6760804	3.24	0.001	1.423077	4.204791
everppenr	.4383243	.110532	-3.27	0.001	.2673921	.7185261
everemppr	1.661232	.593431	1.42	0.155	.8248234	3.345795
privcomp0	1.638948	.6948821	1.17	0.244	.7139572	3.76234
civlocgov0	4.410831	2.331781	2.81	0.005	1.56507	12.43103
jbsecto0	1.739209	.9442644	1.02	0.308	.6000824	5.040719
NorthE	1.508752	.5405682	1.15	0.251	.7475532	3.045043
NorthW	.8741567	.3614482	-0.33	0.745	.3887162	1.96583
SouthW	.9649435	.3911105	-0.09	0.930	.4360068	2.135554
London	.5356323	.251928	-1.33	0.184	.2130663	1.346539
Midland	1.289233	.4398285	0.74	0.456	.6606016	2.516073
Scot	.7218097	.3878911	-0.61	0.544	.2517666	2.069414
Wales	2.779611	1.224248	2.32	0.020	1.172416	6.590012
age53	1.15116	1.158827	0.14	0.889	.1600535	8.279538
age54	1.414151	1.307727	0.37	0.708	.2308623	8.662414
age55	1.160919	1.079326	0.16	0.872	.1876831	7.180894
age56	5.285503	4.139582	2.13	0.034	1.138752	24.5326
age57	3.372408	2.768198	1.48	0.139	.6749044	16.85148
age58	6.13953	4.858417	2.29	0.022	1.301819	28.95473
age59	3.477671	2.861863	1.51	0.130	.693128	17.44872
age60	9.850626	7.87639	2.86	0.004	2.055218	47.21389
age61	9.283986	7.619873	2.71	0.007	1.858262	46.38333
age62	6.190907	5.223463	2.16	0.031	1.184592	32.35488
age63	17.71997	14.70143	3.46	0.001	3.485466	90.08764
age64	17.52085	15.1687	3.31	0.001	3.210897	95.60575
ln_varg						
Gamma var.	.9632755	.5294371	1.82	0.069	.3280286	2.828716

```
--------------------------------------------------------------------
LR test of Gamma var. = 0: chibar2(01) = 4.12856
Prob.>=chibar2 = .021083
```

7.6 OVERVIEW

The primary focus of this chapter is the role of health in determining retirement behaviours. To this end we consider the role of a measure of health limitations (hlltyes) and a measure of underlying latent health stock (latsah) constructed from the results of a pooled ordered probit model of self-assessed health on specific health problems. This provides a means of purging self-assessed health of measurement error. Both these variables are lagged one period to avoid problems of simultaneity. We also condition on the first period's health status so that the estimated effect of lagged health can be interpreted as a health shock. Further, we consider the health of a respondent's spouse or partner. Clearly, this can only be defined should a respondent have a spouse or partner and therefore needs to be interpreted alongside the estimated effect of the marital status variable (marcoup).

For health limitations we observe a large, positive and highly significant effect. This implies that the hazard of retiring is greater for individuals experiencing a shock to health that leads to a health limitation. For our constructed measure of underlying latent health we observe an effect of less than 1, which is statistically significant. The latent health scale is increasing in health so that the coefficient implies that the retirement hazard increases as health decreases. Again this is interpreted as a shock to health. For both models, the estimated coefficients on spousal health are not significant and accordingly for men, there is insufficient evidence that the decision to retire is a function of spousal health. In this application, unobserved heterogeneity does not appear to play a substantial role in the timing of early retirement among men.

Part IV

Panel data

8 Health and wages

SYNOPSIS

This chapter covers linear regression models for panel data. A sub-sample of the BHPS is used to estimate classical Mincerian wage equations that are augmented by measures of self-reported health. The estimators include random and fixed effects approaches as well as the Hausman–Taylor and related instrumental variable approaches.

8.1 INTRODUCTION

To illustrate the use of a range of linear panel data estimators this chapter presents an empirical model of the impact of health on wage rates using data from the British Household Panel Survey (BHPS). Comparatively little research, particularly using data on developed economies, has investigated the effect of health on income, or as in the example presented here, the effect of health on wage rates. There are, however, a number of reasons why health may impact on wages. First, increases in health are assumed to lead to increases in productivity, which, in turn, should be reflected in an increased wage rate. Second, apart from their direct effects, an employer may perceive health to be correlated with unobservable attributes of an individual, which affect productivity and accordingly offer higher wages to healthier employees. Third, irrespective of actual productivity, employers may discriminate against unhealthy individuals.

The example is of interest as it allows us to estimate and compare a number of linear panel data estimators. These range from pooled OLS estimates, through random and fixed effects estimators to instrumental variable generalised least squares estimators that attempt to account for the potential endogenous relationship between health and wage rates. The latter estimators are of particular interest as they rely on instruments that are internal to the model. The example is based on Contoyannis and Rice (2001) where further details of the methods and approaches to estimation can be found. Additional relevant reading can be found in Baltagi (2005: chapter 7).

8.2 BHPS SAMPLE AND VARIABLES

To illustrate the methods we draw on the first six waves of the BHPS. The BHPS has been described in earlier chapters and does not require further elaboration. Our empirical analysis makes use of a sample of the BHPS consisting of individuals who were in employment (part-time or full-time) in each of the six waves and, importantly, for whom information was available in each wave to enable the construction of an average hourly wage. After removing individuals for whom data was missing on key variables used on the model, our balanced sample consists of 1,625 individuals; 833 males and 792 females.

Throughout we attempt to abstract from issues of labour supply, and confine our analysis to the impact of health status on labour productivity, as proxied by average hourly wages. This is likely to underestimate the full effect of health status on *expected* wages, as those individuals who leave the labour force are likely to have poorer health compared to individuals who continue in employment.

Wage rates

The BHPS does not contain an hourly wage variable and as such we constructed hourly wages as follows. First, we divided usual gross monthly pay including overtime (using BHPS variable paygu) derived from the main job of an individual by the number of hours worked per month in their main job, again including overtime (derived from BHPS variables jbhrs and jbot). We obtain the hourly wage in a secondary job (j2has indicates a secondary job, j2pay is the pay and j2hrs are the hours worked) analogously and constructed an overall average wage by taking a weighted average of the hourly wage in the main and secondary jobs with weights equal to the proportions of total working time spent in their main and secondary jobs. Using this procedure we obtain a measure of 'maximum average' productivity; those individuals with relatively low wages are more likely to supplement their income with another job, which may be more highly paid, while those who receive relatively high average wages in their main job should be, *ceteris paribus*, less likely to seek a second job. The Stata code to perform these calculations is as follows:

```
generate hrsmthn=jbhrs*4.33+jbot*4.33   // hrs month, main job
generate wagenorm=paygu/hrsmthn         // wage rate, normal job
generate wagejb2=0                      // wages, 2nd job
replace wagejb2=(j2pay/j2hrs) if j2has ==1
/* generate proportion of hours in normal job */
generate propnorm=hrsmthn/(hrsmthn+j2hrs)
generate propothr=j2hrs/(hrsmthn+j2hrs) if j2hrs>0
```

```
generate wage=(propnorm*wagenorm) + (propothr*wagejb2)
generate lnwage=ln(wage)
```

Our model of wages and our approach to estimation relies on specifying time varying and time-invariant regressors. For the instrumental variables approaches we employ we are further required to partition each of the set of regressors into exogenous and endogenous component sets. We discuss time varying and time invariant regressors in turn.

Time-varying regressors

Of particular relevance to this study are two BHPS survey instruments on health status measured as self-assessed health and subjective well-being via the General Health Questionnaire (GHQ). Self-assessed health is defined by a response to the question: 'Please think back over the last 12 months about how your health has been. Compared to people of your own age, would you say that your health has on the whole been excellent/good/fair/poor/very poor?'. From the responses to this question, we create three dummy variables coded to one if an individual has excellent health (sahex), has good health (sahgd), or has fair or worse than fair health (sahfp). Note that in our sample the categories representing poor and very poor health contained less than 4 per cent of all responses and hence were combined with the category representing fair health. It is hypothesised that increasing health has a positive relationship with wages and as such we expect that the coefficient on excellent and good health will be positive with a larger coefficient on excellent health.

Create dummy variables for self-assessed health as follows:

```
recode hlstat -9 -1 = .
tabulate hlstat , gen(sahdm)
rename sahdm1 sahex
rename sahdm2 sahgd
rename sahdm3 sahf
rename sahdm4 sahp
rename sahdm5 sahvp
generate sahfp = sahf + sahp + sahvp
```

The GHQ was originally developed as a screening instrument for psychiatric illness but is often used as an indicator of subjective well-being. There are 12 individual elements to the shortened GHQ: concentration, sleep loss due to worry, perception of role, capability in decision making, whether constantly under strain, perception of problems in overcoming difficulties, enjoyment of day-to-day activities, ability to face problems, loss of confidence, self-worth, general happiness, and whether suffering depression or unhappiness. Respondents are asked to indicate on a four-point ordinal scale how they have *recently* felt with respect to the item in question. A Likert scale is then used to obtain an overall score by summing the responses to each question. We use a composite measure derived from the results of this questionnaire, which is increasing in ill-health (hlghq1). We expect the coefficient on this variable to be negative. We hypothesise that health status is endogenous in our model of wages.

Two variables are constructed to represent union status based on whether the individual has a recognised workplace union which covers pay and conditions for the type of job in which the individual is employed. The first variable takes a value of one where an individual is a member of a workplace union, and zero otherwise (covmem). The second variable is set to one where a recognised union exists but the individual is not a member, and zero otherwise (covnon). These are contrasted against a baseline of no union representation.

On-the-job training is likely to have a positive impact on wages and accordingly we construct a variable indicating whether an individual has undertaken any training or education related to their current employment. Given the expectation that training will not immediately impact on wages we include the lagged value of this variable (ljtrain).

To capture labour market experience and tenure, we include a quadratic function of both age and experience (age, agesqrd, exp, expsqrd). Age should capture a general labour market experience and tenure effect. A more direct measure of experience is also calculated as the number of years in which an individual has been doing the same job with their current employer. Conditional on age, this variable captures the effect of within-job tenure and specific (on-the-job) training. We expect positive coefficients for the levels of each of these variables with their effects declining over the life-cycle leading to a concave function in both experience and age (see Mincer, 1974).

To account for the possible geographical segmentation of wages, we include a series of regional dummy variables. We also include a binary variable to indicate workforce sector to distinguish between the public and private sectors (jobpriv). It is possible that this variable is endogenous. We include a measure of the number of employees at the individual's place of work (jbsize).

We include indicators of marital status (widow, divsep, nvrmar) to capture household economies of scale and productivity effects that are not captured by other variables and a variable that measures the number of children aged between 0 and 4 years of age (kids04). Previous research has found a positive and significant coefficient for the presence of children in the household for men and a negative and significant coefficient for women. We also include a vector of binary variables to indicate occupational status (prof, manag, skillnm, skllm), which are assumed to be endogenous given the likelihood of selection into job types on the basis of unobserved characteristics, which also impact on wages. Finally, we include a vector of time dummies to control for aggregate productivity effects and inflation.

Time-invariant regressors

Ethnic status is included as an exogenous time invariant variable coded one if the respondent is white and zero otherwise (white). Previous work has found a gradient in wages across educational attainment and as such we include indicators of the highest academic qualification achieved (Harkness, 1996). Responses are categorised into one of the following: degree or higher degree (deg), Higher national diploma or equivalent (hndct), 'A' levels or equivalent (alevel), or 'O' levels or equivalent (ocse). The baseline category consists of respondents with no formal qualifications. In order to reduce the demands on the data, we use only the indicator of whether an individual has a degree or higher degree when utilising the instrumental variable estimators. Our expectation is that educational attainment is endogenous in wages, which is consistent with previous research (e.g. Hausman and Taylor, 1981; Cornwell and Rupert, 1988; Baltagi and Khanti-Akom, 1990).

Table 8.1 presents the variables used in the analysis together with their respective definitions.

Descriptive statistics

To allow for heterogeneity in coefficients by gender, we split the sample by men and women. In the following, we only consider the analysis for men. The reader is referred to Contoyannis and Rice (2001) for results for women. Summary statistics for the full sample (includes both full time and part time workers) of men are presented in Table 8.2. Note that less than 2 per cent of men work part-time. Produce summary statistics as follows:

```
drop if male ~= 1
summarize wage lnwage age exp jbsize SouthW London Midland ///
    NorthW NorthE Scot Wales covmem covnon jobpriv ljtrain ///
    widow divsep nvrmar kids04 white deg ocse alevel hndct ///
    hlghq1 sahex sahgd prof manag skllnm skllm jobpt
```

8.3 EMPIRICAL MODEL AND ESTIMATION

We specify a Mincerian wage function such that the natural logarithm of wages is a function of individual level socioeconomic variables that are either time-varying or time-invariant (Mincer, 1974). This can be represented as follows:

$$w_{it} = x_{it}\beta + z_i\gamma + \alpha_i + \eta_{it}, \quad i = 1,2,...N; \ t = 1,2,...T \tag{8.1}$$

In equation (8.1), i indexes individuals, while t indexes time periods (waves of the BHPS). w_{it} represents the logarithm of hourly wages, x_{it} is a $1 \times K$ vector of time-varying regressors including age, work experience and health. z_i is a $1 \times G$ vector of time invariant regressors including qualifications and ethnicity. β and γ are suitably conformed vectors of parameters. α_i is an individual specific and time-invariant error component, assumed to be normally distributed with zero mean and variance, σ_α^2. Similarly, η_{it}, is a classical mean zero disturbance, assumed to be distributed as $N(0, \sigma_\eta^2)$. We further assume that η_{it} is uncorrelated

Table 8.1 Variable labels and definitions

Label	Definition
Wage	Average hourly wage
age	Age in years
exp	Duration of spell in current job in years
jbsize	Number of employees at workplace
SouthW	Regional indicator: 1 = lives in Southwest
London	Regional indicator: 1 = lives in London
Midland	Regional indicator: 1 = lives in Midlands
NorthW	Regional indicator: 1 = lives in Northwest
NorthE	Regional indicator: 1 = lives in Northeast
Scot	Regional indicator: 1 = lives in Scotland
Wales	Regional indicator: 1 = lives in Wales
covmem	Unionisation indicator: 1 = Covered union member
covnon	Unionisation indicator: 1 = Covered non-member
jobpriv	Sector indicator: 1 = Employed in the private sector
ljtrain	Training indicator: 1 = Received education or training related to current employment in the previous period
widow	Marital status indicator: 1 = Widowed
divep	Marital status indicator: 1 = Divorced or separated
nvrmar	Marital status indicator: 1 = Never married
kids04	Number of children in the household aged 0–4
white	Ethnicity indicator: 1 = White
deg	Education indicator: 1 = Highest academic qualification is degree or higher degree
ocse	Education indicator: 1 = Highest academic qualification is O level/CSE
alevel	Education indicator: 1 = Highest academic qualification is A level
hndct	Education indicator: 1 = Highest academic qualification is HND or equivalent
hlghql	General Health Questionnaire: Likert Scale score
sahex	Health Indicator: 1 = Self-Assessed health reported as excellent
sahgd	Health Indicator: 1 = Self-Assessed health reported as good
prof	Occupation Indicator: 1 = Professional
manag	Occupation Indicator: 1 = Managerial
skllnm	Occupation Indicator: 1 = Skilled non-Manual
skllm	Occupation Indicator: 1 = Skilled Manual
jobpt	Employment Indicator: 1 = Part-time employee

Table 8.2 Summary statistics for full sample of observations

```
------------------------------------------------------------------
Variable |      Obs       Mean    Std. Dev.        Min        Max
---------|--------------------------------------------------------
    wage |     4165   8.194638    4.380659   1.018966   55.85513
  lnwage |     4165   1.993639    .4588185   .0187881   4.022761
     age |     4165   39.20144    10.08049         17         73
     exp |     4165   5.990876    6.508984          0         44
  jbsize |     4165   298.7509    326.8744        1.5       1000
---------|--------------------------------------------------------
  SouthW |     4165   .0979592    .2972951          0          1
  London |     4165   .0965186    .2953366          0          1
 Midland |     4165   .1687875    .3746091          0          1
  NorthW |     4165   .1054022    .3071078          0          1
  NorthE |     4165   .1567827    .3636394          0          1
---------|--------------------------------------------------------
    Scot |     4165   .0821128    .2745695          0          1
   Wales |     4165   .0533013    .2246607          0          1
  covmem |     4165   .4328932    .4955357          0          1
  covnon |     4165   .1623049    .3687746          0          1
 jobpriv |     4165   .7310924     .443445          0          1
---------|--------------------------------------------------------
  ljtrain |    4165   .4055222    .4910518          0          1
   widow |     4165   .0031212    .0557876          0          1
  divsep |     4165   .0456182    .2086808          0          1
  nvrmar |     4165   .1601441    .3667836          0          1
  kids04 |     4165   .2110444    .4840124          0          3
---------|--------------------------------------------------------
   white |     4165   .9759904    .1530973          0          1
     deg |     4165     .15006    .3571731          0          1
    ocse |     4165   .3229292     .467652          0          1
  alevel |     4165   .2340936    .4234818          0          1
   hndct |     4165   .0804322    .2719938          0          1
---------|--------------------------------------------------------
  hlghq1 |     4165   10.15534    4.483037          0         36
   sahex |     4165   .3082833    .4618397          0          1
   sahgd |     4165   .5246098     .499454          0          1
    prof |     4165   .0888355    .2845404          0          1
   manag |     4165   .3361345    .4724422          0          1
---------|--------------------------------------------------------
  skllnm |     4165   .1476591    .3548043          0          1
   skllm |     4165   .2953181    .4562404          0          1
   jobpt |     4165   .0127251     .112099          0          1
```

with the regressors and the individual specific effects, α_i. The effects, α_i may be correlated with all or part of the vectors x and z. For the instrumental variable estimators, we employ we partition the vectors x and z into exogenous and endogenous components (refer to equation (8.2)).

Assuming the error disturbances are uncorrelated with the regressors, we first estimate the model by OLS, which under this assumption will be unbiased and consistent. The parameter estimates will, however, be inefficient as OLS ignores the fact that we have panel data of repeated cross-sections and hence errors are correlated within individuals. Use the following commands to produce the results presented in Table 8.3:

```
clonevar y=lnwage
global xvars "age agesqrd exp expsqrd jbsize covmem covnon
 jobpriv ljtrain widow divsep nvrmar kids04 hlghql sahex sahgd
 prof manag skllnm skllm white deg SouthW London Midland NorthW
 NorthE Scot Wales yr9293 yr9394 yr9495 yr9596"
regress y $xvars
```

From the OLS results, we can see that coefficients on self-assessed general health exhibit the expected positive sign. The coefficient on excellent health is significant at the 1 per cent level while the estimated coefficient is not significant for good health (both are contrasted against a baseline of fair, poor and very poor health). While the estimated coefficient on psychological health is negative, reflecting an increase in ill-health related to a decrease in wages, the coefficient fails to attain statistical significance.

Also of interest are the coefficients on the occupational status variables with the results showing clearly a gradient associated with increased wages as we move from skilled manual, through skilled non-manual and managerial to professional occupational status. The baseline category represents unskilled, part-skilled and the armed forces. Employees of larger organisations appear to attract higher wages as do employees who are members of a union. Job training exhibits the expected positive coefficient and is significant at the 1 per cent level. As expected, higher qualification (deg) is associated with higher wage rates. Compared to the South East (baseline category), workers in other regions, with the exception of London, command lower wage rates. Note that the year dummies exhibit a positive gradient, presumably reflecting wage inflation over the period of observation.

The estimated coefficients on age, agesqrd and on exp and expsqrd imply the expected significant concave relationships with the logarithm of hourly wages. The impact of the number of employees in the workplace also significantly increases wages, as does unionisation, with the expected positive differential between those that are union members and those non-members that are covered by union bargaining and negotiation. The coefficient on the private sector dummy is positive but insignificant. The coefficients on the marital status variables suggest that compared to the baseline of married or living with a partner, being divorced or separated together with individuals who have never married tend to have lower wages.

Table 8.3 OLS on full sample of observations

```
  Source |       SS     df         MS       Number of obs =    4165
---------|----------------------------       F( 33,  4131) =   96.64
   Model | 381.906058    33  11.5729108      Prob > F      =  0.0000
Residual | 494.675966  4131 .119747268       R-squared     =  0.4357
---------|----------------------------       Adj R-squared =  0.4312
   Total | 876.582024  4164  .210514415      Root MSE      = .34605
```

```
       y |      Coef.  Std. Err.      t   P>|t|   [95% Conf. Interval]
---------|------------------------------------------------------------
     age |  .0373693  .0039577    9.44   0.000    .02961    .0451286
  agesqrd| -.0382722  .0047281   -8.09   0.000   -.0475418 -.0290027
     exp |  .0087803  .0021496    4.08   0.000    .004566   .0129946
  expsqrd| -.0322945  .0081515   -3.96   0.000   -.0482759 -.0163131
   jbsize|  .0001552  .0000172    9.05   0.000    .0001216  .0001889
   covmem|  .1117475  .0142312    7.85   0.000    .0838467  .1396483
   covnon|  .0100673  .0166159    0.61   0.545   -.0225089  .0426435
  jobpriv|  .0147592  .0143509    1.03   0.304   -.0133763  .0428947
  ljtrain|   .044326  .0113303    3.91   0.000    .0221126  .0665394
    widow|  .0854187  .097766     0.87   0.382   -.1062554  .2770928
   divsep| -.0876587  .0262608   -3.34   0.001   -.1391439 -.0361734
   nvrmar|  -.073663  .0172395   -4.27   0.000   -.1074617 -.0398644
   kids04|  .0642412  .0121042    5.31   0.000    .0405105  .0879719
   hlghq1|   -.00124  .0012663   -0.98   0.328   -.0037225  .0012426
    sahex|  .0656882  .0171545    3.83   0.000    .032056   .0993203
    sahgd|  .0233362  .0154557    1.51   0.131   -.0069654  .0536378
     prof|  .5432044  .0253148   21.46   0.000    .4935738  .592835
    manag|  .5127876  .019243    26.65   0.000    .475061   .5505143
   skllnm|  .2903433  .0208847   13.90   0.000    .2493979  .3312886
    skllm|  .1402549  .0182848    7.67   0.000    .104407   .1761029
    white| -.0260942  .0357905   -0.73   0.466   -.0962629  .0440745
      deg|  .1705886  .0172554    9.89   0.000    .1367587  .2044186
   SouthW| -.0718187  .0206931   -3.47   0.001   -.1123883 -.0312492
   London|  .0763798  .0210362    3.63   0.000    .0351375  .1176221
  Midland|  -.147842  .0174673   -8.46   0.000   -.1820874 -.1135966
   NorthW| -.0702431  .0201296   -3.49   0.000   -.1097079 -.0307782
   NorthE| -.0683254  .0178897   -3.82   0.000   -.1033988 -.033252
     Scot| -.1351816  .0220309   -6.14   0.000   -.178374  -.0919892
    Wales| -.0913026  .0262802   -3.47   0.001   -.1428259 -.0397792
   yr9293|  .0240372  .0169829    1.42   0.157   -.0092584  .0573327
   yr9394|  .0678777  .0170392    3.98   0.000    .0344717  .1012838
   yr9495|  .0925407  .0171145    5.41   0.000    .0589871  .1260943
   yr9596|   .130982  .0171871    7.62   0.000    .0972859  .164678
    _cons|  .6758936  .0883556    7.65   0.000    .502669   .8491182
```

While OLS is consistent under the assumption of no correlation between the regressors and the error terms, we have noted that it is inefficient as our model (8.1) specifies a random effects (RE) or variance components structure to the error. We can estimate this model using the xtreg command with the option, re. Here xt specifies that we wish to estimate a panel data model (cross-sections in time) and the re option specifies a random effects specification of the error disturbance as in (8.1). Before proceeding to estimation, we first specify the data in panel format with multiple waves (identified using wavenum) per individual (identified by pid) using xtset. The following commands specify the data in the required format, estimate the random effects model and store these for later use. The results are shown in Table 8.4.

```
xtset pid wavenum
xtreg y $xvars , re
estimates store raneff
```

The RE estimates of the self-assessed health variables are smaller than the corresponding OLS estimates. However, the estimates of the standard errors are also smaller resulting in the estimate of excellent health being significant at the 5 per cent level while good health remains non-significant but exhibits the expected positive coefficient. Interestingly, the estimate of psychological well-being, while still exhibiting a negative coefficient is significant at the 5 per cent level under the RE estimator. The majority of the other variables retain similar interpretations to the OLS estimates, albeit mostly at a slightly increased level of significance. Note that the majority of unexplained variation lies at the time invariant individual level, rho = 0.67, indicating a large degree of unobserved individual heterogeneity in log wages. Evidence of heterogeneity to this extent provides support for the use of panel data approaches over OLS.

To help motivate the estimators we will use when relaxing the assumption that the regressors are uncorrelated with the individual unobserved effect, it is useful to re-write our model specification (8.1) in the following way:

$$w_{it} = x_{1it}\beta_1 + x_{2it}\beta_2 + z_{1i}\gamma_1 + z_{2i}\gamma_2 + \alpha_i + \eta_{it}, \quad i = 1,2,...N; \ t = 1,2,...T \ (8.2)$$

where, x_1 is a $1 \times k_1$ vector of exogenous time varying variables and x_2 is a $1 \times k_2$ vector of endogenous variables ($k_1 + k_2 = K$). Similarly, z_1 and z_2 are vectors of exogenous and endogenous time invariant variables of length $1 \times g_1$ and $1 \times g_2$ ($g_1 + g_2 = G$) respectively. The partitioning of x and z into exogenous and endogenous components is based on a priori considerations. Throughout η_{it} is assumed to be uncorrelated with the regressors and the individual specific effects, α_i.

An obvious way of estimating a model where we wish to relax the assumption that the regressors are uncorrelated with the individual specific error component, α_i, is to use the within-groups (or fixed effects) panel data estimator. A main

Table 8.4 RE on full sample of observations

```
------------------------------------------------------------------
Random-effects GLS regression          Number of obs      =    4165
Group variable (i): pid                Number of groups   =     833
R-sq: within  = 0.1244                 Obs per group: min =       5
      between = 0.4513                                avg =     5.0
      overall = 0.3923                                max =       5
Random effects u_i ~ Gaussian          Wald chi2(33)      = 1142.51
corr(u_i, X)      = 0 (assumed)         Prob > chi2        =  0.0000
------------------------------------------------------------------
```

y	Coef.	Std. Err.	z	P>|z|	[95% Conf. Interval]	
age	.0507045	.0059669	8.50	0.000	.0390095	.0623995
agesqrd	-.0533491	.0071466	-7.46	0.000	-.0673562	-.0393419
exp	.0044801	.0019612	2.28	0.022	.0006362	.008324
expsqrd	-.0205011	.0078083	-2.63	0.009	-.0358051	-.0051971
jbsize	.0000765	.0000178	4.31	0.000	.0000417	.0001114
covmem	.0829266	.0169693	4.89	0.000	.0496674	.1161857
covnon	.0191547	.0161448	1.19	0.235	-.0124885	.0507979
jobpriv	.0171332	.0193016	0.89	0.375	-.0206972	.0549637
ljtrain	.0164079	.0077434	2.12	0.034	.0012311	.0315846
widow	.0034152	.0889423	0.04	0.969	-.1709085	.1777389
divsep	-.0585176	.0316685	-1.85	0.065	-.1205867	.0035515
nvrmar	-.0413766	.0206926	-2.00	0.046	-.0819334	-.0008197
kids04	.0187232	.0105703	1.77	0.077	-.0019941	.0394405
hlghq1	-.0021245	.0010031	-2.12	0.034	-.0040905	-.0001586
sahex	.0277526	.0138943	2.00	0.046	.0005203	.0549849
sahgd	.0128728	.0114762	1.12	0.262	-.0096202	.0353658
prof	.2589516	.0259969	9.96	0.000	.2079986	.3099046
manag	.2419512	.0199481	12.13	0.000	.2028536	.2810488
skllnm	.1542511	.0213966	7.21	0.000	.1123146	.1961876
skllm	.065302	.0164493	3.97	0.000	.033062	.097542
white	-.0090221	.0687363	-0.13	0.896	-.1437427	.1256984
deg	.2955493	.0309714	9.54	0.000	.2348465	.3562521
SouthW	-.0835608	.0372552	-2.24	0.025	-.1565796	-.0105419
London	.0579975	.0356839	1.63	0.104	-.0119417	.1279367
Midland	-.1461243	.0314533	-4.65	0.000	-.2077716	-.0844771
NorthW	-.110799	.0365343	-3.03	0.002	-.182405	-.039193
NorthE	-.0880494	.0329058	-2.68	0.007	-.1525435	-.0235552
Scot	-.166324	.0412882	-4.03	0.000	-.2472475	-.0854006
Wales	-.1048742	.0464365	-2.26	0.024	-.1958882	-.0138602
yr9293	.0274477	.0099184	2.77	0.006	.008008	.0468873
yr9394	.0709793	.010141	7.00	0.000	.0511034	.0908552
yr9495	.099696	.0104665	9.53	0.000	.079182	.1202099
yr9596	.1396777	.0108529	12.87	0.000	.1184065	.1609489
_cons	.622221	.1387916	4.48	0.000	.3501946	.8942475

```
--------------------------------------------------------------
sigma_u |.27807532
sigma_e |.19494339
    rho |.67048195  (fraction of variance due to u_i)
```

advantage of this approach is that even in the presence of such correlation, the estimator is consistent. However, it is inefficient as it dispenses with degrees of freedom – one for each individual in the estimation – and, perhaps more importantly, it does not identify the coefficients, γ_1 and γ_2, on the time-invariant variables, z_1 and. z_2.

To estimate the fixed effects model we use the same command as we used for the random effects estimator but specify `fe` rather than `re`. We also drop `age` from the list of variables due to collinearity with the set of time dummies. This arises due to having a balanced sample of individuals and a fixed effects specification.

```
global xvars_fe "agesqrd exp expsqrd jbsize covmem covnon
 jobpriv ljtrain widow divsep nvrmar kids04 hlghq1 sahex sahgd
 prof manag skllnm skllm SouthW London Midland NorthW NorthE
 Scot Wales yr9293 yr9394 yr9495 yr9596"

xtreg y $xvars_fe , fe
estimates store fixeff
```

The results are shown in Table 8.5. If we turn to the estimates of the health variables, we can see that for psychological well-being the FE estimate is very close to the RE estimate. However, the FE estimate is less efficient and as such the associated standard error is slightly larger but the parameter estimate still retains statistical significance at the 5 per cent level. Conversely, the parameter estimates on self-assessed excellent and good health are 50 and 30 per cent less than their respective estimates from the RE model. Note that neither parameter is statistically significant at the 5 per cent level using FE estimation.

Also of interest are the occupational status variables. While the gradient remains apparent having accounted for endogeneity using FE, and the parameter estimates lead us to reject the null hypotheses of zero coefficients, the absolute magnitudes are much diminished. The observed difference between the RE and FE estimates suggest there is positive selection into occupational categories, which may reflect differing time preference, attitudes to risk or other unobserved factors, which are positively correlated with wage rates.

Note that ethnicity (`white`) and educational attainment (`deg`) are dropped from the FE estimation due to them being collinear with the unobserved fixed effects.

We may wish to test formally the difference between the parameters obtained from the RE and FE estimators. Under the hypothesis of correct specification of (8.1) and no correlation between x and α_i, the FE estimates of β should be close to the RE results. This can be tested formally using the Hausman test (Hausman, 1978) which is constructed as $M = \mathbf{q}' \operatorname{cov}(\mathbf{q})^{-1}\mathbf{q}$ where $\mathbf{q} = \hat{\boldsymbol{\beta}}_{FE} - \hat{\boldsymbol{\beta}}_{RE}$ and $\operatorname{cov}(\mathbf{q})$ = $\operatorname{cov}(\hat{\boldsymbol{\beta}}_{FE}) - \operatorname{cov}(\hat{\boldsymbol{\beta}}_{RE})$ where M is asymptotically distributed under H_0 as χ_K^2. Significant differences between the two vectors suggest mis-specification and points to the use of fixed effects or instrumental variables techniques to overcome endogeneity. Note however that the Hausman test compares only the coefficients on the time varying regressors and does not consider time-invariant regressors as

Table 8.5 FE on full sample of observations

```
-----------------------------------------------------------------
Fixed-effects (within) regression      Number of obs     =    4165
Group variable (i): pid                Number of groups  =     833
R-sq: within  = 0.1455                 Obs per group: min =      5
      between = 0.0143                               avg =     5.0
      overall = 0.0065                               max =       5
                                       F(30,3302)        =   18.74
corr(u_i, Xb) = -0.7347                Prob > F          =  0.0000
-----------------------------------------------------------------
       y |     Coef. Std. Err.      t  P>|t|  [95% Conf. Interval]
---------|-------------------------------------------------------
 agesqrd | -.0481303  .0110108  -4.37  0.000  -.0697189  -.0265416
     exp |  .0038217  .0020683   1.85  0.065  -.0002335   .0078769
  expsqrd | -.0166481  .0084153  -1.98  0.048  -.0331478  -.0001484
   jbsize |  .0000411  .0000197   2.09  0.037   2.49e-06   .0000797
   covmem |  .0781241  .0212441   3.68  0.000   .0364712   .1197769
   covnon |   .023711  .0177723   1.33  0.182  -.0111349   .0585568
  jobpriv |   .038906  .0273345   1.42  0.155  -.0146884   .0925003
  ljtrain |  .0063068  .0077064   0.82  0.413  -.0088029   .0214165
    widow | -.0339277  .0938112  -0.36  0.718  -.2178617   .1500064
   divsep | -.0270047  .0377882  -0.71  0.475  -.1010954    .047086
   nvrmar |  .0058038  .0252186   0.23  0.818  -.0436419   .0552495
   kids04 |  .0037053  .0110879   0.33  0.738  -.0180345   .0254452
   hlghq1 | -.0023311  .0010253  -2.27  0.023  -.0043415  -.0003208
    sahex |  .0137109  .0142684   0.96  0.337  -.0142649   .0416868
    sahgd |  .0090108  .0115573   0.78  0.436  -.0136495   .0316711
     prof |  .0849804  .0293286   2.90  0.004   .0274764   .1424844
    manag |  .0819904  .0228365   3.59  0.000   .0372153   .1267655
   skllnm |  .0398242  .0241793   1.65  0.100  -.0075837   .0872321
    skllm |  .0384736  .0172874   2.23  0.026   .0045784   .0723688
   SouthW |  .1282471  .1028712   1.25  0.213  -.0734507   .3299449
   London | -.0244918   .075733  -0.32  0.746  -.1729803   .1239966
  Midland |  .1212739  .0919738   1.32  0.187  -.0590576   .3016054
   NorthW | -.2957556   .104505  -2.83  0.005  -.5006567  -.0908545
   NorthE |  .1319611  .1263534   1.04  0.296  -.1157777      .3797
     Scot | -.1917346  .2015783  -0.95  0.342  -.5869657   .2034965
    Wales | -.0445275  .1150586  -0.39  0.699   -.270121    .181066
   yr9293 |   .075379  .0127044   5.93  0.000   .0504696   .1002883
   yr9394 |  .1668088  .0194975   8.56  0.000   .1285804   .2050372
   yr9495 |  .2442047  .0275099   8.88  0.000   .1902666   .2981428
   yr9596 |  .3313773  .0361766   9.16  0.000   .2604465   .4023081
    _cons |  2.487739  .1770019  14.05  0.000   2.140695   2.834784
---------|-------------------------------------------------------
  sigma_u | .62393645
  sigma_e | .19491991
      rho | .9110821   (fraction of variance due to u_i)
-----------------------------------------------------------------
F test that all u_i=0: F(832, 3302) = 12.41 Prob > F = 0.0000
```

these are eliminated through fixed effects estimation. In circumstances where the Hausman test fails to reject the null, the use of instrumental variables estimation may still remain productive where it is believed that the time-invariant regressors were endogenous with respect to the unobserved individual effect. Further, one may wish to restrict the test to a subset of time-varying regressors deemed, a priori, to be correlated with α_i, (x_2), as the test has low power when including all regressors.

The commands, estimate store randeff and estimate store fixeff were used previously to store the estimates from the random effects and fixed effects estimations. By calling on these estimates, the Hausman test is invoked by typing:

```
hausman fixeff raneff
```

This produces the following set of results:

```
Note: the rank of the differenced variance matrix (29) does not
equal the number of coefficients being tested (30); be sure
        this is what you expect, or there may be problems
computing the test. Examine the output of your estimators for
        anything unexpected and possibly consider scaling your
variables so that the coefficients are on a similar scale.
```

	--- Coefficients ----			
	(b)	(B)	(b-B)	sqrt(diag(V_b-V_B))
	fixeff	raneff	Difference	S.E.
agesqrd	-.0481303	-.0533491	.0052188	.0083763
exp	.0038217	.0044801	-.0006584	.0006568
expsqrd	-.0166481	-.0205011	.0038529	.003138
jbsize	.0000411	.0000765	-.0000355	8.46e-06
covmem	.0781241	.0829266	-.0048025	.012781
covnon	.023711	.0191547	.0045562	.0074297
jobpriv	.038906	.0171332	.0217727	.0193552
ljtrain	.0063068	.0164079	-.0101011	.
widow	-.0339277	.0034152	-.0373429	.0298298
divsep	-.0270047	-.0585176	.0315129	.0206169
nvrmar	.0058038	-.0413766	.0471804	.014415
kids04	.0037053	.0187232	-.0150179	.0033483
hlghql	-.0023311	-.0021245	-.0002066	.0002126
sahex	.0137109	.0277526	-.0140416	.0032461
sahgd	.0090108	.0128728	-.003862	.0013669
prof	.0849804	.2589516	-.1739712	.0135766
manag	.0819904	.2419512	-.1599608	.0111165
skllnm	.0398242	.1542511	-.1144269	.0112616
skllm	.0384736	.065302	-.0268284	.0053176
SouthW	.1282471	-.0835608	.2118079	.0958881

London |	-.0244918	.0579975	-.0824893	.0667993
Midland |	.1212739	-.1461243	.2673982	.0864284
NorthW |	-.2957556	-.110799	-.1849566	.0979108
NorthE |	.1319611	-.0880494	.2200105	.1219934
Scot |	-.1917346	-.166324	-.0254105	.1973046
Wales |	-.0445275	-.1048742	.0603467	.1052717
yr9293 |	.075379	.0274477	.0479313	.007939
yr9394 |	.1668088	.0709793	.0958295	.0166527
yr9495 |	.2442047	.099696	.1445088	.025441
yr9596 |	.3313773	.1396777	.1916996	.0345103

```
                    b = consistent under Ho and Ha; obtained from xtreg
 B = inconsistent under Ha, efficient under Ho; obtained from xtreg

Test: Ho: difference in coefficients not systematic

        chi2(29) = (b-B)'[(V_b-V_B)^(-1)](b-B)
                 =    308.47
     Prob>chi2 =    0.0000
     (V_b-V_B is not positive definite)
```

A common problem encountered with using the Hausman test is that for any finite sample, we have no reason to believe that the matrix, $\text{cov}(\mathbf{q}) = \text{cov}(\hat{\boldsymbol{\beta}}_{FE}) - \text{cov}(\hat{\boldsymbol{\beta}}_{RE})$, is positive definite (PD). If it is not PD then inverting the matrix is difficult and a standard application of the Hausman test may not lead to a reliable test statistic. An alternative test, which is asymptotically equivalent to the Hausman test, is an augmented regression. There are several forms of this test and the one used here is based on the following regression:

$$w_{it} = \bar{x}_i \lambda_1 + \left(x_{it} - \bar{x}_i\right)\lambda_2 + \alpha_i + \eta_{it}, \quad i = 1,2,\ldots N; \ t = 1,2,\ldots T \quad (8.3)$$

Under the null hypothesis that $\lambda_1 = \lambda_2$, (8.3) collapses to the RE model. Rejection of the null suggests an FE estimator (a Mundlak (1978) type specification). Tests of the joint equivalence of the parameter estimates can be obtained using a Wald test. A program to perform this test is provided in the Appendix and is invoked as a Stata .do file. It can be run by specifying the set of time-varying regressors to be tested along with the dependent variable and personal identifier as global variables as follows:

```
global depvar "y"
global varlist "agesqrd exp expsqrd jbsize covmem covnon
 jobpriv ljtrain widow divsep nvrmar kids04 hlghq1 sahex sahgd
 prof manag skllnm skllm SouthW London Midland NorthW NorthE
 Scot Wales"
global id "pid"

do "hausman_alt.do"
```

This returns the following chi-squared statistic: `chi2(26)` `=` `582.80;` `Prob` `>` `chi2` `=` `0.0000`, rejecting the RE specification.

Finally, we estimate the model using instrumental variables procedures suggested by Hausman and Taylor (HT: 1981) and Amemiya and MaCurdy (AM: 1986). These methods rely on specifying instruments for the endogenous variables x_2 and z_2. The idea is that by finding instruments for the endogenous variables, the HT and AM estimators are at least as precise as the fixed effects estimator but may avoid the inconsistency of the RE estimator. Further, they allow estimation of the time invariant regressors.

The HT estimator specifies the following instruments:

$$\mathbf{A}_{HT} = \left((\mathbf{x}_{1it} - \overline{\mathbf{x}}_{1i}), (\mathbf{x}_{2it} - \overline{\mathbf{x}}_{2i}), \overline{\mathbf{x}}_{1i}, \mathbf{z}_{1i} \right)$$

Accordingly, the parameters, β_1, are identified by the instruments, $(x_{1it} - \overline{x}_{1i})$, while β_2 are identified by the instruments $(x_{2it} - \overline{x}_{2i})$. γ_1 and γ_2 are identified by z_1 and $\overline{x}_{1i}$ respectively. Hence z_1 acts as its own instrument (z_1 are assumed exogenous), while the time invariant endogenous regressors, z_2 are instrumented by the within-individual means of the exogenous time varying regressors. For identification we require that $k \geqslant g_2$.

The resulting estimator has the benefit of allowing the estimation of time-invariant variables whilst also allowing for some of the time-varying and time-invariant regressors to be correlated with the individual unobserved error component. Since instruments are derived from variables internal to the model, we do not have to search for external instruments that are relevant and valid, something that is often hard to achieve in practice. However, the relevance of the instrument set formed by the HT method may be weak, particularly for the endogenous time invariant variables. Note, however, that in principle one could add external exogenous variables to the instrument set should they be available. We do not pursue this option here.

The HT estimator is both consistent and more efficient than the FE estimator if the model is overidentified and the partition of the variables into exogenous and endogenous factors is correct, however it is inconsistent if some of the assumed exogenous variables are correlated with α_i. We can test for this using a Hausman test comparing the results of the FE estimator with the HT estimator. Under the null that the overidentifying conditions are valid, a test statistic analogous to M above is, in general, asymptotically distributed as $\chi^2_{k_1-g_2}$.

To implement the Hausman and Taylor estimator in Stata, use the following command, taking care to specify the set of assumed endogenous variables using the option `endog( )`:

```
xthtaylor y $xvars, endog(hlghql sahex sahgd prof        ///
          manag skllnm skllm deg)
```

The results are presented in Table 8.6. It is worth noting that the estimates differ slightly from those presented in Contoyannis and Rice (2001). This is due to the

Table 8.6 Hausman and Taylor IV estimator on full sample of observations

```
-----------------------------------------------------------------------
Hausman-Taylor estimation                Number of obs      =     4165
Group variable (i): pid                  Number of groups   =      833
                                         Obs per group: min =        5
                                                          avg =        5
                                                          max =        5
Random effects u_i ~ i.i.d.              Wald chi2(33)      =   696.15
                                         Prob > chi2        =   0.0000
-----------------------------------------------------------------------
```

y	Coef.	Std. Err.	z	P>|z|	[95% Conf.	Interval]
TVexogenous						
age	.0489733	.0082305	5.95	0.000	.0328417	.0651049
agesqrd	-.0485502	.0094985	-5.11	0.000	-.0671668	-.0299336
exp	.0042259	.0018978	2.23	0.026	.0005062	.0079456
expsqrd	-.0178106	.0076873	-2.32	0.021	-.0328775	-.0027438
jbsize	.0000436	.0000179	2.43	0.015	8.45e-06	.0000787
covmem	.0811579	.0188851	4.30	0.000	.0441437	.118172
covnon	.0240216	.0161374	1.49	0.137	-.0076071	.0556504
jobpriv	.0420076	.0238761	1.76	0.079	-.0047886	.0888038
ljtrain	.0073522	.0071123	1.03	0.301	-.0065876	.0212919
widow	-.026912	.0859373	-0.31	0.754	-.195346	.141522
divsep	-.0354284	.0340369	-1.04	0.298	-.1021394	.0312826
nvrmar	-.0045849	.0225685	-0.20	0.839	-.0488184	.0396486
kids04	.0038084	.0101422	0.38	0.707	-.0160699	.0236867
SouthW	.0369901	.0714148	0.52	0.604	-.1029803	.1769605
London	-.006764	.0582383	-0.12	0.908	-.120909	.1073809
Midland	.003599	.0609756	0.06	0.953	-.115911	.1231091
NorthW	-.2086427	.0707734	-2.95	0.003	-.3473561	-.0699294
NorthE	-.0132267	.070732	-0.19	0.852	-.1518589	.1254055
Scot	-.2005994	.0952262	-2.11	0.035	-.3872392	-.0139596
Wales	-.0376191	.08313	-0.45	0.651	-.2005508	.1253126
yr9293	.0266645	.0093332	2.86	0.004	.0083716	.0449573
yr9394	.0690092	.0106304	6.49	0.000	.048174	.0898445
yr9495	.0978933	.012466	7.85	0.000	.0734604	.1223263
yr9596	.1361645	.0146102	9.32	0.000	.1075291	.1647999
TVendogenous						
hlghq1	-.0023573	.0009477	-2.49	0.013	-.0042147	-.0004999
sahex	.0137715	.013198	1.04	0.297	-.012096	.0396391
sahgd	.0093465	.0106911	0.87	0.382	-.0116078	.0303007
prof	.0871921	.0270631	3.22	0.001	.0341494	.1402348
manag	.0843504	.0210682	4.00	0.000	.0430575	.1256432
skllnm	.0415992	.0223248	1.86	0.062	-.0021565	.085355
skllm	.0384621	.0159865	2.41	0.016	.0071291	.0697952

Table 8.6 continued

```
TIexogenous  |
      white |  .1573687  .1910952   0.82  0.410  -.217171   .5319083
TIendogenous |
        deg |  1.216191  .2594526   4.69  0.000   .7076734  1.724709
            |
      _cons |  .3718601  .2701572   1.38  0.169  -.1576382   .9013585
-------------|-----------------------------------------------------------
    sigma_u |.86751264
    sigma_e |.19403442
        rho |.95235631   (fraction of variance due to u_i)
---------------------------------------------------------------------------
note: TV refers to time varying; TI refers to time invariant.
```

different sample sizes used and the Stata version of the HT and AM estimators employing an estimator of the variance components that differs from that used by Contoyannis and Rice.

Amemiya and MaCurdy (AM: 1986) suggest a potentially more efficient estimator than that of HT. Whilst HT uses the means of the time-varying exogenous variables to identify the parameters of the time-invariant endogenous regressors, AM's approach is to use the level of each regressor at each time period. If N denotes the number of individuals in the panel then let $x_1{}^*$ be an $NT \times TK$ matrix where each column contains values of x_{kit} for a single time period. For example, the ktth column of $x_{1t}^* = (x_{k1t}, \ldots, x_{k1t}, \ldots, x_{kNt}, \ldots, x_{kNt})$ for each $k \in K$. The construction of this instrument set is best illustrated using an example. Suppose we have two individuals, each of whom we observe for three time periods. Further assume we have a set of observations, which for individual 1 consists of the values (34, 54, 23) and for individual 2 the values (37, 56, 25). The resulting instrument set would be formed from the final three columns of the matrix resulting from the following transformation:

$$\begin{bmatrix} 1 & 1 & 34 \\ 1 & 2 & 54 \\ 1 & 3 & 23 \\ 2 & 1 & 37 \\ 2 & 2 & 56 \\ 2 & 3 & 25 \end{bmatrix} \rightarrow \begin{bmatrix} 1 & 1 & 34 & 54 & 23 \\ 1 & 2 & 34 & 54 & 23 \\ 1 & 3 & 34 & 54 & 23 \\ 2 & 1 & 37 & 56 & 25 \\ 2 & 2 & 37 & 56 & 25 \\ 2 & 3 & 37 & 56 & 25 \end{bmatrix}$$

This leads to an instrument set for the AM estimator defined as:

$$A_{AM} = \left((x_{1it} - \bar{x}_{1i}), (x_{2it} - \bar{x}_{2i}), x_{1i}^*, z_{1i} \right)$$

While HT use each x_i variable as two instruments, AM use each of these variables as $(T+1)$ instruments. Following the same reasoning as used to ascertain the conditions for existence of the HT estimator, it can be seen that the order condition for the AM estimator is $Tk_1 \geqslant g_2$. Although the AM estimator, if consistent, is no less efficient than the HT estimator, consistency requires a stronger exogeneity assumption. HT only requires that the means of the x_1 variables be uncorrelated with the unobserved effects, α_i, while the AM estimator requires the variables to be uncorrelated at each point in time. The extra instruments add explanatory power to the reduced form model for z_2 if there is variation over time in the correlation of x_1 and z_2. Again, using a Hausman test we are able to test the extra exogeneity assumptions by comparing the HT and AM estimators (for details to this application, see Contoyannis and Rice, 2001).

The AM estimator is implemented in a similar fashion to the HT estimator by using the `amacurdy` option, but note the requirement to state the variable name that identifies the cross-sectional time periods specified via `xtset`.

```
xthtaylor y $xvars, endog(hlghq1 sahex sahgd prof       ///
    manag skllnm skllm deg) amacurdy
```

A further refinement to the instrument set was suggested by Breusch, Mizon and Schmidt (BMS: 1989) who, following AM, make greater use of the time-varying endogenous variables by treating x_2 in a manner similar to the AM treatment of x_1. We do not pursue this refinement here. Contoyannis and Rice (2001) show the efficiency gains from moving from the AM to BMS estimator for the example of health and wages described in this chapter.

Results from implementing the HT estimator in Table 8.6 can be compared to those from the AM estimator in Table 8.7. Focusing on the endogenous time-varying variables, we can see that the coefficients on the health variables retain the expected signs and mimic closely the corresponding estimates observed for the FE estimator. This is the case for both the HT and AM estimates. Similarly, estimates obtained for occupational class reflect those obtained from the FE estimator. However, for all estimates we observed efficiency gains from using the instrumental variables approach with greater gains observed for AM than HT.

To aid comparison across the different estimators, the sets of results are replicated in Table 8.8. It is noteworthy that the FE and instrumental variables estimates are consistently lower than the RE estimates, with the within estimate for `sahex` 50 per cent lower than that obtained using RE. This may indicate positive correlation between the individual effects and self-assessed health, with those individuals that are more productive, or at least able to obtain relatively high wages, having unobserved characteristics, which lead to better self-assessed health.

The coefficient estimates on educational attainment (`deg`) show an interesting trend across the different estimators and indicate a rate of return to having a degree of between 0.3 (RE) to 1.2 (HT). Interestingly, the coefficient using the HT instrument set is around four times the magnitude of the corresponding RE estimate. This differential diminishes as stronger exogeneity assumptions are employed using the AM estimator. The results would appear to suggest that individuals who obtain a degree or higher degree appear to be compensating for

Table 8.7 Men – Amemiya and MaCurdy IV estimator on full sample of observations

```
-----------------------------------------------------------------------
Amemiya-MaCurdy estimation                Number of obs     =    4165
Group variable (i): pid                   Number of groups  =     833
                                          Obs per group: min =       5
                                                         avg =       5
                                                         max =       5
Random effects u_i ~ i.i.d.               Wald chi2(33)     = 706.71
                                          Prob > chi2       = 0.0000
-----------------------------------------------------------------------
```

y	Coef.	Std. Err.	z	P>|z|	[95% Conf.	Interval]
TVexogenous						
age	.0501906	.0081281	6.17	0.000	.0342598	.0661214
agesqrd	-.0509899	.009349	-5.45	0.000	-.0693136	-.0326663
exp	.0040201	.0018758	2.14	0.032	.0003436	.0076965
expsqrd	-.0174739	.0076038	-2.30	0.022	-.0323771	-.0025707
jbsize	.0000448	.0000177	2.53	0.011	.0000101	.0000796
covmem	.0793588	.0186716	4.25	0.000	.0427631	.1159546
covnon	.0237346	.0159644	1.49	0.137	-.007555	.0550242
jobpriv	.0361759	.0235155	1.54	0.124	-.0099136	.0822655
ljtrain	.0079132	.0070329	1.13	0.261	-.0058709	.0216973
widow	-.0268362	.0850174	-0.32	0.752	-.1934672	.1397948
divsep	-.032636	.0336543	-0.97	0.332	-.0985972	.0333253
nvrmar	-.0033698	.0223218	-0.15	0.880	-.0471197	.0403801
kids04	.0043819	.0100316	0.44	0.662	-.0152796	.0240434
SouthW	.0129475	.0700543	0.18	0.853	-.1243564	.1502515
London	.0017632	.0575254	0.03	0.976	-.1109845	.114511
Midland	-.0119789	.0600301	-0.20	0.842	-.1296358	.1056779
NorthW	-.2069535	.0700134	-2.96	0.003	-.3441771	-.0697298
NorthE	-.0204878	.0699192	-0.29	0.770	-.1575269	.1165512
Scot	-.193395	.0941696	-2.05	0.040	-.377964	-.008826
Wales	-.04507	.0821892	-0.55	0.583	-.206158	.1160179
yr9293	.0273557	.0092296	2.96	0.003	.009266	.0454454
yr9394	.0704982	.0105015	6.71	0.000	.0499155	.0910808
yr9495	.1001087	.0123033	8.14	0.000	.0759946	.1242228
yr9596	.1393102	.014404	9.67	0.000	.1110789	.1675414
TVendogenous						
hlghql	-.0023621	.0009371	-2.52	0.012	-.0041988	-.0005255
sahex	.0137238	.013053	1.05	0.293	-.0118595	.0393072
sahgd	.0092508	.0105751	0.87	0.382	-.0114761	.0299777
prof	.0916372	.0267275	3.43	0.001	.0392523	.1440221
manag	.0891452	.0207941	4.29	0.000	.0483894	.129901
skllnm	.0450761	.0220462	2.04	0.041	.0018664	.0882858
skllm	.039213	.0158023	2.48	0.013	.008241	.0701849

Table 8.7 continued

```
TIexogenous  |
       white |  .0645989   .1857891   0.35  0.728   -.2995411    .4287389
TIendogenous |
         deg |  .7392345   .1832807   4.03  0.000     .380011    1.098458
             |
        _cons |  .5320254   .2603319   2.04  0.041    .0217842   1.042266
-------------|----------------------------------------------------------
     sigma_u |  .86751264
     sigma_e |  .19403442
         rho |  .95235631  (fraction of variance due to u_i)
------------------------------------------------------------------------
note: TV refers to time varying; TI refers to time invariant.
```

unobserved characteristics which would otherwise reduce their wages (a result supported by others; see Hausman and Taylor (1981), Cornwell and Rupert (1988), and Baltagi and Khanti-Akom (1990)). This might be rationalised by considering a model where schooling or educational attainment is assumed to be endogenously determined in models of wages.

The set of results is in line with those obtained by Cornwell and Rupert and Baltagi and Khanti-Akom who use data from the Panel Study of Income Dynamics and who also find the efficiency gains from the AM estimator (and an extension to the BMS estimator) to be attached to the coefficient of the time-invariant endogenous variables, and the estimated coefficient to gradually approach the GLS estimates as one moves from HT to AM to BMS. For our results, the AM estimate of the standard error of the coefficient on deg is around 70 per cent of that for the HT estimator. This appears appropriate given that the additional AM instruments are time-invariant and hence the majority of their additional explanatory power will impact on time-invariant variables.

More generally, while avoiding the potential bias and inconsistency, the application of the HT and AM estimators allows us to retain a similar level of precision as the RE estimator. With the exception of educational attainment standard errors of the other variables differ negligibly from the RE specification.

8.4 OVERVIEW

The primary focus of this chapter is the role of health in determining wages and to this end considers both self-assessed general health and a measure of psychological well-being on hourly wages using data from the British Household Panel Survey. Using a Mincerian wage function to specify the key determinants of wages, we estimate the impact of health by employing fixed effects estimation together with random effects instrumental variable panel data estimators. Instruments are

Table 8.8 Men – comparison across estimators

NT = 4165 N = 833	OLS	RE	FE	HT	AM
age	.037	.051	_	.049	.050
	(.0040)	(.0060)		(.0082)	(.0081)
agesqrd	-.038	-.053	-.048	-.049	-.051
	(.0047)	(.0071)	(.0110)	(.0095)	(.0093)
exp	.009	.004	.004	.004	.004
	(.0021)	(.0020)	(.0021)	(.0019)	(.0019)
expsqrd	-.032	-.021	-.017	-.018	-.017
	(.0082)	(.0078)	(.0084)	(.0077)	(.0076)
jbsize	.00016	.00008	.00004	.00004	.00004
	(.00002)	(.00002)	(.00002)	(.00002)	(.00002)
covmem	.112	.083	.078	.081	.079
	(.0142)	(.0170)	(.0212)	(.0189)	(.0187)
covnon	.010	.019	.024	.024	.024
	(.0166)	(.0161)	(.0178)	(.0161)	(.0160)
jobpriv	.015	.017	.039	.042	.036
	(.0144)	(.0193)	(.0273)	(.0239)	(.0235)
ljtrain	.044	.016	.006	.007	.008
	(.0113)	(.0077)	(.0077)	(.0071)	(.0070)
widow	.085	.003	-.034	-.027	-.027
	(.0978)	(.0889)	(.0938)	(.0859)	(.0850)
divsep	-.088	-.059	-.027	-.035	-.033
	(.0263)	(.0317)	(.0378)	(.0340)	(.0337)
nvrmar	-.074	-.041	.006	-.005	-.003
	(.0172)	(.0207)	(.0252)	(.0226)	(.0223)
kids04	.064	.019	.004	.004	.004
	(.0121)	(.0106)	(.0111)	(.0101)	(.0100)
Hlghq1	-.001	-.002	-.002	-.002	-.002
	(.0013)	(.0010)	(.0010)	(.0009)	(.0009)
sahex	.066	.028	.014	.014	.014
	(.0172)	(.0139)	(.0143)	(.0132)	(.0131)
sahgd	.023	.013	.009	.009	.009
	(.0155)	(.0115)	(.0116)	(.0107)	(.0106)
prof	.543	.259	.085	.087	.092
	(.0253)	(.0260)	(.0293)	(.0271)	(.0267)
manag	.513	.242	.082	.084	.089
	(.0192)	(.0199)	(.0228)	(.0211)	(.0208)
skllnm	.290	.154	.040	.042	.045
	(.0209)	(.0214)	(.0242)	(.0223)	(.0220)
skllm	.140	.065	.038	.038	.039
	(.0183)	(.0164)	(.0173)	(.0160)	(.0158)
white	-.026	-.009	_	.157	.064
	(.0358)	(.0687)		(.1911)	(.1858)
deg	.171	.296	_	1.216	.739
	(.0173)	(.0310)		(.2595)	(.1833)

1 Age was dropped from the within regression due to perfect collinearity with the year dummies.
2 Constant, year and regional dummies suppressed.
3 Standard errors are given in parentheses.
4 `agesqrd = age2/100`, `expsqrd = exp2/100`.

derived through transformations of variables internal to the model as suggested by Hausman and Taylor (1981), and Amemiya and MaCurdy (1986). Results from these regressions show that reduced psychological health reduces hourly wages for the sample of men. We also find that the majority of the efficiency gains from the use of these instrumental variables estimators fall on the time-invariant endogenous variables, in the case presented here, measures of academic attainment.

APPENDIX

Note: save file as `hausman_alt.do`.

```
/* .do file to estimate an alternative to the Hausman test of fixed
versus random effects */
/* See Baltagi (2005, p67) and Davidson and MacKinnon (1993, p89) */
/* Based on program of Vince Wiggins' posting on the STATA list archive
9 Feb 2004 */

local depvar $depvar
local varlist $varlist
local id $id

tokenize `varlist'
local i 1
while "``i''" != "" {
        qui by `id': egen double M`i' = mean(``i'')
        qui by `id': gen double D`i' = ``i'' - M`i'
        local newlist `newlist' M`i' D`i'

        local i = `i' + 1
}

xtreg `depvar' `newlist' , re i($id)
tempname b
matrix `b' = e(b)

qui test M1 = D1 , notest  // clear test
local i 2
while "``i''" != "" {
        if `b'[1, colnumb(`b', "M`i'")] != 0 &  ///
          `b'[1, colnumb(`b', "D`i'")] != 0 {
          qui test M`i' = D`i' , accum notest
        }

        local i = `i' + 1

}
test
drop `newlist'
```

9 Modelling the dynamics of health

SYNOPSIS

This chapter works with the same sub-sample of the BHPS that was used in Chapter 2. It shows how to estimate nonlinear models for binary-dependent variables using both static and dynamic specifications of the models. Ways of dealing with unobservable individual heterogeneity are illustrated. These include pooled and random effects probits and the conditional logit model. The outcome of interest is a binary measure of health problems and the focus of the analysis is on socioeconomic gradients in health.

9.1 INTRODUCTION

Panel data on individual self-reported health can be used to estimate nonlinear models for binary and ordered dependent variables. These models can be based on static or on dynamic specifications. This chapter follows a similar structure to the paper by Contoyannis *et al.* (2004b) that was introduced in Chapter 2, but rather than analysing an ordered categorical measure of self-assessed health, the focus is on a binary measure of limiting health problems. To illustrate the methods, we use a panel data model for a binary measure of health applied to data drawn from the first eight waves of the British Household Panel Survey (BHPS) and derived from the question 'does health limit your daily activities?'

As the analysis estimates models that are designed for panel data begin, as in Chapter 2, by specifying the individual (i) and time indexes (t) and using these to sort the data so that observations are listed by waves within individuals:

```
xtset pid wavenum
sort pid wavenum
```

The dependent variable is based on the BHPS variable `hllt`. This needs to be checked, by running descriptive statistics and tabulating the raw data, and then recoded to deal with missing values and cases where there was no answer. Note that in the raw data the variable is coded as 1 for 'yes' and 2 for 'no'. This is recoded to the more usual 0/1 scale so that it is recognised as a standard binary variable by the software:

```
summarize hllt
```

Variable	Obs	Mean	Std. Dev.	Min	Max
hllt	64741	1.840194	.4104114	-9	2

```
tabulate hllt
```

hllt	Freq.	Percent	Cum.
missing	20	0.03	0.03
not answered	2	0.00	0.03
yes	10,120	15.63	15.67
no	54,599	84.33	100.00
Total	64,741	100.00	

```
clonevar hprob=hllt
recode hprob -9=.
recode hprob -1=.
recode hprob 2=0
summarize hprob
```

Variable	Obs	Mean	Std. Dev.	Min	Max
hprob	64719	.1563683	.363207	0	1

The final `summarize` command describes the binary variable that is used in the econometric models.

The next command creates the first of a series of `globals` to provide a shorthand label for the list of regressors that are used in the econometric models. The list includes measures of gender (`male`), marital status (`widowed nvrmar divsep`), educational attainment (`deghdeg hndalev ocse`), household size and composition (`hhsize nch04 nch511 nch1218`), a cubic function of age (`age age2 age3`), race (`nonwhite`), professional group (`prof mantech skillmn ptskill unskill armed`) and the logarithm of equivalised real income (`lninc`):

```
global xvars "male widowed nvrmar divsep deghdeg hndalev
   ocse hhsize nch04 nch511 nch1218 age age2 age3 nonwhite
   prof mantech skillmn ptskill unskill armed lninc"
```

Recall the following code that was used in Chapter 2 to create indicators of whether observations are in the balanced and unbalanced estimation samples. These variables will be needed again below:

```
quietly probit hprob $xvars
generate insampm = 0
recode insampm 0 = 1 if e(sample)
sort pid wavenum
generate constant = 1
by pid: egen Ti = sum(constant) if insampm == 1
drop constant
sort pid wavenum
by pid: gen nextwavem = insampm[_n+1]
generate allwavesm = .
recode allwavesm . = 0 if Ti ~= 8
recode allwavesm . = 1 if Ti == 8
generate numwavesm = .
replace numwavesm = Ti
```

To make the Stata code generic, so that it is it easier to adapt the code for other applications of the same models, create a copy of the dependent variable hprob as the new dependent variable (y) in this command:

```
clonevar y=hprob
```

Before estimating the panel data regressions, it is helpful to use xtsummarize to derive summary statistics that exploit the panel dimension of the dataset and that separate the between-individual (cross-sectional) and within-individual (time-series) variation in the dependent and independent variables. This is done for the full sample and for the balanced panel (allwavesm==1):

```
xtsummarize y $xvars
```

Variable		Mean	Std. Dev.	Min	Max		Observations	
y	overall	.1563683	.363207	0	1		N =	64719
	between		.3065844	0	1		n =	10264
	within		.2242743	-.7186317	1.031368		T-bar =	6.30544
male	overall	.461485	.4985182	0	1		N =	64741

```
         between |            .499175           0           1 |   n =    10264
          within |                  0    .461485    .461485 | T-bar = 6.30758
                 |                                           |
widowed  overall | .0881745 .2835507           0           1 |   N =    66323
         between |           .2834152           0           1 |   n =    10264
          within |           .0879394 -.7868255   .9631745 | T-bar = 6.46171
                 |                                           |
nvrmar   overall | .1633672 .3697031           0           1 |   N =    66323
         between |           .3589536           0           1 |   n =    10264
          within |            .131913 -.7116328   1.038367 | T-bar = 6.46171
                 |                                           |
divsep   overall | .0682116 .2521106           0           1 |   N =    66323
         between |            .224614           0           1 |   n =    10264
          within |           .1215966 -.8067884   .9432116 | T-bar = 6.46171
                 |                                           |
deghdeg  overall | .0964536 .2952141           0           1 |   N =    82112
         between |           .2952267           0           1 |   n =    10264
          within |                  0   .0964536   .0964536 |   T =        8
                 |                                           |
hndalev  overall | .2024552 .4018321           0           1 |   N =    82112
         between |           .4018492           0           1 |   n =    10264
          within |                  0   .2024552   .2024552 |   T =        8
                 |                                           |
ocse     overall | .2724084 .4452016           0           1 |   N =    82112
         between |           .4452206           0           1 |   n =    10264
          within |                  0   .2724084   .2724084 |   T =        8
                 |                                           |
hhsize   overall | 2.788357 1.329707           1          11 |   N =    64741
         between |             1.2373           1   10.66667 |   n =    10264
          within |           .5415378 -2.711643   9.413357 | T-bar = 6.30758
                 |                                           |
nch04    overall | .1443753 .4196944           0           4 |   N =    64741
         between |           .3263182           0         2.5 |   n =    10264
          within |           .2747743 -1.998482   2.519375 | T-bar = 6.30758
                 |                                           |
nch511   overall | .2597736 .6145583           0           6 |   N =    64741
         between |           .5198938           0        5.25 |   n =    10264
          within |           .3368913 -2.597369   3.402631 | T-bar = 6.30758
                 |                                           |
nch1218  overall | .1833151 .4861762           0           4 |   N =    64741
         between |           .3828021           0         2.5 |   n =    10264
          within |           .3109858 -1.691685   2.808315 | T-bar = 6.30758
                 |                                           |
age      overall | 46.95723 17.77155          15         100 |   N =    64741
         between |           18.34678          16          97 |   n =    10264
          within |           2.180959  32.15723   52.24294 | T-bar = 6.30758
```

```
                |                                                    |
age2    overall | 25.20804  18.17837        2.25        100 |   N =      64741
        between |           18.86734        2.56      94.09 |   n =      10264
         within |           2.165909    10.62004   32.12929 | T-bar =  6.30758
                |                                                    |
age3    overall | 15.01471  15.53261       .3375        100 |   N =      64741
        between |            16.2452       .4096    91.2673 |   n =      10264
         within |           1.978015     4.10103   24.99951 | T-bar =  6.30758
                |                                                    |
nonwhite overall | .0619641  .2410919          0          1 |   N =      82112
        between |           .2411022           0          1 |   n =      10264
         within |                  0    .0619641   .0619641 |   T =          8
                |                                                    |
lninc   overall | 9.497943  .6664307  -.1312631   13.12998 |   N =      64101
        between |           .5793668    4.692182   12.13122 |   n =      10261
         within |            .364328    2.399066   12.70143 | T-bar =  6.24705
                |                                                    |
prof    overall | .0342062  .1817598          0          1 |   N =      64579
        between |           .1470494           0          1 |   n =      10264
         within |           .1034673  -.8407938   .9092062 | T-bar =   6.2918
                |                                                    |
mantech overall | .1843943  .3878084          0          1 |   N =      64579
        between |            .322583           0          1 |   n =      10264
         within |           .2093004  -.6906057   1.059394 | T-bar =   6.2918
                |                                                    |
skillmn overall | .1229037  .3283292          0          1 |   N =      64579
        between |           .2790731           0          1 |   n =      10264
         within |           .1849436  -.7520963   .9979037 | T-bar =   6.2918
                |                                                    |
ptskill overall | .0859258  .2802566          0          1 |   N =      64579
        between |           .2232924           0          1 |   n =      10264
         within |           .1838036  -.7890742   .9609258 | T-bar =   6.2918
                |                                                    |
unskill overall | .0262624  .1599159          0          1 |   N =      64579
        between |           .1231267           0          1 |   n =      10264
         within |           .1093333  -.8487376   .9012624 | T-bar =   6.2918
                |                                                    |
armed   overall | .0007588  .0275354          0          1 |   N =      64579
        between |           .0301781           0          1 |   n =      10264
         within |           .0180176   -.713527   .8757588 | T-bar =   6.2918
                |                                                    |
```

```
xtsummarize y $xvars if allwavesm==1
```

Variable		Mean	Std. Dev.	Min	Max		Observations
y	overall	.1444193	.351518	0	1	N =	48560
	between		.2707188	0	1	n =	6070
	within		.2242471	-.7305807	1.019419	T =	8
male	overall	.4494234	.4974406	0	1	N =	48560
	between		.4974764	0	1	n =	6070
	within		0	.4494234	.4494234	T =	8
widowed	overall	.0806219	.2722564	0	1	N =	48560
	between		.2571574	0	1	n =	6070
	within		.0894603	-.7943781	.9556219	T =	8
nvrmar	overall	.143925	.3510173	0	1	N =	48560
	between		.3244268	0	1	n =	6070
	within		.1340729	-.731075	1.018925	T =	8
divsep	overall	.0681837	.2520635	0	1	N =	48560
	between		.2211882	0	1	n =	6070
	within		.1209083	-.8068163	.9431837	T =	8
deghdeg	overall	.1143328	.3182183	0	1	N =	48560
	between		.3182412	0	1	n =	6070
	within		0	.1143328	.1143328	T =	8
hndalev	overall	.2253707	.4178305	0	1	N =	48560
	between		.4178606	0	1	n =	6070
	within		0	.2253707	.2253707	T =	8
ocse	overall	.2866557	.452204	0	1	N =	48560
	between		.4522365	0	1	n =	6070
	within		0	.2866557	.2866557	T =	8
hhsize	overall	2.808979	1.302575	1	10	N =	48560
	between		1.184421	1	8.625	n =	6070
	within		.5422633	-2.691021	9.433979	T =	8
nch04	overall	.149547	.4222539	0	4	N =	48560
	between		.3119503	0	2	n =	6070
	within		.2846039	-1.600453	2.524547	T =	8

```
nch511    overall | .2696664 .6204588          0          4 |   N =   48560
          between |          .511909            0      3.375 |   n =    6070
          within  |          .350651  -1.980334  2.894666 |   T =        8
                  |                                        |

nch1218   overall | .1843904 .4860323          0          4 |   N =   48560
          between |          .3667978           0        2.5 |   n =    6070
          within  |          .3189141  -1.69061   2.80939 |   T =        8
                  |                                        |

age       overall | 46.87016 17.02794         15        100 |   N =   48560
          between |          16.87426        18.5       96.5 |   n =    6070
          within  |          2.29154   42.74516  51.87016 |   T =        8
                  |                                        |

age2      overall | 24.86757 17.28749       2.25        100 |   N =   48560
          between |          17.13723       3.475     93.175 |   n =    6070
          within  |          2.283685  18.18257  31.69257 |   T =        8
                  |                                        |

age3      overall | 14.55261 14.59312      .3375        100 |   N =   48560
          between |          14.4457        .6623    90.0152 |   n =    6070
          within  |          2.076254  4.973107  24.53741 |   T =        8
                  |                                        |

nonwhite  overall | .0324547 .1772062          0          1 |   N =   48560
          between |          .177219            0          1 |   n =    6070
          within  |                 0  .0324547  .0324547 |   T =        8
                  |                                        |

lninc     overall | 9.528054 .6414354   3.324561    12.9514 |   N =   48560
          between |          .5398719   6.994533   12.13122 |   n =    6070
          within  |          .3464387   4.887086   12.58706 |   T =        8
                  |                                        |

prof      overall | .0351936 .1842707          0          1 |   N =   48560
          between |          .1498151           0          1 |   n =    6070
          within  |          .1073049  -.8398064  .9101936 |   T =        8
                  |                                        |

mantech   overall | .1932867 .3948799          0          1 |   N =   48560
          between |          .3306547           0          1 |   n =    6070
          within  |          .2159014  -.6817133  1.068287 |   T =        8
                  |                                        |

skillmn   overall | .1224465 .3278041          0          1 |   N =   48560
          between |          .2686998           0          1 |   n =    6070
          within  |          .1877934  -.7525535  .9974465 |   T =        8
                  |                                        |

ptskill   overall | .0852348 .2792336          0          1 |   N =   48560
          between |          .2076425           0          1 |   n =    6070
          within  |          .1867143  -.7897652  .9602348 |   T =        8
                  |                                        |
```

unskill	overall		.0272446	.1627972	0	1		N =	48560
	between			.1173912	0	1		n =	6070
	within			.1128016	-.8477554	.9022446		T =	8
armed	overall		.0004119	.0202904	0	1		N =	48560
	between			.0120002	0	.625		n =	6070
	within			.016362	-.6245881	.8754119		T =	8

Notice that for time invariant variables, such as educational qualifications (deghdeg, hndalev, ocse), there is no within-individual variation. Notice also that for most of the time-varying variables there is more between- than within-individual variation.

Comparing the results for the full sample with those from the balanced sample (allwavesm==1) helps to reveal any systematic differences in the observable characteristics of the samples. The balanced sample is a little healthier than the full sample, with 0.154 reporting health problems in the full sample and 0.144 in the balanced sample. For many of the observed characteristics, the differences in means are small but, for example, the balanced sample is better educated with a higher proportion of university graduates (deghdeg). The issue of non-response and attrition bias is pursued in Chapter 10.

9.2 STATIC MODELS

Our models apply to a binary dependent variable: 'does health limit your daily activities?'. There are repeated measurements for each wave ($t = 1, \ldots, T$) for a sample of n individuals ($i = 1, \ldots, n$), and the binary dependent variable y_{it} can be modelled in terms of a continuous latent variable y_{it}^*,

$$y_{it} = I(y_{it}^* > 0) = I(x_{it}\beta + u_{it} > 0)$$

where $I(.)$ is a binary indicator function. The error term u_{it} could be allowed to be freely correlated over time or the correlation structure could be restricted. A common specification is the error components model which splits the error into a time-invariant individual random effect (RE), α_i, and a time-varying idiosyncratic random error, ϵ_{it},

$$y_{it} = I(y_{it}^* > 0) = I(x_{it}\beta + \alpha_i + \epsilon_{it} > 0)$$

The idiosyncratic error term could be autocorrelated, for example following an AR(l) process, $\epsilon_{it} = \rho\epsilon_{it-1} + \eta_{it}$, or it could be independent over t (giving the standard random effects model).

Pooled specification

The most simple specification is to proceed as if the u_{it} are independent over t and to use a pooled probit model. This applies the standard cross section probit estimator, even though there are repeated observations for the same individual. So, the marginal probability of reporting a health problem at wave t is given by:

$$P(y_{it} = 1 \mid x_{it}) = \Phi(x_{it}\beta)$$

The log-likelihood for the pooled model implicitly assumes that observations are independent across waves and uses the simple product of these marginal distributions. If, as is likely, observations are in fact correlated within individuals this joint distribution will be mis-specified and hence the estimates will not be maximum likelihood estimates (MLE). However, the marginal distributions for each wave are correctly specified even though the joint distribution across waves is incorrectly specified. The properties of the quasi-maximum likelihood estimator (QMLE), which applies in this case, mean that the pooled probit estimates are consistent even though the log-likelihood function is incorrect. However, the conventional ML estimates of the standard errors will not be consistent and these need to be replaced by sandwich estimates that are robust to clustering within-individuals (robust cluster(pid)).

The first results are for the unbalanced panel:

```
dprobit y $xvars, robust cluster(pid)
```

Notice that, as in the first edition of this book, the model is estimated here using the dprobit command rather than the standard probit command. The latter would report the coefficients from the linear index (the latent variable equation) while dprobit automatically presents the results as partial effects, evaluated at the sample means of the regressors: dprobit computes marginal effects, based on derivatives, for continuous variables and average effects, based on differences, for discrete regressors. This means that the reported results can be given a quantitative as well as a qualititative interpretation. For example, those with university degrees (deghdeg) have an estimated partial effects of –0.056: meaning that the probability of reporting a limiting illness is around 0.056 lower for those with degrees than those without qualifications (the reference category), holding other factors in the model constant at their sample means. One note of caution here is that this benchmark may not be very meaningful when the dummy variables relate to mutually exclusive sets of categories such as educational qualifications, marital status and occupational group, where each individual can only belong to one category at a time. This creates a problem of interpretation with the standard approach to computing partial effects. The command dprobit can still be used in Stata 12 but is no longer supported as an official Stata command. A better alternative is to use the new margins command with the following syntax:

Table 9.1 Pooled probit model, unbalanced panel

```
------------------------------------------------------------------------
Probit regression, reporting marginal effects    Number of obs =   63918

                                                 Wald chi2(22) = 1981.96
                                                 Prob > chi2   =  0.0000
Log pseudolikelihood = -24044.138                Pseudo R2     =  0.1325
                         (standard errors adjusted for clustering on pid)
------------------------------------------------------------------------
```

	Robust						
y |	dF/dx	Std. Err.	z	P>|z|	x-bar	[95% C.I.	]
male*|	.0088301	.0057147	1.55	0.122	.461294	-.00237	.020031
widowed*|	-.0033601	.0089857	-0.37	0.711	.089646	-.020972	.014252
nvrmar*|	.0203347	.0092692	2.27	0.023	.160659	.002167	.038502
divsep*|	.0351431	.0109542	3.45	0.001	.069151	.013673	.056613
deghdeg*|	-.0563287	.0078981	-6.02	0.000	.108295	-.071809	-.040849
hndalev*|	-.044868	.0067819	-6.08	0.000	.21526	-.05816	-.031576
ocse*|	-.0551473	.0062399	-8.15	0.000	.279765	-.067377	-.042917
hhsize |	-.0002887	.0029376	-0.10	0.922	2.78962	-.006046	.005469
nch04 |	-.0265443	.0065124	-4.07	0.000	.145014	-.039308	-.01378
nch511 |	-.0093574	.0049476	-1.89	0.059	.260115	-.019054	.00034
nch1218 |	-.0062888	.0053513	-1.18	0.240	.182969	-.016777	.0042
age |	.0225194	.0032899	6.86	0.000	46.9753	.016071	.028968
age2 |	-.0382381	.0064794	-5.91	0.000	25.2308	-.050937	-.025539
age3 |	.0225046	.0039697	5.67	0.000	15.0369	.014724	.030285
nonwhite*|	.0927335	.014889	7.24	0.000	.045527	.063552	.121915
prof*|	-.0781306	.0082116	-6.61	0.000	.034263	-.094225	-.062036
mantech*|	-.0916388	.0049077	-15.19	0.000	.184142	-.101258	-.08202
skillmn*|	-.1020752	.0044425	-16.49	0.000	.12308	-.110782	-.093368
ptskill*|	-.0856117	.004574	-13.86	0.000	.086048	-.094577	-.076647
unskill*|	-.0852802	.0064642	-8.54	0.000	.026299	-.09795	-.07261
armed*|	-.0981824	.0286635	-1.65	0.100	.000767	-.154362	-.042003
lninc |	-.0327962	.0034939	-9.38	0.000	9.4974	-.039644	-.025948

```
------------------------------------------------------------------------
  obs. P |  .1563879
  pred. P |  .1233529 (at x-bar)
------------------------------------------------------------------------
```

(*) dF/dx is for discrete change of dummy variable from 0 to 1

z and P>|z| correspond to the test of the underlying coefficient being 0

```
global xvars_f "i.male i.widowed i.nvrmar i.divsep
    i.deghdeg i.hndalev i.ocse hhsize nch04 nch511 nch1218
    c.age c.age#c.age c.age#c.age#c.age i.nonwhite lninc
    i.prof i.mantech i.skillmn i.ptskill i.unskill i.armed"

probit y $xvars_f, robust cluster(pid)
margins, dydx(*)
```

Table 9.2 Pooled probit model, average partial effects

```
-----------------------------------------------------------------
Average marginal effects                    Number of obs  =   63918
Model VCE      : Robust

Expression     : Pr(y), predict()
dy/dx w.r.t. : 1.male 1.widowed 1.nvrmar 1.divsep 1.deghdeg
1.hndalev 1.ocse hhsize nch04 nch511 nch1218 age 1.nonwhite lninc
1.prof 1.mantech 1.skillmn 1.ptskill 1.unskill 1.armed
-----------------------------------------------------------------
```

	dy/dx	Delta-method Std. Err.	z	P>|z|	[95% Conf.Interval]	
1.male	.0090361	.0058476	1.55	0.122	-.002425	.0204972
1.widowed	-.0034448	.009228	-0.37	0.709	-.0215313	.0146417
1.nvrmar	.0206306	.0093277	2.21	0.027	.0023487	.0389125
1.divsep	.0352543	.010788	3.27	0.001	.0141103	.0563984
1.deghdeg	-.0597098	.0086896	-6.87	0.000	-.0767411	-.0426785
1.hndalev	-.0468731	.0072177	-6.49	0.000	-.0610195	-.0327266
1.ocse	-.0576365	.0066422	-8.68	0.000	-.0706549	-.0446181
hhsize	-.0002954	.0030064	-0.10	0.922	-.0061879	.005597
nch04	-.0271661	.0066712	-4.07	0.000	-.0402414	-.0140909
nch511	-.0095766	.0050652	-1.89	0.059	-.0195043	.0003511
nch1218	-.0064361	.0054769	-1.18	0.240	-.0171706	.0042984
age	.0031783	.0002205	14.41	0.000	.0027461	.0036105
1.nonwhite	.0905072	.0139931	6.47	0.000	.0630812	.1179333
lninc	-.0335645	.0035733	-9.39	0.000	.040568	-.026561
1.prof	-.0857477	.0098567	-8.70	0.000	-.1050665	-.0664289
1.mantech	-.0980571	.005472	-17.92	0.000	-.1087821	-.0873322
1.skillmn	-.1117445	.0052014	-21.48	0.000	-.1219391	-.1015498
1.ptskill	-.0938087	.0053881	-17.41	0.000	-.1043692	-.0832482
1.unskill	-.0948978	.0080287	-11.82	0.000	-.1106337	-.0791618
1.armed	-.1126294	.0397463	-2.83	0.005	-.1905308	-.0347281

```
Note: dy/dx for factor levels is the discrete change from the base level.
```

This will compute partial effects for each observation using the actual value of their regressors and then report a table of the average partial effects, averaged across the sample values, along with standard error computed using the delta method. A new global list of regressors is used to allow for factor variables: so that categorical variables are identified as such (using `i.`) and continuous variables are identified (using `c.`). The use of the notation for interactions (#) to specify the square and cubed values of age means that the overall partial effect for `age` is computed, rather than separate effects for `age`, age^2 and age^3, which would be misleading.

Table 9.3 Pooled probit model, balanced panel

```
-------------------------------------------------------------------
Average marginal effects                    Number of obs  =   48540
Model VCE    : Robust
```

```
Expression   : Pr(y), predict()
dy/dx w.r.t. : 1.male 1.widowed 1.nvrmar 1.divsep 1.deghdeg
1.hndalev 1.ocse hhsize nch04 nch511 nch1218 age 1.nonwhite lninc
1.prof 1.mantech 1.skillmn 1.ptskill 1.unskill
```

		Delta-method				
	dy/dx	Std. Err.	z	P>|z|	[95% Conf.	Interval]
1.male	.0050369	.0069237	0.73	0.467	-.0085332	.018607
1.widowed	-.0084638	.0111203	-0.76	0.447	-.0302592	.0133317
1.nvrmar	.029315	.0114331	2.56	0.010	.0069065	.0517236
1.divsep	.0219563	.0123682	1.78	0.076	-.0022849	.0461975
1.deghdeg	-.0588002	.009905	-5.94	0.000	-.0782136	-.0393868
1.hndalev	-.0410284	.0083376	-4.92	0.000	-.0573697	-.0246871
1.ocse	-.0509534	.0078148	-6.52	0.000	-.0662702	-.0356367
hhsize	-.0019795	.0036374	-0.54	0.586	-.0091088	.0051497
nch04	-.0320456	.0077427	-4.14	0.000	.0472211	-.0168702
nch511	-.0164406	.0060667	-2.71	0.007	-.028331	-.0045501
nch1218	-.0088923	.0062894	-1.41	0.157	-.0212193	.0034346
age	.0023358	.0002704	8.64	0.000	.0018058	.0028659
1.nonwhite	.0941703	.0210466	4.47	0.000	.0529197	.1354209
lninc	-.0403837	.0044475	-9.08	0.000	-.0491007	-.0316667
1.prof	-.0861446	.0105689	-8.15	0.000	-.1068593	-.0654299
1.mantech	-.0938139	.0061599	-15.23	0.000	-.105887	-.0817407
1.skillmn	-.1048499	.0058821	-17.83	0.000	-.1163786	-.0933211
1.ptskill	-.089563	.0059876	-14.96	0.000	-.1012984	-.0778276
1.unskill	-.0841483	.0091775	-9.17	0.000	-.1021359	-.0661606

```
Note: dy/dx for factor levels is the discrete change from the base level.
```

The set of results in Table 9.3 are for the balanced panel (where `allwavesm==1`). These are fairly similar to the results for the unbalanced panel although note that the variable `armed` is dropped from the analysis as it has no variation within this smaller sample:

```
global xvars_f "i.male i.widowed i.nvrmar i.divsep
    i.deghdeg i.hndalev i.ocse hhsize nch04 nch511 nch1218
    c.age c.age#c.age c.age#c.age#c.age i.nonwhite lninc
    i.prof i.mantech i.skillmn i.ptskill i.unskill"

probit y $xvars_f if allwavesm==1, robust cluster(pid)
margins, dydx(*)
```

Correlated effects

In the pooled probit model, the individual effect (α_i) is subsumed into the overall error term. The model assumes that the individual effect is independent of the observed regressors, an assumption that will often be questionable in applied work. An approach to dealing with individual effects that are correlated with the regressors is to specify $E(\alpha \mid x)$ directly. For example, in dealing with a random effects probit model Chamberlain (1980) suggests using,

$$\alpha_i = x_i\alpha + u_i, \quad u_i \sim iid(0, \sigma^2)$$

where $x_i = (x_{i1}, ..., x_{iT})$, the values of the regressors for every wave of the panel, and $\alpha = (\alpha_1, ..., \alpha_T)$. This approach will work with the pooled probit model as well. Then, by substitution, the distribution of y_{it} conditional on x_i but marginal to α_i has the probit form,

$$P(y_{it} = 1 \mid x_i) = \Phi[(x_{it}\beta + x_i\alpha)]$$

In other words, the pooled probit model is augmented by adding x_i. A special case of this approach, associated with earlier work by Mundlak (1978) uses the within-individual means of the regressors rather than separate values for each wave; implicitly setting the correlation between α_i and x to be constant over time. This can be implemented in Stata by using `egen` to create new variables for the within-means. To illustrate, here we only take the within-mean of log(income) (`lninc`):

```
by pid: egen mlninc=mean(lninc)
```

Then this is added to the list of regressors:

```
global xvarm "$xvars mlninc"
global xvarm_f "$xvars_f mlninc"
```

The new list of regressors is used to re-run the pooled probit model:

```
probit y $xvarm_f, robust cluster(pid)
margins, dydx(*)
```

Results could be obtained for the balanced sample using the option if
allwavesm==1 within the command:

```
probit y $xvarm_f if allwavesm==1, robust cluster(pid)
margins, dydx(*)
```

Table 9.4 Mundlak specification of pooled probit model, unbalanced panel

```
-----------------------------------------------------------------------
Average marginal effects                      Number of obs  =   63918
Model VCE     : Robust


Expression    : Pr(y), predict()
dy/dx w.r.t.  : 1.male 1.widowed 1.nvrmar 1.divsep 1.deghdeg 1.hndalev
1.ocse hhsize nch04 nch511 nch1218 age 1.nonwhite lninc 1.prof
1.mantech 1.skillmn 1.ptskill 1.unskill 1.armed mlninc
-----------------------------------------------------------------------
```

	dy/dx	Delta-method Std. Err.	z	P>|z|	[95% Conf. Interval]	
1.male	.0091126	.0058378	1.56	0.119	-.0023294	.0205546
1.widowed	-.0052963	.0091722	-0.58	0.564	-.0232734	.0126809
1.nvrmar	.0194462	.0092847	2.09	0.036	.0012486	.0376439
1.divsep	.0298888	.0106507	2.81	0.005	.0090138	.0507637
1.deghdeg	-.0496407	.0092789	-5.35	0.000	-.0678269	-.0314545
1.hndalev	-.0393064	.007481	-5.25	0.000	-.0539689	-.0246439
1.ocse	-.0524258	.0067736	-7.74	0.000	-.0657018	-.0391499
hhsize	-.0002932	.0029997	-0.10	0.922	-.0061725	.0055862
nch04	-.0304999	.0067279	-4.53	0.000	-.0436863	-.0173135
nch511	-.0139472	.005127	-2.72	0.007	-.023996	-.0038983
nch1218	-.0096625	.0054975	-1.76	0.079	-.0204375	.0011124
age	.0030788	.0002213	13.91	0.000	.0026451	.0035125
1.nonwhite	.0866315	.0139856	6.19	0.000	.0592202	.1140429
lninc	.0020563	.0030461	0.68	0.500	-.003914	.0080265
1.prof	-.0811688	.0102395	-7.93	0.000	-.1012378	-.0610998
1.mantech	-.0932294	.0055973	-16.66	0.000	-.1041999	-.0822588
1.skillmn	-.1103428	.0052282	-21.11	0.000	-.1205899	-.1000957
1.ptskill	-.0933268	.0053962	-17.29	0.000	-.1039031	-.0827504
1.unskill	-.0956556	.0079172	-12.08	0.000	-.111173	-.0801382
1.armed	-.1067143	.0430561	-2.48	0.013	-.1911028	-.0223258
mlninc	-.0606182	.0064736	-9.36	0.000	-.0733063	-.0479301

Note: dy/dx for factor levels is the discrete change from the base level.

The impact of moving to the Mundlak specification, for both unbalanced and balanced samples, is to dramatically reduce the size and statistical significance of current income (lninc), while the effect of mean income (mlninc) is larger and statistically significant.

Random effects specification

Using the pooled model gives estimates of the coefficients and partial effects that are consistent and robust to clustering within individuals. However, using the error components assumption of the random effects model can provide more efficient estimates and provide information on how much of the random variability in health is attributable to the individual effect. Assuming that α and ϵ are normally distributed and independent of x gives the random effects probit model (REP). In this case, α can be integrated out to give the sample log-likelihood function by taking the expectation over all the possible values of α weighted by their probability density:

$$\ln L = \sum_{i=1}^{n} \left\{ \ln \int_{-\infty}^{+\infty} \prod_{t=1}^{T} \left(\Phi \left[d_{it} (x_{it} \beta + \alpha) \right] \right) f(\alpha) \, d\alpha \right\}$$

where $d_{it} = 2y_{it} - 1$. This expression contains an integral which can be approximated by Gauss-Hermite quadrature. Assuming $\alpha \sim N(0, \sigma_{\alpha}^2)$, the contribution of each individual to the sample likelihood function is

$$L_i = \int_{-\infty}^{+\infty} \frac{1}{\sqrt{2\pi\sigma_{\alpha}^2}} \exp\left(-\frac{\alpha^2}{2\sigma_{\alpha}^2} \right) \{ g(\alpha) \} \, d\alpha$$

where

$$g(\alpha) = \prod_{t=1}^{T} \Phi \left[d_{it} (x_{it} \beta + \alpha) \right].$$

Use the change of variables, $\alpha = (\sqrt{(2\sigma_{\alpha}^2)})z$ to give

$$L_i = \frac{1}{\sqrt{\pi}} \int_{-\infty}^{+\infty} \exp(-z^2) \left\{ g\left(\sqrt{2\sigma_{\alpha}^2} z \right) \right\} \, dz$$

As it takes the generic form

$$\int_{-\infty}^{+\infty} \exp(-z^2) f(z) \, dz$$

this expression is suitable for Gauss-Hermite quadrature and can be approximated as a weighted sum,

Table 9.5 Random effects probit model, unbalanced panel

```
---------------------------------------------------------------------
Random-effects probit regression      Number of obs      =     63918
Group variable: pid                   Number of groups   =     10261
Random effects u_i ~ Gaussian         Obs per group: min =         1
                                                     avg =       6.2
                                                     max =         8
                                      Wald chi2(22)      =   2061.94
Log likelihood = -17660.529           Prob > chi2        =    0.0000
---------------------------------------------------------------------
         y |    Coef. Std. Err.      z  P>|z| [95% Conf.Interval]
-----------|---------------------------------------------------------
      male | -.068407  .0463141  -1.48  0.140  -.159181   .0223669
   widowed | -.1264621 .0645666  -1.96  0.050 -.2530102   .0000861
    nvrmar |  .1066773 .0594807   1.79  0.073 -.0099028   .2232574
    divsep |  .2014393 .0611405   3.29  0.001  .0816062   .3212724
   deghdeg | -.5995837 .0913787  -6.56  0.000 -.7786827  -.4204846
   hndalev | -.4059626 .0667015  -6.09  0.000 -.5366951    -.27523
      ocse | -.5149269 .0604481  -8.52  0.000  -.633403  -.3964508
    hhsize | -.0020348 .0182919  -0.11  0.911 -.0378862   .0338167
     nch04 | -.1222856  .039881  -3.07  0.002 -.2004508  -.0441204
    nch511 | -.0489116 .0312363  -1.57  0.117 -.1101336   .0123104
   nch1218 |  .0107046 .0323285   0.33  0.741 -.0526581   .0740672
       age |  .1002324 .0229562   4.37  0.000  .0552392   .1452257
      age2 | -.1776026 .0455258  -3.90  0.000 -.2668315  -.0883737
      age3 |  .1374486 .0282381   4.87  0.000  .0821029   .1927943
  nonwhite |  .7778495 .0943377   8.25  0.000   .592951   .9627479
    lninc  | -.1152506 .0221819  -5.20  0.000 -.1587263  -.0717749
      prof | -.6250288 .1004205  -6.22  0.000 -.8218493  -.4282082
   mantech | -.5893524 .0477677 -12.34  0.000 -.6829753  -.4957295
    skillmn | -.6970076 .0519449 -13.42 0.000 -.7988177  -.5951975
   ptskill |  -.516419 .0515398 -10.02  0.000 -.6174352  -.4154029
    unskill | -.4063891 .0806847  -5.04 0.000 -.5645281    -.24825
     armed |  -1.25614 .7707957  -1.63  0.103 -2.766872   .2545917
     _cons | -2.813959 .4078622  -6.90  0.000 -3.613355 -2.014564
-----------|---------------------------------------------------------
  /lnsig2u |  1.064185  .034794                .9959895    1.13238
-----------|---------------------------------------------------------
   sigma_u |  1.702491 .0296182                1.645419   1.761542
       rho |  .7434894 .0066357                .7302693   .7562778
---------------------------------------------------------------------
Likelihood-ratio test of rho=0: chibar2(01) = 1.3e+04 Prob >=
chibar2 = 0.000
```

$$L_i \approx \frac{1}{\sqrt{\pi}} \sum_{j=1}^{m} w_j g\left(\left(\sqrt{2\sigma_\alpha^2}\right) a_j\right)$$

where the weights (w_j) and abscissae (a_j) are tabulated in standard mathematical references and m is the number of nodes or quadrature points (see e.g. Butler and Moffitt, 1982).

In Stata, the random effects probit model is estimated using the xtprobit command. The default is to use 12 quadrature points ($m = 12$). Whether or not

Table 9.6 Random effects probit model, partial effects

```
------------------------------------------------------------------
Average marginal effects                    Number of obs  =   63918
Model VCE  : OIM


Expression  : Pr(y=1 assuming u_i=0), predict(pu0)
dy/dx w.r.t. : 1.male 1.widowed 1.nvrmar 1.divsep 1.deghdeg
1.hndalev 1.ocse hhsize nch04 nch511 nch1218 age 1.nonwhite lninc
1.prof 1.mantech 1.skillmn 1.ptskill 1.unskill 1.armed
------------------------------------------------------------------
```

	Delta-method					
	dy/dx	Std. Err.	z	P>|z|	[95% Conf.Interval]	
1.male	-.0057229	.0038566	-1.48	0.138	-.0132818	.001836
1.widowed	-.0101907	.0049874	-2.04	0.041	-.0199658	-.0004156
1.nvrmar	.0093618	.0054427	1.72	0.085	-.0013058	.0200293
1.divsep	.0183656	.0060386	3.04	0.002	.0065303	.030201
1.deghdeg	-.0387069	.0045239	-8.56	0.000	-.0475736	-.0298402
1.hndalev	-.0296944	.0043191	-6.88	0.000	-.0381597	-.0212291
1.ocse	-.0372534	.0039318	-9.47	0.000	-.0449596	-.0295471
hhsize	-.0001713	.0015399	-0.11	0.911	-.0031895	.0028469
nch04	-.0102938	.0033675	-3.06	0.002	-.016894	-.0036936
nch511	-.0041173	.0026303	-1.57	0.118	-.0092726	.001038
nch1218	.0009011	.0027214	0.33	0.741	-.0044328	.006235
age	.0047146	.000236	19.98	0.000	.004252	.0051771
1.nonwhite	.0897107	.0141145	6.36	0.000	.0620468	.1173746
lninc	-.0097016	.0018939	-5.12	0.000	-.0134136	-.0059896
1.prof	-.0388674	.0045225	-8.59	0.000	-.0477313	-.0300035
1.mantech	-.0387946	.0027243	-14.24	0.000	-.044134	-.0334551
1.skillmn	-.0433402	.0027044	-16.03	0.000	-.0486407	-.0380397
1.ptskill	-.0347719	.0029305	-11.87	0.000	-.0405156	-.0290282
1.unskill	-.0283315	.0046473	-6.10	0.000	-.0374401	-.0192229
1.armed	-.0564692	.0135002	-4.18	0.000	.082929	-.0300093

```
------------------------------------------------------------------
```
Note: dy/dx for factor levels is the discrete change from the base level.

this is sufficient can be checked by following up the estimation with the command quadchk:

```
xtprobit y $xvars
```

Table 9.5 reports estimates of the coefficients, rather than partial effects, so the magnitudes of these cannot be compared directly with the previous results from the margins command. Notice the estimated value of rho, the intra-class correlation coefficient, is 0.74. This implies that 74 per cent of the unexplained variation in limiting health problems is attributed to the individual effect: suggesting a high degree of persistence.

Partial effects for the random effects model can be computed using margins: In this case, the unobserved individual effect is set equal to zero in the computation of the partial effect:

```
quietly xtprobit y $xvars_f
margins, dydx(*) predict(pu0)
```

The results reported for the random effects model in Tables 9.5 and 9.6 use the Stata default of 12 quadrature points in the computation of the log-likelihood. The reliability of the approximation provided by this default should be checked using:

```
quadchk
```

	Fitted quadrature 12 points	Comparison quadrature 8 points	Comparison quadrature 16 points	
		Quadrature check		
Log likelihood	-17660.529	-17674.674	-17666.489	
		-14.145767	-5.9601469	Difference
		.00080098	.00033748	Relative difference
y: 1.male	-.06840702	-.08749627	-.07229908	
		-.01908925	-.00389206	Difference
		.27905389	.05689558	Relative difference
y: 1.widowed	-.12646204	-.13672184	-.12739765	
		-.0102598	-.00093561	Difference
		.08112947	.00739835	Relative difference
y: 1.nvrmar	.10667732	.10800212	.10766119	
		.0013248	.00098387	Difference
		.01241879	.00922286	Relative difference

```
y:              .20143927    .20227768    .20212328
1.divsep                     .0008384     .00068401  Difference
                             .00416206    .00339561  Relative difference
------------------------------------------------------------------
y:             -.59958367   -.65962592   -.60937313
1.deghdeg                   -.06004225   -.00978946  Difference
                             .10013989    .01632709  Relative difference
------------------------------------------------------------------
y:             -.40596255   -.44665747   -.40745292
1.hndalev                   -.04069492   -.00149038  Difference
                             .10024304    .00367121  Relative difference
------------------------------------------------------------------
y:              -.5149269   -.56234637   -.51781252
1.ocse                      -.04741947   -.00288562  Difference
                             .09208972    .00560394  Relative difference
------------------------------------------------------------------
y:             -.00203475   -.00221855   -.00170093
hhsize                      -.0001838     .00033383  Difference
                             .09032953   -.16406204  Relative difference
------------------------------------------------------------------
y:             -.12228561   -.12413096   -.12358415
nch04                       -.00184536   -.00129854  Difference
                             .01509055    .01061894  Relative difference
------------------------------------------------------------------
y:             -.04891163   -.05024594   -.04936914
nch511                      -.00133431   -.00045752  Difference
                             .02728006    .009354    Relative difference
------------------------------------------------------------------
y:              .01070457    .01097057    .01101278
nch1218                      .00026599    .0003082   Difference
                             .02484856    .02879156  Relative difference
------------------------------------------------------------------
y:              .10023249    .09446371    .10145595
age                         -.00576877    .00122346  Difference
                            -.05755392    .01220624  Relative difference
------------------------------------------------------------------
y:             -.00177603   -.00164639   -.00178507
c.age#c.age                  .00012964   -9.047e-06  Difference
                            -.07299372    .00509381  Relative difference
------------------------------------------------------------------
y:              .00001374    .00001326    .00001373
c.age#c.ag~e                -4.898e-07   -1.043e-08  Difference
                            -.03563739   -.00075912  Relative difference
------------------------------------------------------------------
```

```
y:                .77784946    .84497829     .78394352
1.nonwhite                     .06712883     .00609406  Difference
                               .08630054     .00783449  Relative difference
---------------------------------------------------------------------
y:               -.11525057   -.11568523    -.11532721
lninc                         -.00043466    -.00007664  Difference
                               .0037714      .000665    Relative difference
---------------------------------------------------------------------
y:               -.62502876   -.6388425     -.63047536
1.prof                        -.01381374    -.00544659  Difference
                               .02210096     .00871415  Relative difference
---------------------------------------------------------------------
y:               -.58935242   -.60013885    -.59355142
1.mantech                     -.01078643    -.004199    Difference
                               .01830217     .00712477  Relative difference
---------------------------------------------------------------------
y:                -.6970076   -.70501664    -.70079633
1.skillmn                     -.00800904    -.00378873  Difference
                               .0114906      .0054357   Relative difference
---------------------------------------------------------------------
y:               -.51641904   -.5199544     -.51802272
1.ptskill                     -.00353536    -.00160369  Difference
                               .00684592     .0031054   Relative difference
---------------------------------------------------------------------
y:               -.40638906   -.4016918     -.40663231
1.unskill                      .00469726    -.00024325  Difference
                              -.01155852     .00059856  Relative difference
---------------------------------------------------------------------
y:                -1.25614    -1.2914429    -1.2659452
1.armed                       -.03530292    -.00980516  Difference
                               .02810429     .00780579  Relative difference
---------------------------------------------------------------------
y:               -2.8139602   -2.9018704    -2.8421885
_cons                         -.08791018    -.0282283   Difference
                               .03124073     .01003152  Relative difference
---------------------------------------------------------------------
lnsig2u:          1.0641845    1.2008751     1.0654595
_cons                          .13669057     .00127495  Difference
                               .1284463      .00119806  Relative difference
---------------------------------------------------------------------
```

There are noticeable discrepancies in the estimates as the number of quadrature points is increased from 8, through 12, to 16: this is especially so for the estimate of the variance component (lnsig2u). So, from now on we will sacrifice computational speed for the sake of improved accuracy and use a higher value,

Table 9.7 Random effects probit model, balanced panel

Random-effects probit regression		Number of obs	= 48560
Group variable: pid		Number of groups	= 6070
Random effects u_i ~ Gaussian		Obs per group: min	= 8
		avg	= 8.0
		max	= 8
		Wald chi2(22)	= 1057.70
Log likelihood = -12658.807		Prob > chi2	= 0.0000

y	Coef.	Std. Err.	z	P>|z|	[95% Conf.	Interval]
male	-.137526	.0600844	-2.29	0.022	-.2552892	-.0197627
widowed	-.2750502	.081051	-3.39	0.001	-.4339073	-.1161931
nvrmar	.1747472	.0721603	2.42	0.015	.0333155	.3161788
divsep	.1326133	.0739637	1.79	0.073	-.0123528	.2775794
deghdeg	-.6741616	.1138071	-5.92	0.000	-.8972195	-.4511038
hndalev	-.4031788	.084484	-4.77	0.000	-.5687644	-.2375933
ocse	-.5117548	.0776616	-6.59	0.000	-.6639687	-.359541
hhsize	-.0135029	.0221293	-0.61	0.542	-.0568757	.0298698
nch04	-.1299107	.0467738	-2.78	0.005	-.2215856	-.0382358
nch511	-.09292	.0372624	-2.49	0.013	-.1659529	-.0198871
nch1218	-.0050837	.0381611	-0.13	0.894	-.079878	.0697106
age	.1345589	.0291518	4.62	0.000	.0774223	.1916954
age2	-.2613823	.0582076	-4.49	0.000	-.3754671	-.1472976
age3	.1919869	.0364747	5.26	0.000	.1204977	.2634761
nonwhite	.8720133	.1527948	5.71	0.000	.5725411	1.171485
lninc	-.1536363	.0273598	-5.62	0.000	-.2072604	-.1000122
prof	-.6204882	.1200459	-5.17	0.000	-.8557738	-.3852026
mantech	-.5406016	.0546603	-9.89	0.000	-.6477339	-.4334694
skillmn	-.6680123	.0604897	-11.04	0.000	-.78657	-.5494547
ptskill	-.4780211	.0597771	-8.00	0.000	-.5951821	-.36086
unskill	-.3162826	.0903005	-3.50	0.000	-.4932684	-.1392968
armed	-5.98649	1293.72	-0.00	0.996	-2541.631	2529.658
_cons	-2.741733	.5125339	-5.35	0.000	-3.746281	-1.737185
/lnsig2u	1.089163	.0436431			1.003624	1.174702
sigma_u	1.723886	.0376179			1.651711	1.799216
rho	.748224	.0082217			.7317705	.7639938

Likelihood-ratio test of rho=0: chibar2(01) = 1.0e+04 Prob >= chibar2 = 0.000

24 points, in subsequent estimation of the random effects model (using `intp(24)`). For example, applied to the balanced sample (see Table 9.7):

```
xtprobit y $xvars if allwavesm==1, intp(24)
```

The random effects probit model has two important limitations: it relies on the assumptions that the error components have a normal distribution and that errors are not correlated with the regressors. One way in which normality can be relaxed is to use a finite mixture model (see Deb, 2001). This approach is not pursued here but is presented in the context of models for health care utilisation in Chapters 11 and 12.

The possibility of correlated effects can be dealt with by using conditional (fixed effects) approaches or by parameterising the effect. To implement the latter approach, these random effects models are now augmented by the Mundlak specification to allow for individual effects that are correlated with the within-individual means of the regressors (in our case `lninc`), shown here for the unbalanced sample:

```
xtprobit y $xvarm, intp(24)
```

The outcome matches the results for the pooled models; current income (`lninc`) is no longer statistically or quantitatively significant but mean income is (Table 9.8).

Simulation-based inference

The random effects probit model only involves a univariate integral. More complex models, for example where the error term ϵ_{it} is assumed to follow an AR(1) process, lead to sample log-likelihood functions that involve higher order integrals. Monte Carlo simulation techniques can be used to deal with the computational intractability of nonlinear models, such as the panel probit model and the multinomial probit. Popular methods of simulation-based inference include classical maximum simulated likelihood (MSL) estimation, and Bayesian Markov chain Monte Carlo (MCMC) estimation (see Contoyannis *et al.* (2004a) for further details).

Recall that the general version of our model is,

$$y_{it} = 1(y^*_{it} > 0) = 1(x_{it}\beta + u_{it} > 0)$$

This implies that the probability of observing the sequence $y_{i1} \dots y_{iT}$ for a particular individual is,

$$\text{Prob}\left(y_{i1}, \dots, y_{iT}\right) = \int_{ai1}^{bi1} \dots \int_{aiT}^{biT} f\left(u_{i1}, \dots, u_{iT}\right) du_{iT}, \dots, du_{i1}$$

with $a_{it} = -x_{it}\beta$, $b_{it} = \infty$ if $y_{it} = 1$ and $a_{it} = -\infty$, $b_{it} = -x_{it}\beta$ if $y_{it} = 0$. The sample likelihood L is the product of these integrals, L_i, over all n individuals. In certain

Table 9.8 Mundlak specification of random effects probit model, unbalanced panel

```
-------------------------------------------------------------------
Random-effects probit regression        Number of obs    =   63918
Group variable: pid                      Number of groups =   10261
Random effects u_i ~ Gaussian            Obs per group: min =      1
                                                        avg =    6.2
                                                        max =      8
                                         Wald chi2(23)    = 1925.22
Log likelihood = -17617.39               Prob > chi2      =  0.0000
-------------------------------------------------------------------
        y |     Coef. Std. Err.      z   P>|z|  [95% Conf. Interval]
----------|--------------------------------------------------------
     male | -.0577968  .0477614   -1.21  0.226  -.1514074   .0358137
  widowed | -.1538475  .0650542   -2.36  0.018  -.2813513  -.0263437
   nvrmar |  .1046518  .0603352    1.73  0.083  -.0136032   .2229067
   divsep |   .162023  .0619962    2.61  0.009   .0405127   .2835333
  deghdeg | -.3839513  .0975236   -3.94  0.000  -.5750939  -.1928086
  hndalev | -.2590567  .0707369   -3.66  0.000  -.3976986  -.1204149
     ocse | -.4211945  .0633842   -6.65  0.000  -.5454253  -.2969637
   hhsize | -.0056109  .0184857   -0.30  0.761  -.0418422   .0306203
    nch04 | -.1480287  .0403041   -3.67  0.000  -.2270234  -.0690341
   nch511 |  -.084541  .0317945   -2.66  0.008   -.146857   -.022225
  nch1218 | -.0121762  .0327311   -0.37  0.710   -.076328   .0519756
      age |  .1233354  .0234352    5.26  0.000   .0774033   .1692675
     age2 |  -.214472  .0463371   -4.63  0.000   -.305291   -.123653
     age3 |  .1535348  .0286472    5.36  0.000   .0973873   .2096823
 nonwhite |   .746045  .0965554    7.73  0.000   .5567998   .9352901
   lninc | -.0069751   .024986   -0.28  0.780  -.0559468   .0419965
     prof | -.5764358  .1020997   -5.65  0.000  -.7765475  -.3763241
  mantech | -.5521883  .0485833  -11.37  0.000  -.6474099  -.4569668
   skillmn |  -.692272   .052512  -13.18  0.000  -.7951937  -.5893504
  ptskill | -.5194847  .0519613  -10.00  0.000   -.621327  -.4176424
  unskill |  -.417743  .0813965   -5.13  0.000  -.5772772  -.2582089
    armed | -1.132051  .7710094   -1.47  0.142  -2.643202   .3790994
   mlninc | -.5223113  .0534092   -9.78  0.000  -.6269913  -.4176312
    _cons |  .6409717  .5427155    1.18  0.238  -.4227311   1.704675
----------|--------------------------------------------------------
 /lnsig2u |  1.064986  .0371032                  .9922653   1.137707
----------|--------------------------------------------------------
  sigma_u |  1.703173  .0315965                  1.642357   1.766241
      rho |  .7436422  .0070733                  .7295351   .7572584
-------------------------------------------------------------------
Likelihood-ratio test of rho=0: chibar2(01) = 1.3e+04 Prob >= chibar2 = 0.000
```

cases, such as the random effects probit model, L_i can be evaluated by quadrature. In general, the T-dimensional integral L_i cannot be written in terms of univariate integrals that are easy to evaluate. Gaussian quadrature works well with low dimensions but computational problems arise with higher dimensions. Multivariate quadrature uses the Cartesian product of univariate evaluation points and the number of evaluation points increases exponentially. Instead Monte Carlo (MC) simulation can be used to approximate integrals that are numerically intractable. This includes numerous models derived from the multivariate normal distribution (the panel probit, multinomial and multivariate probit, panel ordered probit and interval regression, panel Tobit, etc.). MC approaches use pseudo-random selection of evaluation points and computational cost rises less rapidly than with quadrature (see Contoyannis *et al.*, 2004a, for details). Maximum simulated likelihood estimation of a dynamic version of random effects probit model, which allows for autocorrelation in the error term, is available through Mark Stewart's user-written program `redpace`. This is discussed at the end of this chapter.

The conditional logit model

The conditional logit estimator uses the fact that the within-individual sum $\Sigma_t y_{it}$ is a sufficient statistic for α_i (see e.g., Chamberlain, 1980). This means that conditioning on $\Sigma_t y_{it}$ allows a consistent estimator for β to be derived.

Using the logistic function,

$$P\left(y_{it}=1 \mid x_{it}, \alpha_i\right)=F\left(x_{it}\beta+\alpha_i\right)=\frac{\exp\left(x_{it}\beta+\alpha_i\right)}{1+\exp\left(x_{it}\beta+\alpha_i\right)}$$

Then, for example in the case where $T = 2$, it is possible to show that,

$$P\left((0,1)\mid (0,1) \text{ or } (0,1)\right)=\frac{\exp\left(\left(x_{i2}-x_{i1}\right)\beta\right)}{1+\exp\left(\left(x_{i2}-x_{i1}\right)\beta\right)}$$

This implies that a standard logit model can be applied to differenced data and the individual effect is swept out. In practice, conditioning on those observations that make a transition – (0,1) or (1,0) – and discarding those that do not – (0,0) or (1,1) – means that identification of the models relies on those observations where the dependent variable changes over time.

The conditional logit estimator is implemented by the following commands, shown here for the unbalanced panel. The `group` command specifies the individual identifier:

```
clogit y $xvars, group(pid)
```

This estimator uses variation over time in the dependent and independent variables, so time invariant variables like education are excluded.

Table 9.9 Conditional logit model, unbalanced panel

```
--------------------------------------------------------------------
Conditional (fixed-effects)                  Number of obs =   18715
logistic regression
                                             LR chi2(17)   =  738.64
                                             Prob > chi2   =  0.0000
Log likelihood = -6596.2496                  Pseudo R2     =  0.0530
--------------------------------------------------------------------
```

y	Coef.	Std. Err.	z	P>|z|	[95% Conf. Interval]	
male	0 (omitted)					
widowed	-.3154202	.1599588	-1.97	0.049	-.6289337	-.0019068
nvrmar	.0193504	.1505804	0.13	0.898	-.2757818	.3144826
divsep	.0326484	.1376459	0.24	0.813	-.2371327	.3024294
deghdeg	0 (omitted)					
hndalev	0 (omitted)					
ocse	0 (omitted)					
hhsize	.0380896	.0402778	0.95	0.344	-.0408535	.1170327
nch04	-.2100883	.0823633	-2.55	0.011	-.3715174	-.0486592
nch511	-.1190588	.0696115	-1.71	0.087	-.2554949	.0173773
nch1218	-.0001332	.066743	-0.00	0.998	-.1309471	.1306806
age	.0686033	.0639068	1.07	0.283	-.0566518	.1938584
age2	-.0158264	.1301669	-0.12	0.903	-.2709489	.239296
age3	.1330778	.0814011	1.63	0.102	-.0264654	.2926211
nonwhite	0 (omitted)					
lninc	-.0566095	.0450624	-1.26	0.209	-.1449302	.0317111
prof	-.6692921	.2205286	-3.03	0.002	-1.10152	-.2370639
mantech	-.6218778	.1017862	-6.11	0.000	-.8213751	-.4223804
skillmn	-.7479047	.1067488	-7.01	0.000	-.9571285	-.5386809
ptskill	-.5458931	.1018646	-5.36	0.000	-.745544	-.3462422
unskill	-.2297057	.1566425	-1.47	0.143	-.5367193	.0773079
armed	-18.26525	8574.293	-0.00	0.998	-16823.57	16787.04

9.3 DYNAMIC MODELS

To model dynamics in self-reported health problems, we use dynamic panel probit specifications on both the balanced and unbalanced samples. We include previous health problems in our empirical models in order to capture state dependence and the model can be interpreted as a first order Markov process. The latent variable specification of the model that we estimate can be written as:

$$y_{it}^* = x_{it}\beta + \gamma y_{it-1} + \alpha_i + \epsilon_{it} \quad (i = 1, \dots, N; \ t = 2, \dots, T_i)$$

where x_{it} is the set of observed variables, which may be associated with the health indicator. To capture state dependence, y_{it-1} is an indicator for the individual's health state in the previous wave and γ is the parameter to be estimated. α_i is an individual-specific and time-invariant random component. The error term ϵ_{it} is a time- and individual-specific error term, which is assumed to be normally distributed and uncorrelated across individuals and waves and uncorrelated with α_i. ϵ_i is assumed to be strictly exogenous, that is, the x_{it} are uncorrelated with ϵ_{is} for all t and s. The model can be estimated using pooled or random effects specifications. As we do not have a natural scale for the latent variable, the variance of the idiosyncratic error term is restricted to equal one.

Correlated effects and initial conditions

To allow for the possibility that the observed regressors may be correlated with the individual effect we parameterise the individual effect (Mundlak, 1978; Chamberlain, 1984; Wooldridge, 2005). This allows for correlation between the individual effects and the means of the regressors. In addition, because we are estimating dynamic models, we need to take account of the problem of initial conditions. Heckman (1981) describes two assumptions that are typically invoked concerning a discrete time stochastic process with binary outcomes. The same issues arise with an ordered categorical variable. The first assumption is that the initial observations are exogenous variables. This is invalid when the error process is not serially independent and the first observation is not the true initial outcome of the process. In our case, the latter condition is violated, while the former is unlikely to be correct. Treating the lagged dependent variable as exogenous when these assumptions are incorrect leads to inconsistent estimators. The second assumption is that the process is in equilibrium such that the marginal probabilities have approached their limiting values and can be therefore assumed time-invariant. This assumption is untenable when non-stationary variables such as age and time trends are included in the model, as we do here.

Wooldridge (2005) has suggested a convenient approach to deal with the initial conditions problem in nonlinear dynamic random effects models by modelling the distribution of the unobserved effect conditional on the initial value and any exogenous explanatory variables. This conditional maximum likelihood (CML) approach results in a likelihood function based on the joint distribution of the observations conditional on the initial observations. Parameterising the distribution of the unobserved effects leads to a likelihood function that is easily maximised using pre-programmed commands with standard software (e.g. Stata). However, it should be noted that the CML approach does specify a complete model for the unobserved effects and may therefore be sensitive to misspecification.

We implement this approach by parameterising the distribution of the individual effects as:

$$\alpha_i = \alpha_0 + \alpha_1 y_{i1} + \alpha_2 \bar{x}_i + u_i$$

where $\bar{x}_i$ is the average over the sample period of the observations on the exogenous variables. u_i is assumed to be distributed $N(0,\sigma_u^2)$ and independent of the x variables, the initial conditions, and the idiosyncratic error term (ϵ_{it}). Substitution gives a model that has a random effects structure, with the regressors at time t augmented to include the initial value y_{i1} and $\bar{x}_i$. Three features should be noted. First, this specification implies that the identified coefficients of any time-invariant regressors are composite effects of the relevant elements of β and α_2. Second, all time dummies must be dropped from $\bar{x}_i$ to avoid perfect collinearity. Third, the estimates of α_1 are of direct interest as they are informative about the relationship between the individual effect and initial health problems.

A new global is required for the list of regressors in the dynamic specification that includes lagged health problems (hprobt_1):

```
by pid: gen hprobt_1=hprob[_n-1]

global xvard "hprobt_1 male widowed nvrmar divsep deghdeg
    hndalev ocse hhsize nch04 nch511 nch1218 age age2 age3
    nonwhite prof mantech skillmn ptskill unskill armed
    lninc"
```

and in factor form:

```
global xvard_f "i.hprobt_1 i.male i.widowed i.nvrmar
    i.divsep i.deghdeg i.hndalev i.ocse hhsize nch04 nch511
    nch1218 c.age c.age#c.age c.age#c.age#c.age i.nonwhite
    i.prof i.mantech i.skillmn i.ptskill i.unskill i.armed
    lninc"
```

This is augmented by the initial value of health problems and the within-means of the regressors in the Mundlak–Wooldridge specification:

```
global xvarw "hprobt_1 male widowed nvrmar divsep deghdeg
    hndalev ocse hhsize nch04 nch511 nch1218 age age2 age3
    nonwhite lninc prof mantech skillmn ptskill unskill
    armed hprobt1 mlninc"

global xvarw_f "i.hprobt_1 i.male i.widowed i.nvrmar
    i.divsep i.deghdeg i.hndalev i.ocse hhsize nch04 nch511
    nch1218 c.age c.age#c.age c.age#c.age#c.age i.nonwhite
    lninc i.prof i.mantech i.skillmn i.ptskill i.unskill
    i.armed i.hprobt1 mlninc"
```

The dynamic versions of the pooled probit models can be compared with and without the correlated effects specifications, shown here for the unbalanced sample and reported in Tables 9.10 and 9.11:

```
probit y $xvard_f, robust cluster(pid)
margins, dydx(*)

probit y $xvarw_f, robust cluster(pid)
margins, dydx(*)
```

Table 9.10 Dynamic pooled probit model, unbalanced panel

```
-------------------------------------------------------------------------
Average marginal effects                      Number of obs  =    52904
Model VCE   : Robust
Expression  : Pr(y), predict()
dy/dx w.r.t. : 1.hprobt_1 1.male 1.widowed 1.nvrmar 1.divsep
1.deghdeg 1.hndalev 1.ocse hhsize nch04 nch511 nch1218 age 1.nonwhite
1.prof 1.mantech 1.skillmn 1.ptskill 1.unskill 1.armed lninc
-------------------------------------------------------------------------
```

	dy/dx	Delta-method Std. Err.	z	P>|z|	[95% Conf. Interval]	
1.hprobt_1	.532866	.0083208	64.04	0.000	.5165575	.5491744
1.male	.0046733	.0029531	1.58	0.114	-.0011146	.0104611
1.widowed	-.004685	.0046856	-1.00	0.317	-.0138686	.0044985
1.nvrmar	.0104637	.0047555	2.20	0.028	.0011431	.0197842
1.divsep	.014615	.0054509	2.68	0.007	.0039314	.0252985
1.deghdeg	-.0282595	.0051585	-5.48	0.000	-.03837	-.018149
1.hndalev	-.0223879	.0039793	-5.63	0.000	-.0301872	-.0145886
1.ocse	-.0255839	.0036464	-7.02	0.000	-.0327307	-.0184371
hhsize	-.0009008	.0017018	-0.53	0.597	-.0042363	.0024348
nch04	-.011271	.0041299	-2.73	0.006	-.0193655	-.0031765
nch511	-.0035192	.0029205	-1.20	0.228	-.0092434	.002205
nch1218	-.0022209	.0033784	-0.66	0.511	-.0088424	.0044006
age	.0015698	.000116	13.54	0.000	.0013425	.0017971
1.nonwhite	.0349215	.0072198	4.84	0.000	.020771	.049072
1.prof	-.0517023	.0071606	-7.22	0.000	-.0657369	-.0376678
1.mantech	-.0499044	.0037983	-13.14	0.000	-.0573489	-.0424599
1.skillmn	-.0607288	.0041614	-14.59	0.000	-.0688849	-.0525726
1.ptskill	-.0445636	.0043233	-10.31	0.000	-.0530372	-.03609
1.unskill	-.0448483	.0068626	-6.54	0.000	-.0582989	-.0313978
1.armed	-.1004936	.033213	-3.03	0.002	-.1655898	-.0353974
lninc	-.0169851	.0022015	-7.72	0.000	-.0213	-.0126703

Note: dy/dx for factor levels is the discrete change from the base level.

Table 9.11 Dynamic pooled probit model with initial conditions, unbalanced panel

```
----------------------------------------------------------------------
Average marginal effects                       Number of obs  =   52873
Model VCE    : Robust


Expression   : Pr(y), predict()
dy/dx w.r.t. : 1.hprobt_1 1.male 1.widowed 1.nvrmar 1.divsep
1.deghdeg 1.hndalev 1.ocse hhsize nch04 nch511 nch1218 age 1.nonwhite
lninc 1.prof 1.mantech 1.skillmn 1.ptskill 1.unskill 1.armed
1.hprobt1 mlninc
----------------------------------------------------------------------
              |              Delta-method
              |     dy/dx  Std. Err.      z  P>|z|   [95% Conf. Interval]
----------------------------------------------------------------------
  1.hprobt_1 |   .409278   .0095966   42.65  0.000    .3904689    .4280871
      1.male |  .0054681   .0031146    1.76  0.079   -.0006363    .0115726
   1.widowed |   -.00714   .0049456   -1.44  0.149   -.0168331    .0025531
    1.nvrmar |  .0093069   .0048926    1.90  0.057   -.0002825    .0188963
    1.divsep |  .0103028   .0057158    1.80  0.071       -.0009    .0215057
   1.deghdeg | -.0172777   .0056969   -3.03  0.002   -.0284435   -.0061119
   1.hndalev | -.0151248   .0043194   -3.50  0.000   -.0235907   -.0066589
     1.ocse  | -.0172187   .0038956   -4.42  0.000   -.0248539   -.0095835
      hhsize | -.0006575   .0017476   -0.38  0.707   -.0040828    .0027678
       nch04 | -.0101209   .0041998   -2.41  0.016   -.0183523   -.0018894
      nch511 | -.0041341   .0030589   -1.35  0.177   -.0101294    .0018613
     nch1218 | -.0020169   .0034603   -0.58  0.560   -.0087989    .0047652
         age |  .0014882   .0001235   12.05  0.000     .001246    .0017303
  1.nonwhite |  .0236736   .0077875    3.04  0.002    .0084104    .0389368
       lninc | -.0006271   .0030312   -0.21  0.836   -.0065681     .005314
      1.prof | -.0480057   .0073162   -6.56  0.000   -.0623453   -.0336662
   1.mantech | -.0432508   .0039308  -11.00  0.000   -.0509549   -.0355466
   1.skillmn | -.0550406    .004244  -12.97  0.000   -.0633587   -.0467225
   1.ptskill | -.0382929   .0044698   -8.57  0.000   -.0470535   -.0295324
   1.unskill | -.0381228   .0067079   -5.68  0.000   -.0512701   -.0249755
     1.armed | -.0935585   .0291691   -3.21  0.001   -.1507289   -.0363882
   1.hprobt1 |  .1488894   .0073102   20.37  0.000    .1345617    .1632171
      mlninc | -.0258873   .0044321   -5.84  0.000   -.0345739   -.0172006
----------------------------------------------------------------------
```

Note: dy/dx for factor levels is the discrete change from the base level.

Table 9.12 Dynamic random effects probit model with initial conditions, unbalanced panel

```
------------------------------------------------------------------
Random-effects probit regression       Number of obs     =    52873
Group variable: pid                     Number of groups  =     9206
Random effects u_i ~ Gaussian           Obs per group: min =        1
                                                       avg =      5.7
                                                       max =        7
                                        Wald chi2(25)     =  4901.31
Log likelihood = -13548.211             Prob > chi2       =   0.0000
------------------------------------------------------------------
        y |      Coef. Std. Err.      z    P>|z|    [95% Conf. Interval]
----------|-------------------------------------------------------
 hprobt_1 |   .6974313   .030937   22.54  0.000   .6367959    .7580667
     male |   .0255973  .0346093    0.74  0.460  -.0422357    .0934304
  widowed |  -.1323981  .0569915   -2.32  0.020  -.2440994   -.0206969
   nvrmar |   .0789663  .0519397    1.52  0.128  -.0228337    .1807662
   divsep |   .1058997   .055889    1.89  0.058  -.0036407    .2154401
  deghdeg |  -.1862324  .0700717   -2.66  0.008  -.3235704   -.0488944
  hndalev |  -.1653953  .0510583   -3.24  0.001  -.2654677   -.0653228
     ocse |  -.1948831  .0454736   -4.29  0.000  -.2840098   -.1057565
   hhsize |  -.0095942  .0175606   -0.55  0.585  -.0440124    .0248239
    nch04 |  -.0881623  .0395569   -2.23  0.026  -.1656924   -.0106322
   nch511 |  -.0521964  .0300721   -1.74  0.083  -.1111366    .0067438
  nch1218 |  -.0018007  .0342217   -0.05  0.958   -.068874    .0652726
      age |   .1171514  .0211812    5.53  0.000   .0756371    .1586657
     age2 |  -.2101253  .0414902   -5.06  0.000  -.2914446   -.1288061
     age3 |   .1333247  .0254212    5.24  0.000   .0835001    .1831494
 nonwhite |   .3036623  .0756773    4.01  0.000   .1553376    .4519871
    lninc |  -.0190591  .0270133   -0.71  0.480  -.0720042     .033886
     prof |  -.5192575  .0952192   -5.45  0.000  -.7058836   -.3326313
  mantech |  -.4188696   .045548   -9.20  0.000  -.5081421   -.3295971
   skillmn |  -.558578   .050971  -10.96  0.000  -.6584794   -.4586766
  ptskill |  -.3857378  .0505056   -7.64  0.000  -.4847269   -.2867487
  unskill |  -.3173095   .080716   -3.93  0.000  -.4755099    -.159109
    armed |   -1.12913  .8644246   -1.31  0.191  -2.823371    .5651116
  hprobt1 |   1.804311  .0567231   31.81  0.000   1.693136    1.915486
   mlninc |  -.2958688  .0451845   -6.55  0.000  -.3844288   -.2073088
    _cons |  -.9789592  .4414853   -2.22  0.027  -1.844254   -.1136639
----------|-------------------------------------------------------
 /lnsig2u |   .0031027  .0548073                 -.1043177    .1105231
----------|-------------------------------------------------------
  sigma_u |   1.001553  .0274462                  .9491781    1.056817
      rho |   .5007757  .0137018                  .4739442    .5276027
------------------------------------------------------------------
Likelihood-ratio test of rho=0: chibar2(01) = 1335.28 Prob >= chibar2 = 0.000
```

Table 9.13 Dynamic random effects probit model with initial conditions, partial effects
```
--------------------------------------------------------------------
Average marginal effects                    Number of obs  =    52873
Model VCE   : OIM


Expression  : Pr(y=1 assuming u_i=0), predict(pu0)
dy/dx w.r.t. : 1.hprobt_1 1.male 1.widowed 1.nvrmar 1.divsep
1.deghdeg 1.hndalev 1.ocse hhsize nch04 nch511 nch1218 age 1.nonwhite
lninc 1.prof 1.mantech 1.skillmn 1.ptskill 1.unskill 1.armed
1.hprobt1 mlninc
--------------------------------------------------------------------
             |              Delta-method
             |    dy/dx  Std. Err.      z   P>|z|  [95% Conf. Interval]
--------------------------------------------------------------------
 1.hprobt_1 |  .0891638  .0064883   13.74  0.000   .0764469   .1018807
     1.male |  .0023986  .0032489    0.74  0.460  -.0039691   .0087663
  1.widowed | -.0119236  .0049425   -2.41  0.016  -.0216108  -.0022365
   1.nvrmar |  .0075603  .0050922    1.48  0.138  -.0024202   .0175407
   1.divsep |  .0102621  .0056127    1.83  0.067  -.0007387   .0212629
  1.deghdeg | -.0164664  .0058623   -2.81  0.005  -.0279564  -.0049765
  1.hndalev | -.0149227  .0044482   -3.35  0.001   -.023641  -.0062044
     1.ocse | -.0176853  .0040147   -4.41  0.000  -.0255541  -.0098166
     hhsize | -.0008975  .0016428   -0.55  0.585  -.0041172   .0023223
      nch04 |  -.008247  .0037058   -2.23  0.026  -.0155102  -.0009838
     nch511 | -.0048826  .0028134   -1.74  0.083  -.0103967   .0006315
    nch1218 | -.0001684  .0032012   -0.05  0.958  -.0064427   .0061058
        age |  .0019317  .0001551   12.46  0.000   .0016278   .0022357
 1.nonwhite |  .0318134  .0088527    3.59  0.000   .0144625   .0491643
      lninc | -.0017829  .0025266   -0.71  0.480   -.006735   .0031693
     1.prof | -.0409115  .0063717   -6.42  0.000  -.0533999  -.0284232
  1.mantech | -.0353849  .0035665   -9.92  0.000  -.0423752  -.0283947
  1.skillmn | -.0449388  .0036462  -12.32  0.000  -.0520851  -.0377925
  1.ptskill | -.0323083  .0038419   -8.41  0.000  -.0398383  -.0247782
  1.unskill | -.0266887  .0061387   -4.35  0.000  -.0387204   -.014657
    1.armed |  -.073782  .0390398   -1.89  0.059  -.1502987   .0027347
  1.hprobt1 |   .378103  .0151811   24.91  0.000   .3483486   .4078575
     mlninc | -.0276765  .0042648   -6.49  0.000  -.0360354  -.0193177
--------------------------------------------------------------------
```
Note: dy/dx for factor levels is the discrete change from the base level.

There is some reduction in the partial effect of lagged health (`hprob_1`) when the adjustment for initial conditions is included: from around 0.54 to around 0.41. But the state dependence effect remains large.

Similarly, the random effects specifications can also be extended to include dynamics using the Wooldridge specification. This leads to a much lower estimate of state dependence (see Table 9.12):

```
xtprobit y $xvarw, intp(24)
```

Table 9.13 reports partial effects computed by:

```
quietly xtprobit y $xvarw_f, intp(24)
margins, dydx(*) predict(pu0)
```

The Heckman estimator

The Wooldridge approach is attractive for its simplicity but an alternative strategy for dealing with the initial conditions problem, which makes weaker assumptions, is the estimator proposed by Heckman (1981). This has been implemented as a Stata command by Stewart (2006). The Heckman estimator specifies a reduced form for the latent variable in the initial wave, which includes a vector of exogenous variables (z_{i1}):

$$y_{i1}^* = z_{i1}\pi + \theta\alpha_i + \epsilon_{i1}$$

These exogenous variables should ideally include some instruments that do not appear in the main equation. This is problematic for our empirical application with the limited sub-sample of BHPS variables that we have available.

Then the log-likelihood can be written in terms of the joint probability of the observed sequence of 1s and 0s, with α_i integrated out:

$$\ln L = \sum_{i=1}^{n}\left\{\ln\int_{-\infty}^{+\infty}\left(\Phi\left[d_{i1}(z_{i1}\pi + \theta\alpha)\right]\right)\prod_{t=2}^{T}\left(\Phi\left[d_{it}(x_{it}\beta + \gamma y_{it-1} + \alpha)\right]\right)f(\alpha)\,d\alpha\right\}$$

Like the conventional random effects probit model, this version of the model can be estimated by Gauss-Hermite quadrature.

For example using:

```
findit redpace
```

will locate the reference to the program in the Stata Journal and allow it to be installed:

```
st0106 from http://www.stata-journal.com/software/sj6-2
```

First a global has to be specified for the list of instruments used to predict the initial value. Note also that the program requires that the value of the lagged dependent variable should be set to zero for the first wave of data:

```
global z0 "malet1 widowedt1 nvrmart1 divsept1 deghdegt1
    hndalevt1 ocset1 hhsizet1 nch04t1 nch511t1 nch1218t1
    aget1 age2t1 age3t1 nonwhitet1 proft1 mantecht1
    skillmnt1 ptskillt1 unskillt1 armedt1 lninct1"
replace hprobt_1=0 if wavenum==1
```

Then the model could be estimated using the command redpace, which specifies the individual (i) and time indices (t) as subcommands along with the number of replications to be used in the maximum simulated likelihood estimation. The lagged dependent variable should appear first in the list of regressors. The command is only available for use with balanced panels and that is the sample used here:

```
redpace y $xvard ($z0) if allwavesm==1, i(pid)          ///
        t(wavenum) rep(200) noauto
```

The subcommand noauto specifies that the random effects version of the model should be used, assuming that the error term is serially independent. The command allows more general versions to be estimated: the default is a first-order autoregressive process and a moving average model can be selected by the option mavg. The MSL estimation used by the command is computationally demanding and can be extremely slow to run. The simulation methods can be modified to use antithetics (with the option seg(2)) or Halton quasirandom sequences rather than pseudo-random numbers (with the option halton). The seed for the pseudo-random draws can be set using seed(#).

9.4 OVERVIEW

This chapter shows how regression models for panel data can be extended to deal with categorical dependent variables, illustrated by a binary health outcome from the BHPS data. In static specifications persistence in the dependent variable is modelled through a time-invariant individual effect. This may be assumed to be uncorrelated with the regressors, as in the pooled and random effects probit models. Correlated effects can be modelled using the Mundlak–Chamberlain approach or the conditional logit model. Dynamic models allow for state dependence as well as unobserved heterogeneity. In dynamic models, the individual effect will be correlated with lagged outcomes creating the initial conditions problem. This can be addressed using the approaches suggested by Heckman and by Wooldridge.

10 Non-response and attrition bias

SYNOPSIS

This chapter extends the analysis of the sub-sample of the BHPS from Chapter 9 but shifts the emphasis to the potential problems created by sample attrition in panel data. The chapter defines the problem of non-response and attrition and provides a descriptive analysis of attrition in the BHPS. It shows how to test for attrition bias and illustrates how inverse probability weights provide one way of dealing with the problem.

10.1 INTRODUCTION

The objective of this chapter is to explore the existence of health-related non-response in panel data and its consequences for modelling the association between socioeconomic status (SES) and health problems. It builds on the same sample of data and the results reported in the previous chapter and on a paper by Jones *et al.* (2006), which analyses self-assessed health rather than health problems.

Using panel data, such as the British Household Panel Survey (BHPS), to analyse longitudinal models of health problems creates a risk that the results will be contaminated by bias associated with longitudinal non-response. There are drop-outs from the panels at each wave and some of these may be related directly to health: due to deaths, serious illness and people moving into institutional care. In addition, other sources of non-response may be indirectly related to health, for example divorce may increase the risk of non-response and also be associated with poorer health than average. The long-term survivors who remain in the panel are likely to be healthier on average compared to the sample at wave 1. The health of survivors will tend to be higher than the population as a whole and their rate of decline in health will tend to be lower. Also, the SES of the survivors may not be representative of the original population who were sampled at wave 1. Failing to account for non-response may result in misleading estimates of the relationship between health and socioeconomic characteristics.

The pattern of non-response can be tabulated to show how the sample size and composition evolves across the eight waves of the BHPS. The data used to construct the table include the number of observations that are available at each wave and the corresponding number of drop-outs and re-joiners between waves. These are expressed as wave-on-wave survival and drop-out rates. The survival rate is the percentage of original sample members remaining at wave *t*. The drop-out rate is the percentage of the number of drop-outs between waves *t*–1 and *t* to the number of observations at *t*–1. The raw drop-out rate excludes re-joiners, while the net drop-out rate includes them. These are measures are constructed from the indicator of non-response insampm, which was created in Chapter 9. Here the variable is recoded to system missing (.) for the non-responders:

```
generate miss=insampm
replace miss=. if insampm==0
```

Then the user-written program table calculates the statistics that are needed, looping through the waves of the panel (see Appendix):

```
table
```

Running the program produces the following output, which can be used to tabulate the number of individuals in the sample at each wave, the number of drop outs, the number of rejoinders, the survival rate and the raw drop-out rate and the net drop-out rate (see Table 1 in Jones *et al.*, 2006):

```
wavenum == 2
No. individuals at wave = 1 = 10247
No. individuals at wave = 2 = 8954
Survival rate = .87381673 Drop outs = 1410 Re-joiners = 117
Raw Attrition rate = .13760125 Net Attrition rate = .12618327

wavenum == 3
No. individuals at wave = 2 = 8954
No. individuals at wave = 3 = 8024
Survival rate = .78305846 Drop outs = 1036 Re-joiners = 106
Raw Attrition rate = .11570248 Net Attrition rate = .10386419

wavenum == 4
No. individuals at wave = 3 = 8024
No. individuals at wave = 4 = 7874
Survival rate = .76842003 Drop outs = 237 Re-joiners = 87
Raw Attrition rate = .02953639 Net Attrition rate = .01869392

wavenum == 5
No. individuals at wave = 4 = 7874
No. individuals at wave = 5 = 7451
Survival rate = .72713965 Drop outs = 518 Re-joiners = 95
Raw Attrition rate = .06578613 Net Attrition rate = .05372111
```

```
wavenum == 6
No. individuals at wave = 5 = 7451
No. individuals at wave = 6 = 7379
Survival rate = .7201132 Drop outs = 168 Re-joiners = 96
Raw Attrition rate = .02254731 Net Attrition rate = .00966313

wavenum == 7
No. individuals at wave = 6 = 7379
No. individuals at wave = 7 = 7128
Survival rate = .69561823 Drop outs = 341 Re-joiners = 90
Raw Attrition rate = .04621222 Net Attrition rate = .03401545

wavenum == 8
No. individuals at wave = 7 = 7128
No. individuals at wave = 8 = 6861
Survival rate = .66956182 Drop outs = 358 Re-joiners = 91
Raw Attrition rate = .05022447 Net Attrition rate = .03745791
```

Drop-out rates are highest between waves 1 and 2, with a raw attrition rate of 14 per cent, and the rate tends to decline over time, with a rate of 5 per cent between waves 7 and 8. By wave 8 the original sample of 10,247 has been reduced to 6,861.

Nicoletti and Peracchi (2005) provide a taxonomy of reasons for non-participation in surveys. Non-response can arise due to:

1 Demographic events such as death.
2 Movement out of scope of the survey such as institutionalisation or emigration.
3 Refusal to respond at subsequent waves.
4 Absence of the person at the address.
5 Other types of non-contact.

To these points, we would add item non-response for any of the variables used in the model of health problems, which eliminates these observations from the sample. The notion of attrition, commonly used in the survey methods literature, is usually restricted to points 3, 4 and 5. However, our concern is with any longitudinal non-response that leads to missing observations in the panel data regression analysis. In fact, it is points 1 and 2 – death and incapacity – that are likely to be particularly relevant as sources of health-related non-response. The original sample consists of those who provide a full interview and usable information on health problems at the first wave of the BHPS. Non-response encompasses all of those who fail to provide usable observations for the model of health problems at subsequent waves.

We take a representative sample of individuals at wave 1 and follow them for the eight years of the BHPS sample used in our application. The sample of interest is those n original individuals observed over a full T-year period ($T = 8$). A fully observed sample from this population would consist of nT observations. Due to non-response we only observe $\Sigma_{i=1}^{n} T_i$ observations. The reasons for having incomplete observations include attrition (as conventionally defined in the survey methods literature) as well as individuals becoming ineligible, due to incapacity or death. This creates a problem of *incidental truncation*: we are interested in the association between health and SES for our *n* individuals over the full *T* waves. However, the more frail individuals are more likely to die or drop-out before the end of the observation period, and their levels of health problems and SES are unobservable. This means that the remaining observed sample of survivors may contain less frail individuals – this is the source of potential bias in the relationship between health and SES across our sample of individuals.

10.2 TESTING FOR NON-RESPONSE BIAS

To provide an initial test for non-response bias we use the simple variable addition tests proposed by Verbeek and Nijman (1992, p. 688). These tests work by constructing variables that reflect the pattern of survey response provided by each individual respondent. Recall from Chapter 2 that we created indicators of whether an individual appears in the next wave (nextwavem) and whether they appear in the balanced panel (allwavesm), along with the number of waves that the individual is in the panel (Ti):

```
sort pid wavenum
by pid: gen nextwavem = insampm[_n+1]
generate allwavesm = .
recode allwavesm . = 0 if Ti ~= 8
recode allwavesm . = 1 if Ti == 8
generate numwavesm = .
replace numwavesm = Ti
```

Each of these three variables is an indicator of how the individual responds to the survey. There should be no intrinsic reason that survey response should have an effect on the individual's health. However if there is selection bias, such that those who do not respond have systematically different health than those who do, there will be a statistical association between the new variables and individuals' health. The tests work by adding the new variables to the pooled and random effects probit models, which are estimated with the unbalanced sample. The statistical significance of the added variables provides a test for non-response bias. This can be done for both static and dynamic specifications. The models are run quietly as we are only interested in the test statistics and test is used to compute a chi-squared test:

```
* i) WITH Ti
quietly probit y $xvard Ti, robust cluster(pid)
test Ti=0
```

```
( 1)  Ti = 0
        chi2( 1) =   23.08
      Prob > chi2 =   0.0000

quietly xtprobit y $xvars Ti, intp(24)
test Ti=0

( 1) [hprob]Ti = 0
        chi2( 1) =   1.95
      Prob > chi2 =   0.1624

* ii) WITH ALLWAVESM
quietly probit y $xvars allwavesm, robust cluster(pid)
test allwavesm=0

( 1) allwavesm = 0
          chi2( 1) =   15.12
        Prob > chi2 =   0.0001

quietly xtprobit y $xvars allwavesm, intp(24)
test allwavesm=0

( 1) [hprob]allwavesm = 0
          chi2( 1) =   6.92
        Prob > chi2 =   0.0085

* iii) WITH Sit+1
quietly probit y $xvars nextwavem, robust cluster(pid)
test nextwavem=0

 ( 1) nextwavem = 0
          chi2( 1) =   32.35
        Prob > chi2 =   0.0000

quietly xtprobit y $xvars nextwavem, intp(24)
test nextwavem=0

 ( 1) [hprob]nextwavem = 0
          chi2( 1) =   30.84
        Prob > chi2 =   0.0000

* DYNAMIC MUNDLAK/WOOLDRIDGE VERSION

* i) WITH Ti
quietly probit y $xvarw Ti, robust cluster(pid)
test Ti=0
```

```
( 1)  Ti = 0

          chi2 ( 1)  =   7.50
        Prob > chi2 =   0.0062


quietly xtprobit y $xvarw Ti, intp(24)
test Ti=0

( 1)  [hprob]Ti = 0

          chi2 ( 1)  =   3.58
        Prob > chi2 =   0.0584


* ii) WITH ALLWAVESM
quietly probit y $xvarw allwavesm, robust cluster(pid)
test allwavesm=0

( 1)  allwavesm = 0

          chi2 ( 1)  =   9.80
        Prob > chi2 =   0.0017


quietly xtprobit y $xvarw allwavesm, intp(24)
test allwavesm=0

( 1)  [hprob]allwavesm = 0

          chi2 ( 1)  =   6.60
        Prob > chi2 =   0.0102


* iii) WITH Sit+1
quietly probit y $xvarw nextwavem, robust cluster(pid)
test nextwavem=0

 ( 1)  nextwavem = 0

        chi2 ( 1)  =   16.01
      Prob > chi2 =   0.0001


quietly xtprobit y $xvarw nextwavem, intp(24)
test nextwavem=0

 ( 1)  [hprob]nextwavem = 0

          chi2 ( 1)  =   19.02
        Prob > chi2 =   0.0000
```

With a couple of exceptions for the random effects models, these tests reject the null hypothesis ($p < 0.05$): suggesting that there is a problem of attrition bias.

The intuition behind these tests is that, if non-response is random, indicators of an individual's pattern of survey responses (r) should not be associated with the outcome of interest (y) after controlling for the observed covariates (x): in other words, it tests a conditional independence condition:

$$E(y \mid x, r) = E(y \mid x)$$

In practice r is replaced by the constructed variables `Ti`, `allwavesm` and `Tld`.

Additional evidence can be provided by Hausman-type tests that compare estimates from the balanced and unbalanced samples. In the absence of non-response bias these estimates should be comparable, but non-response bias may affect the unbalanced and balanced samples differently leading to a contrast between the estimates. It should be noted that the variable addition tests and Hausman-type tests may have low power; they rely on the sample of observed outcomes for y_{it} and will not capture non-response associated with idiosyncratic shocks that are not reflected in observed past health (Nicoletti, 2006).

10.3 ESTIMATION

To try and allow for non-response we adopt a strategy based on the inverse probability weighted (IPW) estimator (see Robins *et al.*, 1995; Fitzgerald *et al.*, 1998; Moffitt *et al.*, 1999; Wooldridge, 2002a, 2002b). This approach is grounded in the notion of missing at random or ignorable non-response (Rubin, 1976; Little and Rubin, 1987). Use r as an indicator of response ($r = 1$ if observed, 0 otherwise) and y and x as the outcome and covariates of interest. Then:

(i) *Missing completely at random (MCAR)* is defined by:

$$P(r = 1 \mid y, x) = P(r = 1)$$

(ii) *Missing at random (MAR)* is defined by:

$$P(r = 1 \mid y, x) = P(r = 1 \mid x)$$

The latter implies that, after conditioning on observed covariates, the probability of non-response does not vary systematically with the outcome of interest. By Bayes rule, the MAR condition can be inverted to give:

$$P(y \mid x, r = 1) = P(y \mid x)$$

This result provides a rationale for the Verbeek and Nijman (1992) approach to testing: which tests whether r has a place in the model for y, after conditioning on the observables x.

Fitzgerald *et al.* (1998) extend the notion of ignorable non-response by introducing the concepts of selection on observables and selection on unobservables.

This requires an additional set of observables, z, that are available in the data but not included in the regression model for y. Selection on observables is defined by Fitzgerald *et al.* (1998) by the conditional independence condition:

$$P(r = 1 \mid y, x, z) = P(r = 1 \mid x, z)$$

Selection on unobservables occurs if this conditional independence assumption does not hold. Selection on unobservables, also termed informative, non-random or non-ignorable non-response, is familiar in the econometrics literature where the dominant approach to non-response follows the sample selection model (Heckman, 1976; Hausman and Wise, 1979). This approach relies on the z being 'instruments' that are good predictors of non-response and that satisfy the exclusion restriction $P(y \mid x, z) = P(y \mid x)$. This is quite different from the selection on observables approach that seeks z's, which are endogenous to y. It is worth mentioning that linear fixed effects panel estimators are consistent, in the presence of selection on unobservables, so long as the non-ignorable non-response is due to time-invariant unobservables (see e.g. Verbeek and Nijman, 1992).

The validity of the selection on observables approach hinges on whether the conditional independence assumption holds and non-response can be treated as ignorable, once z is controlled for. If the condition does hold, consistent estimates can be obtained by weighting the observed data by the inverse of the probability of response, conditional on the observed covariates (Robins *et al.*, 1995). This gives more weight to individuals who have a high probability of non-response, as they are under-represented in the observed sample.

Fitzgerald *et al.* (1998) make it clear that this approach will be applicable when interest centres on a structural model for $P(y \mid x)$ and that the z's are deliberately excluded from the model, even though they are endogenous to the outcome of interest. They suggest lagged dependent variables as an obvious candidate for z. Rotnitzky and Robins (1997) offer a similar interpretation when they describe possible candidates for z being intermediate variables in the causal pathway from x to y. This property implies that it would not be sensible to use solely 'field variables' such as changes in interviewer as candidates for the additional observables. These kinds of variables may be good predictors of non-response but are unlikely to be associated with SAH. Horowitz and Manski (1998) show that if the observables (z) are statistically independent of y, conditional on (x, $r = 1$), then the weighted estimates reduce to the unweighted ones. This would explain why no difference between weighed and unweighted estimates may be reported in empirical analyses that use inappropriate variables for z.

In our application we are interested in the distribution of health problems conditional on SES, rather than the distribution conditional on SES and on other indicators of morbidity. We use past morbidity among our z variables. Of course, this approach will break down if an individual suffers an unobserved health shock, which occurs after their previous interview, that leads them to drop out of the survey and that is not captured by conditioning on lagged measures of morbidity. In this case non-response would remain non-ignorable even after conditioning on z. It is possible to test the validity of the selection on observables approach. The first step is to test whether the z's do predict non-response; this is done by testing their significance in probit models for non-response at each wave of the panel. The second is to do Hausman-type tests to compare the coefficients from the weighted and unweighted estimates. In addition, the probit models for health problems can be compared in terms of the magnitudes of estimated partial effects.

Implementation of the Fitzgerald *et al.* (1998) form of the ignorability condition implies that x is observable when $r = 0$. In the case of the kind of unit non-response we are dealing with in the BHPS, non-response means that there is missing data for the current period covariates (x) as well as health problems (y). So we implement a stronger form of conditional independence $P(r = 1 \mid y, x, z) = P(r = 1 \mid z)$ as proposed by Wooldridge (2002a). To compute the IPW estimator we estimate (probit) equations for response ($r_{it} = 1$) versus non-response ($r_{it} = 0$) at each wave, $t = 2,\ldots,T$, conditional on a set of characteristics (z_{i1}) that are measured for all individuals at the first wave. As described above, this relies on selection on observables and implies that non-response can be treated as ignorable non-response, conditional on z_{i1} (Fitzgerald *et al.*, 1998; Wooldridge, 2002b, p. 588). Selection on observables requires that z_{i1} contains variables that predict non-response and that are correlated with the outcome of interest but which are deliberately excluded from the model for health.

In practice z_{i1} includes the initial values of all of the regressors in the health equation. Also it includes initial values of hprob and of the other indicators of morbidity. In addition, z_{i1} includes initial values of the respondent's activity status, occupational socioeconomic group and region. The following code is used to create variables that contain the initial values of the regressors at wave 1:

```
sort pid wavenum
foreach X of varlist male widowed nvrmar divsep deghdeg    ///
    hndalev ocse hhsize nch04 nch511 nch1218 age age2 age3  ///
    nonwhite selfemp unemp retired matleave famcare         ///
    student ltsick prof mantech skillmn ptskill unskill     ///
    armed lninc hlghq1 hprob {
      by pid: gen `X't1 = `X'[1]
}
```

These are included in a global variable list:

```
global z1 "malet1 widowedt1 nvrmart1 divsept1 deghdegt1
    hndalevt1 ocset1 hhsizet1 nch04t1 nch511t1 nch1218t1
    aget1 age2t1 age3t1 nonwhitet1 selfempt1 unempt1
    retiredt1 matleavet1 famcaret1 studentt1 ltsickt1 proft1
    mantecht1 skillmnt1 ptskillt1 unskillt1 armedt1 lninct1
    hlghq1t1 hprobt1 sexzero sfazero spozero svpzero"
```

These variables are used in a sequence of probit models for response versus non-response: so the dependent variable is `insampm`, which indicates whether an observation is in the estimation sample at each wave. The probits are estimated at each wave of the panel, from wave 2 to wave 8, using the full sample of individuals who are observed at wave 1. The whole loop is executed quietly as its purpose is just to create the new variable `ipw`: the inverse of the fitted probability of responding. For the purposes of illustration, we have shown how the inverse Mills ratios (`imr`) could also be created and saved if this procedure was being used to do Heckman-type sample selection correction:

```
forvalues j = 2(1)8 {
    quietly probit insampm $z1 if (wavenum == `j')
    predict p`j' , p
    predict lc`j', xb
    generate imr`j'=normalden(lc`j')/normprob(lc`j')
    generate ipw`j' = 1/p`j'
}

generate imr = 0
forvalues k = 2(1)8 {
    replace imr = imr`k' if wavenum == `k'
}

generate ipw = 1
forvalues k = 2(1)8 {
    replace ipw = ipw`k' if wavenum == `k'
}

summ ipw imr
```

Variable	Obs	Mean	Std. Dev.	Min	Max
ipw	79487	1.338138	.9675544	1	168.3076
imr	79487	.3600614	.2231152	0	2.836962

The summary statistics show that the weights (`ipw`) vary from 1 to 168. The inverse of the fitted probabilities from these models, $1/\hat{p}_{it}$, are then used to weight observations in the IPW-ML estimation of the pooled probit model using:

$$\log L = \sum_i^n \sum_t^T \frac{r_{it}}{\hat{p}_{it}} \log L_{it}$$

Wooldridge (2002a) shows that, under the ignorability assumption:

$$P(r_{it} = 1 \mid y_{it}, x_{it}, z_{i1}) = P(r_{it} = 1 \mid z_{i1}), \quad t = 2,...,T$$

the IPW-ML estimator is $\sqrt{(n)}$-consistent and asymptotically normal. Wooldridge (2002a) also shows that using the estimated $\hat{p}_{it}$ rather than the true p_{it} and ignoring the implied adjustment to the estimated standard errors leads to 'conservative inference' so that the standard errors are larger than they would be with an adjustment for the use of fitted rather than true probabilities (see also Robins *et al.*, 1995). The results presented below use the unadjusted standard errors produced by Stata.

This IPW-ML estimator is implemented by adding the `pweight` subcommand to the probit model. The dynamic pooled probit model, with Mundlak–Wooldridge specification, is estimated for the unbalanced and balanced samples. These results can be compared to the unweighted estimates from Chapter 9:

```
probit y $xvarw_f [pweight=ipw], robust cluster(pid)
margins, dydx(*)
```

For the balanced sample:

```
probit y $xvarw_f [pweight=ipw] if allwavesm==1,          ///
    robust cluster(pid)
margins, dydx(*)
```

A comparison of these results with the unweighted equivalents shows some differences in the estimated partial effects, but these tend to be very small in magnitude.

The IPW-ML estimator can be adapted to allow the elements of z to be updated and change across time, for example adding z variables measured at $t–1$ to predict response at t. This should improve the power of the probit models to predict non-response and hence make the ignorability assumption more plausible. In this case the probit model for non-response at wave t is estimated relative to the sample that is observed at wave $t–1$. This relies on non-response being an absorbing state and is therefore confined to 'monotone attrition' where respondents never re-enter the panel. Also, because estimation at each wave is based on the selected sample observed at the previous wave, the construction of inverse probability weights has to be adapted. The predicted probability weights are constructed cumulatively using $\hat{p}_{it} = \hat{\pi}_{i1} \times \hat{\pi}_{i2} \ldots \times \hat{\pi}_{it}$, where the $\hat{\pi}_{it}$ denote the fitted selection probabilities from each wave. In this version of the estimator the ignorability condition has to be extended to include future values of y and x (see Wooldridge, 2002b, p. 589). Once again, Wooldridge shows that omitting a correction to the asymptotic variance estimator leads to conservative inference.

The IPW approach is attractive as it is easy to apply in the context of nonlinear models, such as the probit model, and only requires a re-weighting of the data. In contrast to the published longitudinal weights that are supplied with the BHPS, our IPW weights are model-specific and specifically designed for the outcome of interest and the associated problem of health-related non-response; although the validity of the approach depends on the credibility of the ignorability assumption.

Table 10.1 Dynamic pooled probit with IPW, unbalanced panel

```
----------------------------------------------------------------------
Average marginal effects                        Number of obs  =   51711
Model VCE     : Robust


Expression    : Pr(y), predict()
dy/dx w.r.t. : 1.hprobt_1 1.male 1.widowed 1.nvrmar 1.divsep
1.deghdeg 1.hndalev 1.ocse hhsize nch04 nch511 nch1218 age 1.nonwhite
lninc 1.prof 1.mantech 1.skillmn 1.ptskill 1.unskill
         1.armed 1.hprobt1 mlninc
----------------------------------------------------------------------
             |               Delta-method
             |    dy/dx   Std. Err.      z   P>|z|   [95% Conf. Interval]
-------------|--------------------------------------------------------
  1.hprobt_1 |  .4156299   .0099212   41.89  0.000   .3961847   .4350751
      1.male |  .0065968    .003311    1.99  0.046   .0001073   .0130862
   1.widowed | -.0042886   .0055307   -0.78  0.438  -.0151287   .0065514
    1.nvrmar |  .0075218   .0052938    1.42  0.155  -.0028538   .0178975
    1.divsep |   .010032   .0059682    1.68  0.093  -.0016655   .0217295
   1.deghdeg | -.0190164   .0059673   -3.19  0.001  -.0307122  -.0073206
   1.hndalev | -.0164473    .004554   -3.61  0.000  -.0253729  -.0075217
      1.ocse | -.0177046   .0041302   -4.29  0.000  -.0257997  -.0096095
      hhsize | -.0015178   .0018857   -0.80  0.421  -.0052138   .0021781
       nch04 | -.0100077   .0044838   -2.23  0.026  -.0187958  -.0012195
      nch511 | -.0022076   .0032664   -0.68  0.499  -.0086096   .0041943
     nch1218 | -.0009432   .0036702   -0.26  0.797  -.0081368   .0062503
         age |  .0016227   .0001638    9.91  0.000   .0013016   .0019438
  1.nonwhite |   .021485   .0092579    2.32  0.020   .0033399   .0396301
       lninc | -.0016746    .003316   -0.51  0.614  -.0081738   .0048245
      1.prof | -.0513953   .0077624   -6.62  0.000  -.0666094  -.0361813
   1.mantech | -.0458272     .00412  -11.12  0.000  -.0539022  -.0377522
   1.skillmn | -.0579069   .0045755  -12.66  0.000  -.0668748   -.048939
   1.ptskill | -.0413284   .0047505   -8.70  0.000  -.0506392  -.0320176
   1.unskill | -.0412901   .0071519   -5.77  0.000  -.0553076  -.0272726
     1.armed | -.0961439   .0342944   -2.80  0.005  -.1633597  -.0289281
   1.hprobt1 |  .1537521   .0076713   20.04  0.000   .1387165   .1687876
      mlninc | -.0239711   .0047779   -5.02  0.000  -.0333356  -.0146066
----------------------------------------------------------------------
```
Note: dy/dx for factor levels is the discrete change from the base level.

Table 10.2 Dynamic pooled probit with IPW, balanced panel

```
------------------------------------------------------------------------
Average marginal effects                     Number of obs  =    41888
Model VCE      : Robust


Expression    : Pr(y), predict()
dy/dx w.r.t.  : 1.hprobt_1 1.male 1.widowed 1.nvrmar 1.divsep
1.deghdeg 1.hndalev 1.ocse hhsize nch04 nch511 nch1218 age 1.nonwhite
lninc 1.prof 1.mantech 1.skillmn 1.ptskill 1.unskill
        1.hprobt1 mlninc
------------------------------------------------------------------------
             |             Delta-method
             |    dy/dx    Std. Err.      z    P>|z|   [95% Conf. Interval]
-------------|----------------------------------------------------------
 1.hprobt_1  |  .4269664   .0112508   37.95   0.000    .4049153    .4490175
     1.male  |  .0050278    .003645    1.38   0.168   -.0021164    .0121719
  1.widowed  | -.0043794   .0061646   -0.71   0.477   -.0164619     .007703
   1.nvrmar  |  .0074812   .0058804    1.27   0.203   -.0040442    .0190066
   1.divsep  |  .0044418   .0064885    0.68   0.494   -.0082755     .017159
  1.deghdeg  | -.0157322   .0066336   -2.37   0.018   -.0287339   -.0027305
  1.hndalev  | -.0107915   .0049725   -2.17   0.030   -.0205375   -.0010456
     1.ocse  | -.0131651   .0045129   -2.92   0.004   -.0220102     -.00432
     hhsize  | -.0031585   .0020987   -1.51   0.132   -.0072718    .0009548
      nch04  | -.0117968   .0049173   -2.40   0.016   -.0214346    -.002159
     nch511  | -.0052488   .0036178   -1.45   0.147   -.0123395     .001842
    nch1218  |  .0005327   .0039348    0.14   0.892   -.0071794    .0082448
        age  |  .0012125     .00018    6.74   0.000    .0008598    .0015652
 1.nonwhite  |  .0188658   .0112848    1.67   0.095   -.0032521    .0409837
      lninc  | -.0051224   .0037113   -1.38   0.168   -.0123964    .0021516
     1.prof  | -.0568593   .0079055   -7.19   0.000   -.0723537   -.0413649
  1.mantech  | -.0436969   .0043791   -9.98   0.000   -.0522797   -.0351141
  1.skillmn  | -.0524152   .0048943  -10.71   0.000   -.0620079   -.0428226
  1.ptskill  | -.0413899   .0050751   -8.16   0.000    -.051337   -.0314428
  1.unskill  | -.0344767   .0075941   -4.54   0.000   -.0493609   -.0195925
  1.hprobt1  |  .1539984   .0086122   17.88   0.000    .1371188     .170878
     mlninc  | -.0235986   .0053856   -4.38   0.000   -.0341542    -.013043
------------------------------------------------------------------------
```

Note: dy/dx for factor levels is the discrete change from the base level.

Jones *et al.* (2006) show that there is clear evidence of health-related non-response in both the BHPS and ECHP. In general, individuals in poor initial health are more likely to drop out, although for younger groups non-response is associated with good health. Furthermore, variable addition tests provide evidence of non-response bias in the models of SAH. Nevertheless a comparison of estimates based on the balanced samples, the unbalanced samples and corrected for non-response using inverse probability weights shows that, in many cases, substantive differences in the magnitudes of the average partial effects of lagged health, income and education are small. Similar findings have been reported concerning the limited influence of non-response bias in models of income dynamics and various labour market outcomes and on measures of social exclusion such as poverty rates and income inequality indices.

10.4 OVERVIEW

The problem of non-response is common in social surveys and in the case of longitudinal data, where there are repeated observations on the same individual, it is compounded by loss to follow-up or attrition. Attrition bias can arise when drop-outs from panel data are non-random. This chapter describes ways of testing for attrition bias in panel data regressions and outlines the use of inverse probability weights as one method to adjust for attrition. The methods are illustrated for the same binary measure of health that was analysed in Chapter 9.

APPENDIX

User-written program table

```
program define table
    {
      quietly summ miss if wavenum == 1
      scalar N0 = r(N)
      forvalues j = 2(1)8 {
        display "wavenum == "`j'
        quietly summ miss if (wavenum == `j'-1)
        scalar N1 = r(N)
        quietly summ miss if (wavenum==`j' & miss[_n-1]~= .)
        scalar N2 = r(N)
        quietly summ miss if (wavenum==`j' & miss[_n-1]== .)
        scalar N3 = r(N)
        quietly summ miss if (wavenum == `j')
        scalar N4 = r(N)
        scalar dropout = N1 - N2
        scalar rejoiner = N3
```

```
        scalar rattr = ((N1 - N2)/N1)
        scalar nattr = ((N1 - N4)/N1)
        scalar surv = N4/N0
        display "No. individuals at wave = " `j'-1 " = " N1
        display "No. individuals at wave = " `j' " = " N4
        display "Survival rate = " surv " Drop outs = "      ///
          dropout " Re-joiners = " rejoiner
        display "Raw Attrition rate = " rattr                ///
          "Net Attrition rate = " nattr
        display " "
          }
}
end
```

Part V

Health care data

11 Models for count data

SYNOPSIS

This chapter describes the use of count data models for utilisation of health care. It covers the basic count data model, the Poisson model and several other more flexible specifications that have been proposed to account for special features of health care use data such as overdispersion and excess zeros. Most studies of health care use have used either cross-sectional data or ignored their panel structure. This chapter considers also some recent proposals to account for this structure using the latent class framework. We illustrate the application of these methods using a sub-sample of the European Community Household Panel (ECHP).

11.1 INTRODUCTION

Many empirical analyses of the use of health care services, use as dependent variable a count variable (non-negative integer valued count $y = 0,1,\ldots$) such as the number of visits to a physician (sometimes detailed by type of physician), number of hospital stays or number of drug prescriptions. In the recent literature, there are various examples of empirical modelling of count measures of health care. The data on health care utilisation typically contain a large proportion of zero observations, as well as a long right tail of individuals who make heavy use of health care. The basic count data regression model is the Poisson. This model has been shown to be too restrictive for modelling health care utilisation and more general specifications have been preferred.

This chapter illustrates the use of count data models to model health care utilisation. These models are applied to Portuguese data taken from waves 2 to 5 of the European Community Household Panel (ECHP), covering the years 1995 to 1998. The dependent variable is the number of visits to a specialist in the previous 12 months (y).

Empirical studies of health care utilisation usually consider as regressors variables that measure: need/morbidity (more commonly, self-assessed health status, typically with five categories, but also indicators of chronic conditions and limited activity, days of sickness/restricted activity and, ideally, albeit less commonly available in survey data, objective health measures); age (accounting for imperfect health status measurement); sex (accounting for sex-specific health care requirements and also for tastes); ability to pay (income, wealth) and other socio-demographic factors such as marital status, education level attained, labour market status and job characteristics. Some studies have also considered the price of health care and characteristics of insurance coverage and, less commonly, due to lack of data, time costs and accessibility.

In this chapter, we consider a restricted list of covariates, as the main goal is to illustrate the practical issues involved in the various methodologies. When interpreting the results, we should therefore bear in mind that the estimated effects may be capturing effects of omitted variables. The explanatory variables considered here are: age in years, a dummy variable for sex (male), the logarithm of household income (lhincome) and a dummy variable that equals one if self-assessed health status in the previous period was bad or very bad (lsahbad), and zero if that was very good, good or fair. The ECHP income variable is total net household income. Here, this variable is deflated by national consumer price indices (CPI), making it comparable across the panel, and by purchasing power parities (PPP), which would have allowed for comparability across countries. The income variable is further deflated by the OECD-modified equivalence scale in order to account for household size and composition. In order to make the syntax in the remainder of this chapter more general, it is useful to create a global list of regressors:

```
global xvars "age male lhincome lsahbad"
```

11.2 THE POISSON MODEL

The basic count data model is the Poisson model. The dependent variable y_i is assumed to follow a Poisson distribution, with mean λ_i, defined as a function of the covariates x_i. In particular, the model is defined by the density:

$$f(y_i \mid x_i) = \frac{\exp(-\lambda_i)\lambda_i^{y_i}}{y_i!}$$

where the conditional mean λ_i is usually defined as:

$$\lambda_i = E[y_i \mid x_i] = \exp(x_i\beta)$$

The conditional variance equals the conditional mean, reflecting the equidispersion property of the Poisson distribution:

$$V[y_i \mid x_i] = \lambda_i = \exp(x_i\beta)$$

Estimate a Poisson regression model for the number of visits to the specialist (y) using the following command:

```
poisson y $xvars
```

Table 11.1 shows the results of maximum likelihood estimation of the Poisson regression model. The output contains the estimated coefficients, standard errors and resulting z-ratios for each explanatory variable. The coefficients are those in the linear index $x_i\beta$, while the expected number of visits is a nonlinear function of that. Thus, the elements of β are not measured in the original units of the count variable and estimation of the absolute effects of a given variable on the number of doctor visits requires the transformation of the estimates. The coefficients can nevertheless be used to analyse the qualitative impacts of the variables considered, and they can also be interpreted as semi-elasticities. For example, reporting bad or very bad health is associated with 90 per cent more specialist visits, compared to reporting very good, good or fair health. Since our income variable is log-transformed, the respective coefficient can actually be interpreted as the income elasticity (with 1 per cent increase in income associated with 0.36 per cent increase in specialist visits). In line with the findings of previous analyses of health care utilisation, the results also show positive and significant effects of age and being a female.

Table 11.1 Poisson regression

```
--------------------------------------------------------------------
Poisson regression                        Number of obs =    32164
                                          LR chi2(4)    = 9782.96
                                          Prob > chi2   =  0.0000
Log likelihood = -66421.47                Pseudo R2     =  0.0686
--------------------------------------------------------------------
       y |   Coef.   Std. Err.    z   P>|z|   [95% Conf. Interval]
--------------------------------------------------------------------
     age |  .0023812  .0003307   7.20  0.000   .001733    .0030295
    male | -.3564767  .0107427 -33.18  0.000  -.3775321  -.3354214
lhincome |  .3606307  .0078924  45.69  0.000   .3451618   .3760996
 lsahbad |  .9008154  .0120738  74.61  0.000   .8771512   .9244795
   _cons | -3.212611  .072741  -44.17  0.000  -3.35518   -3.070041
--------------------------------------------------------------------
```

The marginal effect of a continuous explanatory variable x_k is given by:

$$\frac{\partial E[y_i \mid x_i]}{\partial x_{ik}} = \beta_k \exp(x_i\beta).$$

The incremental effect of a binary variable is given by:

$$\frac{\Delta E[y_i \mid x_i]}{\Delta x_{ik}} = \exp\left(x_i\beta^{|x_{ik}=1}\right) - \exp\left(x_i\beta^{|x_{ik}=0}\right)$$

These marginal and incremental effects depend on the value of the explanatory variables. The command `margins` can be used to obtain these effects evaluated at particular values of x_i, or to obtain the average of them over the whole sample – i.e. average marginal effects. The latter is the default option and returns the following results (as noted in previous chapters, in order to obtain incremental effects for factor variables, one should identify such variables explicitly in the model estimation, which we do here silently):

```
quietly poisson y age i.male lhincome i.lsahbad
margins, dydx(*)
```

Table 11.2 Average marginal effects from Poisson regression

```
-----------------------------------------------------------------------
Average marginal effects                    Number of obs  =    32164
Model VCE     : OIM
Expression    : Predicted number of events, predict()
dy/dx w.r.t.  : age 1.male lhincome 1.lsahbad
-----------------------------------------------------------------------
            |            Delta-method
            |   dy/dx   Std. Err.    z   P>|z|   [95% Conf. Interval]
------------|----------------------------------------------------------
       age  | .0028024  .0003895   7.19  0.000    .002039   .0035657
    1.male  | -.4081553 .0120304 -33.93  0.000  -.4317344  -.3845762
  lhincome  | .4244059  .0095409  44.48  0.000   .4057061   .4431058
 1.lsahbad  | 1.289022  .0215042  59.94  0.000   1.246875   1.33117
-----------------------------------------------------------------------
```

Note: dy/dx for factor levels is the discrete change from the base level.

The Poisson model implies equality of the conditional mean and conditional variance. This is called the equidispersion property and it has been shown to be too restrictive in many empirical applications. In case of over- or underdispersion, the maximum likelihood estimator will still give consistent estimates of β, as long as the conditional mean is well-specified. However, the resulting estimates of the standard errors are biased.

As an alternative approach, an appeal to the Poisson pseudo-maximum likelihood estimator (PMLE) can be used. The estimator for β is defined by the first-order conditions of the MLE but the distribution need not be Poisson. In other words, the Poisson mean assumption is maintained but the restriction of equi-dispersion is not imposed. This is done by using an alternative estimator for the covariance matrix (different functional forms can be assumed for the conditional variance of y_i, see, for example, Cameron and Trivedi, 1998). The option `robust` specifies that the covariance matrix should be estimated using the Huber–White sandwich estimator:

```
poisson y $xvars, robust
```

Table 11.3 shows the results of the Poisson pseudo-maximum likelihood estimation. The coefficient estimates result from maximum likelihood estimation, so they are the same as above, while the standard errors result from the Huber–White sandwich estimator.

Table 11.3 Poisson regression with robust standard errors

```
-----------------------------------------------------------------
Poisson regression                        Number of obs =     32164
                                          Wald chi2(4)  =   1594.92
                                          Prob > chi2   =    0.0000
Log pseudolikelihood = -66421.47          Pseudo R2     =    0.0686
-----------------------------------------------------------------
              |              Robust
         y |   Coef.   Std. Err.    z   P>|z|   [95% Conf. Interval]
----------|------------------------------------------------------
       age |  .0023812  .0009238   2.58  0.010   .0005706   .0041919
      male | -.3564767  .0318036 -11.21  0.000  -.4188107  -.2941428
  lhincome |  .3606307  .0228243  15.80  0.000   .3158958   .4053656
   lsahbad |  .9008154  .0367396  24.52  0.000   .8288072   .9728236
     _cons | -3.212611  .2122474 -15.14  0.000  -3.628608  -2.796613
-----------------------------------------------------------------
```

The literature on modelling of health care utilisation has shown that the Poisson model is usually too restrictive. This has motivated the use of different parametric distributions that can account for the features of the data that are inconsistent with the Poisson. Cameron and Trivedi (1998) list the most common departures from the standard Poisson model. Some of these deal with problems that often arise when modelling count measures of health care utilisation such as: failure of the equidispersion property (due, for example, to unobserved heterogeneity); 'excess zeros' problem (higher observed frequency of zeros than is consistent with the Poisson); and multimodality (which can arise if observations are drawn from different populations). The remainder of this chapter covers generalisations of the Poisson model that have been used to overcome its limitations for modelling health care utilisation.

11.3 THE NEGATIVE BINOMIAL MODEL

Cameron and Trivedi (1998) note that one of the reasons for the failure of the Poisson regression is unobserved heterogeneity. Neglected unobserved hetero-geneity leads to overdispersion and an excess of zeros. This heterogeneity can be modelled as a continuous mixture of the Poisson distribution, by specifying the mean as $E[y_i | x_i] = \lambda_i \eta_i$, with λ_i a deterministic function of the covariates, normally defined as above, and η_i a random term, which distribution should be defined. If $E(\eta_i) = 1$, the Poisson mixture retains the same mean as the Poisson,

λ_i. While, in the Poisson model, $y_i \mid x_i$ follows a Poisson distribution, in the mixture model, this distribution is assumed for $y_i \mid x_i, \eta_i$. Defining the distribution of η_i, one can obtain the marginal distribution of $y_i \mid x_i$. The negative binomial (NB) model results from assuming that η_i follows a gamma distribution with variance α (for the derivation, see, for example, Cameron and Trivedi, 1998, 2005). The associated probability of observing the count y_i is then:

$$ f\left(y_i \mid x_i\right) = \frac{\Gamma\left(\alpha^{-1} + y_i\right)}{\Gamma\left(\alpha^{-1}\right)\Gamma\left(y_i + 1\right)} \left(\frac{\alpha^{-1}}{\lambda_i + \alpha^{-1}}\right)^{\alpha^{-1}} \left(\frac{\lambda_i}{\lambda_i + \alpha^{-1}}\right)^{y_i} $$

where $\Gamma(.)$ is the gamma function. The first two conditional moments are:

$$ E[y_i \mid x_i] = \lambda_i \quad \text{and} \quad V[y_i \mid x_i] = \lambda_i + \alpha\lambda_i^2 $$

With $\lambda_i = \exp(x_i\beta)$ and α a constant overdispersion parameter to be estimated, this specification corresponds to the most commonly used version of the NB regression model, the NB2 (Cameron and Trivedi, 1998). This is the default in Stata and is the version adopted here. Another, less used, version of the NB model specifies the conditional mean in the same way but assumes a linear variance function $V[y_i \mid x_i] = \lambda_i + \alpha\lambda_i$. In both cases, the NB model nests the Poisson model, which corresponds to $\alpha = 0$.

Estimate the NB2 model and save estimation results for later use:

```
nbreg y $xvars
estimates store nb
```

The estimation results of the NB2 model are shown in Table 11.4. The conditional mean function is defined in the same way as in the Poisson model, so the coefficients have the same interpretation. The estimate for the overdispersion parameter α equals 3.46 and the log-likelihood-ratio test shown at the bottom of the table decisively rejects the null hypothesis that it equals zero. This means that the equidispersion property imposed by the Poisson model is rejected. The estimated coefficients show only small differences, compared to the Poisson model, while the estimated standard errors and t-ratios are substantially different.

Following the estimation of the model, calculate average marginal and incremental effects on the expected number of specialists visits in the same way as for the Poisson:

```
quietly nbreg y age i.male lhincome i.lsahbad
margins, dydx(*)
```

The alternative NB1 specification can be obtained by using the option `dispersion(constant)`. A generalisation of the NB2 model, not often considered by researchers, is obtained allowing α to vary with the regressors. In particular, $\log(\alpha)$ is parameterised as a linear combination of the regressors:

Table 11.4 Negative binomial model

```
--------------------------------------------------------------------
Negative binomial regression                 Number of obs =    32164
                                              LR chi2(4)    = 1830.26
                                              Prob > chi2   =  0.0000
Log likelihood = -42753.001                   Pseudo R2     =  0.0210
--------------------------------------------------------------------
         y |      Coef.  Std. Err.      z   P>|z|  [95% Conf. Interval]
-----------+--------------------------------------------------------
       age |   .0064446  .0007321    8.80  0.000   .0050097   .0078795
      male |  -.4560705  .0238621  -19.11  0.000  -.5028394  -.4093016
  lhincome |     .30484  .0158709   19.21  0.000   .2737336   .3359463
   lsahbad |   .8853403  .0286717   30.88  0.000   .8291449   .9415358
     _cons |  -2.893422  .1444795  -20.03  0.000  -3.176596  -2.610247
-----------+--------------------------------------------------------
  /lnalpha |   1.241131  .0146867                  1.212345   1.269916
-----------+--------------------------------------------------------
     alpha |   3.459523  .0508091                  3.361358   3.560554
--------------------------------------------------------------------
Likelihood-ratio test of alpha=0: chibar2(01) = 4.7e+04 Prob>=chibar2 = 0.000
```

Table 11.5 Average marginal effects from negative binomial model

```
--------------------------------------------------------------------
Average marginal effects                      Number of obs  =    32164
Model VCE    : OIM
Expression   : Predicted number of events, predict()
dy/dx w.r.t. : age 1.male lhincome 1.lsahbad
--------------------------------------------------------------------
           |           Delta-method
           |    dy/dx   Std. Err.      z   P>|z|   [95% Conf. Interval]
-----------+--------------------------------------------------------
       age |  .0076794  .0008919    8.61  0.000   .0059314   .0094274
    1.male | -.5221253  .0280462  -18.62  0.000  -.5770948  -.4671558
  lhincome |  .3632484  .0200375   18.13  0.000   .3239757   .4025212
 1.lsahbad |  1.255948  .0539748   23.27  0.000    1.15016   1.361737
--------------------------------------------------------------------
Note: dy/dx for factor levels is the discrete change from the base level.
```

```
gnbreg y $xvars, lna($xvars)
estimates store gnb
```

Table 11.6 shows significant coefficients for all covariates in the overdispersion equation. All the variables have estimated coefficients with opposite signs on the conditional mean function and on the overdispersion function.

According to Gurmu (1997), 'although the NB model is superior to the Poisson in that it allows for overdispersion, it is inadequate in various practical situations'.

Table 11.6 Generalised negative binomial model

```
------------------------------------------------------------------------
Generalized negative binomial regression       Number of obs  =    32164
                                               LR chi2(4)     =  1571.10
                                               Prob > chi2    =   0.0000
Log likelihood = -42307.817                    Pseudo R2      =   0.0182
------------------------------------------------------------------------
       y    |      Coef. Std. Err.      z   P>|z|   [95% Conf. Interval]
------------+-----------------------------------------------------------
y           |
       age  |   .0040104   .0007655    5.24  0.000    .0025101   .0055107
      male  |  -.4007285   .0254426  -15.75  0.000   -.450595   -.3508619
  lhincome  |   .3771582   .0171184   22.03  0.000    .3436068   .4107096
   lsahbad  |   .8455891    .027503   30.75  0.000    .7916842    .899494
     _cons  |  -3.406211   .1585513  -21.48  0.000   -3.716966  -3.095456
------------+-----------------------------------------------------------
lnalpha     |
       age  |  -.0071049   .0009375   -7.58  0.000   -.0089424  -.0052673
      male  |   .5215486    .030414   17.15  0.000    .4619383   .5811589
  lhincome  |  -.4503186   .0209182  -21.53  0.000   -.4913176  -.4093196
   lsahbad  |   -.389146   .0340555  -11.43  0.000   -.4558936  -.3223985
     _cons  |   5.436645   .1920486   28.31  0.000    5.060237   5.813053
------------------------------------------------------------------------
```

Gurmu notes that there is evidence of poor fit in counts models with excess zeros and long-tailed distributions. The assumption that the zeros and positive observations are generated by the same process has been shown to be too restrictive in the case of health care utilisation. Pohlmeier and Ulrich (1995), who model the number of visits to a doctor, argue that the decision of first contact and the frequency of visits may be determined by two different processes. The different nature of the zeros and the positive observations has been taken into account by two alternative approaches: zero-inflated models and, especially, hurdle models. These specifications are presented below.

11.4 ZERO-INFLATED MODELS

We now turn to models that allow for the possibility that the zeros are generated by a different process than the positives. An important aim of these models is to solve the problem of excess zeros, i.e. the occurrence of even more zeros than predicted by the NB model (Cameron and Trivedi, 2005). We start with the one that has been least popular in applied health economics (see, for example, Sarma and Simpson, 2006, for a comparison with some other specifications considered in this chapter). The zero-inflated model gives more weight to the probability that the count variable equals zero. It incorporates an underlying mechanism that splits individuals between non-users, with probability q, and potential users, with probability $1-q$. The probability function for the zero-inflated Poisson model is a mixture of the standard Poisson model, $f^{P}(y\,|\,x)$, and a degenerate distribution concentrated at zero:

$$g(y_i\,|\,x_i) = 1(y_i = 0)q + (1-q)f^{P}(y_i\,|\,x_i)$$

A more general specification is obtained when the NB model, instead of the Poisson, is used for the number of visits of potential users, ZINB. In both cases, the conditional mean is:

$$E[y_i\,|\,x_i] = (1-q)\lambda_i,$$

where $\lambda_i = \exp(x_i\beta)$. Zero-inflated Poisson (ZIP) and NB (ZINB) models can be estimated by maximum likelihood. The simplest version is the ZIP with constant zero-inflation probability q. Stata reparameterises q to ensure that it lies between 0 and 1. By default the reparameterisation is $q = \exp(\gamma_0)/[1 + \exp(\gamma_0)]$, which corresponds to a logit model with just a constant term, γ_0. Estimation results show the estimate of γ_0. Choosing the option vuong when estimating the model returns the test statistic of the Vuong test that $q = 0$ with the estimation results, which allows the comparison of the ZIP and Poisson models:

```
zip y $xvars, inflate(_cons) vuong
```

As can be seen in Table 11.7, the Vuong test of ZIP against the Poisson model clearly favours the zero-inflated specification. This shows evidence of a split between potential users and non-users of specialist visits. With constant zero-inflation probability, the coefficients of the ZIP can also be interpreted as semi-elasticities. The estimated results for this model are substantially different from the ones obtained previously with the basic Poisson model.

Marginal effects of continuous variables and incremental effects of binary variables are different from what was shown above for the Poisson and NB models, because of the different mean function:

$$\frac{\partial E[y_i\,|\,x_i]}{\partial x_{ik}} = \beta_k(1-q)\,\exp(x_i\beta)$$

$$\frac{\Delta E[y_i\,|\,x_i]}{\Delta x_{ik}} = (1-q)\,\exp\left(x_i\beta^{|x_{ik}=1}\right) - (1-q)\,\exp\left(x_i\beta^{|x_{ik}=0}\right)$$

These can also be obtained with the command margins:

```
quietly zip y age i.male lhincome i.lsahbad,          ///
      inflate(_cons) vuong
margins, dydx(*)
```

Table 11.7 Zero-inflated Poisson model with constant zero-inflation probability

```
------------------------------------------------------------------------
Zero-inflated poisson regression              Number of obs =    32164
                                              Nonzero obs   =    11266
                                              Zero obs      =    20898
Inflation model = logit                       LR chi2(4)    = 1900.46
Log likelihood = -51057.84                    Prob > chi2   =  0.0000
------------------------------------------------------------------------
        y |     Coef.  Std. Err.      z   P>|z|   [95% Conf. Interval]
----------|-------------------------------------------------------------
y         |
      age | -.0007622    .000364  -2.09   0.036   -.0014757  -.0000487
     male |  -.070633   .0118146  -5.98   0.000   -.0937892  -.0474768
 lhincome |  .0947423   .0083167  11.39   0.000    .0784419   .1110427
  lsahbad |  .5153494   .0125093  41.20   0.000    .4908315   .5398672
    _cons |   .199003   .0776417   2.56   0.010    .0468281   .3511779
----------|-------------------------------------------------------------
inflate   |
    _cons |  .5093962   .0124118  41.04   0.000    .4850695   .5337229
------------------------------------------------------------------------
Vuong test of zip vs. standard Poisson:     z =   37.55 Pr>z = 0.0000
```

Table 11.8 Average marginal effects from zero-inflated Poisson model with constant zero-inflation probability

```
------------------------------------------------------------------------
Average marginal effects                      Number of obs =    32164
Model VCE    : OIM
Expression   : Predicted number of events, predict()
dy/dx w.r.t. : age 1.male lhincome 1.lsahbad
------------------------------------------------------------------------
          |    Delta-method
          |     dy/dx  Std. Err.      z   P>|z|   [95% Conf. Interval]
----------|-------------------------------------------------------------
      age | -.0008478  .0004054  -2.09   0.037   -.0016423  -.0000532
   1.male | -.0783062  .0129987  -6.02   0.000   -.1037832  -.0528293
 lhincome |  .1053789  .0092016  11.45   0.000    .0873441   .1234137
1.lsahbad |  .6500464  .0181296  35.86   0.000     .614513   .6855798
------------------------------------------------------------------------
Note: dy/dx for factor levels is the discrete change from the base level.
```

The model can be further extended to allow for the zero-inflation probability (q) to depend on explanatory variables, x_{1i}, $q(x_{1i}\beta_1)$. However, researchers often report problems in obtaining convergence when the same set of regressors is included in the splitting mechanism and the potential users' density (see, e.g., Grootendorst, 1995, and Gerdtham, 1997), i.e., with $x_{1i} = x_i$. We illustrate this specification here, which is not problematic in this particular application. By default, Stata uses a logit specification for the probability of being a non-user, conditional on the variables listed in the option inflate(), so $q(x_i\beta_1) = \exp(x_i\beta_1)/[1 + \exp(x_i\beta_1)]$:

```
zip y $xvars, inflate($xvars)
```

The results in Table 11.9 show evidence that the split between potential users and non-users of specialist visits is influenced by all covariates considered. Younger males, as well as individuals with lower incomes and those in better health, tend to have a higher probability of being non-users.

Table 11.9 Zero-inflated Poisson model with variable zero-inflation probability

```
-----------------------------------------------------------------------
Zero-inflated poisson regression            Number of obs =     32164
                                            Nonzero obs   =     11266
                                            Zero obs      =     20898
Inflation model = logit                     LR chi2(4)    =   1617.98
Log likelihood = -50028.94                  Prob > chi2   =    0.0000
-----------------------------------------------------------------------
        y |       Coef. Std. Err.      z   P>|z|   [95% Conf. Interval]
-----------------------------------------------------------------------
y         |
      age |   -.0016061   .0003606   -4.45  0.000   -.0023127   -.0008994
     male |   -.0246478   .0115466   -2.13  0.033   -.0472788   -.0020168
 lhincome |    .0628027   .0080689    7.78  0.000    .0469879    .0786174
  lsahbad |    .4836837   .0124048   38.99  0.000    .4593707    .5079967
    _cons |    .5299433   .0747959    7.09  0.000     .383346    .6765406
-----------------------------------------------------------------------
inflate   |
      age |   -.0087677    .000786  -11.16  0.000   -.0103081   -.0072272
     male |    .6159362   .0255089   24.15  0.000    .5659397    .6659327
 lhincome |   -.5068374   .0195151  -25.97  0.000   -.5450863   -.4685885
  lsahbad |   -.7045381   .0317606  -22.18  0.000   -.7667878   -.6422884
    _cons |    5.232266    .177915   29.41  0.000    4.883559    5.580973
-----------------------------------------------------------------------
```

Estimation of the ZINB is achieved using similar commands. We do not show results of the model with constant zero-inflation probability, which is rejected against the more flexible version with zero-inflation dependent on covariates. As above, we request that the Vuong test against the null NB model be performed, option vuong, as well as a likelihood ratio (LR) test against the null ZIP model (i.e. of significance of the overdispersion parameter α in the NB model for potential users), option zip:

```
zinb y $xvars, inflate($xvars) vuong zip
estimates store zinb
```

Estimates are shown in Table 11.10. The LR test rejects the null of $\alpha = 0$, i.e. the nested ZIP. On the other hand, the Vuong test favours the ZINB against the NB without zero-inflation. The estimated coefficients in the NB model for the potential users differ considerably from the ones obtained with the NB regression without zero-inflation (Table 11.4). For example, the simpler specification indicated a negative and significant effect of being male on the expected number of

Table 11.10 Zero-inflated NB model for number of specialist visits with variable zero-inflation probability

```
-------------------------------------------------------------------------
Zero-inflated negative binomial                 Number of obs   =   32164
regression

                                                Nonzero obs     =   11266
                                                Zero obs        =   20898
Inflation model = logit                         LR chi2(4)      =  507.28
Log likelihood = -42218.81                      Prob > chi2     =  0.0000
-------------------------------------------------------------------------
         y |      Coef. Std. Err.     z    P>|z|   [95% Conf. Interval]
-------------------------------------------------------------------------
y          |
       age | -.0043025   .0008231  -5.23   0.000   -.0059159   -.0026892
      male |  -.027775   .0284726  -0.98   0.329   -.0835804    .0280304
  lhincome |  .2112907    .018254  11.58   0.000    .1755135     .247068
   lsahbad |  .6247848   .0296696  21.06   0.000    .5666334    .6829361
     _cons | -1.347752    .174639  -7.72   0.000   -1.690038   -1.005465
-----------+-------------------------------------------------------------
inflate    |
       age | -.0426388   .0031538 -13.52   0.000   -.0488201   -.0364576
      male |  1.816027   .1017853  17.84   0.000    1.616532    2.015523
  lhincome |  -.598092   .0437903 -13.66   0.000   -.6839195   -.5122646
   lsahbad | -2.279397   .2978691  -7.65   0.000   -2.863209   -1.695584
     _cons |  5.282505   .4004838  13.19   0.000    4.497572    6.067439
-----------+-------------------------------------------------------------
  /lnalpha |  .8565125   .0281352  30.44   0.000    .8013685    .9116566
-----------+-------------------------------------------------------------
     alpha |  2.354934   .0662566                   2.228589    2.488441
-------------------------------------------------------------------------
Likelihood-ratio test of alpha=0: chibar2(01) = 1.6e+04 Pr>=chibar2 = 0.0000
Vuong test of zinb vs. standard negative binomial: z =  15.09 Pr>z = 0.0000
```

specialist visits. In the ZINB, the negative coefficient of male on the number of visits of potential users is not significant, while there is evidence that males have a substantially larger probability of being non-users.

Computation of marginal effects of continuous variables and incremental effects of binary variables on the expected number of specialist visits needs to account for the fact that the same variables enter the inflation function and the conditional mean function of potential users. After some manipulation, including using the chain rule for derivative of a product, marginal effects are given by:

$$\frac{\partial E[y_i \mid x_i]}{\partial x_{ik}} = \beta_k \left[1 - q(x_i\beta_1)\right] \exp(x_i\beta) -$$

$$\beta_{1k} \left[1 - q(x_i\beta_1)\right] q(x_i\beta_1) \exp(x_i\beta)$$

Incremental effects are obtained in a straightforward way:

$$\frac{\Delta E[y_i \mid x_i]}{\Delta x_{ik}} = \left[1 - q\left(x_i\beta_1^{|x_{ik}=1}\right)\right] \exp\left(x_i\beta^{|x_{ik}=1}\right) -$$

$$\left[1 - q\left(x_i\beta_1^{|x_{ik}=0}\right)\right] \exp\left(x_i\beta^{|x_{ik}=0}\right)$$

where $q(x_i\beta_1)$ is as defined above. This model is however also supported by margins, which estimates directly effects on the overall expected number of visits:

```
quietly zinb y age i.male lhincome i.lsahbad,                    ///
      inflate(age i.male lhincome i.lsahbad)
margins, dydx(*)
```

Table 11.11 Average marginal effects from zero-inflated NB model with variable zero-inflation probability

```
-------------------------------------------------------------------
Average marginal effects                    Number of obs  =    32164
Model VCE     : OIM
Expression    : Predicted number of events, predict()
dy/dx w.r.t.  : age 1.male lhincome 1.lsahbad
-------------------------------------------------------------------
```

	Delta-method					
	dy/dx	Std. Err.	z	P>|z|	[95% Conf. Interval]	
age	.003116	.0008153	3.82	0.000	.0015182	.0047139
1.male	-.4019505	.0272433	-14.75	0.000	-.4553463	-.3485546
lhincome	.3620779	.0192245	18.83	0.000	.3243985	.3997572
1.lsahbad	1.365602	.0553793	24.66	0.000	1.25706	1.474143

Note: dy/dx for factor levels is the discrete change from the base level.

11.5 HURDLE MODELS

The hurdle model implies that the count measure of health care utilisation is a result of two different decision processes. The first part specifies the decision to seek care, and the second part models the amount of health care for those individuals who receive some care. This can be interpreted as a principal–agent type model, where the physician (the agent) determines utilisation on behalf of the patient (the principal) once initial contact is made. Thus, it is assumed that the decision to seek care is taken by the individual, while the level of care depends also on supply factors. On statistical grounds, it has also been shown in the literature on health care utilisation that the two-part hurdle model is often a better starting point than the NB class, given the high proportion of zeros that often remains even after allowing for overdispersion (e.g. Pohlmeier and Ulrich, 1995; Grootendorst, 1995; Gerdtham, 1997).

The hurdle model for count data was proposed by Mullahy (1986). The participation decision and the positive counts are determined by two different processes $f_1(.)$ and $f_2(.)$. Formally:

$$g(0) = f_1(0)$$

$$g(y_i) = \frac{1 - f_1(0)}{1 - f_2(0)} f_2(y_i), \quad y_i > 0$$

The log-likelihood of the hurdle model is given by:

$$\ln L = \sum_{y_i=0} \ln \left[f_1(0) \right] + \sum_{y_i>0} \ln \left\{ \left[1 - f_1(0) \right] \frac{f_2(y_i)}{1 - f_2(0)} \right\}$$

$$= \underbrace{\left\{ \sum_{y_i=0} \ln \left[f_1(0) \right] + \sum_{y_i>0} \ln \left[1 - f_1(0) \right] \right\}}_{\ln L_1} + \underbrace{\sum_{y_i>0} \ln \left[\frac{f_2(y_i)}{1 - f_2(0)} \right]}_{\ln L_2}$$

The two parts of the hurdle model can therefore be estimated separately. The participation decision, $\Pr[y > 0]$, is determined by binary model, with log-likelihood $\ln L_1$. This could be any binary model but here we follow what has been the most common choice, the logit (this corresponds to a model where the zeros are determined by an NB2 model, with overdispersion parameter fixed to 1). The second decision determines the amount of use of health care, given participation, and is modelled by a truncated-at-zero count data model, with log-likelihood $\ln L_2$. This is to be estimated over the sample of positive observations, for which the probability of observing y, conditional on $y > 0$, is $g(y \mid y > 0) = f_2(y)/[1 - f_2(0)]$. The typical choice has been the truncated negative binomial, especially NB2, and this is the option we illustrate here. The mean in this model is the product of the probability of positives and the conditional mean of the zero-truncated density.

There have been numerous applications of the hurdle model in the context of health care utilisation. In Mullahy's original proposal (1986), the underlying distribution for both stages is the Poisson, i.e. the probability of observing a zero $(g(0) = f_1(0))$ is specified as in a Poisson model, and the positives are determined by another truncated-at-zero Poisson model. Pohlmeier and Ulrich (1995) argue that it is necessary to account for remaining unobserved heterogeneity, since 'supply side effects are rarely well captured in household data at the micro level'. Thus, these authors use the NB1 distribution for both stages of the model, instead of the Poisson. They use this specification to test distributional assumptions (against Mullahy's Poisson-hurdle) and the equality of the two parts of the decision-making process (Poisson-hurdle against Poisson; and NB1-hurdle against NB1, thus assessing the importance of allowing the number of physician visits to be determined by two different processes).

Gurmu (1997) notes a possible practical problem related to the hurdle model. When the sample size is small or the proportion on zeros is very high, it might be difficult to estimate the second part of the model. Gurmu suggests that, in this case, the researchers should focus on modelling the first stage, using binary models.

Estimate the hurdle logit-NB2 model using the user-written command hnblogit (Hilbe, 2005) and save the estimation results:

```
hnblogit y $xvars
estimates store hnb
```

Table 11.12 Logit-NB2 hurdle model

```
------------------------------------------------------------------
Negative Binomial-Logit Hurdle Regression      Number of obs =    32164
                                                Wald chi2(4)  =  2108.32
Log likelihood = -42275.99                      Prob > chi2   =   0.0000
------------------------------------------------------------------
             |    Coef.  Std. Err.     z   P>|z|  [95% Conf. Interval]
-------------|----------------------------------------------------
logit        |
         age |  .0081008  .0007538  10.75  0.000   .0066234   .0095782
        male | -.6061246  .0246338 -24.61  0.000  -.6544059  -.5578432
    lhincome |   .51122   .0188779  27.08  0.000    .47422     .54822
     lsahbad |  .7879607  .0308416  25.55  0.000   .7275122   .8484092
       _cons | -5.348587  .1721853 -31.06  0.000  -5.686064  -5.01111
-------------|----------------------------------------------------
negbinomial  |
         age | -.0008151  .0008804  -0.93  0.355  -.0025407   .0009106
        male | -.0487244   .029037  -1.68  0.093  -.1056359   .0081872
    lhincome |  .0627813  .0190673   3.29  0.001   .0254102   .1001525
     lsahbad |  .6155092  .0314509  19.57  0.000   .5538665   .6771519
       _cons |  -.187232  .1784201  -1.05  0.294   -.536929   .162465
-------------|----------------------------------------------------
    /lnalpha |  .7778783  .0566324  13.74  0.000   .6668808   .8888759
------------------------------------------------------------------
AIC Statistic =    2.629
```

Table 11.12 shows a positive effect of age, income and poor health and a negative effect of male on the probability of visiting a specialist (equation `logit`). It also shows that, conditional on having at least one visit, the expected number of visits increases significantly with poor health and income (equation `negbinomial`). The negative effect of male is only significant at 10 per cent, while the effect of age is non-significant.

The command `hnblogit` is not supported by `margins` but the latter can be used after the commands `logit` and `ztnb` (zero-truncated NB) which estimate the two parts of the hurdle models separately (by maximising, respectively, $\ln L_1$ and $\ln L_2$). The logit model has as dependent variable an indicator of whether the number of specialist visits is greater than zero. It is however not necessary to create this new variable since the `logit` command in Stata makes the necessary transformation automatically. The zero-truncated model, however, will return an error message if one does not request explicitly that the model be estimated only for positive observations ('`if  y>0`'). As above, estimate both models indicating which are the factor variables and then request the computation of average marginal effects. For the zero-truncated model, request average marginal effects on the expected number of visits, conditional on being positive (option `cm`):

```
quietly logit y age i.male lhincome i.lsahbad
margins, dydx(*)
quietly ztnb y age i.male lhincome i.lsahbad if y>0
margins, dydx(*) predict(cm)
```

Table 11.13 Average marginal effects on probability of receiving some health care from first part of hurdle model (Logit)

```
-----------------------------------------------------------------------
Average marginal effects                         Number of obs =    32164
Model VCE      : OIM
Expression     : Pr(y), predict()
dy/dx w.r.t. : age 1.male lhincome 1.lsahbad
-----------------------------------------------------------------------
                |             Delta-method
                |    dy/dx  Std. Err.       z  P>|z|  [95% Conf. Interval]
----------------|------------------------------------------------------
        age |  .0017121  .0001583   10.81  0.000   .0014017    .0020224
     1.male | -.1290776  .0051558  -25.04  0.000  -.1391827   -.1189724
   lhincome |  .1080432  .0038329   28.19  0.000   .1005309    .1155555
  1.lsahbad |  .1774785   .007081   25.06  0.000   .1636001     .191357
-----------------------------------------------------------------------
```

Note: dy/dx for factor levels is the discrete change from the base level.

Table 11.14 Average marginal effects on conditionally positive number of visits from second part of hurdle model (truncated NB2)

```
--------------------------------------------------------------------
Average marginal effects                    Number of obs  =   11266
Model VCE     : OIM
Expression    : Conditional mean of n|n>0, predict(cm)
dy/dx w.r.t.  : age 1.male lhincome 1.lsahbad
--------------------------------------------------------------------
            |         Delta-method
            |    dy/dx  Std. Err.     z   P>|z|  [95% Conf. Interval]
------------|-------------------------------------------------------
       age  | -.0017863  .0019295  -0.93  0.355  -.005568   .0019955
    1.male  |  -.106149  .0629232  -1.69  0.092 -.2294763   .0171782
  lhincome  |  .1375889  .0418665   3.29  0.001   .055532   .2196459
1.lsahbad   |  1.454354   .084784  17.15  0.000   1.28818   1.620527
--------------------------------------------------------------------
```

Note: dy/dx for factor levels is the discrete change from the base level.

11.6 FINITE MIXTURE/LATENT CLASS MODELS

Deb and Trivedi (1997) propose the use of finite mixture models as an alternative to the hurdle models in empirical modelling of health care utilisation. In a more recent paper, Deb and Trivedi (2002) point out that 'a more tenable distinction for typical cross-sectional data may be between an "infrequent user" and a "frequent user" of medical care, the difference being determined by health status, attitudes to health risk, and choice of lifestyle'. They argue that this is a better framework than the hurdle model, which distinguishes more starkly between users and non-users of care.

Deb and Trivedi (1997) point out a number of advantages of the finite mixture approach. It provides a natural representation since each latent class can be seen as a 'type' of individual, while still accommodating heterogeneity within each class. It can also be seen as a discrete approximation of an underlying continuous mixing distribution, which does not need to be specified. Furthermore, the number of points of support needed for the finite mixture model is low, usually two or three.

In the finite mixture (latent class) formulation of unobserved heterogeneity, the latent classes are assumed to be based on the person's latent long-term health status, which may not be well captured by proxy variables such as self-perceived health status and chronic health conditions (Cameron and Trivedi, 1998). The two-point finite mixture model suggests the dichotomy between the 'healthy' and the 'ill' groups, whose demands for health care are characterised by, respectively, low mean and low variance and high mean and high variance. Jiménez-Martín *et al.* (2002) agree with the advantages of the finite mixture model described above but also note a disadvantage. Namely, while the hurdle model is a natural extension of an economic model (the principal–agent model), the finite mixture model is driven by statistical reasoning.

In a latent class (LC) model, the population is assumed to be divided in C distinct populations in proportions $\pi_1, \ldots, \pi_C$, where $\sum_{j=1}^{C} \pi_j = 1$, $0 \leqslant \pi_j \leqslant 1$, $j = 1, \ldots, C$. The C-point finite mixture model is given by:

$$g\left(y_i \mid x_i; \pi_1, \ldots, \pi_C; \theta_1, \ldots, \theta_C\right) = \sum_{j=1}^{C} \pi_j f_j\left(y_i \mid x_i; \theta_j\right)$$

where the mixing probabilities π_j are estimated along with all the other parameters of the model, the elements of class-specific parameter vectors $\theta_1, \ldots, \theta_C$.

The latent class NB2 (LCNB) model assumes that each of the component distributions follows a NB2 model with mean $\lambda_{j,i}$ and overdispersion parameter α_j. So, we have:

$$f_j\left(y_i \mid x_i; \theta_j\right) = \frac{\Gamma\left(\alpha_j^{-1} + y_i\right)}{\Gamma\left(\alpha_j^{-1}\right)\Gamma\left(y_i + 1\right)} \left(\frac{\alpha_j^{-1}}{\lambda_{j,i} + \alpha_j^{-1}}\right)^{\alpha_j^{-1}} \left(\frac{\lambda_{j,i}}{\lambda_{j,i} + \alpha_j^{-1}}\right)^{y_i}$$

where $\theta_j = (\alpha_j, \beta_j)$, $\lambda_{j,i} = \exp(x_i \beta_j)$, α_j are overdispersion parameters, usually allowed to differ across latent classes, like slopes and constant terms in β_j. Unconditionally on the latent class the individual belongs to, the mean equals:

$$E\left[y_i \mid x_i\right] = \sum_{j=1}^{C} \pi_j \lambda_{j,i}$$

In the most general specification, all elements of the vectors β_j are allowed to vary across latent classes. However, more parsimonious specifications can arise from restrictions on the elements of $\theta_j = (\alpha_j, \beta_j)$, $j = 1, \ldots, C$. For example, the slope parameters can be restricted to be equal across all latent classes.

The number of classes in a finite mixture model is commonly chosen according to information criteria, such as the AIC and BIC. First, the standard negative binomial model is estimated, followed by the LC model with $C = 2$. The number of points of support C is chosen such that there is no further improvement in the information criterion when C is increased. In most applications, C equals 2 or 3. In this chapter, we illustrate the estimation of the LCNB just with $C = 2$.

We estimate the latent class NB2 model by maximum likelihood using the Broyden-Fletcher-Goldfarb-Shanno (BFGS) quasi-Newton algorithm. This can be done with the user-written command fmm (Deb, 2007) with option technique (bfgs). We find this algorithm works better in our case, but the default Newton–Raphson algorithm may also work well in some cases. The fmm command accommodates other latent class count data models, the LC Poisson and the LC NB1. Obtain and save results for the LC NB2 in the following way:

```
fmm y $xvars, components(2) mixtureof(negbin2) technique(bfgs)
estimates store lcnb
```

Due to the possibility of convergence to local maxima in latent class models, estimation should be repeated using different sets of starting values. Option shift() can be used to request alternative starting values based on the default algorithm, while with option from() users can specify their own choice of starting values (Deb, 2007). One option is to obtain them as combinations of the estimates of the one component version of the model (nbreg), which we illustrate in Section 11.7 in the estimation of the panel data LCNB.

The output presented in Table 11.15 shows the covariate coefficients and overdispersion parameter of the NB2 for class 1 (equation component1 and alpha1) and for class 2 (equation component2 and alpha2). The estimated class proportions are 0.681 (pi1) and 0.319 (pi2). All variables have coefficients of the same sign in both classes but they are all larger in absolute value, and more significant, for class 1.

Table 11.15 LCNB model with two latent classes

```
--------------------------------------------------------------------------
2 component Negative Binomial-2 regression     Number of obs  =    32164
                                               Wald chi2(8)   =  1107.96
Log likelihood = -42411.029                    Prob > chi2    =   0.0000
--------------------------------------------------------------------------
```

y	Coef.	Std. Err.	z	P>|z|	[95% Conf.	Interval]
component1						
age	.0113389	.0020648	5.49	0.000	.007292	.0153858
male	-1.078325	.0839914	-12.84	0.000	-1.242945	-.9137047
lhincome	1.150537	.0862307	13.34	0.000	.9815276	1.319546
lsahbad	1.424943	.0815151	17.48	0.000	1.265177	1.58471
_cons	-11.38737	.8204704	-13.88	0.000	-12.99546	-9.779276
component2						
age	.0030273	.0011168	2.71	0.007	.0008385	.0052162
male	-.1926466	.0364107	-5.29	0.000	-.2640102	-.121283
lhincome	.0810607	.027165	2.98	0.003	.0278183	.1343031
lsahbad	.6691553	.0437128	15.31	0.000	.5834797	.7548308
_cons	-.0533662	.2635908	-0.20	0.840	-.5699946	.4632623
/imlogitpi1	.7585781	.1239134	6.12	0.000	.5157122	1.001444
/lnalpha1	.9906783	.0465074	21.30	0.000	.8995256	1.081831
/lnalpha2	.4796346	.0811258	5.91	0.000	.320631	.6386382
alpha1	2.693061	.1252472			2.458436	2.950077
alpha2	1.615484	.1310574			1.377997	1.8939
pi1	.6810449	.0269168			.6261446	.7313424
pi2	.3189551	.0269168			.2686576	.3738554

We can compute fitted values for each latent class and analyse their summary statistics:

```
predict y_c1, equation(component1)
predict y_c2, equation(component2)
summarize y_c1 y_c2
drop y_c1 y_c2
```

The mean fitted value and the minimum value are substantially larger for class 2 (see Table 11.16). The maximum fitted value for class 1 is larger than for class 2 but y_c2 is larger than y_c1 for all but 1 per cent of the observations. Therefore, we refer to class 1 and class 2 as low users and high users, respectively.

Table 11.16 Summary statistics of fitted values by latent class (LCNB)

Variable	Obs	Mean	Std. Dev.	Min	Max
y_c1	32164	.6029914	.968401	.0007493	37.56749
y_c2	32164	2.499268	.9451077	1.221003	5.648476

The equality of the coefficients of all covariates across latent classes can be tested using a Wald test:

```
test [component1=component2]
```

The output shows clear rejection of the null hypothesis:

```
( 1)  [component1]age - [component2]age = 0
( 2)  [component1]male - [component2]male = 0
( 3)  [component1]lhincome - [component2]lhincome = 0
( 4)  [component1]lsahbad - [component2]lsahbad = 0

          chi2(4)    =   248.89
        Prob > chi2 =   0.0000
```

It was already noted that the estimated coefficients are larger in absolute value for class 1 (low users). Tests of equality of coefficients of individual covariates across classes can be performed in order to test whether the coefficients are significantly larger for low users. For example, for income:

```
test [component1]lhincome = [component2]lhincome
```

There is clear evidence that the income coefficient is larger for low users:

```
( 1)   [component1]lhincome - [component2]lhincome = 0
            chi2( 1)   =   133.37
         Prob > chi2 =   0.0000
```

Similar results (not shown) are obtained for the other three regressors.

Marginal effects and incremental effects conditional on latent class *j* are defined in the same way as for the Poisson and the negative binomial:

$$\frac{\partial E_j\left[y_i \mid x_i\right]}{\partial x_{ik}} = \beta_{jk} \, \exp\left(x_i\beta_j\right)$$

$$\frac{\Delta E_j\left[y_i \mid x_i\right]}{\Delta x_{ik}} = \exp\left(x_i\beta_j^{|x_{ik}=1}\right) - \exp\left(x_i\beta_j^{|x_{ik}=0}\right)$$

while effects unconditionally on latent class are an average of the above, weighted by the respective class proportion, π_j.

The fmm model is supported by the margins command but does not allow for factor variables. We can obtain average marginal effects for continuous variables, conditional on each latent class, as well as unconditionally:

```
margins, dydx(age lhincome) predict(equation(component1))
margins, dydx(age lhincome) predict(equation(component2))
margins, dydx(age lhincome)
```

Table 11.17 Average marginal effects of continuous regressors from LCNB model – latent class 1

```
------------------------------------------------------------------------
Warning: cannot perform check for estimable functions.

Average marginal effects                        Number of obs   =   32164
Model VCE    : OIM
Expression   : predicted mean: component1, predict(equation(component1))
dy/dx w.r.t. : age lhincome
------------------------------------------------------------------------
            |            Delta-method
            |     dy/dx   Std. Err.      z    P>|z|    [95% Conf. Interval]
------------|-----------------------------------------------------------
        age |   .0068373  .0013185    5.19   0.000    .004253    .0094215
   lhincome |   .6937638  .0547859   12.66   0.000    .5863854   .8011421
------------------------------------------------------------------------
```

Table 11.18 Average marginal effects of continuous regressors from LCNB model –
        latent class 2

```
-----------------------------------------------------------------------
Warning: cannot perform check for estimable functions.

Average marginal effects                    Number of obs  =    32164
Model VCE    : OIM
Expression   : predicted mean: component2, predict(equation(component2))
dy/dx w.r.t. : age lhincome
-----------------------------------------------------------------------
             |           Delta-method
             |    dy/dx    Std. Err.    z   P>|z|   [95% Conf. Interval]
-------------|---------------------------------------------------------
         age |  .0075661   .0027412   2.76  0.006   .0021933   .0129388
    lhincome |  .2025924   .0679498   2.98  0.003   .0694132   .3357715
-----------------------------------------------------------------------

Warning: cannot perform check for estimable functions.
```

Table 11.19 Average marginal effects of continuous regressors from LCNB model

```
-----------------------------------------------------------------------
Average marginal effects                    Number of obs  =    32164
Model VCE    : OIM

Expression   : predicted mean, predict()
dy/dx w.r.t. : age lhincome
-------------|---------------------------------------------------------
             |           Delta-method
             |    dy/dx   Std. Err.    z   P>|z|    [95% Conf. Interval]
-------------|---------------------------------------------------------
         age |  .0070697  .0009758   7.25  0.000    .0051573   .0089822
    lhincome |  .5371023  .0300633  17.87  0.000    .4781793   .5960252
-----------------------------------------------------------------------
```

For the binary variables, for example, for `male`, we can compute average
incremental effects in the following way:

```
preserve
replace male = 1
predict e_male1_1,  equation(component1)
predict e_male1_2,  equation(component2)
predict e_male1
replace male = 0
predict e_male0_1,  equation(component1)
predict e_male0_2,  equation(component2)
```

```
predict e_male0
generate ie_fmm_1 = e_male1_1-e_male0_1
generate ie_fmm_2 = e_male1_2-e_male0_2
generate ie_fmm = e_male1-e_male0
summarize ie_fmm_1 ie_fmm_2 ie_fmm
```

Table 11.20 Average incremental effects of male from LCNB model

Variable	Obs	Mean	Std. Dev.	Min	Max
ie_fmm_1	32164	-.5614774	.7663682	-27.03394	-.0004944
ie_fmm_2	32164	-.4756935	.168064	-1.004859	-.2407496
ie_fmm	32164	-.5341162	.5555374	-18.71578	-.077125

The hurdle and the LCNB models are usually compared using information criteria (AIC and BIC). As noted above, these criteria are also used to choose the number of latent classes in the LCNB. Here we compare the fit of all specifications considered so far, including the less common ZINB and generalised NB models:

```
estimates stats nb gnb zinb hnb lcnb
```

Table 11.21 shows that the AIC and the BIC improve considerably when two latent classes are considered, instead of the one component NB model. In practice, we should now move on to a model with three latent classes and set C equal to the number beyond which the information criteria do not improve. The AIC and BIC for the two-component LCNB are substantially larger than those shown above for the hurdle model, which means that the latter specification is preferred according to these criteria. However, the zero-inflated NB model provides the best fitting, with the same number of parameters as the hurdle, and more parsimonious than the LCNB. Further insight into the quality of fit of these models could be obtained through comparison of their fitted frequencies with observed frequencies

Table 11.21 AIC and BIC of alternative models

Model	Obs	ll(null)	ll(model)	df	AIC	BIC
nb	32164	-43668.13	-42753	6	85518	85568.27
gnb	32164	-43093.37	-42307.82	10	84635.63	84719.42
zinb	32164	-42472.45	-42218.81	11	84459.62	84551.79
hnb	32164	.	-42275.99	11	84573.98	84666.15
lcnb	32164	.	-42411.03	13	84848.06	84956.98

Note: N=Obs used in calculating BIC; see [R] BIC note

with the user-written command by Long and Freese (2006) `countfit y $xvars,`
`nbreg zinb` (results not shown here), for NB and ZINB, and manually for the
other models.

Recent empirical studies of health care utilisation have provided comparisons
between the performance of the hurdle model and the latent class model. In the
empirical applications in Deb and Trivedi (1997, 2002), it is found that a two-
point mixture of NB is sufficient to explain health care counts very well and
outperforms the NB hurdle. Deb and Holmes (2000) and Gerdtham and Trivedi
(2001) also present evidence in favour of the finite mixture model against the hurdle
model. Jiménez-Martín *et al.* (2002) however show that, in some cases, the hurdle
model can provide better results than the finite mixture model. They compare the
hurdle and the finite mixture specifications for visits to specialists and GPs in 12
EU countries. It is found that the finite mixture model performs better for the visits
to GPs while the hurdle model is preferred for specialists. Sarma and Simpson
(2006) also present evidence in favour of the hurdle model vs. latent class model
for specialists and vice-versa for general physicians (GPs) but, for specialists, like
here, the ZINB outperforms both.

11.7 LATENT CLASS MODELS FOR PANEL DATA

Recent empirical studies have used the latent class framework to model binary
indicators of health care utilisation in a panel data context (or with multiple
binary responses in a cross-section). Atella *et al.* (2004) model the probability of
visiting three types of physician jointly. Individuals are assumed to belong to
different latent classes. Within each latent class, the decision to visit each physician
type follows a probit distribution. An example of a binary mixture model with
panel data is the discrete random effects probit. Deb (2001) uses a latent class
model where only the constant varies across classes. The discrete random effects
probit is a discrete approximation of the distribution of the unobserved family
effects in the random effects probit. Bago d'Uva (2005) uses the latent class
approach to account for individual unobserved heterogeneity in panel data
models for access to and utilisation of primary care. Conditional on the latent
class, it is assumed that the probability of visiting a GP in a given year is determined by the logit model. In the model for the number of GP visits, as the
information on the dependent variable is grouped, an aggregated NB is used for
each latent class. In the context of smoking behaviour, Clark and Etilé (2006)
use the latent class framework to approximate the continuous distribution of
the individual effects in a dynamic random effects bivariate probit model. Clark
et al. (2005) develop a latent class ordered probit model for reported well-being,
in which individual time invariant heterogeneity is allowed both in the intercept
and in the income effect.

This section illustrates the application of two latent class models for panel data:
the latent class NB and the latent class hurdle. The panel structure is accounted
for in the formulation of the mixture, and the latent class framework represents

individual unobserved time-invariant heterogeneity. In other words, the distribution of the individual effects is approximated by a discrete distribution. Furthermore, the model accommodates heterogeneity in the slopes, as these can be allowed to vary across latent classes. We do not cover other more conventional panel data models for count data such as random effects or fixed effects Poisson and negative binomial (see, for example, Cameron and Trivedi, 2005, and, for Stata applications, Cameron and Trivedi, 2009). Other alternatives not considered here are the random effects hurdle model proposed by Van Ourti (2004) and, more recently, the fixed-effects latent class Poisson model (Deb and Trivedi, 2011), and the fixed-effects zero-inflated Poisson model (Majo and Van Soest, 2011).

This chapter uses a panel of individuals across time. Individuals i are observed T_i times. Let y_{it} represent the number of visits in year t. Denote the observations of the dependent and explanatory variables over the panel as $y_i = [y_{i1}, \ldots, y_{iT_i}]$ and $x_i = [x_{i1}, \ldots, x_{iT_i}]$. Consider that individual i belongs to a latent class $j, j = 1, \ldots, C$, and that individuals are heterogeneous across classes. Given the class that individual i belongs to, the dependent variable in a given year t, y_{it} has density $f_j(y_{it} \mid x_{it}; \theta_j)$, with θ_j vectors of parameters specific to each class. Given class j, the joint density of the dependent variable over the observed periods is a product of T_i independent densities $f_j(y_{it} \mid x_{it}; \theta_j)$. The probability of belonging to class j is π_{ij}, where $0 < \pi_{ij} < 1$ and $\sum_{j=1}^{C} \pi_{ij} = 1$. Unconditionally on the latent class, the individual belongs to, the joint density of $y_i = [y_{i1}, \ldots, y_{iT_i}]$ is given by:

$$g\left(y_i \mid x_i; \pi_{i1}, \ldots, \pi_{iC}; \theta_1, \ldots, \theta_C\right) = \sum_{j=1}^{C} \pi_{ij} \prod_{t=1}^{T_i} f_j\left(y_{it} \mid x_{it}; \theta_j\right)$$

In most empirical applications of latent class model to health care utilisation, class membership probabilities are taken as fixed parameters $\pi_{ij} = \pi_j, j = 1, \ldots, C$, to be estimated along with $\theta_1, \ldots, \theta_C$ (Deb and Trivedi, 1997, 2002; Deb and Holmes, 2000; Deb, 2001; Jiménez-Martín *et al.*, 2002, Atella *et al.*, 2004). This assumption is analogous to a random effects or random parameters specification that assumes that individual heterogeneity is uncorrelated with the regressors.

There are currently no Stata built-in or user-written commands for estimation of latent class models for panel data. We define specific programs for this purpose. As the panel data models that we use here assume that each individual belongs to the same latent class throughout the panel, specification of the likelihood becomes simpler if we convert the data from the usual long form (where each row represents one period t for individual i, identified here by variable `pidc`, and each column represents one variable z) to wide form (where each row represents one individual and variable z across periods $1, \ldots, T$ is represented by columns $z1, \ldots, zT$). First we recode the variable `wave` so that the remaining code is valid for panels with waves numbered 1 to 4, after which we apply the `reshape` command:

```
replace wave=wave-1
reshape wide y $xvars , i(pidc) j(wave)
```

The output displayed after this command describes clearly the transformations that `reshape` performs in the dataset:

```
(note: j = 1 2 3 4)

Data                        long  ->  wide
-----------------------------------------------------------------------------
Number of obs.             32164  ->  8041
Number of variables            8  ->  22
j variable (4 values)       wave  ->  (dropped)
xij variables:
                               y  ->  y1 y2 ... y4
                             age  ->  age1 age2 ... age4
                            male  ->  male1 male2 ... male4
                        lhincome  ->  lhincome1 lhincome2 ... lhincome4
                         lsahbad  ->  lsahbad1 lsahbad2 ... lsahbad4
-----------------------------------------------------------------------------
```

Create new lists of variables to be used in the estimation of latent class models for panel data:

```
global xvar1 "age1 male1 lhincome1 lsahbad1"
global xvar2 "age2 male2 lhincome2 lsahbad2"
global xvar3 "age3 male3 lhincome3 lsahbad3"
global xvar4 "age4 male4 lhincome4 lsahbad4"
```

Latent class negative binomial model for panel data

Specification of the latent class NB model for panel data (LCNB-Pan) is completed by defining the component densities in the same way as for the LCNB model above:

$$f_j\left(y_{it} \mid x_{it}; \theta_j\right) = \frac{\Gamma\left(\alpha_j^{-1} + y_{it}\right)}{\Gamma\left(\alpha_j^{-1}\right)\Gamma\left(y_{it} + 1\right)} \left(\frac{\alpha_j^{-1}}{\lambda_{j,it} + \alpha_j^{-1}}\right)^{\alpha_j^{-1}} \left(\frac{\lambda_{j,it}}{\lambda_{j,it} + \alpha_j^{-1}}\right)^{y_{it}},$$

where, also as above, for each latent class j, $j = 1, \ldots, C$, $\theta_j = (\alpha_j, \beta_j)$, α_j are over-dispersion parameters, and $\lambda_{j,it} = \exp(x_{it}\beta_j)$.

This model differs, however, from the LCNB (Deb and Trivedi, 1997, 2002) presented above, in that it accounts for the panel structure of the data. Comparison of the fit of non-nested models LCNB and LCNB-Pan shows the extent to which it is relevant to account for the panel data structure in the latent class frame-work.

The program `lcnb_pan` defines the log-likelihood of a model with two latent classes and a NB2 for each class. The program is specific to a balanced panel with 4 waves and is to be applied to a panel dataset in wide form. It is shown in the

Appendix. Save it in a separate Stata .do file called 'lcnb_pan.do', and then call it using the following command:

```
run "lcnb_pan.do"
```

The program lcnb_pan does not account for the assumption of the LCNB-Pan that the parameters contained in $\theta_j, j = 1,2$, are constant throughout the panel, which has to be done through specification of constraints to be imposed in the estimation of the model below:

```
constraint drop _all
global i=1
foreach wave in 2 3 4 {
    foreach var in $xvars {
        constraint $i [xb1]`var'1=[xb1_w`wave']`var'`wave'
        global i=$i+1
        constraint $i [xb2]`var'1=[xb2_w`wave']`var'`wave'
        global i=$i+1
    }
    constraint $i [xb1]_cons=[xb1_w`wave']_cons
    global i=$i+1
    constraint $i [xb2]_cons=[xb2_w`wave']_cons
    global i=$i+1
    constraint $i [alpha1]_cons=[alpha1_w`wave']_cons
    global i=$i+1
    constraint $i [alpha2]_cons=[alpha2_w`wave']_cons
    global i=$i+1
}
global i=$i-1
```

As noted above, to avoid local maxima in latent class models, one should repeat estimation using different sets of starting values. Here, we illustrate the preparation of starting values equal to the estimates of nbreg for both classes, except for the constant terms, which are defined as the constant term of nbreg multiplied by (1+d_init) and (1-d_init). In order to start the estimation from $\pi_1 = 0.5$, the starting value for $\log(\pi_1/(1 - \pi_1))$ is 0 (scalar initpi=0). For the LCNB-Pan, we also need to initialise the parameters corresponding to waves 2 to 4, constrained to be the same as the ones for wave 1. Use initc1, initc2 as vectors of initial values for waves 1 to 4:

```
estimates restore
matrix bnb = e(b)
scalar d_init=.20
matrix initc1=(bnb[1,1..e(k)-2],                          ///
    (1+d_init)*bnb[1,e(k)-1],e(alpha))
```

```
matrix initc2=(bnb[1,1..e(k)-2],                           ///
    (1-d_init)*bnb[1,e(k)-1],e(alpha))
scalar initpi=0
matrix initlcpan=(initc1,initc2, initpi,                   ///
    initc1,initc1,initc1, initc2,initc2,initc2)
```

With the syntax below, the LCNB-Pan is estimated and the parameters of interest are displayed. The option constraints(1-$i) imposes the specified constraints during estimation. When nooutput is specified as an option in ml maximize, Stata suppresses the display of the final results and shows just the iteration log. The output can then be specified using the options of the command ml display. The option diparm(pi,invlogit p) determines that the displayed table of results is to include not only the estimate of $\log(\pi_1/(1 - \pi_1))$ (constant term in equation pi) but also of π_1. The option neq(5) requests that only the estimation results for the first five equations (xb1, alpha1, xb2, alpha2 and pi) be displayed. The omitted results correspond to the parameters for waves 2 to 4, restricted to be the same as for wave 1:

```
ml model lf lcnb_pan (xb1: $xvars1)(alpha1:)              ///
                     (xb2: $xvars1)(alpha2:) (pi:)        ///
(xb1_w2: $xvars2) (alpha1_w2:)                            ///
(xb1_w3: $xvars3) (alpha1_w3:)                            ///
(xb1_w4: $xvars4) (alpha1_w4:)                            ///
(xb2_w2: $xvars2) (alpha2_w2:)                            ///
(xb2_w3: $xvars3) (alpha2_w3:)                            ///
(xb2_w4: $xvars4) (alpha2_w4:),                           ///
  technique(bfgs) constraints(1-$i)
ml init initlcpan, skip copy
ml maximize, nooutput
ml display, neq(5) diparm(pi,invlogit p)
```

Table 11.22 shows estimation results for the LCNB-Pan. It is interesting to compare these with the estimates of the LCNB in Table 11.15. Class proportions and parameters for class 2 are more precisely estimated in the panel data model, while for class 1 that is the case of all parameters except for the overdispersion parameter. All coefficients have the same signs as in the LCNB. The magnitudes of the effects of male, income and poor health in class 1 are substantially larger in the pooled LCNB. The panel model provides a better fit to the data, with the same number of parameters.

In order to compute fitted values, predict $x_{it}\beta_j$ for each latent class and each wave, then reshape back to long form and compute fitted values and the respective summary statistics (see Table 11.23):

```
predict xb1_1, equation(xb1)
predict xb2_1, equation(xb2)
```

Table 11.22 LCNB-Pan with two latent classes

```
--------------------------------------------------------------------
                                      Number of obs  =   8041
                                      Wald chi2(0)   =      .
Log likelihood = -41061.181           Prob > chi2    =      .
```

(Stata also displays the list of constraints imposed, not shown here)

```
--------------------------------------------------------------------
             |    Coef.  Std. Err.     z   P>|z|  [95% Conf. Interval]
-------------|------------------------------------------------------
xb1          |
        age1 |  .0174695  .0019129   9.13  0.000   .0137203   .0212187
       male1 | -.6839307  .0616763 -11.09  0.000  -.8048139  -.5630474
   lhincome1 |  .514844   .0545542   9.44  0.000   .4079197   .6217683
    lsahbad1 |  .5056444  .0734561   6.88  0.000   .3616731   .6496156
       _cons |  -6.2993   .5233294 -12.04  0.000  -7.325007  -5.273594
-------------|------------------------------------------------------
alfa1        |
       _cons | 4.744802   .2623315  18.09  0.000   4.230641   5.258962
-------------|------------------------------------------------------
xb2          |
        age1 |  .0028421  .0009119   3.12  0.002   .0010547   .0046295
       male1 | -.1875385  .0305506  -6.14  0.000  -.2474165  -.1276604
   lhincome1 |  .1509927  .0180485   8.37  0.000   .1156182   .1863671
    lsahbad1 |  .614637   .0299928  20.49  0.000   .5558521   .6734219
       _cons | -.6166755  .170176   -3.62  0.000  -.9502143  -.2831367
-------------|------------------------------------------------------
alfa2        |
       _cons | 1.246937   .0374331  33.31  0.000   1.173569   1.320304
-------------|------------------------------------------------------
pi           |
       _cons |  .5839477  .0530388  11.01  0.000   .4799934   .6879019
-------------|------------------------------------------------------
         /pi |  .6419753  .0121906                 .6177463   .6655
--------------------------------------------------------------------
```

Table 11.23 Summary statistics of fitted values by latent class (LCNB-Pan)

```
--------------------------------------------------------------------
    Variable |   Obs     Mean      Std. Dev.     Min        Max
-------------|------------------------------------------------------
        y_c1 |  32164  .3580019   .2416036     .015022    3.212535
        y_c2 |  32164  2.521117   .8735082     .9543253   6.53659
--------------------------------------------------------------------
```

```
foreach wave in 2 3 4 {
        predict xb1_`wave', equation(xb1_w`wave')
        predict xb2_`wave', equation(xb2_w`wave')
}
reshape long y $xvars xb1_ xb2_ , i(pidc) j(wave)
generate y_c1=exp(xb1_)
generate y_c2=exp(xb2_)
drop xb1_ xb2_
summarize y_c1 y_c2
drop y_c1 y_c2
```

The mean fitted value, maximum and minimum values are substantially larger for class 2, to which we can refer to as class of high users (see Table 11.23). The disparity between the mean fitted values in the LCNB-Pan is larger than what was shown in Table 11.15 for the LCNB.

In order to assess the extent to which the two classes respond differently to the covariates considered, we can perform tests of equality of coefficients. When considered jointly, the coefficients of the two classes of users are significantly different:

```
test [xb1=xb2]

 ( 1)  [xb1]age1 - [xb2]age1 = 0
 ( 2)  [xb1]male1 - [xb2]male1 = 0
 ( 3)  [xb1]lhincome1 - [xb2]lhincome1 = 0
 ( 4)  [xb1]lsahbad1 - [xb2]lsahbad1 = 0

         chi2( 4)  =   146.51
       Prob > chi2 =   0.0000
```

In particular, the estimated coefficient of income is significantly higher for low users:

```
test [xb1]lhincome1 = [xb2]lhincome1

 ( 1)  [xb1]lhincome1 - [xb2]lhincome1 = 0

         chi2( 1) =   44.71
       Prob > chi2 =   0.0000
```

The same can be said of the coefficients of male and age (not shown here). No significant difference is found between the estimated coefficients of lsahbad for high and low users:

```
test [xb1]lsahbad1 = [xb2]lsahbad1

( 1)  [xb1]lsahbad1 - [xb2]lsahbad1 = 0

        chi2( 1) =   1.91
      Prob > chi2 =   0.1670
```

The LCNB-Pan can be compared to the one component NB and the LCNB by means of the information criteria AIC and BIC:

```
estimates store lcnb_pan
estimates stats nb lcnb lcnb_pan
```

Table 11.24 shows that the LCNB-Pan performs better than the NB according to information criteria, which provides evidence of unobserved individual heterogeneity. The panel version of the latent class model outperforms the LCNB. Given that the ZINB was shown to provide the best fit amongst the cross-sectional models, it would also be interesting to consider panel data versions of zero-inflated models such as the fixed-effects ZIP model proposed by Majo and Van Soest (2011).

Table 11.24 AIC and BIC of NB, LCNB and LCNB-Pan (with two latent classes)

Model		nobs	ll(null)	ll(model)	df	AIC	BIC
nb	|	32164	-43668.13	-42753	6	85518	85568.27
lcnb	|	32164	.	-42411.03	13	84848.06	84956.98
lcnb_pan	|	8041	.	-41061.18	13	82148.36	82239.26

Latent class hurdle model for panel data

Bago d'Uva (2006) proposes a model that combines the hurdle and the finite mixture models in a single specification. Following the latent class model, it is assumed that each individual is a draw from one of a finite number of classes. Then, for each class, the hypothesis that the decision concerning the number of visits is taken in two steps is not discarded. Individual health care use in a given period is therefore specified as a two-stage decision process, conditional on the latent class.

More formally, conditionally on the class that the individual belongs to, the number of visits in period t, y_{it}, is assumed to be determined by a hurdle model. In this example, as in Section 11.5, we use a hurdle logit-NB2 model. Formally, for each component j, $j = 1,\ldots,C$, it is assumed that the probability of zero visits and the probability of observing y_{it} visits, given that y_{it} is positive, are given by the following expressions:

$$f_j\left(0\mid x_{it};\beta_{j1}\right)=\left(\lambda_{j1,it}+1\right)^{-1}$$

$$f_j\left(y_{it}\mid y_{it}>0;x_{it};\alpha_j,\beta_{j2}\right)=\frac{\Gamma\left(\alpha_j^{-1}+y_{it}\right)\left(\alpha_j\lambda_{j2,it}+1\right)^{-\alpha_j^{-1}}\left(1+\alpha_j^{-1}\lambda_{j2,it}\right)^{-y_{it}}}{\Gamma\left(\alpha_j^{-1}\right)\Gamma\left(y_{it}+1\right)\left[1-\left(\alpha_j\lambda_{j2,it}+1\right)^{-\alpha_j^{-1}}\right]}$$

where $\lambda_{j1,it} = \exp(x_{it}\beta_{j1})$, $\lambda_{j2,it} = \exp(x_{it}\beta_{j2})$, and α_j are overdispersion parameters. So, in this case, $\theta_j = (\beta_{j1},\beta_{j2},\alpha_j)$. Unconditionally on the latent class the individual belongs to, the joint density of $y_i = [y_{i1},\dots,y_{iT_i}]$ is obtained by replacing the component densities in $g(y_i\mid x_i; \pi_{i1},\dots,\pi_{iC};\theta_1,\dots,\theta_C)$ defined above. It can easily be shown that the resulting log-likelihood is not separable into the log-likelihoods of a binary and a truncated part, as the standard hurdle, so the full model should be estimated jointly.

Having $[\beta_{j1},\beta_{j2}] \neq [\beta_{l1},\beta_{l2}]$ for $j \neq l$, reflects the differences between latent classes. It can be assumed that all slopes are the same, varying only the constant terms, $\beta_{j1,0}$ and $\beta_{j2,0}$, and the overdispersion parameters α_j. This represents a case where there is unobserved individual heterogeneity but not in the responses to the covariates (as in the model used in Deb, 2001). The most flexible version allows α_j and all elements of β_{j1} and β_{j2} to vary across classes.

Estimation of the LCH-Pan also requires a specific program (lchurdle_pan, shown in the Appendix). Again, we present a program for a model with two latent classes and four waves of data, which can be easily extended to a specification with more classes and a longer panel. Having previously saved the program in a .do file called 'lchurdle_pan.do', call it using the following command:

```
run "lchurdle_pan.do"
```

As in the lcnb2_pan, impose the constraints that the parameters are the same throughout the panel.

```
constraint drop _all
global i=1
foreach wave in 2 3 4 {
  foreach part in prob trunc {
    foreach var in $xvars {
      constraint $i [xb1_`part']`var'1              ///
          =[xb1_`part'_w`wave']`var'`wave'
      global i=$i+1
      constraint $i [xb2_`part']`var'1              ///
          =[xb2_`part'_w`wave']`var'`wave'
      global i=$i+1
    }
```

```
      constraint $i [xb1_`part'] cons=[xb1_`part'_w`wave'] cons
      global i=$i+1
      constraint $i [xb2_`part'] cons=[xb2_`part'_w`wave'] cons
      global i=$i+1
      }
      constraint $i [alpha1]_cons=[alpha1_w`wave'] cons
      global i=$i+1
      constraint $i [alpha2]_cons=[alpha2_w`wave'] cons
      global i=$i+1
}
constraint list
global i=$i-1
```

This program also requires that the dataset is in wide form so we return to this
form prior to estimation:

```
reshape wide y $xvars , i(pidc) j(wave)
```

Before estimating the model, we define initial values for the parameters, using
the estimates of the hurdle model (Table 11.12). The vector initlchurdle is
constructed in a similar way as initlcpan above, except that now we need to
initialise the parameters of the binary part (initc1_prob, initc2_prob) and
of the truncated part (initc1_trunc, initc2_trunc). Here, we use starting
values equal to the estimates of the two parts of the hurdle logit-NB2 from
hnblogit (logit and negbinomial, respectively) for both classes, except for
the constant terms, which are defined as the constant terms of hnblogit multiplied
by (1+d_init) and (1-d_init), respectively, for class 1 and class 2. Here we
also save the number of parameters of the hurdle model (k_hurdle) for later use.
The initial value for α_1 and α_2 is defined as exp([lnalpha]_cons) since the
command hnblogit saves the estimate of ln (α) and not of α:

```
estimates restore hnb
matrix bhnb = e(b)
scalar k_hurdle = e(k)
matrix blogit_slopes = bhnb[1,1..(e(k)-3)/2]
matrix blogit_c = [logit]_cons
matrix btrunc_slopes = bhnb[1,(e(k)+1)/2..e(k)-2]
matrix btrunc_c = [negbinomial]_cons
matrix btrunc_a = exp([lnalpha]_cons)

scalar d_init=.2
matrix initc1_prob =(blogit_slopes,(1+ d_init)*blogit_c)
matrix initc2_prob =(blogit_slopes,(1- d_init)*blogit_c)
matrix initc1_trunc=(btrunc_slopes,(1+ d_init)*btrunc_c,btrunc_a)
matrix initc2_trunc=(btrunc_slopes,(1- d_init)*btrunc_c,btrunc_a)
```

```
matrix initpi=0
matrix initlchurdle=(initc1_prob,initc1_trunc,                    ///
                     initc2_prob,initc2_trunc,                    ///
                     initpi,                                      ///
                     initc1_prob,initc1_prob,initc1_prob,         ///
                     initc2_prob,initc2_prob, initc2_prob,        ///
                     initc1_trunc,initc1_trunc,initc1_trunc, ///
                     initc2_trunc,initc2_trunc,initc2_trunc)
```

As noted above, starting values can be specified in many different ways and estimation should be repeated with different sets of starting values in order to avoid local maxima.

The log-likelihood defined by program lchurdle_pan is maximised, starting from the vector initlchurdle. This program specifies equations for the binary part and the truncated part of the hurdle model as well as for pi, which in this case is constant. The estimation results are saved in vector blchurdle. Again, the full set of estimation results is suppressed (nooutput) and only the relevant parameters are shown (neq(6) diparm(pi,invlogit p)):

```
ml model lf lchurdle_pan
(xb1_prob: $xvars1) (xb1_trunc: $xvars1) (alpha1:)            ///
(xb2_prob: $xvars1) (xb2_trunc: $xvars1) (alpha2:) (pi:)      ///
(xb1_prob_w2:$xvars2 (xb1_prob_w3:$xvars3)                    ///
(xb1_prob_w4:$xvars4 (xb2_prob_w2:$xvars2)                    ///
(xb2_prob_w3:$xvars3) (xb2_prob_w4: $xvars4)                  ///
(xb1_trunc_w2:$xvars2) (alpha1_w2:)                           ///
(xb1_trunc_w3:$xvars3) (alpha1_w3:)                           ///
(xb1_trunc_w4:$xvars4) (alpha1_w4:)                           ///
(xb2_trunc_w2:$xvars2) (alpha2_w2:)                           ///
(xb2_trunc_w3:$xvars3) (alpha2_w3:)                           ///
(xb2_trunc_w4:$xvars4) (alpha2_w4:),                          ///
 technique(bfgs) constraints(1-$i)
ml init initlchurdle, skip copy
ml maximize, nooutput
ml display, neq(6) diparm(pi,invlogit p)
estimates store lchurdle_pan
```

The estimation results of the LCH-Pan are presented in Table 11.25, with class proportions estimated as 0.653 and 0.347, respectively, for class 1 and class 2. Consistently across classes and in both parts, positive effects are estimated for age, income and poor health, while there are negative effects for males. The coefficients in the binary part are more significant than those in the truncated part, for both classes.

Table 11.25 LCH-Pan (with two latent classes), with constant class membership

```
---------------------------------------------------------------------
                                   Number of obs   =      8041
                                   Wald chi2(0)    =        .
Log likelihood = -40674.74         Prob > chi2     =        .
```

(Stata also displays the list of constraints imposed, not shown here)

	Coef.	Std. Err.	z	P>|z|	[95% Conf.	Interval]
xb1_prob						
age1	.0165935	.0015292	10.85	0.000	.0135964	.0195906
male1	-.683093	.0541969	-12.60	0.000	-.7893169	-.5768691
lhincome1	.6353438	.0438232	14.50	0.000	.5494519	.7212356
lsahbad1	.474868	.0588503	8.07	0.000	.3595235	.5902125
_cons	-7.661458	.4069215	-18.83	0.000	-8.45901	-6.863907
xb1_trunc						
age1	.0068269	.001723	3.96	0.000	.0034498	.0102039
male1	-.3500083	.0588734	-5.95	0.000	-.4653981	-.2346186
lhincome1	.0175322	.0402518	0.44	0.663	-.0613598	.0964242
lsahbad1	.1685644	.0555284	3.04	0.002	.0597307	.277398
_cons	-.1151454	.3876669	-0.30	0.766	-.8749586	.6446679
alpha1						
_cons	.2188574	.0597116	3.67	0.000	.1018248	.3358899
xb2_prob						
age1	.0150065	.001836	8.17	0.000	.011408	.018605
male1	-.8800947	.0596438	-14.76	0.000	-.9969945	-.7631949
lhincome1	.462893	.0358158	12.92	0.000	.3926954	.5330906
lsahbad1	.8976633	.0677867	13.24	0.000	.7648038	1.030523
_cons	-3.801972	.3272878	-11.62	0.000	-4.443444	-3.1605
xb2_trunc						
age1	.0017156	.0010958	1.57	0.117	-.0004322	.0038634
male1	-.0598784	.0359852	-1.66	0.096	-.1304081	.0106512
lhincome1	.089013	.0225199	3.95	0.000	.0448748	.1331512
lsahbad1	.5809951	.037379	15.54	0.000	.5077337	.6542565
_cons	-.133006	.2079016	-0.64	0.522	-.5404857	.2744738
alpha2						
_cons	1.641227	.0983986	16.68	0.000	1.448369	1.834085
/pi	.6529417	.0116303			.6298105	.6753726

We compare the models LCNB-Pan, LCH-Pan and standard hurdle model according to information criteria, displaying the results for the new model together with the ones stored earlier:

```
estimates stats lcnb_pan hnb lchurdle_pan
```

The LCH-Pan outperforms the LCNB-Pan, even penalising for the larger number of parameters (see Table 11.26). Recall that these criteria are usually considered in the choice of the number of latent classes. We can compare the AIC of the LCH-Pan with those of the (degenerate) one class hurdle model to assess whether moving from one class to two classes improves this criterion. We can also compare the BIC of the LCH-Pan with that of the hurdle model but in this case not the one that is given directly by estimates stats (as this uses N equal to the number of observations 32,164, rather than individuals, 8041), but the BIC computed manually 84650.895. Both AIC and BIC are considerable larger for the hurdle than for the LCH-Pan shown in Table 11.25, providing evidence of unobserved time-invariant heterogeneity within the hurdle framework.

Table 11.26 AIC and BIC of LCNB-Pan, hurdle and LCH-Pan

Model		nobs	ll(null)	ll(model)	df	AIC	BIC
lcnb_pan	|	8041	.	-41061.18	13	82148.36	82239.26
hnb	|	32164	.	-42275.99	11	84573.98	84666.15
lchurdle_pan	|	8041	.	-40674.74	23	81395.48	81556.3

Note: N=Obs used in calculating BIC; see [R] BIC note

The latent class models estimated so far have assumed constant class membership (π and $1-\pi$), following the most common approach in latent class models for health care utilisation. In the context of panel data models, this is analogous to a random effects or random parameters specification that assumes no correlation between individual heterogeneity and the regressors. A generalisation is obtained when individual heterogeneity is parameterised as a function of time invariant individual characteristics z_i, as in Mundlak (1978). To implement this approach in the case of the latent class model, class membership can be modelled as a multinomial logit (as in, for example, Clark and Etilé, 2006; Clark *et al.*, 2005; Bago d'Uva, 2005):

$$\pi_{ij} = \frac{\exp\left(z_i \gamma_j\right)}{\sum_{g=1}^{C} \exp\left(z_i \gamma_g\right)} , \quad j = 1, \ldots, C ,$$

with $\gamma_C = 0$. This uncovers the determinants of class membership. In a panel data context, this parameterisation provides a way of accounting for the possibility that the observed regressors may be correlated with the individual effect. Let $z_i = \bar{x}_i$ be the average of the covariates across the observed panel. This is in line with what has been done in recent studies to allow for the correlation between covariates and random effects, following the suggestion of authors such as Mundlak (1978). The vectors of parameters $\theta_1, \ldots, \theta_C, \gamma_1, \ldots, \gamma_{C-1}$, are estimated jointly by maximum likelihood.

In order to specify class membership probabilities as functions of $z_i = \bar{x}_i$, create means of the covariates across the panel and the respective list:

```
foreach var in $xvars {
    egen mean`var'=rmean( `var'1 `var'2 `var'3 `var'4)
}
global xvarmean "meanage meanmale meanlhincome meanlsahbad"
```

A possible set of starting values for this model is the set of estimates of the LC hurdle with constant class membership probabilities blchurdle. In vector γ (in $\pi_i = \exp(z_i\gamma)/(1+\exp(z_i\gamma))$, the coefficients of the covariates are initialised as zeros, except for the constant term, which starts at the estimate in the model with constant π. Starting values for γ are defined in vector initpi.

```
estimates restore lchurdle_pan
matrix blchurdle = e(b)
scalar initpi0=[pi]_cons
matrix initpi_slopes=blogit_slopes-blogit_slopes
matrix initpi=(initpi_slopes,initpi0)
matrix initlchurdle=(blchurdle[1,1..k_hurdle*2],              ///
        initpi, blchurdle[1, k_hurdle*2+2..colsof(blchurdle)])
```

Estimation uses again the program lchurdle_pan, except that now the means of the covariates within individual, z_i, are included in the equation that corresponds to π (pi:$xvarsmean). Estimates of the relevant parameters are shown:

```
ml model lf lchurdle_pan
  (xb1_prob: $xvars1) (xb1_trunc: $xvars1) (alpha1:)        ///
  (xb2_prob: $xvars1) (xb2_trunc: $xvars1) (alpha2:)        ///
  (pi:$xvarsmean)                                           ///
  (xb1_prob_w2:$xvars2) (xb1_prob_w3:$xvars3)               ///
  (xb1_prob_w4:$xvars4) (xb2_prob_w2:$xvars2)               ///
  (xb2_prob_w3:$xvars3) (xb2_prob_w4:$xvars4)               ///
  (xb1_trunc_w2:$xvars2) (alpha1_w2:                        ///
  (xb1_trunc_w3:$xvars3) (alpha1_w3:                        ///
  (xb1_trunc_w4:$xvars4) (alpha1_w4:)                       ///
  (xb2_trunc_w2:$xvars2) (alpha2_w2                         ///
  (xb2_trunc_w3:$xvars3) (alpha2_w3:)                       ///
  (xb2_trunc_w4:$xvars4) (alpha2_w4:),                      ///
```

Table 11.27 LCH-Pan (with two latent classes), with variable class membership

```
--------------------------------------------------------------------
                                    Number of obs  =     8041
                                    Wald chi2(0)   =        .
Log likelihood = -40498.679         Prob > chi2    =        .
```

(Stata also displays the list of constraints imposed, not shown here)

```
--------------------------------------------------------------------
             |    Coef.  Std. Err.     z   P>|z|  [95% Conf. Interval]
-------------|------------------------------------------------------
xb1_prob     |
        age1 |  .0208469  .0017624  11.83  0.000   .0173927   .0243012
       male1 | -.4017464  .0697666  -5.76  0.000  -.5384864  -.2650064
   lhincome1 |  .4398147  .0496108   8.87  0.000   .3425793   .5370501
   lsahbad1  |  .1541958  .0630061   2.45  0.014   .0307061   .2776856
       _cons | -6.185561  .4539121 -13.63  0.000  -7.075213   -5.29591
-------------|------------------------------------------------------
xb1_trunc    |
        age1 |  .0067402  .0017525   3.85  0.000   .0033054    .010175
       male1 | -.1621718  .0566563  -2.86  0.004  -.2732161  -.0511275
   lhincome1 | -.0654131  .0402198  -1.63  0.104  -.1442425   .0134163
   lsahbad1  |  .0618253  .0587842   1.05  0.293  -.0533897   .1770403
       _cons |  .5546553  .3834037   1.45  0.148   -.196802   1.306113
-------------|------------------------------------------------------
alfa1        |
       _cons |  .2626437  .0725251   3.62  0.000   .1204971   .4047902
-------------|------------------------------------------------------
xb2_prob     |
        age1 |   .015747  .0024971   6.31  0.000   .0108529   .0206412
       male1 | -.5022037  .0840317  -5.98  0.000  -.6669027  -.3375046
   lhincome1 |   .342913  .0414058   8.28  0.000    .261759   .4240669
   lsahbad1  |  .5231293  .0719303   7.27  0.000   .3821484   .6641101
       _cons |  -2.77847  .3838727  -7.24  0.000  -3.530847  -2.026094
-------------|------------------------------------------------------
xb2_trunc    |
        age1 |  .0029462  .0012085   2.44  0.015   .0005776   .0053148
       male1 |  .0560933  .0418872   1.34  0.181  -.0260041   .1381907
   lhincome1 |  .0446213  .0245924   1.81  0.070   -.003579   .0928215
   lsahbad1  |  .4554031  .0385214  11.82  0.000   .3799026   .5309036
       _cons |   .221972  .2256708   0.98  0.325  -.2203345   .6642786
-------------|------------------------------------------------------
alfa2        |
       _cons |  1.58942  .0925368  17.18  0.000   1.408051   1.770788
-------------|------------------------------------------------------
pi           |
     meanage |  .0191768  .0030117   6.37  0.000   .0132741   .0250796
    meanmale |  .5826916  .1081308   5.39  0.000   .3707592    .794624
meanlhincome | -.5913602  .0785008  -7.53  0.000   -.745219  -.4375014
 meanlsahbad | -1.887485  .1194501 -15.80  0.000  -2.121602  -1.653367
       _cons |  5.144382  .7123858   7.22  0.000   3.748131   6.540632
--------------------------------------------------------------------
```

(command continued from page 331)

```
technique(bfgs) constraints(1-$i)
ml init initlchurdle, skip copy
ml maximize, nooutput
ml display, neq(7)
```

Table 11.27 shows the results displayed after estimation. The results under `pi` correspond to the logit model for the probability of belonging to class 1, within the LC hurdle for specialist visits. All variables are significant, especially `meanlsahbad1`, which is negatively associated with that probability. Income also has a negative effect on the probability of belonging to class 1, while the association with male and age is positive. Since class membership is time invariant in this model and the covariates considered are averages across the panel, the estimated coefficients should be seen as a long-term association with class membership probabilities, unlike the effects on the distribution of the number of visits, conditional on the latent class to which the individual belongs, which represent short-term effects. Except for age, the estimated coefficients of the hurdle model conditional on the latent class (`xbj_prob`, `xbj_trunc` and `alphaj`, for classes $j = 1,2$) are substantially different to those in the model with constant class memberships (Table 11.25). This means that, in the restricted model, the coefficients of the conditional densities were also capturing the long-term effects that are disentangled in the specification that allows the class membership to be associated with the regressors. The estimated effects of `lsahbad` and `lhincome` become smaller throughout. The negative effects of `male` decrease in absolute value (in the second part for class 2, the effect becomes was insignificantly negative and becomes insignificantly positive).

Predictions for the individual probability of belonging to class 1 are computed and summarised, returning an average of 0.684:

```
predict xbpi, equation(pi)
generate pi=exp(xbpi)/(1+exp(xbpi))
summarize pi
drop pi
```

Table 11.28 Summary statistics for individual p in LCH-Pan, with variable class membership

Variable	Obs	Mean	Std. Dev.	Min	Max
pi	8041	.683627	.144993	.1518098	.9766239

As above, the computation of fitted values for each class requires the prediction of the linear indices $x_{it}\beta_{j1}$ and $x_{it}\beta_{j2}$ for each wave:

```
foreach part in prob trunc {
    predict xb1`part'_1, equation(xb1_`part')
    predict xb2`part'_1, equation(xb2_`part')
    foreach wave in 2 3 4 {
        predict xb1`part'_`wave', equation(xb1_`part'_w`wave')
        predict xb2`part'_`wave', equation(xb2_`part'_w`wave')
    }
}
```

Reshape the dataset back to long form and predict the probabilities of having a least one visit and expected number of visits, given that it is positive:

```
reshape long y $xvars xb1prob_ xb2prob_                      ///
                     xb1trunc_ xb2trunc_, i(pidc) j(wave)
generate prob_c1=exp(xb1prob_)/(1+exp(xb1prob_))
generate prob_c2=exp(xb2prob_)/(1+exp(xb2prob_))
drop xb1prob_ xb2prob_
predict a1, equation(alpha1)
predict a2, equation(alpha2)
generate pos_c1=exp(xb1trunc_)                              ///
              /(1-exp(-1/a1*log(a1*exp(xb1trunc_)+1)))
generate pos_c2=exp(xb2trunc_)                              ///
                /(1-exp(-1/a2*log(a2*exp(xb2trunc_)+1)))
drop xb1trunc_ xb2trunc_ a1 a2
```

For each class, the expected total number of visits is obtained as the product of the predictions for the binary and truncated parts and summary statistics are computed:

```
generate y_c1=prob_c1*pos_c1
generate y_c2=prob_c2*pos_c2
summarize prob_c1 pos_c1 y_c1 prob_c2 pos_c2 y_c2
drop prob_c1 pos_c1 y_c1 prob_c2 pos_c2 y_c2
```

The sample averages of predicted utilisation conditional on the latent class, and decomposed into the probability of visiting a specialist at least once and the conditional number of visits, are shown in Table 11.29. The relative differences between latent classes are evident, being larger for the probability of visiting a specialist than for the conditional number of visits. The class of high users, class 2, is predicted to have an average total number of specialist visits, which is more than seven times larger than the one for the class of low users. Looking again at Table 11.27, we see that the longer term poor health and higher incomes are

Table 11.29 Summary statistics of fitted values by latent class in LCH-Pan, with variable class membership

Variable	Obs	Mean	Std. Dev.	Min	Max
prob_c1	32164	.188638	.075541	.0170539	.6131296
pos_c1	32164	1.952122	.1860794	1.576288	2.998953
y_c1	32164	.3769701	.1768027	.0330943	1.311237
prob_c2	32164	.6846681	.107405	.2110134	.9354007
pos_c2	32164	3.906013	.662016	2.914859	5.896165
y_c2	32164	2.719588	.8263522	.6501194	5.333615

associated with the probability of being a high user, while older individuals and males are more likely to be low users.

Test for the equality of coefficients across classes to see whether there are significant differences both in the binary and in the truncated parts:

```
test [xb1_prob=xb2_prob]
test [xb1_trunc=xb2_trunc]

 ( 1)  [xb1_prob]age1 - [xb2_prob]age1 = 0
 ( 2)  [xb1_prob]male1 - [xb2_prob]male1 = 0
 ( 3)  [xb1_prob]lhincome1 - [xb2_prob]lhincome1 = 0
 ( 4)  [xb1_prob]lsahbad1 - [xb2_prob]lsahbad1 = 0

        chi2( 4) =  23.45
      Prob > chi2 =  0.0001

 ( 1)  [xb1_trunc]age1 - [xb2_trunc]age1 = 0
 ( 2)  [xb1_trunc]male1 - [xb2_trunc]male1 = 0
 ( 3)  [xb1_trunc]lhincome1 - [xb2_trunc]lhincome1 = 0
 ( 4)  [xb1_trunc]lsahbad1 - [xb2_trunc]lsahbad1 = 0

        chi2( 4) =  40.75
      Prob > chi2 =  0.0000
```

Individual tests of equality of parameters across classes, coupled with the results in Table 11.27, show us that the effects of poor health are significantly larger for high users, in both the binary and the truncated parts, while the effect of income in the binary part is larger for low users (difference significant at 10 per cent):

```
test [xb1_prob]lhincome1 = [xb2_prob]lhincome1
test [xb1_trunc]lhincome1 = [xb2_trunc]lhincome1
test [xb1_prob]lsahbad1 = [xb2_prob]lsahbad1
test [xb1_trunc]lsahbad1 = [xb2_trunc]lsahbad1
```

```
( 1)  [xb1_prob]lhincome1 - [xb2_prob]lhincome1 = 0

              chi2( 1) =   2.88
           Prob > chi2 =   0.0895


 ( 1)  [xb1_trunc]lhincome1 - [xb2_trunc]lhincome1 = 0

              chi2( 1) =   5.41
           Prob > chi2 =   0.0200


 ( 1)  [xb1_prob]lsahbad1 - [xb2_prob]lsahbad1 = 0

              chi2( 1) =  16.06
           Prob > chi2 =   0.0001


 ( 1)  [xb1_trunc]lsahbad1 - [xb2_trunc]lsahbad1 = 0

              chi2( 1) =  30.25
           Prob > chi2 =   0.0000
```

Similar tests for age show that the effect of age on the probability of visiting a specialist is significantly higher for low users.

Information criteria are displayed for the LCH-Pan and the restricted versions estimated above:

```
estimates store lchurdle_pan_varpi
estimates stats lcnb_pan lchurdle_pan lchurdle_pan_varpi
```

The more general specification, the latent class hurdle model with class membership probabilities modelled as functions of the covariates, is the preferred specification according to information criteria (Table 11.30).

Table 11.30 AIC and BIC of LCNB-Pan and LCH-Pan (with two latent classes) with constant and variable class memberships

Model	nobs	ll(null)	ll(model)	df	AIC	BIC
lcnb_pan	8041	.	-41061.18	13	82148.36	82239.26
lchurdle_pan	8041	.	-40674.74	23	81395.48	81556.3
lchurdle_p~i	8041	.	-40498.68	27	81051.36	81240.15

11.8 OVERVIEW

Poisson regression is the starting point for modelling count data with cross-section data. The model can be extended to deal with the commonly observed phenomena of overdispersion and excess zeros using mixture models, such as the negative binomial, and through zero-inflated or hurdle models. Finite mixture or latent class models provide a semi-parametric approach for dealing with unobserved heterogeneity. This chapter shows how these models can be extended for use with panel data.

The latent class panel data model accounts for the panel feature of the data in a flexible way that assumes no distribution for the unobserved individual effects. It can also be seen as a discrete approximation of an underlying continuous mixing distribution (Heckman and Singer, 1984). The number of points of support needed for the finite mixture model is low, usually two or three. The specification used here allows for correlation between latent heterogeneity and the covariates. The conventional fixed effects models that have been developed for binary dependent variables (conditional logit) and for counts (fixed effects Poisson and NB) also offer a distribution-free approach to the individual heterogeneity that is robust to correlation between covariates and individual effects (see Cameron and Trivedi, 2005, 2009). However, fixed effects models do not identify the effects of time-invariant regressors. Furthermore, although conventional fixed effects models account for intercept heterogeneity, they do not accommodate different responses to the covariates across individuals, while the latent class model accommodates both intercept heterogeneity and slope heterogeneity. A recent development not covered here (Deb and Trivedi, 2011) combines the two approaches in a fixed-effects latent class Poisson.

APPENDIX

Program for latent class negative binomial model for panel data in wide form

This program specifies the log-likelihood of a model with two latent classes and a NB2 for each class. It is specific to a balanced panel with four waves and is to be applied to a panel dataset in wide form. Temporary variables f_j ($j = 1,2$) represent the logarithm of

$$\prod_{i=1}^{T_i} f_j\left(y_{it} \mid x_{it}; \theta_j\right),$$

that is, of the joint density of the dependent variable over the observed periods, where the density for each period is determined by a NB2. The specification of

the model in this way requires that the dataset be converted to wide form, which
we need to do prior to estimation:

```
#delimit ;
capture program drop lcnb_pan;
program define lcnb_pan;
   args      lnf   b1_w1 a1_w1 b2_w1 a2_w1 bpi

                  b1_w2 a1_w2 b1_w3 a1_w3 b1_w4 a1_w4
                  b2_w2 a2_w2 b2_w3 a2_w3 b2_w4 a2_w4;

   tempvar      f_1 f_2 pi;
   gen double `f_1'=0; gen double `f_2'=0;gen double `pi'=0;

   quietly replace `pi' = exp(`bpi')/(1+exp(`bpi'));

   quietly replace `f_1' = lngamma(y1+1/`a1_w1')
                  -lngamma(1/`a1_w1')-lngamma(y1+1)
                  -1/`a1_w1'*log(1+`a1_w1'*exp(`b1_w1'))
                  -y1*log(1+exp(-`b1_w1')/`a1_w1')

                      +lngamma(y2+1/`a1_w2')
                  -lngamma(1/`a1_w2')-lngamma(y2+1)
                  -1/`a1_w2'*log(1+`a1_w2'*exp(`b1_w2'))
                  -y2*log(1+exp(-`b1_w2')/`a1_w2')

                      +lngamma(y3+1/`a1_w3')
                  -lngamma(1/`a1_w3') - lngamma(y3+1)
                  -1/`a1_w3'*log(1+`a1_w3'*exp(`b1_w3'))
                  -y3*log(1+exp(-`b1_w3')/`a1_w3')

                      +lngamma(y4+1/`a1_w4')
                  -lngamma(1/`a1_w4')-lngamma(y4+1)
                  -1/`a1_w4'*log(1+`a1_w4'*exp(`b1_w4'))
                  -y4*log(1+exp(-`b1_w4')/`a1_w4');

   quietly replace `f_2' = lngamma(y1+1/`a2_w1')
                  -lngamma(1/`a2_w1')-lngamma(y1+1)
                  -1/`a2_w1'*log(1+`a2_w1'*exp(`b2_w1'))
                  -y1*log(1+exp(-`b2_w1')/`a2_w1')

                      +lngamma(y2+1/`a2_w2')
                  -lngamma(1/`a2_w2')-lngamma(y2+1)
                  -1/`a2_w2'*log(1+`a2_w2'*exp(`b2_w2'))
```

```
                    -y2*log(1+exp(-`b2_w2')/`a2_w2')

                         +lngamma(y3+1/`a2_w3')
                    -lngamma(1/`a2_w3') - lngamma(y3+1)
                    -1/`a2_w3'*log(1+`a2_w3'*exp(`b2_w3'))
                    -y3*log(1+exp(-`b2_w3')/`a2_w3')

                         +lngamma(y4+1/`a2_w4')
                    -lngamma(1/`a2_w4')-lngamma(y4+1)
                    -1/`a2_w4'*log(1+`a2_w4'*exp(`b2_w4'))
                    -y4*log(1+exp(-`b2_w4')/`a2_w4');

   quietly replace `lnf' =
             log(`pi'*exp(`f_1')+(1-`pi')*exp(`f_2'));

end;
#delimit cr
```

Program for latent class hurdle model for panel data in wide form

The program `lchurdle_pan` specifies the log-likelihood of a model with two latent classes and a hurdle (logit-truncated NB2) for each class. It is specific to a balanced panel with four waves and is to be applied to a panel dataset in wide form. This program extends `lcnb2_pan` by specifying temporary variables `f_1` and `f_2` as the sum of the logarithms of the density of the hurdle model for each period. The list of arguments of the new program contains equations for the binary part of the hurdle model (`b1_pr_w1` to `b1_pr_w4`, and `b2_pr_w1` to `b2_pr_w4`) and for the truncated part (`b1_tr_w1` to `b1_tr_w4`, `b2_tr_w1` to `b2_tr_w4`, `a1_tr_w1` to `a1_tr_w4` and `a2_tr_w1` to `a2_tr_w4`).

```
#delimit ;
capture program drop lchurdle_pan;
program define lchurdle_pan;
   args lnf b1_pr_w1 b1_tr_w1 a1_tr_w1
            b2_pr_w1 b2_tr_w1 a2_tr_w1
            bpi
      b1_pr_w2 b1_pr_w3 b1_pr_w4
      b2_pr_w2 b2_pr_w3 b2_pr_w4
      b1_tr_w2 a1_tr_w2 b1_tr_w3 a1_tr_w3 b1_tr_w4 a1_tr_w4
      b2_tr_w2 a2_tr_w2 b2_tr_w3 a2_tr_w3 b2_tr_w4 a2_tr_w4;

   tempvar    f_1 f_2 pi;
```

```
gen double `f_1'=0;   gen double `f_2'=0;gen double `pi'=0

quietly replace `pi' = exp(`bpi')/(1+exp(`bpi'));

quietly replace `f_1' = (lngamma(y1+1/`a1_tr_w1')
   - lngamma(1/`a1_tr_w1') - lngamma(y1+1)
   - log((1+`a1_tr_w1'*exp(`b1_tr_w1'))^(1/`a1_tr_w1')-1)
   -y1*log(1+exp(-`b1_tr_w1')/`a1_tr_w1')) * (y1>0)
   - log(exp(`b1_pr_w1') +1) + `b1_pr_w1'*(y1>0)


                          +(lngamma(y2+1/`a1_tr_w2')
   -lngamma(1/`a1_tr_w2')- lngamma(y2+1)
   - log((1+`a1_tr_w2'*exp(`b1_tr_w2'))^(1/`a1_tr_w2')-1)
   -y2*log(1+exp(-`b1_tr_w2')/`a1_tr_w2')) * (y2>0)
   - log(exp(`b1_pr_w2') +1) + `b1_pr_w2'*(y2>0)


                          +(lngamma(y3+1/`a1_tr_w3')
   -lngamma(1/`a1_tr_w3')- lngamma(y3+1)
   - log((1+`a1_tr_w3'*exp(`b1_tr_w3'))^(1/`a1_tr_w3')-1)
   -y3*log(1+exp(-`b1_tr_w3')/`a1_tr_w3')) * (y3>0)
   - log(exp(`b1_pr_w3') +1) + `b1_pr_w3'*(y3>0)


                          +(lngamma(y4+1/`a1_tr_w4')
   -lngamma(1/`a1_tr_w4') - lngamma(y4+1)
   - log((1+`a1_tr_w4'*exp(`b1_tr_w4'))^(1/`a1_tr_w4')-1)
   -y4*log(1+exp(-`b1_tr_w4')/`a1_tr_w4')) * (y4>0)
   - log(exp(`b1_pr_w4') +1) + `b1_pr_w4'*(y4>0);

quietly replace `f_2' = (lngamma(y1+1/`a2_tr_w1')
   - lngamma(1/`a2_tr_w1') - lngamma(y1+1)
   - log((1+`a2_tr_w1'*exp(`b2_tr_w1'))^(1/`a2_tr_w1')-1)
   -y1*log(1+exp(-`b2_tr_w1')/`a2_tr_w1')) * (y1>0)
   - log(exp(`b2_pr_w1') +1) + `b2_pr_w1'*(y1>0)


                          +(lngamma(y2+1/`a2_tr_w2')
   -lngamma(1/`a2_tr_w2')- lngamma(y2+1)
   - log((1+`a2_tr_w2'*exp(`b2_tr_w2'))^(1/`a2_tr_w2')-1)
   -y2*log(1+exp(-`b2_tr_w2')/`a2_tr_w2')) * (y2>0)
   - log(exp(`b2_pr_w2') +1) + `b2_pr_w2'*(y2>0)


                          +(lngamma(y3+1/`a2_tr_w3')
   -lngamma(1/`a2_tr_w3')- lngamma(y3+1)
   - log((1+`a2_tr_w3'*exp(`b2_tr_w3'))^(1/`a2_tr_w3')-1)
   -y3*log(1+exp(-`b2_tr_w3')/`a2_tr_w3')) * (y3>0)
```

```
      - log(exp(`b2_pr_w3') +1) + `b2_pr_w3'*(y3>0)


                          +(lngamma(y4+1/`a2_tr_w4')
    -lngamma(1/`a2_tr_w4') - lngamma(y4+1)
    - log((1+`a2_tr_w4'*exp(`b2_tr_w4'))^(1/`a2_tr_w4')-1)
    -y4*log(1+exp(-`b2_tr_w4')/`a2_tr_w4')) * (y4>0)
    - log(exp(`b2_pr_w4') +1) + `b2_pr_w4'*(y4>0);

  quietly replace `lnf' =
            log(`pi'*exp(`f_1')+(1-`pi')*exp(`f_2'));

end;
#delimit cr
```

12 Modelling health care costs

SYNOPSIS

This chapter extends the analysis of health care costs introduced in Chapter 3. It describes the use of nonlinear regression models, generalised linear models and more advanced nonlinear models including finite mixture models. The implementation of these methods is illustrated using a sub-sample of the Medical Expenditure Panel Survey (MEPS). The chapter concludes by considering the relative predictive performance of the various models described. It is highly recommended that Chapter 3 is read before this chapter.

12.1 INTRODUCTION

This chapter introduces advanced methods to model health care cost data. Throughout we make use of the sub-sample of the Medical Expenditure Panel Survey (MEPS) described in Chapter 3 and estimate models with the same specification of the set of explanatory variables as used in the linear and transformed linear regression models. A description of the data can be found in Chapter 1 and discussion of the problems encountered in modelling health care expenditures together with summary statistics for the sub-sample of MEPS data and an exposition of linear regression approaches to modelling cost data were covered in Chapter 3. The methods described in this chapter build on these previous analyses and it is advisable to ensure you are familiar with the content of Chapter 3 before proceeding with this chapter. Once again we focus on positive expenditures only and abstract from the issues encountered where there are observations with zero costs. The latter commonly occur when the cost data represent the population as a whole, rather than just the users of health care, and the distribution will typically have a large mass point at zero (with costs truncated at zero). Modelling expenditure data that contain zeros has typically been achieved using two-part models, where the probability of incurring expenditure is modelled separately to the level of costs conditional on incurring expenditure. Tobit models have also been applied in this context (see Jones, 2000). We do not consider these models in this chapter.

12.2 EXPONENTIAL CONDITIONAL MEAN MODELS

Chapter 3 considered transformations of expenditure data such as the logarithmic or square-root intended to produce a more symmetric distribution that is more suited to linear regression. As an alternative, consider a nonlinear specification of the conditional mean of costs, using an exponential conditional mean (ECM) model:

$$E[y_i \mid x_i] = \mu_i = \phi \exp(x_i \beta)$$

Through the use of the exponential function, the model directly accommodates the non-negative property of health care costs and attempts to address skewness in the data. The ECM model can be estimated in a variety of ways. The most direct is to treat it as a nonlinear regression and estimate by nonlinear least squares (NLS).

Here we estimate the exponential conditional mean model using Stata's `nl` command. First generate a variable to represent the constant in the model:

```
generate one = 1
```

Nonlinear regression models can be estimated in Stata by explicitly specifying the functional form of the model. For the exponential conditional mean model we specify

$$E[y \mid x] = \exp(x\beta) .$$

This is done below by indicating the dependent variable, total expenditures, using the global `y` defined in Chapter 3, together with the set of regressors, `$xvars`, plus the constructed constant term, `one`. The `nolog` command simply suppresses the reporting of the iterations when displaying the results.

```
nl(y=exp({ xb: $xvars one} )), vce(robust) nolog
```

Running this model generates the output in Table 12.1.

Table 12.1 Nonlinear regression: exponential conditional mean model

```
-----------------------------------------------------------------------
Nonlinear regression                        Number of obs =       2955
                                            R-squared      =     0.3519
                                            Adj R-squared =      0.3502
                                            Root MSE       = 11310.88
                                            Res. dev.      = 63539.02
-----------------------------------------------------------------------
                |              Robust
       totexp | Coef.     Std. Err.      t   P>|t|   [95% Conf. Interval]
   ------------|----------------------------------------------------------
       /xb_age | -.0106488  .0058993  -1.81  0.071   -.0222161   .0009184
    /xb_female | -.1688437  .0694458  -2.43  0.015   -.3050109  -.0326766
    /xb_income |  .0011871  .001556    0.76  0.446   -.001864    .0042381
   /xb_suppins |  .0620645  .0693332   0.90  0.371   -.0738819   .1980109
    /xb_phylim |  .3608786  .0871674   4.14  0.000    .1899634   .5317937
    /xb_actlim |  .418535   .0821924   5.09  0.000    .2573747   .5796954
    /xb_totchr |  .1798849  .0250688   7.18  0.000    .1307307   .229039
       /xb_one |  9.01872   .4459337  20.22  0.000    8.144347   9.893093
-----------------------------------------------------------------------
```

We can compare the predictions (on the raw cost scale) with the observed expenditures. These show that the mean of the predictions is slightly greater than the observed mean and that the model performs poorly at predicting the extremes of the distribution of costs.

```
predict nls_yhat if e(sample)
generate e = y-nls_yhat
```

```
   Variable |   Obs      Mean     Std. Dev.        Min        Max
   ----------------------------------------------------------------
     totexp |  2955   7290.235   11990.84           3     125610
   nls_yhat |  2955   7390.977    3829.861    2843.413   33186.44
```

Summarise the distribution of the estimated residuals from the regression and note that these are not centred on zero and are positively skewed and kurtotic:

```
tabstat e , stat (n mean med sd cv iqr sk k mi ma)
```

```
   variable |    N       mean       p50        sd         cv        iqr
   ----------|------------------------------------------------------------
          e |  2955  -100.7416  -2803.197  11297.02  -112.1387  4941.011
   ------------------------------------------------------------------------
```

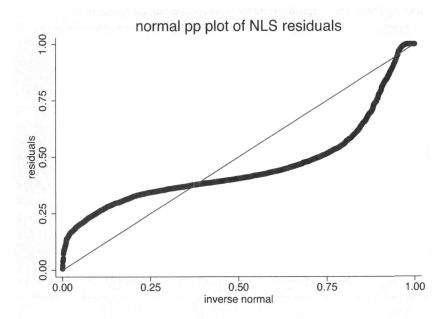

Figure 12.1 Normal probability plot for the exponential conditional mean model.

variable	skewness	kurtosis	min	max
e	4.09167	26.76991	-27938.44	113922.7

A normal probability plot of the residuals is given in Figure 12.1. As can clearly be seen, the plot confirms significant departure from normality.

```
pnorm e, title(normal pp plot of NLS residuals) ytitle(residuals) ///
   xtitle(inverse normal)
```

By specifying the option `variables($xvars one)` in the command line for `nl` compute average marginal effects by using the command `margins`:

```
quietly nl(y=exp({ xb: $xvars one} )), variables($xvars one)   ///

   vce(robust) nolog

margins, dydx(*)
```

By default, `margins` calculates marginal effects by averaging across the values for the independent variables. It will also calculate incremental effects for binary variables such as supplementary insurance status where these are defined as factor variables (using, e.g., `i.suppins` in the regression command line). Nonlinear

Table 12.2 Average marginal effects for exponential conditional mean model

```
--------------------------------------------------------------------
Average marginal effects                    Number of obs  =    2955
Model VCE      : Robust
Expression     : Fitted values, predict()
dy/dx w.r.t. : age female income suppins phylim actlim totchr one
--------------------------------------------------------------------
             |               Delta-method
             |    dy/dx  Std. Err.      z  P>|z|  [95% Conf. Interval]
--------------------------------------------------------------------
       age | -78.70519  44.05295   -1.79  0.074  -165.0474   7.637009
    female | -1247.92   514.0908   -2.43  0.015  -2255.52   -240.3206
    income |  8.773576  11.49311    0.76  0.445   -13.7525   31.29966
   suppins |  458.7171  513.3689    0.89  0.372  -547.4674   1464.902
    phylim |  2667.245  650.6441    4.10  0.000   1392.006   3942.484
    actlim |  3093.383  629.3323    4.92  0.000   1859.914   4326.851
    totchr |  1329.525  184.4679    7.21  0.000   967.9743   1691.075
       one |  66657.15  4193.644   15.89  0.000   58437.76   74876.54
--------------------------------------------------------------------
```

regression using the nl command does not support the specification of factor variables and accordingly, for illustrative purposes, we report marginal effects for variables as if all were continuous. Table 12.2 shows that the estimated marginal effect of having supplementary insurance is US$459; physical limitations is US$2,667, and activity limitations is US$3,093. In general annual health care expenditures for women are US$1,330 less than men. The average marginal effect of income is estimated as US$8.77 (note annual income has been divided by US$1,000). Compute the Akaike information criterion (AIC) for the model to compare against alternative specifications we might wish to use.

```
estat ic
--------------------------------------------------------------------
   Model |  Obs   ll(null)  ll(model)   df      AIC        BIC
---------|----------------------------------------------------------
       . | 2955         .  -31769.51    8   63555.02   63602.95
--------------------------------------------------------------------
Note: N=Obs used in calculating BIC; see [R] BIC note
```

For nonlinear regression models, the link tests for misspecification of the regression model may be augmented by a modified Hosmer and Lemeshow (1980, 1995) test and its variants. The idea is to compute the fitted values and prediction errors for the model on the raw cost scale. These prediction errors can then be regressed on the fitted values, testing whether the slope equals zero. In the modified Hosmer–Lemeshow test, an *F* statistic is used to test for equality of the mean of the prediction errors over, say, deciles of the fitted values, often accompanied by a graphical residual-fitted value plot of the relationship on the cost scale. This can be implemented by regressing the prediction errors on binary indicators for the deciles of the fitted values and testing the joint significance of the coefficients. Implement this test as follows:

```
sort nls_yhat
xtile grp = nls_yhat, nq(10)
quietly tab grp, gen(gr)
regress e gr1-gr10, nocons robust
```

```
Linear regression                          Number of obs =    2955
                                           F( 10,  2945) =    2.93
                                           Prob > F      =  0.0012
                                           R-squared     =  0.0023
                                           Root MSE      =   11302
```

e	Coef.	Robust Std. Err.	t	P>|t|	[95% Conf. Interval]
gr1	-1011.463	228.9363	-4.42	0.000	-1460.354 -562.5718
gr2	-723.6345	299.0319	-2.42	0.016	-1309.967 -137.3018
gr3	-577.0016	367.0632	-1.57	0.116	-1296.728 142.7249
gr4	-109.5147	518.0764	-0.21	0.833	-1125.343 906.3138
gr5	-217.9663	480.3463	-0.45	0.650	-1159.815 723.8822
gr6	-69.46239	618.7333	-0.11	0.911	-1282.656 1143.731
gr7	137.4134	587.3558	0.23	0.815	-1014.256 1289.083
gr8	425.8295	858.0653	0.50	0.620	-1256.639 2108.298
gr9	815.8429	914.7141	0.89	0.373	-977.7009 2609.387
gr10	323.7257	1117.953	0.29	0.772	-1868.322 2515.774

```
testparm gr1-gr10

 ( 1)  gr1 = 0
 ( 2)  gr2 = 0
 ( 3)  gr3 = 0
 ( 4)  gr4 = 0
 ( 5)  gr5 = 0
 ( 6)  gr6 = 0
 ( 7)  gr7 = 0
 ( 8)  gr8 = 0
 ( 9)  gr9 = 0
 (10)  gr10 = 0

       F( 10,  2945) =   2.93
            Prob > F =   0.0012
```

The modified Hosmer–Lemeshow test rejects the null hypothesis that the means of the residuals are jointly equal to zero across the deciles of the fitted values. The coefficients in the above regression are increasing with the deciles of the fitted values, rather than being a random scatter around zero. This suggests that the model overpredicts at low deciles of the distribution of fitted values and underpredicts at high deciles. This is better illustrated in Figure 12.2 and indicates that the nonlinear least-squares estimated exponential conditional mean is not well specified:

```
bysort grp: egen ebar=mean(e)
summarize grp ebar
twoway scatter ebar grp, yline(0) title(ECM)          ///
   ytitle(mean of residuals)                          ///
   xtitle(deciles of fitted values)
```

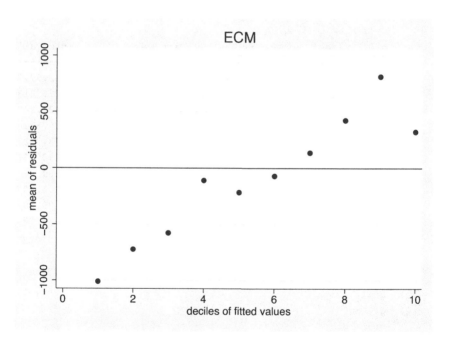

Figure 12.2 Hosmer–Lemeshow plot: nonlinear least squares.

Poisson regression

When the dependent variable is an integer-valued count the Poisson model is an obvious candidate for regression analysis, for example to model the number of encounters with the health care system (see Chapter 11). The model can, however, also be applied to cost data. The Poisson distribution with mean, μ, defined as a function of the covariates x, has the exponential conditional mean (ECM) form:

$$E[y_i \mid x_i] = \mu_i = \exp(x_i\beta).$$

Estimation of the Poisson model can be achieved using quasi-maximum likelihood (QML), which is a consistent estimator so long as the conditional mean is correctly specified. We estimate the model together with the corresponding marginal effects (including incremental effects for factor variables) using the commands set out below. Robust standard errors are applied. Average marginal effects are reported in Table 12.3.

```
quietly poisson y age i.female income i.suppins i.phylim i.actlim ///
    totchr, vce(robust) nolog
margins, dydx(*)
predict pyhat if e(sample)
generate eP = y-pyhat
```

The average marginal effects for the Poisson model are generally similar to those for the NLS estimates of the exponential conditional mean model. However, the effect of supplementary insurance and the total number of chronic conditions is substantively greater for the QML estimator than the NLS estimator. The estimated coefficient on the squared term of the predicted values in a link test for the Poisson model suggests that the model is not well specified. A normal probability plot of the residuals from the Poisson estimation displays a similar relationship to that shown in Figure 12.1 for the NLS estimates of the exponential conditional mean.

Table 12.3 Average marginal effects from Poisson regression

```
-----------------------------------------------------------------------
Average marginal effects                      Number of obs  =     2955
Model VCE     : Robust
Expression    : Predicted number of events, predict()
dy/dx w.r.t.  : age 1.female income 1.suppins 1.phylim 1.actlim totchr
-----------------------------------------------------------------------
```

	dy/dx	Delta-method Std. Err.	z	P>|z|	[95% Conf. Interval]	
age	-67.5529	36.94151	-1.83	0.067	-139.9569	4.851127
1.female	-1413.186	441.4708	-3.20	0.001	-2278.453	-547.9188
income	8.62956	9.459291	0.91	0.362	-9.91031	27.16943
1.suppins	688.7766	430.351	1.60	0.109	-154.6959	1532.249
1.phylim	2708.822	546.0544	4.96	0.000	1638.575	3779.069
1.actlim	3168.856	634.1811	5.00	0.000	1925.884	4411.828
totchr	1602.376	160.6735	9.97	0.000	1287.462	1917.29

Note: dy/dx for factor levels is the discrete change from the base level.

```
linktest, nolog
```

```
Poisson regression                          Number of obs  =        2955
                                            LR chi2(2)     = 6490506.63
                                            Prob > chi2    =     0.0000
Log likelihood = -13045962                  Pseudo R2      =     0.1992
------------------------------------------------------------------------
    totexp |     Coef.  Std. Err.      z  P>|z|   [95% Conf. Interval]
------------------------------------------------------------------------
      _hat |  6.744634  .0126712   532.28  0.000   6.719799   6.769469
    _hatsq | -.3171255  .0006995  -453.36  0.000  -.3184965  -.3157545
      _cons |  -25.9254  .0572576  -452.79  0.000  -26.03762  -25.81317
------------------------------------------------------------------------
```

Application of the modified Hosmer–Lemeshow test fails to reject the null
hypothesis that the means of the residuals are jointly equal to zero across the deciles
of the fitted values ($p = 0.062$). A plot of the mean of the residuals across the deciles
of the fitted values shows no clear discernible pattern (Figure 12.3), although there
are large discrepancies between fitted and actual values at high deciles of the
distribution of fitted values. This suggests that the Poisson QML estimator is an
improvement, for these data, on the NLS estimator considered earlier.

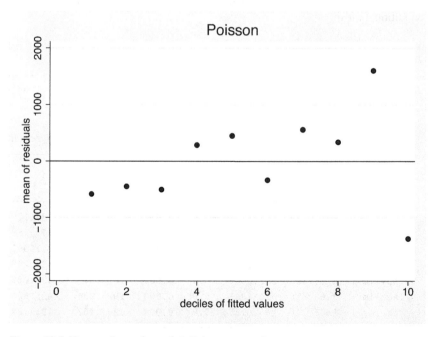

Figure 12.3 Hosmer–Lemeshow plot: Poisson regression.

Hazard models

Estimation routines that are normally applied to duration data can also be applied to cost regressions. Once again, these estimators have the ECM form. Chapter 6 discusses the basic concepts involved in analysing duration data which we do not cover again here.

Exponential and Weibull models

To see how duration models can be applied to cost data first consider the Weibull model, which has the following hazard function:

$$h[y_i \mid x_i] = \rho y_i^{\rho-1} \exp(x_i\beta) ,$$

where ρ is known as the shape parameter. To illustrate the flexibility the Weibull model offers, Figure 12.4 displays the probability density function for different values of the parameters ρ (rho) assuming for simplicity that $\exp(x\beta) = 1$. The parameters of the model can be obtained using maximum likelihood estimation.

The expected conditional mean for the Weibull model is given by:

$$E[y_i \mid x_i] = \exp(x_i\beta)\Gamma(1+\sigma) = \exp(x_i\beta)\Gamma\left(1+\frac{1}{\rho}\right)$$

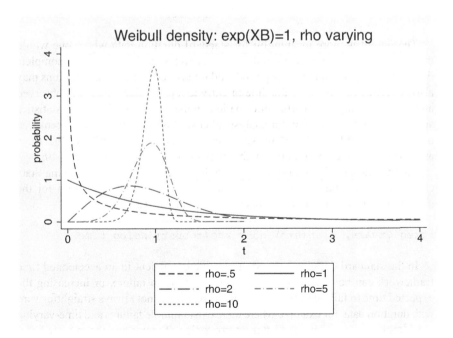

Figure 12.4 Weibull density functions.

where Γ is the gamma function. For the exponential distribution ($\rho = 1$), the conditional mean collapses to

$$E[y \mid x] = \exp(x\beta) \;.$$

To estimate hazard models in Stata we first need to declare the data to represent durations using the `stset` command. The command informs Stata of the key variables and their roles in defining durations and instigates various checks for consistency to ensure these make sense:

```
stset y

    failure event: (assumed to fail at time=totexp)
obs. time interval: (0, totexp]
 exit on or before: failure
-----------------------------------------------------------------
    2955  total obs.
       0  exclusions
-----------------------------------------------------------------
    2955  obs. remaining, representing
    2955  failures in single record/single failure data
2.15e+07  total analysis time at risk, at risk from t =        0
                             earliest observed entry t =        0
                                last observed exit t =     125610
```

The output is more meaningful for standard duration data where one would expect observations to be censored, either due to loss to follow-up or incomplete durations at the end of the study period (right-censored). Individual durations may also be left-censored where the time of entry to a particular state is not observed and hence we only have partial information on the durations. The above statistics summarise such events. For our analysis of costs, however, there are no censored observations and hence the above summary is sparse and informing us that there are 2,955 complete observations with a maximum observation of $125,610.

To estimate a model with an exponential hazard we specify the following Stata commands. The option `time` requests accelerated time to failure form for the estimation. The results for this model are presented in Table 12.4.

```
streg $xvars, dist(exp) nohr vce(robust) nolog time
```

In the standard duration context, a positive coefficient in an accelerated time framework can be interpreted as delaying the time to failure, or increasing the expected time to failure (although this interpretation is not always straightforward with duration data, for example where there exist multiple failures and time-varying covariates). For cost data, the latter interpretation of increasing the expected cost can be used. Accordingly, the model implies that individuals with supplementary

Table 12.4 Exponential hazard function

```
------------------------------------------------------------------
         failure _d: 1 (meaning all fail)
   analysis time _t: totexp

Exponential regression - accelerated failure-time form

No. of subjects   =      2955              Number of obs =    2955
No. of failures   =      2955
Time at risk      =   21542645
                                           Wald chi2(7)  = 458.87
Log pseudolikelihood =  -4963.859          Prob > chi2   = 0.0000
------------------------------------------------------------------
             |                Robust
        _t |   Coef.  Std. Err.    z   P>|z|  [95% Conf. Interval]
---------|--------------------------------------------------------
       age | -.0053813  .0046676  -1.15  0.249  -.0145296   .0037669
    female | -.1906611  .0574585  -3.32  0.001  -.3032777  -.0780444
    income |  .0011287  .0012688   0.89  0.374  -.0013582   .0036155
   suppins |  .1228877  .0599605   2.05  0.040   .0053672   .2404083
    phylim |  .3937388  .0688322   5.72  0.000   .2588301   .5286474
    actlim |  .4206781  .0745528   5.64  0.000   .2745573   .5667989
    totchr |  .2679844  .0219325  12.22  0.000   .2249976   .3109713
     _cons |  8.37466   .3647337  22.96  0.000  7.659795   9.089525
------------------------------------------------------------------
```

insurance have greater expenditures than those without, as do individuals with physical or activity limitations and chronic conditions. We can derive average marginal effects for the model using the command margins. Note, however, we use the option predict(mean time). This ensures that the marginal effects are calculated from predicted values of the model in terms of mean rather than the default median cost. Applying the default would result in the marginal effects representing the impact of covariates on median, rather than mean, costs and hence the marginal effects presented in Table 12.5 would not be comparable to the exponential conditional mean model in Table 12.2.

```
quietly streg age i.female income i.suppins i.phylim i.actlim ///
      totchr, dist(exp) nohr vce(robust) nolog time
margins, dydx(*) predict(mean time)
```

The main difference in the estimated marginal effects is that the impact of supplementary insurance status is approximately twice the size of the estimate for the NLS estimator of exponential conditional mean model and statistically significant at the 5 per cent level.

Table 12.5 Marginal effects from exponential hazard function

```
--------------------------------------------------------------------
Average marginal effects                    Number of obs  =    2955
Model VCE     : Robust
Expression    : Predicted mean _t, predict(mean time)
dy/dx w.r.t.  : age 1.female income 1.suppins 1.phylim 1.actlim totchr
--------------------------------------------------------------------
            |              Delta-method
            |    dy/dx  Std. Err.    z   P>|z|    [95% Conf. Interval]
------------|-------------------------------------------------------
        age | -39.99359  34.88744  -1.15  0.252  -108.3717   28.38454
   1.female | -1441.193  447.8914  -3.22  0.001  -2319.043  -563.3416
     income |  8.388017  9.429084   0.89  0.374  -10.09265   26.86868
  1.suppins |  901.7018  435.2807   2.07  0.038   48.56725   1754.836
   1.phylim |  2834.507  497.9513   5.69  0.000   1858.541   3810.474
   1.actlim |  3228.237  613.5676   5.26  0.000   2025.667   4430.808
      totchr |  1991.633  182.2522  10.93  0.000   1634.425    2348.84
--------------------------------------------------------------------
```

Note: dy/dx for factor levels is the discrete change from the base level.

A link test suggests that the exponential model may not work well for these data:

```
linktest, dist(exp) nolog time

        failure _d:  1 (meaning all fail)
   analysis time _t: totexp

Exponential regression — accelerated failure-time form

No. of subjects   =      2955            Number of obs  =     2955
No. of failures   =      2955
Time at risk      =  21542645
                                         LR chi2(2)     =   937.45
Log likelihood  = -4952.0006             Prob > chi2    =   0.0000
--------------------------------------------------------------------
        _t |     Coef.  Std. Err.    z   P>|z|    [95% Conf. Interval]
-----------|--------------------------------------------------------
      _hat |  5.438368  .8874911   6.13  0.000   3.698918   7.177819
    _hatsq | -.2502384  .0499461  -5.01  0.000   -.348131  -.1523457
      _cons | -19.59979  3.930449  -4.99  0.000  -27.30332  -11.89625
--------------------------------------------------------------------
```

We compute the AIC in the usual way:

```
estat ic

  Model |    Obs      ll(null)    ll(model)    df         AIC        BIC
--------|---------------------------------------------------------------
      . |   2955    -5420.725   -4963.859     8    9943.718   9991.648
        ----------------------------------------------------------------

Note: N=Obs used in calculating BIC; see [R] BIC note
```

The Weibull model can be estimated in a similar way to the exponential hazard function by specifying the Weibull distribution. The results of the model are presented in Table 12.6 with marginal and incremental effects in Table 12.7.

```
streg $xvars, dist(w) nohr vce(robust) nolog time
```

The results in Table 12.6 show that the estimate of ρ is 0.86. A test of the null hypothesis H_0: $\rho = 1$, is equivalent to the test H_0: ln $\rho = 0$, which is firmly rejected at the 1 per cent significance level. This provides further evidence against the exponential form of the hazard. The marginal effects (again specifying predictions of mean rather than median costs) from the Weibull model are, in general, similar to the corresponding effects for the exponential form of the model (Table 12.7). Note, however, that the impact of supplementary insurance is approximately 10 per cent larger than the corresponding estimate from the exponential hazard model.

With the exponential hazard model, a link test suggests the specification of the model is not appropriate. However, the AIC for the Weibull model is preferable to that for the exponential hazard. This is due to the greater flexibility of the Weibull hazard in fitting the cost data by allowing the shape parameter, ρ, to be estimated and not constrained to unity as in the exponential form.

```
linktest, dist(w) time nolog

estat ic

  Model |    Obs      ll(null)    ll(model)    df         AIC        BIC
--------|---------------------------------------------------------------
      . |   2955    -5220.334   -4895.532     9    9809.064   9862.985
        ----------------------------------------------------------------

Note: N=Obs used in calculating BIC; see [R] BIC note
```

Generalised gamma model

Greater flexibility in the parametric modelling of cost data as durations is provided by the generalised gamma model – see Manning *et al.* (2005) and Jones (2011)

Table 12.6 Weibull hazard function

```
----------------------------------------------------------------------
          failure _d: 1 (meaning all fail)
    analysis time _t: totexp
Weibull regression - accelerated failure-time form
No. of subjects      =       2955            Number of obs =      2955
No. of failures      =       2955
Time at risk         =   21542645
                                             Wald chi2(7)  =    533.93
Log pseudolikelihood = -4895.5319            Prob > chi2   =    0.0000
----------------------------------------------------------------------
            |              Robust
         _t |      Coef. Std. Err.      z   P>|z|    [95% Conf. Interval]
------------|---------------------------------------------------------
        age | -.0039805  .0044089   -0.90   0.367   -.0126217   .0046608
     female |  -.177528  .0543361   -3.27   0.001   -.2840248  -.0710311
     income |  .0013189  .0011913    1.11   0.268   -.0010161   .0036538
    suppins |  .1381467  .0565914    2.44   0.015    .0272295   .2490639
     phylim |  .3881499  .0658117    5.90   0.000    .2591614   .5171385
     actlim |  .4176869  .0719666    5.80   0.000    .2766348   .5587389
     totchr |  .2783687  .0209345   13.30   0.000    .2373379   .3193996
      _cons |  8.144623  .3415048   23.85   0.000    7.475286   8.813961
------------|---------------------------------------------------------
      /ln_p |  -.147214   .015515   -9.49   0.000   -.1776228  -.1168052
------------|---------------------------------------------------------
          p |  .8631092  .0133911                    .8372582   .8897585
        1/p |  1.158602  .0179757                    1.123901   1.194375
----------------------------------------------------------------------
```

Table 12.7 Marginal effects from Weibull hazard function

```
----------------------------------------------------------------------
Average marginal effects                      Number of obs =      2955
Model VCE     : Robust
Expression    : Predicted mean _t, predict(mean time)
dy/dx w.r.t.  : age 1.female income 1.suppins 1.phylim 1.actlim totchr
----------------------------------------------------------------------
            |            Delta-method
            |      dy/dx Std. Err.      z   P>|z|    [95% Conf. Interval]
------------|---------------------------------------------------------
        age | -29.33159   32.6131   -0.90   0.368   -93.25209   34.58891
   1.female | -1329.278   418.427   -3.18   0.001    -2149.38  -509.1758
     income |   9.71849  8.780589    1.11   0.268   -7.491149   26.92813
  1.suppins |  1003.328  406.5584    2.47   0.014     206.488   1800.168
   1.phylim |  2768.964  471.2478    5.88   0.000    1845.336   3692.593
   1.actlim |   3174.64  586.8745    5.41   0.000    2024.388   4324.893
     totchr |  2051.271  175.5961   11.68   0.000    1707.109   2395.433
------------|---------------------------------------------------------
```

Note: dy/dx for factor levels is the discrete change from the base level.

Table 12.8 Link test Weibull hazard function

```
                 failure _d:  1 (meaning all fail)
      analysis time _t:  totexp
Weibull regression — accelerated failure-time form
No. of subjects =     2955                   Number of obs =    2955
No. of failures =     2955
Time at risk     = 21542645
                                             LR chi2(2)     =  667.39
Log likelihood =  -4886.641                  Prob > chi2    =  0.0000
```

_t	Coef.	Std. Err.	z	P>|z|	[95% Conf. Interval]	
_hat	5.205148	.9725892	5.35	0.000	3.298908	7.111388
_hatsq	-.2394274	.0552745	-4.33	0.000	-.3477635	-.1310913
_cons	-18.38186	4.264641	-4.31	0.000	-26.7404	-10.02332
/ln_p	-.1436081	.0131899	-10.89	0.000	-.1694599	-.1177564
p	.8662271	.0114255			.8441206	.8889126
1/p	1.154432	.0152269			1.12497	1.184665

for a fuller description of the generalised gamma distribution and its application to cost data. The conditional mean of costs is:

$$E[y_i \mid x_i] = \mu_i = \exp(x_i\beta) \left[\kappa^{2\sigma/\kappa} \frac{\Gamma\left(\dfrac{1}{\kappa^2} + \dfrac{\sigma}{\kappa}\right)}{\Gamma\left(\dfrac{1}{\kappa^2}\right)} \right] = \exp(x_i\beta)\phi .$$

where the parameters κ and σ are two shape parameters which allow for flexibility in the hazard function. A useful property of the generalised gamma model is that it nests more commonly used parametric models, i.e. gamma ($\kappa = \sigma$), Weibull ($\kappa = 1$), exponential ($\kappa = 1, \sigma = 1$), and log-normal ($\kappa = 0$). The model can be estimated in Stata using the streg command. Tests for the restrictions leading to the nested models can be undertaken readily. The conditional variance of the generalised gamma model is proportional to the square of the mean.

Estimate the generalised gamma in accelerated failure time (AFT) form using similar syntax to that used for the exponential and Weibull distributions:

```
streg $xvars, dist(gamma) vce(robust) nolog time
```

This produces the results in Table 12.9.

Table 12.9 Generalised gamma

```
------------------------------------------------------------------------
         failure _d:  1 (meaning all fail)
    analysis time _t:  totexp
Gamma regression — accelerated failure-time form
No. of subjects      =      2955              Number of obs  =    2955
No. of failures      =      2955
Time at risk         =   21542645
                                              Wald chi2(7)   =  856.88
Log pseudolikelihood = -4721.0339             Prob > chi2    =  0.0000
------------------------------------------------------------------------
            |                Robust
        _t  |    Coef.    Std. Err.    z    P>|z|    [95% Conf. Interval]
------------+-----------------------------------------------------------
        age |  .0025294   .0036883   0.69   0.493   -.0046996    .0097584
     female | -.1023316   .0455807  -2.25   0.025   -.1916682   -.0129951
     income |  .0023284   .0010153   2.29   0.022    .0003385    .0043183
    suppins |  .2312114   .046829    4.94   0.000    .1394282    .3229946
     phylim |  .3270578   .0569407   5.74   0.000     .215456    .4386596
     actlim |  .3723807   .0632419   5.89   0.000    .2484289    .4963326
     totchr |  .3507726   .0188153  18.64   0.000    .3138953    .3876499
      _cons |   6.97772   .2886168  24.18   0.000    6.412042    7.543399
------------+-----------------------------------------------------------
    /ln_sig |  .1720063   .0145981  11.78   0.000    .1433945    .2006181
     /kappa |   .200477   .0497499   4.03   0.000    .1029689    .2979851
------------+-----------------------------------------------------------
      sigma |  1.187685   .017338                    1.154185    1.222158
------------------------------------------------------------------------
```

As the exponential and Weibull are nested within the generalised gamma, we can test the restrictions directly. For an exponential distribution, $\kappa = 1$, $\sigma = 1$, which can be tested as follows:

```
test ([kappa]_cons = 1) ([ln_sig]_cons = 0)

( 1)  [kappa]_cons = 1
( 2)  [ln_sig]_cons = 0

       chi2( 2)   =   412.52
     Prob > chi2  =   0.0000
```

The Weibull is less restrictive ($\kappa = 1$), but again a direct test rejects the null hypothesis:

```
test [kappa]_cons = 1
```

```
( 1)  [kappa]_cons = 1

          chi2( 1)  =  258.27
       Prob > chi2 =   0.0000
```

An alternative to the Stata command `streg` is the user written command `gengam2` provided by Anirban Basu (http://faculty.washington.edu/basua/software.html). This code has the advantage of automatically testing the restrictions on the generalised gamma distribution. Implementation of the code and the table of results are given below. The tests of restrictions on the functional form of the generalised gamma distribution are clearly useful but in a particular application may reject all of the nested models. Results from `gengam2` are presented in Table 12.10.

```
gengam2 $xvars, vce(robust) nolog time
```

The generalised gamma allows for additional heteroskedasticity by parameterising σ as a function of covariates, for example $\sigma = \exp(z_i\alpha)$ for a set of regressors z. Manning *et al.* (2005) suggest that this parameterisation is useful when there is evidence that κ is small (<0.1). While $\kappa = 0.2$ in the above application, we allow for heteroskedasticity by parameterising σ as a function of the model regressors using the option `ancillary`:

```
gengam2 $xvars, ancillary($xvars) vce(robust) nolog time
```

The results are presented in Table 12.11. All but the two regressors (`income` and `actlim`) are significant at the 5 per cent level in the parameterisation of sigma. This is supported by a comparison of information criteria which suggests an improved model fit when accounting for heteroskedasticity (AIC = 9349.23 compared to the homoskedastic model with AIC = 9462.07). Again tests of the null hypothesis for the various restrictions required to specify the parametric forms the GGM nests are rejected at conventional significance levels.

12.3 GENERALISED LINEAR MODELS

Much of the recent literature on health care costs has used the generalised linear models (GLMs) framework. GLMs offer flexibility in modelling cost data by allowing the mean and variance function of the expenditures to be directly specified by the analyst.

The first requirement is to specify how the linear index ($x\beta$) relates to the conditional mean function $E[y \mid x]$:

$$E\left[y_i \mid x_i\right] = \mu_i = f\left(x_i\beta\right)$$

Table 12.10 Generalised gamma

```
-----------------------------------------------------------------------
         failure _d: 1 (meaning all fail)
   analysis time _t: totexp
Gamma regression — accelerated failure-time form
No. of subjects        =      2955              Number of obs =     2955
No. of failures        =      2955
Time at risk           =  21542645
                                                Wald chi2(7)  =   856.88
Log pseudolikelihood = -4721.0339               Prob > chi2   =   0.0000
-----------------------------------------------------------------------
           |               Robust
       _t  |    Coef.  Std. Err.      z    P>|z|    [95% Conf. Interval]
-----------+-----------------------------------------------------------
       age | .0025294  .0036883    0.69   0.493  -.0046996    .0097584
    female | -.1023316 .0455807   -2.25   0.025  -.1916682   -.0129951
    income | .0023284  .0010153    2.29   0.022   .0003385    .0043183
   suppins | .2312114  .046829     4.94   0.000   .1394282    .3229946
    phylim | .3270578  .0569407    5.74   0.000   .215456     .4386596
    actlim | .3723807  .0632419    5.89   0.000   .2484289    .4963326
    totchr | .3507726  .0188153   18.64   0.000   .3138953    .3876499
     _cons | 6.97772   .2886168   24.18   0.000   6.412042    7.543399
-----------+-----------------------------------------------------------
   /ln_sig | .1720063  .0145981   11.78   0.000   .1433945    .2006181
    /kappa | .200477   .0497499    4.03   0.000   .1029689    .2979851
-----------+-----------------------------------------------------------
     sigma | 1.187685  .017338                    1.154185    1.222158
-----------------------------------------------------------------------
```

Tests for identifying distributions

```
-----------------------------------------------------------------------
Distributions                     |    chi2      df     Prob>chi2
-----------+-----------------------------------------------------------
Std. Gamma   (kappa = sigma)      |   359.85      1       0.0000
Log Normal   (kappa = 0)          |    16.24      1       0.0001
Weibull      (kappa = 1)          |   258.27      1       0.0000
Exponential (kappa = sigma = 1)   |   412.52      2       0.0000
-----------------------------------------------------------------------
```

New Variables for Schoenfield Residuals created: _h*, _c*

Table 12.11 Generalised gamma with heteroskedasticity

```
          failure _d: 1 (meaning all fail)
   analysis time _t: totexp
Gamma regression — accelerated failure-time form
No. of subjects       =       2955           Number of obs  =      2955
No. of failures       =       2955
Time at risk          =   21542645
                                              Wald chi2(7)   =    818.70
Log pseudolikelihood = -4657.6125             Prob > chi2    =    0.0000
-----------------------------------------------------------------------
            |              Robust
        _t  |    Coef.   Std. Err.     z    P>|z|   [95% Conf. Interval]
------------|----------------------------------------------------------
_t          |
        age |  .0042813  .0035683    1.20   0.230   -.0027123    .011275
     female | -.1191031  .0445216   -2.68   0.007   -.2063638   -.0318424
     income |  .0022251  .0009518    2.34   0.019    .0003596    .0040906
    suppins |  .2291502  .0451373    5.08   0.000    .1406828    .3176176
     phylim |  .3034471  .0554073    5.48   0.000    .1948508    .4120433
     actlim |  .3304209  .0604688    5.46   0.000    .2119041    .4489376
     totchr |  .3423385  .0174877   19.58   0.000    .3080633    .3766137
      _cons |  6.859457  .2749498   24.95   0.000    6.320566    7.398349
------------|----------------------------------------------------------
ln_sig      |
        age | -.0048953   .002343   -2.09   0.037   -.0094874   -.0003032
     female | -.0911431  .0290003   -3.14   0.002   -.1479826   -.0343035
     income | -.0010707  .0007057   -1.52   0.129   -.0024537    .0003124
    suppins | -.0965686  .0297582   -3.25   0.001   -.1548937   -.0382436
     phylim |  .1070153  .0365711    2.93   0.003    .0353372    .1786934
     actlim |  .0639611  .0381274    1.68   0.093   -.0107672    .1386894
     totchr | -.1067555  .0116897   -9.13   0.000   -.1296668   -.0838442
      _cons |  .7806109  .1755318    4.45   0.000    .4365749    1.124647
------------|----------------------------------------------------------
kappa       |
      _cons |  .1280454  .0465183    2.75   0.006    .0368711    .2192197
-----------------------------------------------------------------------
Tests for identifying distributions
-----------------------------------------------------------------------
Distributions                      |     chi2      df    Prob>chi2
-----------------------------------------------------------------------
Std. Gamma  (kappa = sigma)        |    475.23     1      0.0000
Log Normal  (kappa = 0)            |      7.58     1      0.0059
Weibull     (kappa = 1)            |    351.35     1      0.0000
Exponential (kappa = sigma = 1)    |    524.52     2      0.0000
-----------------------------------------------------------------------
New Variables for Schoenfield Residuals created: _h*, _c*
```

With an exponential conditional mean (ECM) we have $\mu = \exp(x\beta)$ and hence $g(\mu) = f^{-1}(\mu) = x\beta$, where $g(.)$ represents the link function which here is the 'log link' function since $g(\mu) = \ln(\mu)$. For the log link we have $\ln(E[y \mid x]) = x\beta$ and hence, $E[y \mid x]) = \exp(x\beta)$, and accordingly the log link implies that the covariates act multiplicatively on the mean (see for example, Blough *et al.*, 1999). Since the link function characterises how the mean on the original cost scale is related to the set of regressors the GLM model does not suffer from the retransformation problem we encountered in Chapter 3 and we can derive predictions on the original scale directly from the model.

Stata provides seven link functions to choose for GLMs, however, our interest in modelling health care costs leads us to focus on the log, identity and power link functions. An identity link function specifies the covariates to act linearly on the conditional mean, whereas the power link allows the analyst to model the conditional mean as a power function of the covariates: $E[y \mid x]) = (x\beta)^\tau$.

An advantage of the GLM approach is that it allows heteroskedasticity to be modelled through the choice of distributional family, albeit this is limited to specifications of the conditional variance that are pre-specified functions of the mean. So the second requirement for GLM estimation is to specify the relationship between the conditional variance and the conditional mean. GLM uses distributions that belong to the linear exponential family, many of which take the form:

$$\text{var}\left[y_i \mid x_i\right] = \nu\left(\mu_i\right) \propto \left(E\left[y_i \mid x_i\right]\right)^\nu$$

Most often, the power parameter, ν, is assumed to take a discrete value, although this is not strictly necessary, and characterises a set of distributional families based on power functions. Common specifications of ν and the distributional family types to which these lead are: Gaussian (constant variance; $\nu = 0$); Poisson (variance proportional to the mean; $\nu = 1$); gamma (variance proportional to the square of the mean; $\nu = 2$); inverse Gaussian (variance proportional to cube of the mean; $\nu = 3$). These distributions allow considerable flexibility in modelling cost data and perhaps the most commonly used specification for health care expenditures is the log link with a gamma variance (Blough *et al.*, 1999; Manning and Mullahy, 2001; Manning *et al.*, 2005).

GLMs can be estimated using quasi-score functions which have the pseudo- or QML property (which do not require the full density to be specified) and importantly estimates are consistent so long as the conditional mean is correctly specified (Gourieroux *et al.*, 1984). Where the mean function of the model is correctly specified, misspecification of the variance function will lead to inefficient parameter estimates and, in the extreme, might cause the estimation routine to fail to converge. If the mean function is misspecified, then the model will fail to fit well the observed data across its full range. In such circumstances the choice of variance function will affect both the efficiency of the estimator and model fit (predictions versus observed data) (Buntin and Zaslavsky, 2004). As the estimator only specifies the mean and variance functions, more efficient estimators may be obtained that make use of correctly specified functions for higher moments, such as the skewness of the distributions.

We estimate a set of models using the GLM framework within Stata: the first has a square root link and gamma type variance (glm, link(power 0.5) family(gamma)) and the others all have log links, coupled with a gamma distribution (glm, l(log) f(gamma)), a Poisson distribution (f(poisson)), and a log-normal distribution (f(normal)). First estimate the model with a square root link and gamma variance as follows:

```
glm y $xvars, l(power 0.5) f(gamma) vce(robust) nolog
predict glmyhat if e(sample), mu
```

This produces the output presented in Table 12.12. Note that the form of the link and variance functions taken are defined in the Stata output as V(u) and g(u) respectively.

The results indicate a statistically significant and positive effect of supplementary insurance on total expenditures. Physical and activity limitations and the number of chronic conditions are also positively associated with health care expenditures. We can compute the average marginal (and incremental) effects by re-estimating the model specifying the set of binary regressors as factor variables

Table 12.12 Generalised linear model; square root link, gamma distribution

```
-------------------------------------------------------------------
Generalized linear models                No. of obs      =     2955
Optimization : ML                        Residual df     =     2947
                                         Scale parameter =  2.314334
Deviance     = 3992.897291               (1/df) Deviance =  1.354902
Pearson      = 6820.342564               (1/df) Pearson  =  2.314334
Variance function: V(u) = u^2            [Gamma]
Link function     : g(u) = u^(0.5)       [Power]
                                         AIC             =  19.47638
Log pseudolikelihood = -28768.35365      BIC             = -19557.33
-------------------------------------------------------------------
             |              Robust
      totexp |     Coef. Std. Err.      z   P>|z|  [95% Conf. Interval]
-------------+-----------------------------------------------------
         age | -.1638597  .177636   -0.92  0.356  -.5120199   .1843005
      female | -5.805946 2.208885   -2.63  0.009  -10.13528  -1.476611
      income |  .0390525 .0485143    0.80  0.421  -.0560337   .1341387
     suppins |  4.602653 2.177238    2.11  0.035   .3353456    8.86996
      phylim |  14.54638 2.828548    5.14  0.000   9.002525   20.09023
      actlim |   19.5701 3.416653    5.73  0.000   12.87358   26.26662
      totchr |  11.30037 .9123141   12.39  0.000    9.51227   13.08848
       _cons |  61.70329 13.91044    4.44  0.000   34.43934   88.96724
-------------------------------------------------------------------
```

and using the post estimation command, `margins, dydx(*)`. The incremental effect of having supplementary insurance is $753; physical limitations is $2,418, and activity limitations is $3,379. In general, annual health care expenditures for women are $960 less than men. The marginal effect of income is estimated as $6.42 (annual income has been divided by $1,000).

There are a number of diagnostic tests that can be applied to GLM models to inform the choice of link and variance functions. To assess the choice of variance function, deviance residuals (deviance residuals are recommended by McCullagh and Nelder (1989) as having the best properties for examining the goodness of fit of a GLM model) from a GLM model can be assessed using normal plots, which plot the residuals against the values they would take if they were normally distributed. If the variance function is chosen correctly then deviance residuals should be approximately normally distributed and follow the 45° line on a normal plot. Compute and display deviance residuals, using a normal plot, as follows:

```
predict e if e(sample), deviance // deviance residuals

pnorm e, title(normal pp plot: glm sqr-gamma)              ///
   ytitle(residuals) xtitle(inverse normal)
```

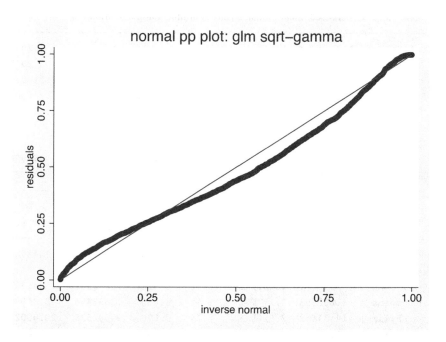

Figure 12.5 Normal pp plot for generalised linear model.

This produces the normal plot seen in Figure 12.5, showing some deviation from normality suggesting that the gamma function may not be the optimal distributional form for these data.

A further test for the adequacy of the variance function for health expenditure data, suggested by Manning and Mullahy (2001), is provided by the Park test (Park, 1966). The idea behind the test is based on the variance function being proportional to the conditional mean. The Park test exploits this relationship by using a regression of $\ln(y_i - \hat{y}_i)^2$ on $\ln(\hat{y}_i)$ and a constant, where $\hat{y}_i$ is obtained from a preliminary GLM regression. For example, for a log link function, this follows since: $\text{var}\,[y\,|\,x] = \omega(\exp(x\beta))^\nu$ and accordingly, $\ln(\text{var}\,[y\,|\,x]) = \ln(\omega) + \nu\ln(\exp(x\beta))$, which can be approximated via the following GLM (with log link) regression: $(y_i - \hat{y}_i)^2 = \alpha + \nu\ln(\hat{y}_i) + \epsilon_i$. The estimated coefficient, $\hat{\nu}$, provides an indication of the appropriate power of the variance function. The following code implements this test:

```
generate e2=(y-glmyhat)^2
generate lnyhat = log(glmyhat)
glm e2 lnyhat, l(log) f(gamma) nolog vce(robust)
```

```
Generalized linear models                No. of obs      =      2955
Optimization    : ML                     Residual df     =      2953
                                         Scale parameter = 27.79775
Deviance        = 12175.92306            (1/df) Deviance = 4.123238
Pearson         = 82086.74136            (1/df) Pearson  = 27.79775
Variance function: V(u) = u^2            [Gamma]
Link function   : g(u)   = ln(u)         [Log]
                                         AIC             = 38.58169
Log pseudolikelihood  = -57002.44441     BIC             = -11422.25
-----------------------------------------------------------------------
             |              Robust
       e2 |      Coef.   Std. Err.      z    P>|z|   [95% Conf. Interval]
----------|------------------------------------------------------------
   lnyhat |   1.651486   .1700116    9.71   0.000    1.318269    1.984703
    _cons |   3.863639   1.521485    2.54   0.011    .8815831    6.845694
-----------------------------------------------------------------------
```

```
test lnyhat == 0    // Gaussian

( 1)  [e2]lnyhat = 0
          chi2( 1)   =     94.36
        Prob > chi2 =    0.0000

test lnyhat == 1    // Poisson

( 1)  [e2]lnyhat = 1
          chi2( 1)   =     14.68
        Prob > chi2 =    0.0001
```

```
test lnyhat == 2    // Gamma

 ( 1)   [e2]lnyhat = 2
            chi2( 1)  =     4.20
          Prob > chi2 =  0.0404

test lnyhat == 3    // Inverse Gaussian

 ( 1)   [e2]lnyhat = 3
            chi2( 1)  =    62.91
          Prob > chi2 =  0.0000
```

These results indicate that the gamma distribution ($\nu = 2$) provides the most appropriate fit to the data. We can, however, see from the regression output that the coefficient estimate, $\hat{\nu} = 1.65$ (lnyhat in the Stata output), although close to 2, is not an integer value. We will see later how we might improve on the fit of the GLM approach in situations where ν takes non-integer values.

Table 12.13 Link test for generalised linear model

```
------------------------------------------------------------------------
Iteration 0:  log pseudolikelihood = -29386.264
Iteration 1:  log pseudolikelihood = -28773.904
Iteration 2:  log pseudolikelihood = -28768.241
Iteration 3:  log pseudolikelihood = -28768.154
Iteration 4:  log pseudolikelihood = -28768.154

Generalized linear models                 No. of obs      =       2955
Optimization   : ML                       Residual df     =       2952
                                          Scale parameter =   2.303409
Deviance       = 3992.497782              (1/df) Deviance =   1.352472
Pearson        = 6799.664121              (1/df) Pearson  =   2.303409

Variance function: V(u) = u^2                [ Gamma]
Link function     : g(u) = u^(0.5)           [ Power]

                                          AIC             =   19.47286
Log pseudolikelihood   = -28768.15389     BIC             = -19597.68
------------------------------------------------------------------------
             |                 Robust
      totexp |      Coef. Std. Err.      z  P>|z|  [95% Conf. Interval]
----------- +-----------------------------------------------------------
       _hat |   1.132209  .2888037    3.92  0.000    .566164    1.698254
     _hatsq |  -.0008243  .0017267   -0.48  0.633   -.0042086     .00256
       _cons |  -4.881946  11.23846   -0.43  0.664  -26.90892   17.14502
------------------------------------------------------------------------
```

Table 12.14 Summary results for alternative GLMs

Link Distribution	(1) Square root Gamma	(2) Log Gamma	(3) Log Poisson	(4) Log Normal
Age	−26.9 (29.3)	−39.9 (34.9)	−67.6 (36.9)	−78.7 (46.9)
Female	−959.9 (369.2)	−1441.2 (447.9)	−1413.2 (441.5)	−1266.1 (545.4)
Income	6.42 (7.97)	8.39 (9.43)	8.63 (9.46)	8.77 (11.02)
Supplementary insurance	752.6 (357.7)	901.7 (435.3)	688.8 (430.4)	455.9 (512.4)
Physical limitations	2417.7 (480.9)	2834.5 (497.9)	2708.8 (546.1)	2616.6 (732.8)
Activity limitations	3378.8 (625.7)	3228.3 (613.6)	3168.9 (634.2)	3232.3 (751.3)
# Chronic conditions	1857.2 (156.4)	1991.6 (182.3)	1602.4 (160.7)	1329.5 (190.7)
Linktest	Pass	Fail	Fail	Fail
Hosmer Lemeshow	Pass	Pass	Pass	Fail
Park test (coef, $\hat{\nu}$)	1.651	1.649	1.407	1.237

A link test using the GLM post-estimation command (`linktest, l(power 0.5) f(gamma) vce(robust)`) fails to reject the square root link function (Table 12.13). Note that the test is implemented using the same link and distributional family as the model being tested. A modified Hosmer–Lemeshow test also fails to reject the specification of the mean function: $F(10, 2945) = 0.45$ ($P = 0.92$).

Table 12.14 presents marginal effects and incremental effects for four specifications of GLMs. The link test rejects the log link but does not reject the square root link. The modified Park tests for these specifications always reject specific integer values of ν, although values of 1 (Poisson) and 2 (gamma) perform best.

Extended estimating equations

Basu and Rathouz (2005) suggest an extension of the GLM approach termed extended estimating equations (EEEs). Their approach estimates the link and variance functions directly using the available data and thereby avoids many of the problems due to misspecification. Accordingly, the analyst is not required to know the appropriate link or distributional family. Instead, the relevant parameters defining the link and variance functions are estimated via ancillary estimating equations.

The model makes use of the Box–Cox transformation for the link function:

$$x_i\beta = \begin{cases} \dfrac{\mu_i^{\lambda} - 1}{\lambda} & \text{if } \lambda \neq 0 \\[2mm] \log\left(\mu_i\right) & \text{if } \lambda = 0 \end{cases}$$

where $\mu_i = E[y_i \mid x_i]$. This is complemented with a general power function specification for the variance:

$$\text{var}\left(y_i \mid x_i\right) = \nu_1 \mu_i^{\nu_2}$$

This allows restrictions corresponding to common distributional family types to be directly tested, for example, $\nu_1 = 1$; $\nu_2 = 1$ corresponds to a Poisson distribution and $\nu_1 > 0$; $\nu_2 = 2$ the gamma type distribution. An alternative is to specify a quadratic function of the variance:

$$\text{var}\left(y_i \mid x_i\right) = \nu_1 \mu_i + \nu_2 \mu_i^2$$

which corresponds to the Poisson distribution when $\nu_1 = 1$ and $\nu_2 = 0$ and the gamma when $\nu_1 = 0$ and $\nu_2 > 0$.

The GLM specifications estimated above are nested within the EEE model, which is implemented in Stata by the user written (by Anirban Basu) program `pglm`. To aid convergence it is recommended to rescale the dependent variable by its mean prior to estimation. The following commands estimate the model on the MEPS data:

```
quietly summ y
generate scyvar = y/r(mean)      // rescale the cost variable
global sc = r(mean)

pglm scyvar $xvars               // estimation via EEE
```

Table 12.15 presents the results of EEE estimation. Note that by default the program models the variance as a power function (the option `vf(q)` must be specified to estimate the variance as a quadratic function of the conditional mean). Robust variance estimates are also reported by default.

The estimate of the Box–Cox parameter for the link function is 0.563 (95% CI: 0.28 to 0.84), suggesting a square root rather than a log transformation. This differs markedly from the estimate obtained in Chapter 3 using the Box–Cox regression model (0.076) and illustrates how misleading the Box–Cox regression can be where the errors are non-normal and heteroskedastic. The estimate of ν_2 (equivalent to ν in the notation adopted for GLM and labelled `theta2` in the output for `pglm`) is 1.67 (95% CI: 1.47 to 1.86) between the Poisson and gamma distributions.

Table 12.15 Extended estimating equations

```
-----------------------------------------------------------------------
Extended GEE with Power Variance Function      No of obs    =    2955
Optimization: Fisher's Scoring                 Residual df  =    2944
Variance:     (theta1*mu^theta2)
Link:         (mu^lambda - 1)/lambda
Std Errors:   Robust
-----------------------------------------------------------------------
   scyvar |    Coef.  Std. Err.    z  P>|z|    [95% Conf. Interval]
----------|------------------------------------------------------------
scyvar    |
     age  | -.0049493  .0040112  -1.23  0.217  -.012811   .0029124
   female | -.1453583  .0495788  -2.93  0.003  -.2425309  -.0481857
   income |   .000872  .0009348   0.93  0.351  -.0009602   .0027043
  suppins |    .10745  .051777    2.08  0.038   .005969    .2089311
   phylim |  .3380732  .068188    4.96  0.000   .2044273   .4717192
   actlim |  .4636564  .0848272   5.47  0.000   .2973982   .6299147
   totchr |   .258112  .0214944  12.01  0.000   .2159838   .3002403
    _cons | -.4452356  .3137634  -1.42  0.156  -1.060201   .1697292
----------|------------------------------------------------------------
lambda    |
    _cons |  .5626705  .1428813   3.94  0.000   .2826282   .8427127
----------|------------------------------------------------------------
theta1    |
    _cons |  2.139191  .1272745  16.81  0.000   1.889738   2.388645
----------|------------------------------------------------------------
theta2    |
    _cons |  1.665464  .1001817  16.62  0.000   1.469112   1.861817
-----------------------------------------------------------------------
```

To compute incremental effects, for example of having supplementary insurance, from the model we can use the post estimation command (pglmpredict) as follows (see Basu, 2005):

```
pglmpredict iesuppins, ie(suppins) var(varsupp) scale($sc)
summ iesuppins varsupp
```

```
   Variable |   Obs      Mean    Std. Dev.      Min       Max
------------|-------------------------------------------------
  iesuppins |  2955    750.4544   187.4197   431.6049  1375.846
    varsupp |  2955   144979.4    87697.86   36997.79   620865.4
```

The incremental effect is estimated to be $750, indicating that the health care costs of Medicare patients with supplementary insurance are on average $750 greater than for those without supplementary insurance. The variable varsupp provides the variance of the incremental effect for each observation, conditional on the set of regressors. To obtain the variance of the overall incremental effect, this needs to be combined with the uncertainty associated with the set of regressors. This is given by the variance of the mean incremental effect (Basu and Rathouz, 2005). For the above application the overall standard error of the incremental effect is given by:

$$\text{se (i.e. suppins)} = \sqrt{\frac{187.42^2}{2955} + 144979} = \sqrt{144991} \approx 381$$

To estimate the marginal effect of a continuous variable such as income, we can use the same post estimation command as above with the option `me()`, that is: `pglmpredict meinc, me(inc) var(varinc) scale($sc)`. The marginal effect of a \$1,000 increase in annual income on health care costs is \$6.12 (95% CI: −\$7.18 to \$19.42). These figures are very similar to those estimated above using a generalised linear model with a square root power function and gamma distributed errors.

12.4 FINITE MIXTURE MODELS

Finite mixture models offer an alternative approach to estimating cost data and are useful in situations where the distribution is thought to be multimodal. In such circumstances the data may be modelled as a mixture of distributions. For example, Deb and Burgess (2007) apply a mixture of gamma distributions to model health care costs. Chapter 11 also considers finite mixture models, but in the context of health care utilisation (count data) where there is a large mass point at zero and a long right hand tail to account for individuals who make heavy use of care.

Assume there exists a set of heterogeneous latent classes $j = 1, \ldots, C$ to which individuals belong but where class membership is unobserved. Assuming homogeneity of individuals within each class conditional on the set of covariates, then the observed costs for individual i have a density $f_j(y_i \mid x_i; \beta_j)$, assumed to take a particular distributional form, for example a gamma distribution. Note that the parameters are specific to each class and accordingly are allowed to vary across the C classes. Denoting the probability of membership to class j as π_{ij} ($0 < \pi_{ij} < 1$ and $\Sigma_{j=1}^{C} \pi_{ij} = 1$), then the density of y_i is given by

$$f\left(y_i \mid x_i; \pi_{i1}, \ldots, \pi_{iC}; \beta_1, \ldots, \beta_C\right) = \sum_{j=1}^{C} \pi_{ij} f_j\left(y_i \mid x_i; \beta_j\right)$$

Heterogeneity in outcomes is reflected in the C mass points of the discrete distribution. Estimation recovers the probability of class membership together with the vectors of parameters, β_j. Typically class membership probabilities are treated as fixed parameters $\pi_{ij} = \pi_j$, but this can be relaxed. Following estimation, the posterior probability of class membership for each individual can be calculated.

These probabilities can then be combined with the predicted costs for the individual in each class to obtain an estimate of the overall predicted cost.

We estimate a two-class (or two component) finite mixture of gamma distributions. This is done using the user-written command fmm written by Partha Deb:

```
fmm y $xvars , vce(robust) components(2) mixtureof(gamma)
```

The results are presented in Table 12.16. The estimated class proportions are 0.752 and 0.248 for class 1 and 2 respectively. The gamma shape parameter is estimated as 1.415 for class 1 and 1.064 for class 2. The former is significantly different to 1 (p-value of H_0: /lnalpha1=0; p-value < 0.05) while the latter is not and could be approximated by an exponential distribution. We compute the fitted values of cost for each individual and for each latent class and analyse the resulting summary statistics. The mean fitted value and the minimum and maximum are substantially larger for class 2 compared to class 1. We might think of class 2 representing high cost users of health care and class 1 representing low cost users.

```
predict yhat1 if e(sample), equation(component1)
predict yhat2 if e(sample), equation(component2)
summarize yhat1 yhat2
```

Variable	Obs	Mean	Std. Dev.	Min	Max
yhat1	2955	4183.367	3242.587	982.8514	33938.95
yhat2	2955	16882.44	9934.911	5427.546	97064.38

The posterior probability that each individual belongs to a given class can be computed and the means confirm the estimated class proportions:

```
predict post1 if e(sample), pos equation(component1)
predict post2 if e(sample), pos equation(component2)
summarize post1 post2
```

Variable	Obs	Mean	Std. Dev.	Min	Max
post1	2955	.7524014	.2673642	4.18e-19	.9615063
post2	2955	.2475986	.2673642	.0384937	1

We can combine the above probabilities of class membership with the fitted values for each class to obtain overall predictions of costs for each individual or alternatively we can compute these directly using command predict. This shows that the mean of the fitted values is below that for observed costs and has a smaller variance.

Table 12.16 Finite mixture model (mixture of gammas)

```
------------------------------------------------------------------------
Fitting Gamma regression model:
Iteration 0:  log pseudolikelihood = -28780.764
Note: Output suppressed
Iteration 3:  log pseudolikelihood = -28759.108
Fitting 2 component Gamma model:
Iteration 0:  log pseudolikelihood = -28758.697 (not concave)
Note: Output suppressed
Iteration 9:  log pseudolikelihood =  -28503.5
2 component Gamma regression              Number of obs  =      2955
                                          Wald chi2(14)  =    685.07
Log pseudolikelihood = -28503.5           Prob > chi2    =    0.0000
------------------------------------------------------------------------
             |            Robust
      totexp |   Coef.  Std. Err.    z   P>|z|   [95% Conf. Interval]
-------------+----------------------------------------------------------
component1   |
         age |  .0101255  .0040455   2.50  0.012   .0021964   .0180545
      female | -.0666263  .0514715  -1.29  0.196  -.1675085   .0342559
      income |  .0031533  .0010063   3.13  0.002    .001181   .0051256
     suppins |  .2982341  .0538201   5.54  0.000   .1927486   .4037197
      phylim |  .2875844  .0664252   4.33  0.000   .1573934   .4177755
      actlim |  .3067102  .0773966   3.96  0.000   .1550157   .4584047
      totchr |  .3590686  .0227799  15.76  0.000   .3144207   .4037165
       _cons |  5.951575  .3285793  18.11  0.000   5.307571   6.595579
-------------+----------------------------------------------------------
component2   |
         age | -.0163599  .0076243  -2.15  0.032  -.0313032  -.0014166
      female | -.2716229  .0892164  -3.04  0.002  -.4464837   -.096762
      income | -.0005708  .0024328  -0.23  0.815  -.0053389   .0041974
     suppins |  .0355457  .0911813   0.39  0.697  -.1431664   .2142578
      phylim |  .3974127  .1021512   3.89  0.000      .1972   .5976253
      actlim |  .4190959  .1035322   4.05  0.000   .2161764   .6220153
      totchr |  .2087046  .0378021   5.52  0.000   .1346138   .2827953
       _cons |  10.22769  .6161151  16.60  0.000   9.020126   11.43525
-------------+----------------------------------------------------------
 /imlogitpi1 |  1.111462  .1855092   5.99  0.000   .7478707   1.475053
   /lnalpha1 |  .3473538  .0422904   8.21  0.000   .2644661   .4302414
   /lnalpha2 |  .0619604  .0554762   1.12  0.264  -.0467709   .1706918
-------------+----------------------------------------------------------
      alpha1 |  1.415317  .0598543         1.302735   1.537629
      alpha2 |   1.06392  .0590222          .954306   1.186125
         pi1 |  .7524016  .0345591         .6787146   .8138242
         pi2 |  .2475984  .0345591         .1861758   .3212854
------------------------------------------------------------------------
```

```
predict yhat if e(sample)
summarize yhat y
```

```
   Variable |       Obs        Mean    Std. Dev.         Min         Max
------------|------------------------------------------------------------
       yhat |      2955    7327.638     4746.84    2301.976    49568.71
     totexp |      2955    7290.235    11990.84           3      125610
```

The finite mixture model assumes homogeneity conditional on class membership, but allows for heterogeneity in response to covariates across classes. This
can be seen in Table 12.16 where the coefficients for many of the covariates
differ across classes. A Wald test of the equality of the coefficients of all covariates across the two latent classes provides a formal test of homogeneous responses
and clearer rejects the null hypothesis:

```
test [component1=component2]
```

```
 ( 1)   [component1]age    - [component2]age    = 0
 ( 2)   [component1]female - [component2]female = 0
 ( 3)   [component1]income - [component2]income = 0
 ( 4)   [component1]suppins - [component2]suppins = 0
 ( 5)   [component1]phylim - [component2]phylim = 0
 ( 6)   [component1]actlim - [component2]actlim = 0
 ( 7)   [component1]totchr - [component2]totchr = 0

            chi2( 7)    =     32.27
          Prob > chi2 =    0.0000
```

Tests of equality of individual coefficients are perhaps more revealing and we
can see that, for example, the impact on latent levels of costs of holding
supplementary insurance is greater for 'low users' of health care (class 1) than
'higher users' (class 2):

```
test [component1=component2]: suppins
```

```
 ( 1)   [component1]suppins - [component2]suppins = 0

            chi2( 1)    =      6.38
          Prob > chi2 =    0.0115
```

Marginal effects are more useful for interpreting the impact of the covariates
within each of the two classes than simply considering coefficients on the latent
scale. These can be obtained using the margins command (however, note that
fmm does not support the specification of factor variables). Again these reveal that
the impact of the regressors differ across classes. In particular, the marginal effect

of both physical and activity limitations are substantially greater in the second class compared to the first. In general the average cost for males in class 2 is far greater than that estimated class 1.

```
margins, dydx(*) predict(eq(component1))
```

```
Warning: cannot perform check for estimable functions.
Average marginal effects                  Number of obs  =    2955
Model VCE      : Robust
Expression     : predicted mean: component1, predict(eq(component1))
dy/dx w.r.t.   : age female income suppins phylim actlim totchr
```

	Delta-method					
	dy/dx	Std. Err.	z	P>|z|	[95% Conf.	Interval]
age	42.35855	17.02217	2.49	0.013	8.995712	75.72139
female	-278.7222	218.6819	-1.27	0.202	-707.3308	149.8863
income	13.19142	4.197588	3.14	0.002	4.964295	21.41854
suppins	1247.623	224.9222	5.55	0.000	806.7833	1688.462
phylim	1203.071	297.4272	4.04	0.000	620.1247	1786.018
actlim	1283.081	346.5094	3.70	0.000	603.9353	1962.227
totchr	1502.116	114.2043	13.15	0.000	1278.279	1725.952

```
margins, dydx(*) predict(eq(component2))
```

```
Warning: cannot perform check for estimable functions.
Average marginal effects                  Number of obs  =    2955
Model VCE   : Robust
Expression  : predicted mean: component2, predict(eq(component2))
dy/dx w.r.t.   : age female income suppins phylim actlim totchr
```

	Delta-method					
	dy/dx	Std. Err.	z	P>|z|	[95% Conf.	Interval]
age	-276.1952	135.5153	-2.04	0.042	-541.8004	-10.5901
female	-4585.657	1570.112	-2.92	0.003	-7663.019	-1508.295
income	-9.635779	41.04294	-0.23	0.814	-90.07846	70.80691
suppins	600.0982	1540.742	0.39	0.697	-2419.701	3619.898
phylim	6709.296	1731.652	3.87	0.000	3315.321	10103.27
actlim	7075.361	1789.176	3.95	0.000	3568.64	10582.08
totchr	3523.443	662.1266	5.32	0.000	2225.698	4821.187

In empirical applications of the finite mixture model the number of classes tends to be small and usually restricted to two or three. The number of classes is commonly chosen according to information criteria, such as the AIC or Bayesian information criterion (BIC). For example, we can extend the above estimation to including three classes. The results are presented in Table 12.18. Inspection of the fitted values for the three classes suggests that the classes now consist of low cost (with low variance) users of health care (class 3), moderate users of care (class 1) and high users of health care (class 2) with the estimated class proportions being 0.597, 0.180 and 0.223 respectively.

```
predict yhat2 if e(sample), equation(component2)
predict yhat3 if e(sample), equation(component3)
summarize yhat1 yhat2 yhat3
```

```
   Variable |      Obs       Mean    Std. Dev.        Min         Max
------------+-------------------------------------------------------
      yhat1 |     2955   5167.072    14720.81    135.2199    306885.2
      yhat2 |     2955   17850.63    9820.906    6146.098    91665.15
      yhat3 |     2955   4303.047    2477.805    1435.611     20725.9
```

Information criteria comparing the two- and three-component models are provided in Table 12.17. The AIC for the three-component model suggests an improved fit over the two-component model, although if we apply the BIC, which carries a greater penalty for the additional parameters of the three component model this is no longer the case. Similarly, we can use information criteria to differentiate between the distributional form chosen for the latent classes. Table 12.17 reports these for both a two- and three-component Gaussian mixture model. This specification appears inferior to the gamma distribution.

Table 12.17 Finite mixture model information criteria

Model	Obser- vations	ll(null)	ll (model)	df	AIC	BIC
2-comp gamma	2955	.	−28503.50	19	57045	57158.83
3-comp gamma	2955	.	−28467.09	29	56992.19	57165.93
2-comp Gaussian	2955	.	−29396.17	19	58830.33	58944.17
3-comp Gaussian	2955	.	−28945.94	29	57949.88	58123.6

Table 12.18 Finite mixture model (three-component mixture of gammas)

```
--------------------------------------------------------------------
Note: Iterations suppressed from output
3 component Gamma regression              Number of obs  =    2955
                                          Wald chi2(21)  =  496.54
Log pseudolikelihood = -28467.093         Prob > chi2    =  0.0000
--------------------------------------------------------------------
```

totexp	Coef.	Robust Std. Err.	z	P>|z|	[95% Conf. Interval]	
component1						
age	.0102666	.013633	0.75	0.451	-.0164534	.0369867
female	.1275259	.1686556	0.76	0.450	-.203033	.4580848
income	.0037725	.0027984	1.35	0.178	-.0017123	.0092574
suppins	.524622	.1475932	3.55	0.000	.2353446	.8138994
phylim	.2737875	.5512956	0.50	0.619	-.8067319	1.354307
actlim	-.2516385	.4211391	-0.60	0.550	-1.077056	.5737789
totchr	.9921498	.2285194	4.34	0.000	.54426	1.44004
_cons	3.912803	1.245443	3.14	0.002	1.471781	6.353826
component2						
age	-.0164495	.0077499	-2.12	0.034	-.0316391	-.0012599
female	-.2658589	.0895924	-2.97	0.003	-.4414567	-.0902611
income	-.0005149	.0024644	-0.21	0.835	-.0053451	.0043153
suppins	.0289152	.0921366	0.31	0.754	-.1516693	.2094997
phylim	.3798167	.1043564	3.64	0.000	.1752819	.5843514
actlim	.4201158	.1041311	4.03	0.000	.2160227	.6242089
totchr	.1869842	.039921	4.68	0.000	.1087404	.265228
_cons	10.26538	.6271207	16.37	0.000	9.036244	11.49451
component3						
age	.0085035	.0048603	1.75	0.080	-.0010226	.0180296
female	-.0928203	.063083	-1.47	0.141	-.2164607	.0308201
income	.0027411	.0011834	2.32	0.021	.0004218	.0050604
suppins	.2191547	.0712548	3.08	0.002	.0794978	.3588115
phylim	.2717615	.1038358	2.62	0.009	.068247	.475276
actlim	.4023513	.1263717	3.18	0.001	.1546673	.6500352
totchr	.232062	.0509516	4.55	0.000	.1321986	.3319254
_cons	6.18609	.4293624	14.41	0.000	5.344556	7.027625
/imlogitpi1	-1.198207	.5626353	-2.13	0.033	-2.300952	-.0954619
/imlogitpi2	-.983005	.1851399	-5.31	0.000	-1.345872	-.6201375
/lnalpha1	.4850216	.1666273	2.91	0.004	.158438	.8116052
/lnalpha2	.1476929	.072301	2.04	0.041	.0059856	.2894002
/lnalpha3	.6233452	.0721764	8.64	0.000	.481882	.7648084
alpha1	1.62421	.2706378			1.171679	2.251519
alpha2	1.159157	.0838082			1.006004	1.335626
alpha3	1.865157	.1346204			1.619119	2.148583
pi1	.1800413	.082556			.0683623	.3965138
pi2	.2232714	.0371389			.1588997	.3042866
pi3	.5966873	.0677978			.463806	.7295686

12.5 COMPARING MODEL PERFORMANCE

In this section, we compare the performance of the estimators described above together with those outlined in Chapter 3 using the sample of MEPS data. The literature contains a number of studies that compare the performance of different estimators for health care cost data. These studies differ in their approach to assessing the performance with some relying on Monte Carlo simulations based on models with known distributional forms, whilst others are based on evaluating predictive performance for models estimated on observational data and assessed using a separate validation sample.

Our approach to comparing model performance follows that of Hill and Miller (2010). For each model, we summarise tests of specification using the Pregibon link test and the Pearson test, which is related to the Hosmer and Lemeshow approach, and test whether the correlation coefficient between the prediction error and the fitted values, on the raw cost scale, equals zero. We summarise the goodness of fit including the R^2 from an auxiliary regression of actual costs on the predicted values on the raw cost scale, as well as the related measure of root mean squared error (RMSE),

$$\text{RMSE} = \sqrt{\frac{\sum_{i=1}^{n}(y_i - \hat{y}_i)^2}{n}}$$

and the mean absolute prediction error (MAPE):

$$\text{MAPE} = \frac{\sum_{i=1}^{n} \text{abs}(y_i - \hat{y}_i)}{n}$$

A potential downside of heavily parameterised models, particularly where these have been constructed using a given dataset, is that they may overfit a particular sample of data and perform poorly in terms of out-of-sample forecasts. When models are to be used for prediction, the Copas test provides a useful guide to out-of-sample performance and guards against overfitting (Blough *et al.*, 1999; Copas, 1983). The Copas test works by randomly splitting the data into an estimation, or training, sample and a forecast, or holdout, sample (see e.g. Buntin and Zaslavsky, 2004). The model is estimated on the former and used to form predictions on the latter. The predictions from the forecast data are then regressed on actual costs to test whether the coefficient on the predictions is significantly different from one over multiple replications of the random sampling. For linear models, evidence of a significant difference suggests a problem of overfitting. In nonlinear models, this might also imply model misspecification (Bilger and Manning, 2011).

We implement the Copas test using the related approach of ν-fold cross validation. This consists of splitting the sample of n individuals into equal groups of size ν – here the sample is split into 100 groups with either 29 or 30 observations in each group. The model is estimated on a sample with $n-\nu$ observations and predictions formed on the remaining sample of ν observations. Where there are 100 groups we can repeat this process 100 times so that fitted values are provided for all observations treated as out-of-sample. The predictions can then be compared to actual costs for evaluation purposes. Performance is assessed using the RMSE, MAPE and mean prediction error (MPE), which captures bias within the forecast sample:

$$\text{MPE} = \frac{\sum_{i=1}^{n}(y_i - \hat{y}_i)}{n}$$

The results of evaluation are reported in Table 12.19. For the link test, Pearson's correlation coefficient, Hosmer–Lemeshow test, and the Copas ν-fold cross validation figures in bold indicate that the model was not rejected by the specification test at the 5 per cent level of statistical significance. The three models which perform best on each criterion of R^2, RMSE, MAPE and MPE, are also highlighted in bold. It is notable that the regression on log costs, the exponential conditional mean models, and the GLMs with a log link all perform poorly according to the link test. The Copas test indicates that the generalised gamma specification suffers from overfitting, but less so once additional heteroskedasticity is specified. OLS on log cost, Poisson regression and GLMs with a log link also perform poorly with these data according to the Copas test.

Not surprisingly, given estimation is based on maximising the R^2, OLS does best on this specific criterion within the estimation sample. The EEE model and the GLM model with square root link and gamma distribution have a similar performance to OLS. The generalised gamma and OLS on the log scale have poor performance on this criterion. A similar pattern is reflected in the RMSE for both the estimation and forecast samples with OLS and EEE performing best, and OLS on the square-root scale and GLM with a square-root link and gamma distribution also performing well. EEE and OLS on the square-root scale also perform well using the MAPE whereas untransformed OLS does less well on this criterion. Bias (MPE) is small for linear regression, the square root transformed regression, Poisson regression (maximum likelihood and GLM) and the EEE model. The bias is substantial for the generalised gamma without additional heteroskedasticity and the generalised beta of the second kind. An interesting finding is that OLS on untransformed cost performs well across the range of criteria applied. EEE and square-root functions also perform well. Stata code used to run the evaluation exercise is available through the web page.

Table 12.19 Comparison of model specification and predictive performance

	Link test p-value	Pearson p-value	Hosmer-Lemeshow p-value	Copas test	R^2	RMSE		MAPE		MPE
	Within sample	Within sample	Within sample	v-fold cross validation	Within sample	Within sample	v-fold cross validation	Within sample	v-fold cross validation	v-fold cross validation
OLS on y	**0.133**	–	0.008	**0.974** (0.608)	**0.116**	**11270**	**11307**	6225	6244	**–1.41**
OLS on ln(y)	0.000	0.000	0.001	0.713 (0.000)	0.095	11499	11515	6330	6342	–218.8
OLS on $\sqrt{y}$	**0.712**	**0.817**	**0.686**	**0.969** (0.545)	0.114	11283	**11310**	**6181**	**6198**	**–1.27**
ECM – NLS	–	**0.350**	0.001	**1.002** (0.968)	0.113	11296	11353	6267	6294	–102.6
ECM – Poisson–ML	0.000	**0.158**	**0.062**	0.897 (0.035)	0.110	11312	11362	6196	6220	**–3.36**
Generalised gamma	0.000	0.000	0.000	0.590 (0.000)	0.093	11676	11714	6429	6452	–403.5
Gen gamma + het	0.000	0.004	**0.266**	0.841 (0.001)	0.106	11354	11395	6221	6245	–39.0
Generalised beta	–	**0.832**		**0.974** (0.621)	0.110	11319	11337	6409	6423	–432.1
GLM sqrt–gamma	**0.633**	**0.343**	**0.922**	**0.934** (0.178)	**0.115**	**11281**	**11311**	**6185**	**6203**	– 29.3
GLM log–gamma	0.000	0.000	**0.050**	0.759 (0.000)	0.106	11390	11432	6254	6276	–147.0
GLM log–normal	0.001	**0.350**	0.001	**1.002** (0.968)	0.113	11295	11353	6267	6294	–102.6
GLM log–poisson	0.000	**0.158**	**0.062**	0.897 (0.035)	0.110	11312	11362	6196	6220	**–3.36**
EEE	–	**0.690**	**0.894**	**0.955** (0.371)	**0.116**	**11274**	**11310**	**6179**	**6200**	–7.06
FMM gamma	–	0.000	**0.120**	0.792 (0.000)	0.104	11382	11423	6218	6238	–42.6

Notes to the table: R^2 denotes the R-squared form a regression of actual costs on the predicted values; RMSE is the root mean squared prediction error on the cost scale, MAPE is the mean absolute prediction error; MPE is the mean prediction error (bias) for the cross-validation predictions. The results for the Copas test with v-fold cross validation are all based on 100 groups of size 29/30. The figures reported are the slope coefficient and the p-value for the test of the null hypothesis that this coefficient equals 1. Numbers in bold indicate that the model was not rejected by the specification test at a 5 per cent level of statistical significance.

12.6 OVERVIEW

This chapter extends the analysis of health care cost data presented in Chapter 3 by considering nonlinear models, which avoid the retransformation problem and offer greater model flexibility. The exponential conditional mean model, where the specification of the conditional mean is proportional to the exponential function, can be estimated by nonlinear least squares and by the Poisson maximum likelihood estimator. The ECM model encompasses hazard models including exponential, Weibull and generalised gamma distributions. The chapter then considers generalised linear models which offer flexibility in modelling cost data by allowing the mean and variance function of expenditures to be directly specified by the analyst and further allow for heteroskedasticity by specifying the variance as a power function of the conditional mean. The extended estimating equation (EEE) is a very general form of a GLM making use of a Box–Cox transformation for the link function. Finally, recent extensions to modelling cost data through finite mixtures models are described. The chapter finishes with a comparative evaluation of the various models using the sample of MEPS data.

Bibliography

Amemiya, T. and MaCurdy, T. (1986) 'Instrumental variable estimation of an error-components model', *Econometrica*, 54: 869–880.

Atella, V., Brindisi, F., Deb, P. and Rosati, F.C. (2004) 'Determinants of access to physician services in Italy: a latent class seemingly unrelated probit approach', *Health Economics*, 13: 657–668.

Au, D., Crossley, T.F. and Schellhorn, M. (2005) 'The effects of health shocks and long-term health on the work activity of older Canadians', *Health Economics*, 14: 999–1018.

Bago d'Uva, T. (2005) 'Latent class models for use of primary care: evidence from a British panel', *Health Economics*, 14: 873–892.

Bago d'Uva, T. (2006) 'Latent class models for health care utilisation', *Health Economics*, 15: 329–343.

Bago d'Uva, T. and Jones, A.M. (2009) 'Health care utilisation in Europe: new evidence from the ECHP', *Journal of Health Economics*, 28: 265–279.

Bago d'Uva, T., van Doorslaer, E., Lindeboom, M. and O'Donnell, O. (2008a) 'Does reporting heterogeneity bias the measurement of health disparities?', *Health Economics*, 17: 351–375.

Bago d'Uva T., O'Donnell, O. and van Doorslaer, E. (2008b) 'Differential health reporting by education level and its impact on the measurement of health inequalities among older Europeans', *International Journal of Epidemiology*, 37: 1375–1383.

Bago d'Uva, T., Lindeboom, M., O'Donnell, O. and van Doorslaer, E. (2011) 'Slipping anchor? Testing the vignettes approach to identification and correction of reporting heterogeneity', *Journal of Human Resources*, 46: 872–903.

Balia, S. and Jones, A.M. (2008) 'Mortality, lifestyle and socio-economic status', *Journal of Health Economics*, 27: 1–26.

Balia, S. and Jones, A.M. (2011) 'Catching the habit: a study of inequality of opportunity in smoking-related mortality', *Journal of the Royal Statistical Society Series A*, 174: 175–194.

Baltagi, B.H. (2005) *Econometric Analysis of Panel Data*, Chichester: John Wiley.

Baltagi, B.H. and Khanti-Akom, S. (1990) 'On efficient estimation with panel data: an empirical comparison of instrumental variables estimators', *Journal of Applied Econometrics*, 5: 401–406.

Basu, A. (2005) 'Extended generalized linear models: simultaneous estimation of flexible link and variance functions', *The Stata Journal*, 5: 501–516.

Basu, A. and Rathouz, P.J. (2005) 'Estimating marginal and incremental effects on health outcomes using flexible link and variance function models', *Biostatistics*, 6: 93–109.

Bazzoli, G.J. (1985) 'The early retirement decision: new empirical evidence on the influence of health', *Journal of Human Resources*, 20: 214–234.

Bilger, M. and Manning, W.G. (2011) 'Measuring overfitting and misspecification in nonlinear models', Health, Econometrics and Data Group Working Paper 11/25, University of York.

Blough, D.K., Madden, C.W. and Hornbrook, M.C. (1999) 'Modeling risk using generalized linear models', *Journal of Health Economics*, 18: 153–171.

Blundell, R., Meghir, C. and Smith, S. (2002) 'Pension incentives and the pattern of early retirement', *Economic Journal*, 112: 153–170.

Börsch-Supan, A. and Jürges, H. (2005) *The Survey of Health, Ageing and Retirement in Europe – Methodology*, Mannheim: MEA.

Bound, J. (1991) 'Self reported versus objective measures of health in retirement models', *Journal of Human Resources*, 26: 107–137.

Bound, J., Schoenbaum, M., Stinebrickner, T.R. and Waidmann, T. (1999) 'The dynamic effects of health on the labor force transitions of older workers', *Labour Economics*, 6: 179–202.

Box, G.E.P. and Cox, D.R. (1964) 'An analysis of transformations', *Journal of the Royal Statistical Society B*, 26: 211–252.

Breusch, T., Mizon, G.E. and Schmidt, P. (1989) 'Efficient estimation using panel data', *Econometrica*, 57: 695–700.

Buntin, M.B. and Zaslavsky, A.M. (2004) 'Too much ado about two-part models and transformation? comparing methods of modelling Medicare expenditures', *Journal of Health Economics*, 23: 525–542.

Butler, J. and Moffitt, R. (1982) 'A computationally efficient quadrature procedure for the one-factor multinomial probit model', *Econometrica*, 50: 761–764.

Butler, J.S., Burkhauser, R.V., Mitchel, J.M. and Pincus, T.P. (1987) 'Measurement error in self-reported health variables', *The Review of Economics and Statistics*, 69: 644–650.

Cameron, A.C. and Trivedi, P.K. (1998) *Regression Analysis of Count Data*, New York: Cambridge University Press.

Cameron, A.C. and Trivedi, P.K. (2005) *Microeconometrics. Methods and Applications*, Cambridge: Cambridge University Press.

Cameron, A.C. and Trivedi, P.K. (2009) *Microeconometrics Using Stata*. Revised edition, College Station, TX: Stata Press.

Cappellari, L. and Jenkins, S.P. (2003) 'Multivariate probit regression using simulated maximum likelihood', *The Stata Journal*, 3: 278–294.

Chamberlain, G. (1980) 'Analysis of covariance with qualitative data', *Review of Economic Studies*, 47: 225–238.

Clark, A. and Etilé, F. (2006) 'Don't give up on me baby: spousal correlation in smoking behaviour', *Journal of Health Economics*, 25: 958–978.

Clark, A., Etilé, F., Postel-Vinay, F., Senik, C. and Van der Straeten, K. (2005) 'Heterogeneity in reported well-being: evidence from twelve European countries', *The Economic Journal*, 115: C118–C132.

Contoyannis, P. and Jones, A.M. (2004) 'Socio-economic status, health and lifestyle', *Journal of Health Economics*, 23: 965–995.

Contoyannis, P. and Rice, N. (2001) 'The impact of health on wages: evidence from the British Household Panel Survey', *Empirical Economics*, 26: 599–622.

Contoyannis, P., Jones, A.M. and Leon-Gonzalez, R. (2004a) 'Using simulation-based inference with panel data in health economics', *Health Economics*, 13: 101–122.

Contoyannis, P., Jones, A.M. and Rice, N. (2004b) 'The dynamics of health in the British Household Panel Survey', *Journal of Applied Econometrics*, 19: 473–503.

Copas, J.B. (1983) 'Regression, prediction and shrinkage', *Journal of the Royal Statistical Society B*, 45: 311–354.

Cornwell, C. and Rupert, P. (1988) 'Efficient estimation with panel data: an empirical comparison of instrumental variables estimators', *Journal of Applied Econometrics*, 3: 149–155.

Cox, B.D., Blaxter, M., Buckle, A.L.J., Fenner, N.P., Golding, J.F., Gore, M., Huppert, F.A., Nickson, J., Roth, M., Stark, J., Wadsworth, M.E.J. and Whichelow, M. (1987) *The Health and Lifestyle Survey*, London: Health Promotion Research Trust.

Cox, B.D., Huppert, F.A. and Whichelow, M.J. (1993) *The Health and Lifestyle Survey: Seven Years On*, Aldershot: Dartmouth.

Crossley, T.F. and Kennedy, S. (2002) 'The reliability of self-assessed health status', *Journal of Health Economics*, 21: 643–658.

Currie, J. and Madrian, B.C. (1999) 'Health, health insurance and the labor market', in Ashenfelter, O. and Card, D. (eds) *Handbook of Labour Economics*, Volume 3, Amsterdam: Elsevier.

Datta Gupta, N., Kristensen, N. and Pozzoli, D. (2010) 'External validation of the use of vignettes in cross-country health studies', *Economic Modelling*, 27: 854–865.

Deaton, A.S. (1997) *The Analysis of Household Data: A Microeconometric approach to Development Policy*, Baltimore, MD: Johns Hopkins Press.

Deb, P. (2001) 'A discrete random effects probit model with application to the demand for preventive care', *Health Economics*, 10: 371–383.

Deb, P. (2007) 'fmm: Stata module to estimate finite mixture models'. Statistical Software Components S456895, Boston College Department of Economics. Downloadable from: http://ideas.repec.org/c/boc/bocode/s456895.html.

Deb, P. and Burgess Jr, J.F. (2007) 'A quasi-experimental comparison of statistical models for health care expenditures.' Hunter College Department of Economics Working Papers, 212.

Deb, P. and Holmes, A.M. (2000) 'Estimates of use and costs of behavioural health care: a comparison of standard and finite mixture models', *Health Economics*, 9: 475–489.

Deb, P. and Trivedi, P.K. (1997) 'Demand for medical care by the elderly: a finite mixture approach', *Journal of Applied Econometrics*, 12: 313–336.

Deb, P. and Trivedi, P.K. (2002) 'The structure of demand for health care: latent class versus two-part models', *Journal of Health Economics*, 21: 601–625.

Deb, P. and Trivedi, P.K. (2011) 'Finite mixture for panels with fixed effects', HEDG Working Paper 03/11, University of York.

Disney, R., Emmerson, C. and Wakefield, M. (2006) 'Ill-health and retirement in Britain: a panel data-based analysis', *Journal of Health Economics*, 25: 621–649.

Drukker, D.M. (2000) 'Box–Cox regression models', *Stata Technical Bulletin*, 54: 27–36.

Duan, N. (1983) 'Smearing estimate: a nonparametric retransformation method', *Journal of the American Statistical Association*, 78: 605–610.

Ettner S.L., Frank, R.G., McGuire, T.G., Newhouse, J.P. and Notman, E. (1998) 'Risk adjustment of mental health and substance abuse payments', *Inquiry* 35: 223–239.

Fitzgerald, J., Gottshalk, P. and Moffitt, R. (1998) 'An analysis of sample attrition in panel data. The Michigan Panel Study on Income Dynamics', *Journal of Human Resources*, 33: 251–299.

Forster, M. and Jones, A.M. (2001) 'The role of tobacco taxes in starting and quitting smoking: duration analysis of British data', *Journal of the Royal Statistical Society Series A*, 164: 517–547.

Gerdtham, U.-G. (1997) 'Equity in health care utilization: further tests based on hurdle models and Swedish micro data', *Health Economics*, 6: 303–319.

Gerdtham, U.G. and Trivedi, P.K. (2001) 'Equity in Swedish health care reconsidered: new results based on the finite mixture model', *Health Economics*, 10: 565–572.

Gourieroux, C.S., Monfort, A. and Trognon, A. (1984). 'Pseudo maximum likelihood methods: theory', *Econometrica*, 52: 680–700.

Greene, W.H. (2003) *Econometric Analysis*, 5th edn, New York: Macmillan.

Grootendorst, P. (1995) 'A comparison of alternative models of prescription drug utilization', *Health Economics*, 4: 183–198.

Grootendorst, P., Feeny, D., and Furlong, W. (1997) 'Does it matter whom and how you ask? Inter and intra-rater agreement in the Ontario health survey', *Journal of Clinical Epidemiology*, 50: 127–136.

Gurmu, S. (1997) 'Semi-parametric estimation of hurdle regression models with an application to medicaid utilizations', *Journal of Applied Econometrics*, 12: 225–242.

Harkness, S. (1996) 'The gender earnings gap: evidence from the UK', *Fiscal Studies*, 17: 1–36.

Hausman, J. (1978) 'Specification tests in econometrics', *Econometrica*, 46: 1251–1271.

Hausman, J. and Taylor, W. (1981) 'Panel data and unobservable individual effects', *Econometrica*, 49: 1377–1398.

Hausman, J. and Wise, D. (1979) 'Attrition bias in experimental and panel data: the Gary Income Maintenance Experiment', *Econometrica*, 47: 455–474.

Heckman, J.J. (1976) 'The common structure of statistical models of truncation, sample selection and limited dependent variables and a simple estimator for such models', *The Annals of Economic and Social Measurement*, 5: 475–492.

Heckman, J. (1981) 'The incidental parameters problem and the problem of initial conditions in estimating a discrete time-discrete data stochastic process', in Manski, C.F. and McFadden, D. (eds), *Structural Analysis of Discrete Data with Econometric Applications*, Cambridge, MA: MIT Press.

Heckman, J. and Singer, B. (1984) 'A method for minimizing the impact of distributional assumptions in econometric models for duration data', *Econometrica*, 52: 271–320.

Hernandez-Quevedo, C., Jones, A.M. and Rice, N. (2004) 'Reporting bias and heterogeneity in self-assessed health. Evidence from the British Household Panel Survey', ECuity III Working Paper #19, Erasmus University.

Hilbe, P. (2005) 'hnblogit: Stata module to estimate negative binomial-logit hurdle regression'. Statistical Software Components S456401, Boston College Department of Economics. Downloadable from: http://ideas.repec.org/c/boc/bocode/s456401.html.

Hill, S.C. and Miller, G.E. (2010). 'Health expenditure estimation and functional form: application of the generalized gamma and extended estimating equation models', *Health Economics*, 19: 608–627.

Horowitz, J.L. and Manski, C.F. (1998) 'Censoring of outcomes and regressors due to survey nonresponse: identification and estimation using weights and imputations', *Journal of Econometrics*, 84: 37–58.

Hosmer, D.W. and Lemeshow, S. (1980) 'Goodness of fit tests for the multiple logistic regression model', *Communications in Statistics – Theory and Methods*, 9: 1043–1069.

Hosmer, D.W. and Lemeshow, S. (1995). *Applied Logistic Regression.* 2nd edn, New York: Wiley.

Jenkins, S.P. (1995) 'Easy estimation methods for discrete-time duration models', *Oxford Bulletin of Economics and Statistics*, 57: 129–138.

Jenkins, S.P. (1997) 'Discrete time proportional hazards regression', STATA Technical Bulletin. STB-39.

Jiménez-Martín, S., Labeaga, J.M. and Martinez-Granado, M. (2002) 'Latent class versus two-part models in the demand for physician services across the European Union', *Health Economics*, 11: 301–321.

Jones, A.M. (2000) 'Health econometrics', in Newhouse, J.P. and Culyer, A.J. (eds), *Handbook of Health Economics*, Amsterdam: Elsevier.

Jones, A.M. (2009) 'Panel data methods and applications to health economics', in Mills, T.C. and Patterson, K. (eds), *Palgrave Handbook of Econometrics. Volume 2*, London: Palgrave Macmillan, pp. 557–631.

Jones, A.M. (2011) 'Models for health care', in Hendry, D. and Clements, M. (eds), *Oxford Handbook of Economic Forecasting*, Oxford: Oxford University Press, pp. 625–654.

Jones, A.M., Koolman, X. and Rice, N. (2006) 'Health-related non-response in the BHPS and ECHP: using inverse probability weighted estimators in nonlinear models', *Journal of the Royal Statistical Society Series A*, 169: 543–569.

Jones, A.M., Rice, N. and Roberts, J. (2010) 'Sick of work or too sick to work? Evidence on self-reported health shocks and early retirement from the BHPS', *Economic Modelling*, 27: 866–880.

Kapteyn, A., Smith, J. and van Soest, A. (2007) 'Self-reported work disability in the US and the Netherlands', *American Economic Review*, 97: 461–473..

Kerkhofs, M.J.M. and Lindeboom, M. (1995) 'Subjective health measures and state dependent reporting errors', *Health Economics*, 4: 221–235.

King, G., Murray, C.J.L., Salomon, J. and Tandon, A. (2004) 'Enhancing the validity and cross-cultural comparability of measurement in survey research', *American Political Science Review*, 98: 184–191.

Knapp, L.G. and Seaks, T.G. (1998) 'A Hausman test for a dummy variable in probit', *Applied Economics Letters*, 5: 321–323.

Kreider, B. (1999) 'Latent work disability and reporting bias', *Journal of Human Resources*, 34: 734–769.

Kristensen, N., and Johansson, E. (2008) 'New evidence on cross-country differences in job satisfaction using anchoring vignettes', *Labour Economics*, 15: 96–117.

Lindeboom, M. (2006) 'Health and work of older workers', in Jones, A.M. (ed.), *Elgar Companion to Health Economics*, Cheltenham: Edward Elgar.

Lindeboom, M. and van Doorslaer, E. (2004) 'Cut-point shift and index shift in self-reported health', *Journal of Health Economics*, 23: 1083–1099.

Little, J.A. and Rubin, D.B. (1987) *Statistical Analysis with Missing Data*, New York: John Wiley.

Long, J.S. and Freese, J. (2006) *Regression Models for Categorical Dependent Variables Using Stata*, 2nd edn, College Station, TX: Stata Press.

McCullagh, P. and Nelder, J.A. (1989) *Generalized Linear Models*, London: Chapman & Hall.

Majo, M.C. and Van Soest, A. (2011) 'The fixed-effects zero-inflated Poisson model with an application to health care utilization', CentER Discussion Paper No. 2011-083, University of Tilburg, The Netherlands.

Manning, W. (1998) 'The logged dependent variable, heteroscedasticity, and the retransformation problem', *Journal of Health Economics*, 17: 283–295.

Manning, W.G. and Mullahy, J. (2001) 'Estimating log models: to transform or not to transform?', *Journal of Health Economics*, 20: 461–494.

Manning, W.G. Duan, N. and Rogers, W.H. (1987) 'Monte Carlo evidence on the choice between sample selection and two-part models', *Journal of Econometrics*, 35: 59–82.

Manning, W.G., Basu, A. and Mullahy, J. (2005) 'Generalized modeling approaches to risk adjustment of skewed outcomes data', *Journal of Health Economics*, 24: 465–488.

Meyer, B.D. (1990) 'Unemployment insurance and unemployment spells', *Econometrica*, 58: 757–782.

Mincer, J. (1974) *Schooling, Experience and Earnings*, NBER, New York: Columbia University Press.

Moffitt, R., Fitzgerald, J. and Gottschalk, P. (1999) 'Sample attrition in panel data: the role of selection observables', *Annales d'Economie et de Statistique*, 55–56: 129–152.

Mullahy, J. (1986) 'Specification and testing in some modified count data models', *Journal of Econometrics*, 33: 341–365.

Mundlak, Y. (1978) 'On the pooling of time series and cross-section data', *Econometrica*, 46: 69–85.

Murray, C.J.L., Ozaltin, E., Tandon, A., Salomon, J., Sadana, R. and Chatterji, S. (2003) 'Empirical evaluation of the anchoring vignettes approach in health surveys', in Murray, C.J.L. and Evans, D.B. (eds), *Health Systems Performance Assessment: Debates, Methods and Empiricism*, Geneva: World Health Organization.

Narendranathan, W. and Stewart, M.B. (1993) 'How does the benefit effect vary as unemployment spells lengthen?', *Journal of Applied Econometrics*, 8: 361–381.

Nicoletti, C. (2006) 'Non-response in dynamic panel data models', *Journal of Econometrics*, 132: 461–489.

Nicoletti, C. and Peracchi, F. (2005) 'A cross-country comparison of survey nonparticipation in the ECHP', *Journal of the Royal Statistical Society Series A*, 168: 763–781.

Nicoletti, C. and Rondinelli, C. (2010) 'The (mis)specification of discrete time duration models with unobserved heterogeneity: a Monte Carlo study', *Journal of Econometrics*, 159: 1–13.

Park, R.E. (1966). 'Estimation with heteroscedastic error', *Econometrica*, 34: 888.

Peracchi, F. (2002) 'The European Community Household Panel: a review', *Empirical Economics*, 27: 63–90.

Pohlmeier, W. and Ulrich, V. (1995) 'An econometric model of the two-part decision making process in the demand for health care', *The Journal of Human Resources*, 30: 339–361.

Pregibon, D. (1980) 'Goodness of link tests for generalized linear models', *Applied Statistics*, 29: 15–24.

Prentice, R. and Gloeckler, L. (1978) 'Regression analysis of grouped survival data with applications to breast cancer data', *Biometrics*, 34: 57–67.

Pudney, S. and Shields, M. (2000) 'Gender, race, pay and promotion in the British nursing profession: estimation of a generalized probit model', *Journal of Applied Econometrics*, 15: 367–399.

Ramsey, J.B. (1969) 'Tests for specification errors in classical linear least squares regression analysis', *Journal of the Royal Statistical Society B*, 31: 350–370.

Riphahn, R.T. (1997) 'Disability, retirement and unemployment: substitute pathways for labour force exit? An empirical test for the case of Germany', *Applied Economics*, 29: 551–561.

Robins, J., Rotnitzky, A. and Zhao, L.P. (1995) 'Analysis of semiparametric regression models for repeated outcomes in the presence of missing data', *Journal of the American Statistical Association*, 90: 106–121.

Rotnitzky, A. and Robins, J. (1997) 'Analysis of semi-parametric regression models with non-ignorable non-response', *Statistics in Medicine*, 16: 81–102.

Rubin, D.B. (1976) 'Inference and missing data', *Biometrika*, 63: 581–592.

Sarma, S. and Simpson, W. (2006) 'A microeconometric analysis of Canadian health care utilization', *Health Economics*, 15: 219–239.

Spitzer, J.J. (1984) 'Variance estimates in models with the Box–Cox transformation: implications for estimation and hypothesis testing', *Review of Economics and Statistics*, 66: 645–652.

Stewart, M. (2006) 'Maximum simulated likelihood estimation of random effects dynamic probit models with autocorrelated errors', *Stata Journal*, 6: 256–272.

Tandon, A., Murray, C.J.L., Salomon, J.A. and King, G. (2003) 'Statistical models for enhancing cross-population comparability. Health systems performance assessment: debates, methods and empiricisms', in Murray, C.J.L. and Evans, D.B. (eds), *Health Systems Performance Assessment: Debates, Methods and Empiricism*, Geneva: World Health Organization.

Taylor, M., Brice, J., Buck, N. and Prentice, E. (1998) *British Household Panel Survey User Manual Volume A: Introduction, Technical Report and Appendices*, Colchester: University of Essex.

Terza, J.V. (1985) 'Ordinal probit: a generalization', *Communications in Statistics*, 14: 1–11.

Train, K.E. (2003) *Discrete Choice Methods with Simulation*, Cambridge: Cambridge University Press.

UNESCO (1997) *International Standard Classification of Education*. Paris: UNESCO.

Van Ourti, T. (2004) 'Measuring horizontal inequity in Belgian health care using a Gaussian random effects two part count data model', *Health Economics*, 13(7): 705–724.

Van Soest, A., Delaney, L., Harmon, X., Kapteyn, A., and Smith, J.P (2011) 'Validating the use of anchoring vignettes for the correction of response scale differences in subjective questions', *Journal of the Royal Statistical Society Series A*, 174: 575–595.

Veazie, P.J., Manning, W.G. and Kane, R.L. (2003) 'Improving risk adjustment for Medicare capitated reimbursement using nonlinear models', *Medical Care*, 41: 741–752.

Verbeek, M. and Nijman, T.E. (1992) 'Testing for selectivity bias in panel data models', *International Economic Review*, 33: 681–703.

White, H. (1980) 'A heteroskedasticity-consistent covariance matrix estimator and a direct test for heteroskedasticity', *Econometrica*, 48: 817–838.

Wilde, J. (2000) 'Identification of multiple equation probit models with endogenous dummy variables', *Economic Letters*, 69: 309–312.

Wooldridge, J.M. (2002a) 'Inverse probability weighted M-estimators for sample stratification, attrition and stratification', *Portuguese Economic Journal*, 1: 117–139.

Wooldridge, J.M. (2002b) *Econometric Analysis of Cross Section and Panel Data*, Cambridge, MA: MIT Press.

Wooldridge, J.M. (2005) 'Simple solutions to the initial conditions problem in dynamic, nonlinear panel data models with unobserved heterogeneity', *Journal of Applied Econometrics*, 20: 39–54.

Index

accelerated failure time (AFT) 156, 157–9, 170–3, 357–8
actuarial adjustment 200–1, 202–3
age *see* socioeconomic status (SES)
Akaike information criterion *see* information criteria (AIC/BIC)
algorithms 312–13
Amemiya and MaCurdy (AM) estimator 236, 238–41, 242
antithetics 276
attrition bias, BHPS 279–80, 290; monotone attrition 287; *see also* non-response bias, BHPS
augmented regression test 235
Australian National Health Survey 69
average marginal effects: exponential conditional mean models 345–6, 353–4; generalised linear models 363–4; hurdle model 310–11; latent class models 315–16; Poisson regression 297–8, 349; *see also* marginal effects
average partial effects (APE) 135–8, 254, 290; *see also* partial effects

bar charts, SAH 15–21
Bayesian information criterion *see* information criteria (AIC/BIC)
Bayesian Markov chain Monte Carlo (MCMC) estimation 265
behavioural model for health 106–7; *see also* mortality
BHPS *see* British Household Panel Survey
bias *see* attrition bias, BHPS; non-response bias, BHPS; reporting heterogeneity

binary variables/regressors 122, 123, 224, 245, 251; comparison of approaches 60; and incremental effects 297, 303, 307, 316–17, 345, 363–4; and smearing estimators 54–5; retirement 198, 199, 203, 205
binomial density function 206, 208
Box–Cox transformation 62–5, 368
box plots 36–7
breathing vignettes *see* vignettes, hypothetical
Breusch, Mizon and Schmidt (BMS) estimator 239, 241
British Household Panel Survey (BHPS) 5–7, 182–93, 222–5, 244–5; *see also* dynamics of health, BHPS; non-response bias, BHPS; retirement, BHPS; wage rates, BHPS
Broyden-Fletcher-Goldfarb-Shanno (BFGS) quasi-Newton algorithm 312

Canadian National Population Health Survey 70
censoring 142, 157, 178, 200–1, 352
chain rule 307
chi-squared tests 116–17, 201, 202, 280–3
class membership: finite mixture models 370–6; latent class models 319, 329, 330–6
clustered sampling 4, 5
complementary log-log functions 204–6, 208, 209–11
conditional independence condition 283, 284–5
conditional logit model 267–8

conditional maximum likelihood (CML)
269–75
conditional mean/variance 54–5, 208–9,
365–6, 368; extended estimating
equations 65, 367–70, 378–9;
generalised gamma model 357;
generalised linear models 38–9, 65, 359,
362–7; negative binomial models 300,
301–2, 308; ordinary least squares 44,
46; Poisson model 296, 298, 349;
Weibull model 351–2; zero-inflated
models 303, 307; *see also* exponential
conditional mean (ECM) models
conservative inference 287
consumer price indices (CPIs) 296
continuous/discrete regressors 50, 57, 60,
252, 315–16
continuous/discrete time *see* duration
models
Copas test 377–9
correlated effects: dynamic pooled probit
model 269, 271–2; static pooled probit
model 256–8, 265
correlation coefficients 113–14, 127–9,
261, 377, 378, 379
count data models 295–6, 337; finite
mixture/latent class models 311–18,
325, 337, 370–6; hurdle models 308–11,
317–18; latent class hurdle models
318–19, 325–36, 339–41; latent class
negative binomial model 318, 320–25,
337–9; negative binomial model
299–302; Poisson model 296–9; zero-
inflated models 302–7, 317–18, 325
covariance 122–3
covariates 30, 44, 55, 127, 192, 331, 333,
337, 353, 359, 362, 373; average partial
effects of 135; and non-response 283,
284, 285; negative binomial model 299,
301–2, 313, 314; Poisson models 298,
305, 349–50; and reporting
heterogeneity 70, 72–9, 81, 83–4, 88,
90, 102; retirement 201, 203, 205, 209
Cox–Snell residuals 153–6, 160–1,
167–70, 176–7
cross-section surveys *see* Health and
Lifestyle Survey (HALS)
cumulative distribution functions (CDFs)
19, 43–4, 142

cumulative hazard functions 142, 176;
smoking cessation 166–73; smoking
initiation 152–64
cut-point shift 70; non-parallel 81–6, 90–2,
98, 99–100; parallel 79–80, 87–90,
93–7, 99–100
cut-points 72–3, 75–6, 77–8, 86, 92–3

data cleaning 148–9
data description, MEPS 31–40
data tabulation, BHPS 21–9
death rates 120–1
deaths data, HALS 5, 107–8, 143, 174;
causes of death 117–20; *see also*
mortality
demographics *see* socioeconomic status
(SES)
density functions 142, 156–7, 206, 208,
258, 296, 319, 326, 337, 339, 370; finite
density estimator 211; kernel density
plot 35–6; Weibull 169, 351–2
density plots 35–6
dependent variables 13–14, 44, 62, 235,
246, 276, 286, 295, 296, 310, 319, 343,
348, 368; binary 122, 123, 205, 244,
245, 251; lagged 269, 276, 284
descriptive statistics/analysis: dynamics of
health 21–9, 245–51; lifestyles and
health 113–21; retirement and health
190, 192–3, 196–7, 200–1; smoking and
mortality 149; wages and health 225;
see also non-response bias, BHPS
deviance residuals 364
diagnostic tests, linear regression models
47–8
discrete/continuous regressors 50, 57, 60,
252, 315–16
discrete/continuous time *see* duration
models
discrete random effects probit model 318
distributional families 362; and extended
estimating equations 367–70
distributions: comparison of models,
health care costs 377–9; cumulative
distribution functions 19, 43–4, 142;
exponential 153–6, 160–1, 167–8,
169–70, 177, 352, 357–8, 371; gamma
209, 212, 300, 355, 357–9, 360–1,
363–6, 367, 370–2, 375–6, 378;

Gompertz 177–81; log-logistic/log-normal 50–1, 153–64, 168–70, 177, 363, 367; Weibull 153–6, 161, 168, 169–73, 177, 357–9

drinking *see* lifestyles

drop-out/survival rates *see* non-response bias, BHPS

Duan's smearing factor 52–5, 60

duration analysis, basic concepts 141–3

duration data: BHPS 182–96; HALS 145–9

duration models: empirical approach 196–201, 202–3; health costs 351–9; lifespan 173–81; smoking cessation 164–73; smoking initiation 150–64; stock sampling/discrete-time hazard analysis 201–16

dynamic models 276, 280; correlated effects/initial conditions 269–75; panel probit 268–9; pooled probit 271–2, 287–9; random effects probit 269–70, 273–5, 318; Heckman estimator 275–6

dynamics of health, BHPS 12–14, 244–51; data tabulation 21–9; dynamic models 268–76; graphical analysis 14–21; static models 251–68

ECHP *see* European Community Household Panel

econometric model, lifestyles and mortality 106–7, 121–38

education *see* socioeconomic status (SES)

empirical cumulative distribution functions (CDFs) 19, 43–4

empirical model, wage rates 225, 228–41

employment *see* socioeconomic status (SES)

endogenous variables/regressors: lifestyles and health 106–7, 121–2, 123, 135, 137–8; retirement and health 186, 194, 196; wages and health 224, 225, 230, 232, 234, 236–43

equidispersion property 297–8, 299, 300

error components model 251

error disturbances 123, 225, 228, 230

error measurement 377, 378–9

error terms 38–9, 47, 72, 86, 107, 122, 135, 157, 194, 230, 265; idiosyncratic 44, 251, 269, 270

European Community Household Panel (ECHP) 7–8, 295–6; *see also* count data models

'excess zeros' 299, 337; *see also* zero-inflated models

exclusion restrictions 78, 123–34, 284

exogenous variables/regressors 52, 107, 122, 123, 127, 130–5, 230, 236, 238–9, 269, 275

explanatory variables/regressors 44, 138, 205, 269, 296, 297–8, 305, 319

exponential conditional mean (ECM) models 343–8, 362, 378–9, 380; hazard models 351–9; Poisson regression 348–50

exponential distributions 153–6, 160–1, 167–8, 169–70, 177, 352, 357–8, 371

exponential hazard function 352–5

extended estimating equations (EEEs) 65, 367–70, 378–9

failure functions *see* survivor/failure functions

field variables 284

finite density estimator 211

finite mixture models 211, 213, 265; class membership 370–6; health care costs 370–6; health care use/count data 311–18, 325, 337

first order stochastic dominance 19

fitted values 39, 47–8, 55, 57–8, 65, 313–14, 346–8, 350, 371, 375; latent class hurdle model for panel data 334–5; latent class negative binomial model for panel data 322–4; model comparison 377–9

fixed effects (FE) estimators 230, 232–4, 239, 242, 284, 337

fixed-effects ZIP model 325

flagging process 5, 75, 108, 109, 143

frailty *see* unobserved heterogeneity

framing/learning effects 69–70

full information maximum likelihood (FIML) 122–3

gamma distribution 209, 212, 300, 355, 357–9, 360–1, 362, 363–6, 367, 368, 370–2, 375–6, 378

gamma frailty 209, 211, 212–13, 215

Gauss-Hermite quadrature 258, 260–3, 265, 267, 275–6
Gaussian distribution 362
Gaussian frailty 211, 215
Gaussian mixture model 375–6
Gaussian random variables 173
gender *see* socioeconomic status (SES)
General Health Questionnaire (GHQ) 223
generalised gamma model 355, 357–9, 360–1, 378–9
generalised linear models (GLMs) 359–70, 380
generalised ordered probit model 70, 77, 79, 81–6, 90, 102–3
Geweke-Hajivassilou-Keane (GHK) simulator 122–3
Gompertz distribution 177–81
Graph Editor 153
graphical analysis, SAH 14–21

HALS *see* Health and Lifestyle Survey
Halton quasirandom sequences 276
Hausman and Taylor (HT) estimator 236–9, 241, 242
Hausman(-type) tests 232, 234–5, 236, 239, 283, 285
hazard analysis, discrete-time 203–16
hazard functions 142, 205; health costs data 351–9; life tables 200–1, 202–3; lifespan/hazard of death 148, 152, 173–81; smoking cessation 164–73; smoking initiation 152–64
Health and Lifestyle Survey (HALS) 3–5, 107–12, 143–9, 174; *see also* mortality
health care costs, MEPS 9, 30, 342–3; comparison of models 377–9; data description 31–40; exponential conditional mean models 343–59, 362, 378–9, 380; finite mixture models 370–6; generalised linear models 359–70, 380; linear regression models 44–65; modelling data 40–4
health care utilisation, ECHP 7, 295–6; *see also* count data models
health limitations 6, 185, 196, 200, 201, 202–3, 208, 211, 213, 215, 217, 244
health measures, SHARE 10–11
health-related behaviours *see* lifestyles
health shocks 196, 213, 217

health stock 185–6, 194–6, 215–17
Health Utility Index (HUI-3) 70
Heckman estimator 275–6
Heckman–Singer frailty 211, 214, 215
Heckman-type tests 286
heterogeneity 230; finite mixture model 370, 373; individual 106–7, 121–3, 330; unobserved (frailty) 205–16, 217, 299–300, 311, 318, 326; *see also* reporting heterogeneity
heteroskedasticity 38–40, 47–8, 54–5, 56, 57, 60, 65, 359, 361, 362
hierarchical ordered probit (HOPIT) model 75–6, 77, 78, 81, 86–92, 98–100, 103–5; one-step estimation 92–8, 99
homogeneity/reporting homogeneity 72–3, 74, 83, 92, 201–2, 370, 373
Hosmer–Lemeshow test 346–8, 350, 377–9
Huber–White sandwich estimator 298–9
hurdle models 308–11, 317–18; latent class 318–19, 325–36, 339–41

ICD-9-CM diagnostic system 117–18
identity link function 362
idiosyncratic error terms 44, 251, 269, 270
ignorability condition 284–5, 287
incidental truncation 280
income *see* socioeconomic status (SES); wage rates, BHPS
incremental effects 50, 52, 54, 55, 57, 136, 298, 300, 345, 355–6; generalised linear models 363–4, 367, 369–70; latent class models 315, 316–17; zero-inflated models 303, 307
independent variables *see* regressors/independent variables
individual heterogeneity 106–7, 121–3, 330
inference, simulation-based 265–7
information criteria (AIC/BIC): count data models 312, 317, 325, 330; health care costs 346, 355, 359, 375; lifestyles and health 123, 127; retirement and health 209, 211, 213, 215; smoking and mortality 156–7, 160–1, 167–70, 176–7
initial conditions: Heckman estimator 275–6; Wooldridge specification 269–75

insurance status, and health care costs 9–10, 42–4, 52, 55, 57, 60
interval regression 86–98
inverse Gaussian distribution 362
inverse probability weighted (IPW) estimator 283, 285, 286–90

Kaplan–Meier (product-limit) estimator 152–6, 166–7, 176, 201, 203
kernel density plot 35–6
kurtosis/skewness 34–8, 46, 49, 65, 343, 344–5

lagged variables 186, 196, 213, 217, 224, 269–70, 275, 276, 284
latent class (LC) models 311–18, 337, 370–6; hurdle, for panel data (LCH-Pan) 318–19, 325–36, 339–41; negative binomial, for panel data (LCNB-Pan) 318, 320–25, 337–9
latent health indices 73, 74, 75, 77, 81, 98–9, 102
latent health stock 185–6, 194–6, 215–17
learning/framing effects 69–70
left-censored spells 142, 352
left truncation 143, 174–5, 178
life tables 200–1, 202–3
lifespan/hazard of death 148, 152, 173–81; *see also* hazard functions
lifestyles, HALS 106–7, 113–17; *see also* mortality
likelihood 81, 170, 178, 204–5, 319; *see also* log-likelihood function; maximum likelihood (estimation) (ML(E))
likelihood ratio (LR) tests 62, 130, 135, 201, 209, 211, 300, 306
linear indices 40, 57, 102, 136, 137, 195, 252, 297, 334, 359
linear regression models: Box–Cox transformation 62–5, 368; comparison of approaches 57, 60–2; diagnostic tests 47–8; logarithmic transformation 49–55, 56, 57, 60–2; ordinary least squares 44–7, 228–30, 242, 378–9; for panel data 221–2, 225, 228–41; square-root transformation 55, 57, 58–9, 60–2
link functions 206, 208, 362, 363, 365, 367, 378; extended estimating equations 65, 367–70, 378–9

link tests 47–8, 377–9; exponential conditional mean models 346–8, 349–50, 354, 355, 357; generalised linear models 365–7
log-likelihood function 169, 178, 204, 208, 265; econometric model 122; generalised ordered probit model 102; Heckman estimator 275; HOPIT model 92, 103; hurdle models 308, 326, 328, 339–41; latent class panel models 320–1, 326, 328, 337–41; multivariate probit model 129, 135; pooled probit model 252; random effects model 258, 261; *see also* likelihood
log link functions *see* link functions
log-log functions, complementary 204–6, 208, 209–11
log-logistic/log-normal distributions 50–1, 153–64, 168–70, 177, 363, 367
logarithmic transformation 35–8, 49–55, 56, 57, 60–2
logit models 70, 72, 160, 318; conditional 267–8; hurdle 308–10, 325–8, 339; multinomial 330–1; zero-inflated 303, 305
longitudinal non-response *see* non-response bias, BHPS
longitudinal/panel datasets 8–10, 342; BHPS 5–7, 182–93, 222–5, 244–5; ECHP 7–8, 295–6; HALS 4–5, 107–12, 143–9, 174

marginal effects 252; exponential conditional mean models 345–6, 353–6; finite mixture model 373–4; generalised linear models 363–4, 367, 370; hurdle models 310–11; latent class models 315–16; linear regression models 44, 50, 51–2, 53, 54, 55–7, 62, 65; negative binomial model 300–1; Poisson regression 297–8, 349; zero-inflated models 303–4, 307
marital status *see* socioeconomic status (SES)
Markov process 268–9
Markov chain Monte Carlo (MCMC) estimation 265
maximum likelihood (estimation) (ML(E)) 50–1, 62–3, 156–7, 194, 205, 252,

297–8, 303, 312, 331, 351; conditional 269–75; full information 122–3; inverse probability weighted 286–7; pseudo-MLE 298–9, 362; quasi-MLE 252, 349–50, 362; simulated 122–3, 265, 267, 276

McMaster Health Utility Index (HUI-3) 70

mean absolute prediction error (MAPE) 377, 378–9

mean prediction error (MPE) 378–9

mean zero disturbance 225, 228, 230

measurement error, SAH 69–70, 182, 193–6; *see also* reporting heterogeneity

Medical Expenditure Panel Survey (MEPS), US 8–10, 342; *see also* health care costs, MEPS

Mills ratios 286

Mincerian wage function 225, 228

missing (completely) at random (M(C)AR) condition 283

mode of administration effects 69

monotone attrition 287

Monte Carlo (MC) simulation 267

morbidity 6, 46, 69–70, 284–5, 296; *see also* self-assessed health (SAH)

mortality 106–7, 141; descriptive analysis, lifestyles and socioeconomic status 113–21; descriptive statistics 149; duration analysis basic concepts 141–3; duration model, smoking cessation 164–73; duration model, smoking initiation 150–64; estimation strategy/econometric model 121–38; Gompertz mortality model 177–81; HALS data and sample 107–12, 143–9, 174; lifespan/hazard of death 148, 152, 173–81

multimodality 299, 370

multinomial logit model 330–1

multinomial probit model 265

multivariate probit models 106, 122, 123, 127–38

multivariate quadrature 267

Mundlak specification 235, 256–8, 265, 266

Mundlak–Wooldridge specification 270, 287

negative binomial (NB) models 299–302; latent class 312–18, 318, 320–25, 330, 337–9; truncated 308–11, 325–8; zero-inflated 303, 305–7, 317–18, 325

Nelson–Aalen cumulative hazard function 152–6, 166–7, 176

Newton–Raphson algorithm 312–13

nonlinear least squares (NLS) 343, 345, 348, 349. 379

nonlinear regression models 47, 343–8

non-parallel cut-point shift 81–6, 90–2, 98, 99–100

non-response bias, BHPS 6, 13, 277–80; estimation 283–90; testing for 280–3

objective health indicators 70

observables/unobservables, selection on 283–5

OECD-modified equivalence scale 8, 296

one-step estimation, HOPIT model 92–8, 99

ordered probit models 70, 72–5, 79–80, 86, 98–100, 194–6, 318; generalised 70, 77, 79, 81–6, 90, 102–3; hierarchical (HOPIT) 75–6, 77, 78, 81, 86–100, 103–5; pooled 13–14, 194–6, 215, 217

ordinary least squares (OLS) 44–8, 55, 61, 62, 228–30, 242, 378–9

over-/underdispersion 297–8, 299–300, 301–2, 306, 308, 312–13, 314, 320, 326, 337

overlapping panel design, MEPS 9

panel data: hurdle model (LCH-Pan) 318–19, 325–36, 339–41; negative binomial model (LCNB-Pan) 318, 320–25, 337–9

panel probit models 265

parallel cut-point shift 79–80, 87–90, 93–7, 99–100

parameterisation 156, 177–8, 211, 265, 269–70, 300–1, 303, 330–1, 359, 377

Park test 365–6

partial effects 74–5, 89–92, 97–8, 100, 252, 255, 258, 260–1, 274–5, 285, 287; average (APE) 135–8, 254, 290

Pearson chi-squared test 116–17

Pearson test 377–9

pension entitlements 188, 208

Poisson distribution/models 348–50, 362, 363, 367, 368, 378–9; for count data 295, 296–9, 309, 312, 319, 337; mixture 299–300; zero-inflated 303–6, 325
Poisson pseudo-maximum likelihood estimator (PMLE) 298–9, 299–300
pooled probit models 252–8, 271–2, 280–3, 286–9; ordered 13–14, 194–6, 215, 217
positive definite (PD) matrix 235
power functions 362, 368–9
Pregibon's link test 47–8, 377–9
principal–agent models 308
probability plots 36–7, 64, 173–4, 345, 349, 364
probit models 159, 160, 285–6, 287; multinomial 265; multivariate/univariate 122–38, 267; panel/dynamic panel 265, 268–9; pooled/dynamic pooled 252–8, 271–2, 280–3, 286–7, 287–9; random effects 256, 258–67, 273–5, 280–3, 318; *see also* ordered probit models
product-limit (Kaplan–Meier) estimator 152–6, 166–7, 176, 201, 203
proportional hazard (PH) models 158, 204–5
pseudo-maximum likelihood estimation (PMLE) 298–9, 362
pseudo-random draws 276
purchasing power parities (PPPs) 296

quadrature, Gauss-Hermite 258, 260–3, 265, 267, 275–6
quasi-maximum likelihood (QML) 252, 349–50, 362

random effects (RE) estimator 230–2, 239, 242, 251
random effects probit (REP) models 256, 258–67, 269–70, 273–5, 280–3, 318
recursive system of equations 107, 121–2
regression models 40–4, 70, 156; Box–Cox 62–5, 368; heteroskedasticity 38–40, 47–8, 54–5, 56, 57, 60, 65, 359, 361, 362; interval regression 86–98; nonlinear 47, 343–8; *see also* linear regression models; logit models; negative binomial (NB) models; Poisson distribution/models; probit models

regressors/independent variables 13–14, 135, 167, 245–51, 255, 296, 345; continuous/discrete 50, 57, 60, 252, 315–16; explanatory 44, 138, 205, 269, 296, 297–8, 305, 319; and initial conditions 269–76; pooled probit model 256–7; time-varying/invariant 223–5, 228, 230, 234–8; *see also* binary variables/regressors; regression models
reporting heterogeneity 69–71, 72–5, 86–7, 99; *see also* vignettes, hypothetical
reporting homogeneity 72–3, 74, 83, 92
RESET test 47, 124–7
residuals, deviance 364
response category cut-point shift *see* cut-point shift
response rates: BHPS 6; HALS 4; *see also* non-response bias, BHPS
retirement, BHPS 182, 217; data preparation/summary 182–93; descriptive statistics 192–3; duration model, empirical approach 196–201, 202–3; duration model, stock sampling/discrete-time hazard analysis 201–16; self-assessed health/latent health stock 193–6
right-censored spells 142, 157, 178, 352
right truncation 143
root mean squared error (RMSE) 377, 378–9

samples/sampling: balanced/unbalanced, BHPS 12, 13, 246–51, 252–6, 257–8, 259, 264–5, 266, 271–3, 276, 283, 288–90; clustered 4, 5; HALS 109–12; stock samples 189–90, 201–4
selection bias *see* non-response bias, BHPS
selection on observables/unobservables 283–5
self-assessed health (SAH), BHPS 5–6, 8, 69–70, 182, 184–6, 193, 193–6, 223; data tabulation 21–9; graphical analysis 14–21; *see also* non-response bias, BHPS; self-reported measures of health
self-reported functional limitations *see* health limitations

self-reported measures of health: standard analysis 72–5; *see also* self-assessed health (SAH), BHPS; vignettes, hypothetical

semi-elasticities 297, 303

SHARE *see* Survey of Health, Ageing and Retirement in Europe

simulation-based inference 265–7

skewness/kurtosis 34–8, 46, 49, 65, 343, 344–5

smearing factors/estimators 49–50, 52–5, 55, 57–62

smoking *see* lifestyles, HALS; mortality

socioeconomic status (SES): BHPS/SAH 6–7, 18–20, 22–9, 183, 186–9, 190–3, 208, 224–7, 245–51, 277–80; ECHP/health care 8, 296; HALS/lifestyles 107, 109, 112, 113–15, 117–21; MEPS/health care costs 9–10, 40–4; SHARE/reporting heterogeneity 11, 72

splitting mechanisms 159–60, 303–4

square root link function 363, 367

square root transformation 35–8, 55, 57, 58–9, 60–2

Stata codes/commands xiii, xviii–xx, 245–6, 322, 343; hazard models 205–16, 352; random effects probit model 260–1; SHARE data 101–2; survival time 197–200; wage rates 222–3

static models 251, 276, 280; conditional logit model 267–8; correlated effects 256–8, 265; pooled specification 252–6; random effects specification 258–65; simulation-based inference 265–7

stock sampling 189–90; duration model 201–4

subjective well-being 223

Survey of Health, Ageing and Retirement in Europe (SHARE) 10–11, 71; *see also* self-reported measures of health

surveys 69–71; *see also* British Household Panel Survey (BHPS); European Community Household Panel (ECHP); Health and Lifestyle Survey (HALS); Medical Expenditure Panel Survey (MEPS), US; Survey of Health, Ageing and Retirement in Europe (SHARE)

survival/drop-out rates *see* non-response bias, BHPS

survivor/failure functions 142–3, 352; life tables 200–1, 202–3; lifespan/hazard of death 148, 152, 173–81; smoking cessation 164–73; smoking initiation 152–64

time-invariant individual random effect 251

time-varying idiosyncratic random error 251

time-varying/invariant regressors 223–5, 228, 230, 234–8

triangular recursive system of equations 107, 121–2

'true health', SAH 70; *see also* cut-point shift

truncated-at-zero models 308–11, 325–8

truncated negative binomial (NB2) model 308–11, 325–8

truncation: incidental 280; left/right 143, 174–5, 178

underdispersion *see* over-/under-dispersion

univariate integrals 265, 267

univariate probit model 122–38

unobserved heterogeneity (frailty) 205–16, 217, 299–300, 311, 319, 326

v-fold cross validation 378–9

variable addition tests 280–3, 290

variables/regressors: continuous/discrete 50, 57, 60, 252, 315–16; exogenous 52, 107, 122, 123, 127, 130–5, 230, 236, 238–9, 269, 275; explanatory 44, 138, 205, 269, 296, 297–8, 305, 319; field 284; Gaussian random 173; lagged 186, 196, 213, 217, 224, 269–70, 275, 276, 284; *see also* binary variables/regressors; dependent variables; endogenous variables/regressors; regressors/independent variables; socioeconomic status (SES)

variance functions *see* conditional mean/variance

vignettes, hypothetical 70–1, 71–2, 75–6; adjusting for reporting heterogeneity 86–7; modelling vignette ratings 76–8, 98–100; non-parallel cut-point shift 81–6, 90–2, 98, 99–100; one-step estimation, HOPIT model 92–8, 99; parallel cut-point shift 79–80, 87–90, 93–7, 99–100

Vuong test 303, 304, 305–6

wage rates, BHPS 221–2, 241–3; empirical model and estimation 225, 228–41; sample and variables 222–5

Wald tests 62, 235–6, 243, 314, 373

wave-on-wave survival/drop-out rates 278–80, 290–1

wealth *see* socioeconomic status (SES)

Weibull distributions 153–6, 161, 168, 169–73, 177, 357–9; density functions 169, 351–2; hazard functions 205, 355, 356–7

whisker plots 36

Wooldridge specifications 269–70, 275, 287

World Health Organization Multi-Country Survey (WHO-MCS) 70

z-tests 127, 130–5

zero-inflation/zero-inflated models 302–7, 317–18, 325

zero truncation/zero-truncated models 308–11, 325–8, 342–3

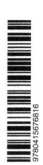